SIMULATION GUIDE

MCSE

MCSE Simulation Guide: Windows NT Server 4 and Enterprise

Exam: 70-067
70-068

Dave Bixler

201 West 103rd Street, Indianapolis, Indiana 46290

MCSE Simulation Guide: Windows NT Server 4 and Enterprise

International Standard Book Number: 1-56205-914-9

Library of Congress Catalog Card Number: 98-87236

Printed in the United States of America

First Printing: *November, 1998*

00 99 98 4 3 2 1

Trademarks

All terms mentioned in this book that are known to be trademarks or service marks have been appropriately capitalized. New Riders cannot attest to the accuracy of this information. Use of a term in this book should not be regarded as affecting the validity of any trademark or service mark.

Warning and Disclaimer

Every effort has been made to make this book as complete and as accurate as possible, but no warranty or fitness is implied. The information provided is on an "as is" basis. The author and the publisher shall have neither liability nor responsibility to any person or entity with respect to any loss or damages arising from the information contained in this book.

EXECUTIVE EDITOR
Mary Foote

ACQUISITIONS EDITOR
Sean Angus

DEVELOPMENT EDITOR
Nancy D. Warner

MANAGING EDITOR
Sarah Kearns

PROJECT EDITOR
Lori Morency

COPY EDITOR
Daryl Kessler

INDEXER
Larry Sweazy

TECHNICAL EDITORS
Marc Savage
Andrew Brice

PROOFREADER
Megan Wade

PRODUCTION
Steve Balle-Gifford
Wil Cruz
Louis Porter, Jr.

Contents at a Glance

Table of Contents

About the Author

Dave Bixler

Dave Bixler is a Senior IT Consultant with one of the largest systems integrators in the United States. He has been active in the networking arena for the last 12 years, working on network designs, server implementations, and network management, as well as Internet security. Dave has also worked on a number of Macmillan books as a contributing author, technical editor, or book reviewer.

Dave's industry certifications include Microsoft's MCPS and MCSE, as well as Novell's CNE for NetWare versions 3.x, 4.x, and IntranetWare, ECNE, and MCNE. Dave also has IBM's PSE, Check Point Software's CCSE, and 3Com's 3Wizard Master certifications. (He takes lots of certification tests!) Dave lives in Cincinnati, Ohio, with his very patient wife Sarah, sons Marty and Nicholas, and two Keeshonds, Zeus and Arcus.

Dedication

I would like to dedicate this book to my family, without whose patience and understanding I would not have made it to the end of this project. Sarah, Marty, and Nicholas...thanks for putting up with me!

Acknowledgments

As much as I would love to take credit for this book, it wouldn't be fair. It was a team project, and without the team, it wouldn't have gotten done.

Sean Angus, thanks for the opportunity, and the support throughout. Easily the best editor I've worked with! It was a joy!

Nancy Warner, whose great development editing helped me make it through all the parts of this process I just didn't understand. It's a much better book for your suggestions!

Marc Savage and Andrew Brice provided excellent technical editing. Thanks for keeping me honest and for helping me fill in the blanks!

My Mom and Dad, for their faith in my abilities...and for asking me "How's the book going?" at least once a week. And my sisters Susan, Laura, and Amy, just so they can see their names in print.

I'd like to also acknowledge two of the people who got me into this line of work. Jim Whoie, the best "big picture" thinker I've ever met, and James Hood, the best technical troubleshooter I know.

A huge thanks to my wife and sons. Sarah, Marty, and Nicholas...thanks for your patience and understanding. Now maybe we can go to Disney World!

And finally, I'd like to acknowledge my fourth grade English teacher, Mrs. Angela "The Moose" Cihiwsky, for reasons that will be obvious to her. Hi Mrs. C.!

Tell Us What You Think!

As the reader of this book, *you* are our most important critic and commentator. We value your opinion and want to know what we're doing right, what we could do better, what areas you'd like to see us publish in, and any other words of wisdom you're willing to pass our way.

As the Executive Editor for the Certification team at Macmillan Computer Publishing, I welcome your comments. You can fax, email, or write to me directly to let me know what you did or didn't like about this book—as well as what we can do to make our books stronger.

Please note that I cannot help you with technical problems related to the topic of this book, and that due to the high volume of mail I receive, I might not be able to reply to every message.

When you write, please be sure to include this book's title and author, as well as your name and phone or fax number. I will carefully review your comments and share them with the author and editors who worked on the book.

Fax: 317-581-4663

Email: `certification@mcp.com`

Mail: Mary Foote
Executive Editor
Certification
Macmillan Computer Publishing
201 West 103rd Street
Indianapolis, IN 46290 USA

Introduction

If you're reading this, you are probably looking to get your Microsoft Certified Systems Engineer certification. And you're probably wondering why you should buy this book rather than another of the dozens of other books that are available. So allow me to take this opportunity to explain exactly what the thinking was behind this book, and let you decide whether it's what you're looking for.

Let me assure you that no one was just sitting around thinking "What the market needs now is another Windows NT certification guide series." There are plenty of excellent books on passing the Windows NT exams on the market already. But there are some major things that the existing books are lacking, and the *Simulation Guide* series addresses this lack in three ways.

First, the *Simulation Guide* series is geared to prepare you for the new, scenario-based questions on the Microsoft exams. The days of "What utility do you use to ..." questions and A, B, C, or D answers are rapidly vanishing. The new series of exam questions is designed to test your ability to apply your knowledge to situations, not simply report on what you memorized from a book. Now you might see a question like this:

> Bob, Mary, and Alice all need to print to a color laser printer, which no one else is allowed access to. Because Bob is the company president's administrative assistant, his jobs need to print immediately, taking precedence over the other users' print jobs. How do you configure the printer?

This question would have four possible answers involving groups and priorities, and would require you to apply your experience and knowledge of configuring printers. The *Simulation Guide* series presents much of this information in a scenario format. Throughout the book you will find real-life scenarios, and a graphs-based simulation of the results.

Speaking of simulation, that is the second strength of this series. Recognizing that not everyone trying to get a Windows NT certification has the resources to set up a Windows NT learning lab in their basement, this series presents much of its information in the form of graphical simulations of actual tasks. As you can see, this presentation of information is radically different from the usual MCSE certification book. In addition, we explore some of the other features of each tool and utility, much as you might while sitting in front of a Windows NT Server. Just as you might click on a button, thinking "I wonder what this does..." our simulation takes you to that next step, with a detailed explanation of how it works.

Finally, this series is an excellent value. In fact, this book is a particularly good value because it encompasses both the Windows NT Server exam (70-67) and the Windows NT Server in the Enterprise exam. If you pick up a Windows NT Server exam guide, and a Windows NT Server in the Enterprise exam, and look up how to create a user, you'll see the steps are identical. The overlap between these two exams is considerable. For that reason, we have combined the two exams into one exam guide.

CHAPTER 1

Planning

This chapter helps you get ready for the "Planning" sections of the Windows NT Server (Exam 70-067) and Windows NT Server Enterprise (Exam 70-068) exams. This chapter is heavily tested on the Enterprise exam, due to the absolute need for planning in an enterprise deployment of Windows NT Server. To Microsoft's credit, installing Windows NT Server can be as easy as loading a word processing application. Unfortunately, that means some people have a tendency of thinking that Windows NT is as easy to use and support as a word processor. Not true. In this chapter you learn about a lot of the things you need to think about before you deploy Windows NT, whether you have 10 users or 10,000.

For Exam 70-067, the Windows NT Server Exam, Microsoft defines "Planning" objectives as follows:

- Plan the disk drive configuration for various requirements including choosing a file system and choosing a fault-tolerance method.
- Windows NT Server offers a number of options for configuring the disk subsystems. In order to successfully pass this section of the exam, you need to be familiar with the FAT and NTFS file systems, as well as how to configure hard drives for a number of different fault-tolerant configurations.
- Choose a protocol for various situations, including TCP/IP, NWLink IPX/SPX Compatible Transport, or NetBEUI.
- Windows NT Server is a terrific operating system, but it's not much good unless you can connect it to the network. This objective stresses familiarity with the three major protocols for Windows NT Server.

For Exam 70-068, the Windows NT Server Enterprise Exam, Microsoft defines "Planning" objectives as follows:

- Plan the implementation of directory services architecture, including selecting the appropriate domain model, supporting a single logon account, and allowing users to access resources in different domains.
- The whole point of an enterprise deployment of Windows NT is ensuring that you properly plan for the directory services architecture. This is the major differentiation between the Planning sections of the Server and Enterprise exams. You can expect a majority of the planning questions on the Enterprise exam to deal with domains, trusts, and ensuring client access to resources.
- Plan the disk drive configuration for various requirements including choosing a fault-tolerance method.
- As in the objective for the 70-067 exam, you need to be familiar with Windows NT's options for configuring disk subsystems. You should be familiar with the FAT and NTFS file systems, as well as how to configure hard drives for a number of different fault-tolerant configurations.
- Choose a protocol for various situations including TCP/IP, TCP/IP with DHCP and WINS, NWLink IPX/SPX Compatible Transport Protocol, Data Link Control (DLC), or AppleTalk.
- The Enterprise exam adds a few more protocols beyond those found on the Server exams list, but the bottom line is the same: You need to know when to use each protocol and why.

This chapter concentrates on three basic topics. First you learn how to plan for your disk configuration, including the file system and fault-tolerant drive configurations. Next you examine what protocols can be used with Windows NT, and why you would want to use them. Finally, you study what could be the most critical section of this chapter if you are taking the Windows NT Server in the Enterprise exam: domains and trust relationships. Get started by looking at the disk configurations.

PLANNING THE DISK CONFIGURATION

This section of the chapter discusses the two main facets of Windows NT Server's disk configurations: choosing the file system and choosing the drive configuration. Windows NT supports the DOS legacy file system, FAT (File Allocation Table), and the file system Microsoft introduced with Windows NT's first release, NTFS (New Technology File System). Windows NT also supports a variety of disk configurations, including striping (RAID Level 0), mirroring (RAID Level 1), and striping with parity (RAID Level 5). Each is discussed in turn.

> **NOTE** Windows NT supports a number of *software* RAID configurations. Be sure not to confuse these with the RAID configurations supported by the hardware vendor's SCSI RAID adapter. It is easy to configure a hardware RAID adapter to support a RAID Level 3, and it will work fine with NT because it happens at the hardware level, before the operating system is involved. RAID 3 is not one of Windows NT's software RAID levels.

Choosing a File System

One of the choices you need to make before you install Windows NT is what file system you plan to use. One choice, FAT, is a legacy file system that is also supported by MS-DOS and Windows 95/98. Although FAT was fine when hard drives averaged 120 MB and MS-DOS was the operating system of choice, it reveals some severe limitations with newer operating systems, larger drives, and the security requirements of today's networked servers. NTFS, on the other hand, is a robust file system that easily supports the largest hard drives on the market as well as fault tolerance and long filenames, and also allows you to implement very granular security to the file level. Take a closer look at FAT and NTFS in the following sections.

> **NOTE** Windows NT Server 3.x also supported HPFS (High Performance File System) for the OS/2 file system. This was a holdover from the times when IBM and Microsoft were co-developing a network operating system. Windows NT 4 no longer supports HPFS. If you are asked to install Windows NT on an HPFS volume, you must either convert the file system to NTFS, or back up the data, delete the partition, install Windows NT on either a FAT or an NTFS volume, and restore the data.

FAT

FAT (File Allocation Table) is a legacy file system from the days of MS-DOS. FAT has some fairly significant limitations:

- **Very Inefficient File Storage.** The FAT file system stores files by breaking the files up into pieces called *clusters.* On a small partition, FAT uses 4 KB clusters to store a file. So an 8 KB file would take up two clusters. Suppose, however, the file size is 5 KB instead of 8 KB. With a 5 KB file, the first 4 KB would be stored in one cluster, and the final 1 KB would be stored in a second cluster. The problem with FAT is that the remaining 3 KB of that second cluster is unusable—it's wasted. Even worse, when FAT encounters larger partitions, such as those that are used in most file servers these days, it can use a cluster of 32 KB, making it possible to waste over 31 KB in a cluster, depending on the file's configuration.

NOTE

FAT, although an inefficient file system, still outperforms NTFS on a partition of under 800 MB. Any partition larger than that causes FAT's inadequacies to make it slower than NTFS. Microsoft recommends a maximum of 400 MB for a FAT partition.

- **Lack of Support for Large Partitions.** FAT is unable to use disk partitions larger than 4 GB. Not a tremendous issue with older drives, but with the recent introduction of 9 GB drives for servers, and 8 GB drives in laptops, FAT's backward-compatibility pluses are rapidly outweighed.

FAT does have one redeeming feature. If you have a Windows NT server with a FAT partition, and there is a problem, you can boot from a DOS floppy disk and access the server's FAT partitions. (Of course, this sends security departments into convulsions.) This can be handy for troubleshooting, but it's not usually enough of a benefit to make FAT a file system of choice.

You might want to use a FAT file system in a server you are planning to multi-boot with DOS or Windows 95/98; these operating systems can't read NTFS partitions. However, configuring a multi-boot production server is generally a bad idea. It might be a better idea for a lab environment.

NOTE

Recently, Microsoft has a new version of FAT that addresses some of the issues surrounding the FAT file system. FAT-32, a 32-bit version of the FAT file system, was introduced with the OEM version of Windows 95, also known as Windows 95 OSR2. Although FAT-32

> resolves a number of FAT's issues, this system cannot be read by Windows NT Server. If you need to install Windows NT Server on a FAT-32 partition, you must back up the data, delete the partition, install NT on a FAT or NTFS partition, and restore the data.

A final note: In order to address FAT's file storage inefficiencies, file compression is often used. Unfortunately, Windows NT cannot recognize compressed FAT partitions. Be sure to uncompress the drive if it is to be accessed by Windows NT.

NTFS

NTFS (New Technology File System) was introduced when Windows NT was released in its 3.1 form. It corrects all of FAT's issues, and contains a number of very attractive options that make it a much better choice than FAT for a file server file system.

NTFS provides the following capabilities:

- **Support for Long File Names.** NTFS does not restrict you to the 8.3 format file names required by DOS or Windows for WorkGroups machines. NTFS maintains backward compatibility with DOS users by using special abbreviations that maintain the 8.3 naming convention. The file name `Simulation Guide.doc` would be abbreviated to `simula~1.doc` for DOS users.
- **Support for Windows NT Security.** NTFS allows granular user and group access control to both files and directories on the local machine. (File sharing security is handled separately.) This is a significant improvement over FAT's complete lack of security. For this reason alone, NTFS is the best choice for a file server file system.
- **Support for Fault-Tolerance.** At one level, disk activity is logged. If there is a hardware problem with the disk controller during a write operation, Windows NT can either try again or back out of the activity. NTFS also supports fault-tolerant disk configurations. You can set up volumes for better performance, fault-tolerance, or a mixture of both.

NTFS is the clear choice for the file system on a production file server.

For the exam, you may be asked what file system to use on an 800 MB (or less) volume to provide better performance. This is kind of a trick question. The answer is FAT because it performs better than NTFS on volumes of that size (refer to the note in the previous section). In real life, however, you would probably use an NTFS volume because in most cases security outweighs the minor performance increase FAT provides.

Converting from FAT to NTFS

When you select an NTFS partition upon installing Windows NT (covered in Chapter 2, "Installation and Configuration"), the partition is formatted with the FAT file system. The first time the server starts after setup has been completed, the FAT partition is converted to NTFS.

If you have a server that has a FAT partition and you want to convert it to NTFS, you can use the `CONVERT` utility, with the following flags:

```
CONVERT.EXE <drive>: /F:NTFS [/V]
```

`<drive>` is the drive letter of the partition to be converted. `/F:NTFS` indicates the partition is to be converted to NTFS. `[/V]` is an optional parameter that places the `CONVERT` utility into verbose mode.

As in the installation partition, this conversion takes place when the server next reboots. After a partition has been converted to NTFS, it cannot be converted back to FAT.

Configuring Disks for Fault-Tolerance and Performance

Now that you understand how to select a file system, consider the different configurations Windows NT allows you to configure under the NTFS file system. You can set up your drives for high performance, for fault-tolerance, or for a combination of both.

Before you start looking at the different configurations, you should review what exactly is meant by Redundant Array of Inexpensive Disks (RAID). With the introduction and proliferation of (relatively) inexpensive file servers based on UNIX and Novell's NetWare in the mid-1980s, a need arose for fault-tolerant disk subsystems. Disk mirroring and duplexing were common, but they were very expensive in terms of disk capacity. Two hard drives are needed for each usable drive. The notion of using a parity drive was introduced, which made fault-tolerance more affordable because you only gave up one drive out of three or more for the capability. The RAID specification was adopted from work done at Berkeley University, and describes the different types of fault-tolerance in terms of RAID levels. The three levels supported by Windows NT are described in the following sections. {*Configuring drives for the following RAID levels is discussed in Chapter 2, "Installation and Configuration."*}

> **NOTE**
> RAID implementations require that all the drives be of the same size.

Striping—RAID 0

Disk striping is not, strictly speaking, a RAID configuration because there is no redundant data. Striping takes the data and *stripes* it (writes one bit to each drive in the stripe set) across all drives in the array, in 64 K units. If implemented properly, striping can deliver very high performance. Some points of striping to consider include the following:

- Striping doesn't suffer from the overhead associated with maintaining a parity bit (RAID-5, or Striping with Parity, discussed later).
- Striping takes advantage of the multiple read/write heads (one for each drive in the array) used for reading and writing the data. This yields the highest possible I/O performance for any disk configuration under Windows NT.
- If the drives/partitions are all the same size, a stripe set's capacity is the same as the total capacity of the drives in the array.
- Because a stripe set has no fault-tolerance capabilities, the risk of data loss goes up every time you add a hard drive. Each additional drive is an additional point of failure.

> **NOTE**
> Unlike most hardware RAID 0 implementations, Windows NT allows you to use drives of different sizes to configure a stripe set. Just remember that each of the partitions must be the same size. For example, if you have a 100 MB partition on one drive, a 500 MB partition on the second, and a 250 MB partition on the third, the stripe set will have a capacity of 300 MB. The rest of the space on the larger two drives is free space.

> **NOTE**
> The Windows NT system partition cannot be contained on a stripe set volume, or a stripe set with parity volume. It can be located on a mirrored partition, however, which is recommended for critical production servers.

Mirroring—RAID 1

Mirroring (RAID 1) is a technology that has been around for quite a while. Common in the early UNIX and NetWare servers, and later in OS/2 and Windows NT, RAID 1 is a mirrored pair of disks, in which one drive contains an exact copy of the data on the other. Write performance suffers with mirroring because each write must be performed for both disks in the pair.

> **NOTE** To implement *disk duplexing,* a variation of RAID 1, add a second controller to the system. Disk duplexing not only improves fault-tolerance by removing the controller as a single point of failure, but also adds an additional data path. This improves performance by allowing concurrent writes to the mirrored disks.

There is a drawback to a RAID 1 implementation: It is an expensive method of fault-tolerance. Granted, the reliability of a RAID 1 implementation is terrific, but available capacity is only half the total capacity of the disks in the array. This limitation makes RAID 1 a very expensive solution to implement.

Striping with Parity—RAID 5

Striping with Parity (RAID 5) provides the best of both the RAID 0 and RAID 1 implementations. RAID 5 works by striping data across a minimum of three drives and a maximum of 32 drives. What makes this approach different from RAID 0 is that, in addition to the data, a parity bit is written as well.

Think of it like this: Assume your piece of data can be represented by the formula X+Y=Z. If you know X, Y, and Z, then you have the solution to the problem—you know what the data is. But what happens if you only know X and Y? You can still calculate Z by inserting the information you have into the formula. That's how RAID 5 works. Because a parity bit is written with each set of data bits, the loss of any single drive is not a loss of data. Although an operating system may no longer have all the data on its drives, it can calculate the missing information by using the data it does have, in conjunction with the formula used to write the data to the drives.

A nice thing about this implementation over RAID 1 is that you get fault-tolerance at a cheaper price. With RAID 1, your capacity is equal to half the total drive capacity. With RAID 5, your capacity is the total number of drives, minus the capacity of one of the drives. Even in its worst case configuration of three drives, you only lose 33% of your capacity, rather than 50%.

Like RAID 0, RAID 5 can take advantage of the multiple drive heads for read/write activity. Due to the overhead associated with writing the parity bit to disk, however, RAID 5's performance is generally slower than RAID 0 or RAID 1.

Choosing the Right Protocol

The next piece of the planning puzzle is to decide which protocol you need to run on your server. This is usually determined by the existing network infrastructure, other equipment with which the server must coexist , present network protocols, and services to be delivered. In many cases, you may need to run two or three protocols in order to coexist with current services on the network. The following sections discuss the features and functions of each of the protocols Windows NT supports. {*TCP/IP and NWLink IPX/SPX Compatible Transport are discussed in greater detail in Chapter 4, "Connectivity." DHCP and DNS are also discussed in depth in that chapter.*}

TCP/IP

TCP/IP is by far the most popular protocol running on networks today. A good rule of thumb is "when in doubt, network with TCP/IP." TCP/IP's popularity can be directly linked to its use as the backbone protocol of the Internet. In addition, features such as DNS (Domain Name Service) and DHCP (Dynamic Host Control Protocol) make TCP/IP more attractive to administrators.

When would you use TCP/IP? TCP/IP is the protocol of choice when you need to connect to the Internet, or when you have a Wide Area Network (WAN) environment without NetWare servers to communicate with. Although TCP/IP's addressing and management can make it a bit more planning-intensive protocol to implement, it is well worth the time and effort.

NWLink IPX/SPX Compatible Transport

NWLink IPX/SPX Compatible Transport is Microsoft's answer to Novell's IPX/SPX protocol family. Novell introduced IPX in the 1980s as the protocol of choice for its NetWare network operating system. A lot of people have complained recently about Novell's reliance on IPX, and its lack of native IP support. It is interesting to note that when Novell released IPX, TCP/IP was still in its infancy. The Internet still consisted of a number of universities and government agencies, and the World Wide Web wasn't even a dream yet. Novell was looking for a protocol that was easy for administrators to use, as well as routable and fast. Because there really wasn't a protocol that fit its needs, Novell came up with IPX. With the large number of Novell NetWare clients around, you will still find IPX running on a lot of company backbones.

So when do you use NWLINK? NWLINK is used whenever you need Novell NetWare coexistence. This can be for migration purposes, or just so the Windows NT server can access IPX-based resources and can be accessed by IPX-based clients.

NetBEUI

NetBEUI is a protocol originally developed by Microsoft and IBM when they were still doing joint development on OS/2. A nonroutable protocol, NetBEUI allows for an easy setup and maintenance of a network. NetBEUI is also a very *chatty* protocol, meaning there are a lot of broadcasts involved with using this protocol.

When do you use NetBEUI? If you have a very small, single-segment network with a limited number of users, and no experienced administrators to set up TCP/IP or IPX, NetBEUI makes a good choice. There is very little administration for NetBEUI beyond installing the protocol.

AppleTalk

Deciding when to use AppleTalk is pretty easy. If you have Apple Macintosh equipment and want to allow it to access your Windows NT server, you probably need AppleTalk. Apple developed AppleTalk when it first introduced networking to the Macintosh platform. A very slow and proprietary protocol, AppleTalk was never accepted outside of the Macintosh platform, and is not used a great deal.

DLC (Data Link Control)

DLC is a Hewlett-Packard protocol that allows Windows NT to connect directly to HP printers across the network. You can use DLC when setting up a server to act as a print server for the network, or NT clients can use it to print directly to the printer, bypassing any Windows NT (or other) queues or print servers. This protocol also spares a network administrator from either configuring TCP/IP for the printer or directly connecting it via cable to a server.

IBM's SNA (Systems Network Architecture) protocol also uses DLC to communicate to IBM mainframes or front-end processors.

Planning the Directory Services (Domain) Architecture

For those of you studying for the Enterprise exam, this is the part of the planning chapter to pay close attention to. When you are ready to deploy your server into a network environment, you need to be familiar with the different ways that Windows NT Server can be configured for authentication and administration. A Windows NT Server can be set up to be a member of a *workgroup* or a *domain.* You should also be familiar with the four types of domain architectures—*single, master, multiple master,* and *complete trust*—and understand the strengths and weaknesses of each. And finally, in order to understand how to set up the multiple domain implementations, you must understand how *trusts* play a part in the Windows NT Directory Services model. Start with a look at the differences between workgroups and domains.

Workgroups Versus Directory Services

Windows NT Servers can be divided into two different architectures: workgroups and directory services. Both architectures have their place in the suite of configurations for Windows NT Server, and each has its own uses, strengths, and weaknesses. The following sections offer a more in-depth look at each of these configurations.

Workgroup

Windows NT Workgroups are collections of Windows NT servers and workstations configured to broadcast as members of the same workgroup. Each server maintains a database of users and each server has to be administered separately. Each user generally maintains his own access controls, and determines which resources will be shared.

The following is a list of advantages of workgroups:

- **Ease of Use.** In many cases, workgroups can be easier to use than domains, due to the lack of the domain controllers. Windows NT's utilities make creating users and sharing resources very intuitive, and well within the abilities of the average user.

- **Cost.** Workgroups tend to be less expensive than domains because there is generally not a need for an administrator, and you also don't need to pay for dedicated hardware for a domain controller.

The following is a list of disadvantages of workgroups:

- **Security.** With many untrained people configuring the access control and sharing of resources, the risk of inadvertently sharing confidential information is greater.
- **Resource Availability.** With information and resources distributed throughout the workgroup, the chances are usually greater that the resource you need will be unavailable. If the boss takes his laptop to Tahiti for his vacation and the sales forecasts are on his shared E: drive, for example, you'll need to wait a couple weeks before you have access to those files.
- **Scalability.** Workgroups do not scale well beyond about 10 or 15 users. Because there is no way to synchronize passwords on each of the member servers (other than manually), you can suddenly find yourself struggling to remember 10 different passwords.

Generally the best environment for a workgroup deployment is in a small office or a single department, where there are a limited number of users, a limited number of machines, and a need to keep costs down.

Although workgroups are still used from time to time, increasing demand for reliable networks and decreasing hardware and software costs are making domains more attractive even to smaller offices.

Directory Services

A domain uses primary and secondary domain controllers to provide user authentication for the entire domain. All resources in the domain are managed with the domain utilities. This overcomes the limitations of the workgroup model. Because there are a number of different domain implementations, each with advantages and disadvantages, you should study them individually in Chapter 3, "Managing Resources." At a higher level, use of the domain architecture is meant to provide several services, as discussed in the following list. {*Domain utilities are discussed in detail in Chapter 3, "Managing Resources."*}

- **Centralized Administration.** Whereas the workgroup model allows every user to manage access to resources for his own machine, the use of domains moves the administration to a central point. Domains require administrators—that is, users with special levels of access who can manage user accounts and access to resources.

- **Single Point of Logon.** With a correctly implemented domain, users need only one user ID and password to access any resource in the network. This is far different from the workgroup model, which requires a user to log on to each machine she wants to access resources on.
- **Access to Resources.** The flip side to single login is the global access to resources. A correctly designed and implemented domain allows access to any resource on the network, as long as the user has the correct permissions.
- **Directory Synchronization.** All the information about users and domain resources are contained in a single database, known as the Security Accounts Manager (SAM) database. This database can be replicated to backup domain controllers throughout the network, allowing for local authentication to the domain from anywhere on the network.

You've learned how domains work in general, so now the subject matter becomes more specific. For testing purposes, think about how you would apply each of these models to a real-world situation. Microsoft is much more interested in testing whether you can apply these models appropriately than in whether you can define them.

Selecting the Appropriate Domain Model

Before you deploy Windows NT Server into a network environment, it is important to understand the needs of the environment, and choose the domain model best suited to meet those needs.

Microsoft has defined four domain models:

- **Single Domain Model.** A single domain is used for user authentication and also contains all the shared resources.
- **Master Domain Model.** One domain is used for user authentication. Additional domains contain shared resources.
- **Multiple Master Domain Model.** Two or more domains perform user authentication. Additional domains contain shared resources.
- **Complete Trust Domain Model.** Multiple domains trust each other to authenticate users and share resources. Each domain contains user accounts and shared resources.

Each of these models has advantages and disadvantages, as discussed in the following sections.

Single Domain Model

The Single Domain model is the building block of the Windows NT Directory Services architecture. This domain is used for user authentication as well as resource management. This is also the simplest implementation, so it's a great place to start with domain implementations. *Figure 1.1* shows a Single Domain implementation. As you can see, the users, computer, and resources are all contained within the same domain.

FIGURE 1.1
An example of a Single Domain architecture.

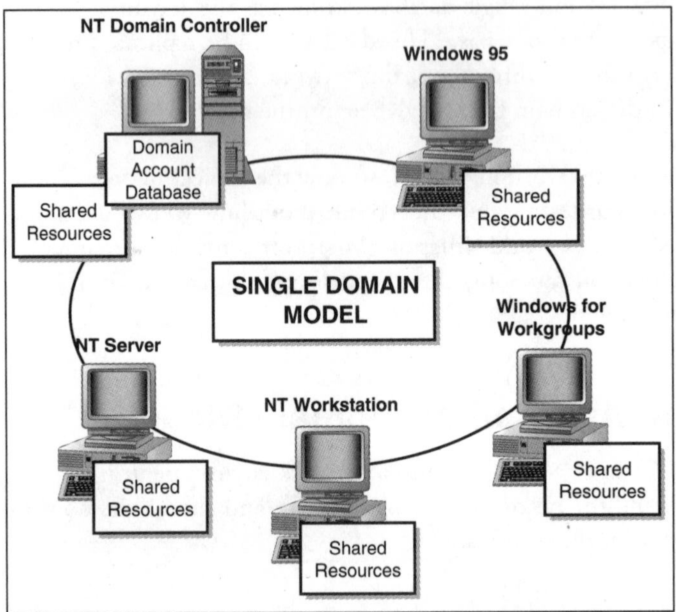

The primary advantage of the Single Domain architecture is its centralized administration. Because all the user and computer accounts exist within the same domain, they can all be managed from that domain.

The following is a list of disadvantages:

- **Scalability.** Although a single domain can theoretically support 40,000 users and computer accounts, things like authentication overhead and browser traffic can frequently cripple the domain before it reaches its theoretical limit.

> **NOTE** An important thing to keep in mind as you prepare for the exam is the two criteria for the maximum size of a domain. A domain can either contain 40,000 users and computer accounts, or it can have a SAM (Security Accounts Manager) database. Calculating the size of the SAM is discussed later in the chapter.

- **Security.** Because all the users and resources exist in the same domain, there is no way to allow local administrators to administer just local resources. Windows NT's administrative permissions do not allow that level of granularity. For example, if you give Phil in Accounting the ability to manage the shares on the Accounting server, you've made him a user administrator as well, whether you intended to or not.
- **Organization.** Although Windows NT has a theoretical limit of around 40,000 accounts, accounts of anywhere near that quantity can cause some problems with the domain organization. The next time you are in User Manager for Domains, look at the list of users and imagine 15,000 of them. If you need to reset a password for John Smith, you need to page through around 13,000 accounts before you get to John's. This does not provide ease of administration.

The Single Domain model works extremely well for smaller networks. Suppose, however, that the number of your users and computer accounts approach the multiple thousands, or you want to allow departments to control access to their resources while maintaining central account administration. It is then time to look at the next model: the Master Domain.

Master Domain Model

The primary function of the Master Domain model is to allow domains to specialize. One domain is devoted entirely to user authentication, whereas the additional domains are used for shared resources. This specialization grants some organizational benefits. Users are all in one domain, but resources such as printers and file servers are in another; this prevents resource domains from having to process user authentication.

Figure 1.2 shows a Master Domain network. Domain A is the Master domain, used for authentication for all logons. Resource domains B and C, which contain the shared resources, *trust* domain A. Trusts are discussed immediately following the directory services discussion.

FIGURE 1.2
An example of a Master Domain architecture.

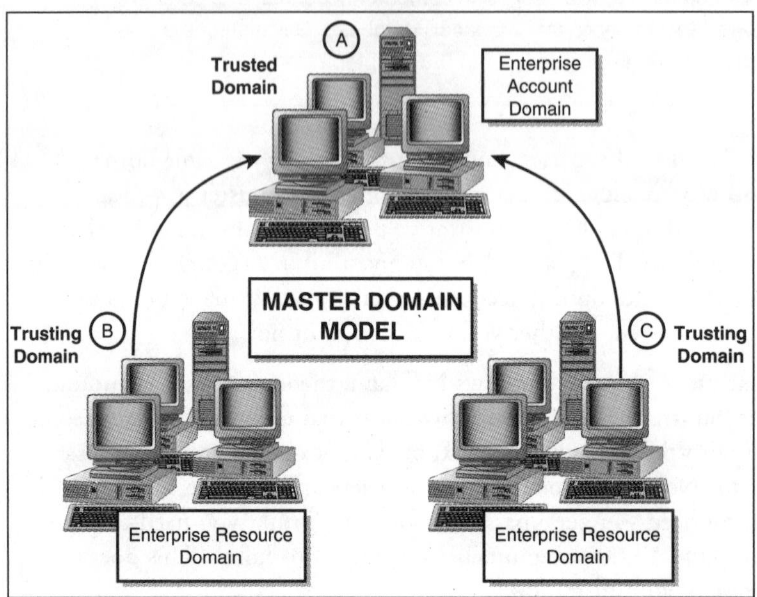

The following is a list of advantages of Master Domain architecture:

- **Centralized Security Management.** Because all user authentications occur from the Master domain, all user account security and resource access control are managed from a single point.
- **Local Management of Resources.** One of the drawbacks of the Single Domain model is the fact that the people who manage resources also have the ability to manage users. By using resource domains, the Master Domain model allows for local administration of resource domains, but maintains user management in the user domain.
- **Global Management of Resources.** This feature appears to contradict the preceding feature, but in fact it does not. Through the use of Global groups in the Master domain, and Local groups in the resource domains, administrators in the Master domain can easily be configured to manage resources located in the resource domains.
- **Better Organization.** Resource domains can be used to organize resources logically. For example, users in the Sales Department might access servers and printers located in the Sales resource domain, whereas their user accounts reside in the Master domain.

The following is a list of disadvantages of the Master Domain architecture:

- **Bottlenecks.** In a large Master Domain implementation, processing user authentication can become a bottleneck during peak utilization times, such as morning or after lunch. This model supports a maximum of 40,000 user accounts in the Master domain. Master domains are often thought of as User domains.
- **Trust Relationships.** Trusts in and of themselves are not necessarily a disadvantage. They do, however, introduce another factor that needs to be configured and maintained. In a Master Domain model, each resource domain trusts the Master domain. The number of trusts is equal to the number of resource domains. Trusts are discussed later in the chapter.

The following is a list of uses of the Master Domain architecture:

- **Larger Networks.** A Master Domain model is appropriate for networks that have outgrown the Single Domain model.
- **Secure Networks.** This is a little misleading because all networks should be secure. The Master Domain model is useful when your security model requires that a limited number of administrators have access to user accounts. If you need to use local administrators for resource management, but don't want them to have access to user accounts, this is the domain model for you.

Multiple Master Domain Model

The Multiple Master Domain model extends the Master Domain model by providing additional logon domains. This is the best method for supporting extremely large organizations.

> **NOTE**
> Microsoft's domain architecture was a Multiple Master domain supporting 40,000+ users worldwide. The next release of Windows NT replaces the domain architecture with a true directory service, so that is the direction the Microsoft network is moving toward.

Figure 1.3 shows a simple network that is organized around two Master domains. Each Master domain supports about half the user and computer accounts.

FIGURE 1.3
An example of a Multiple Master Domain architecture.

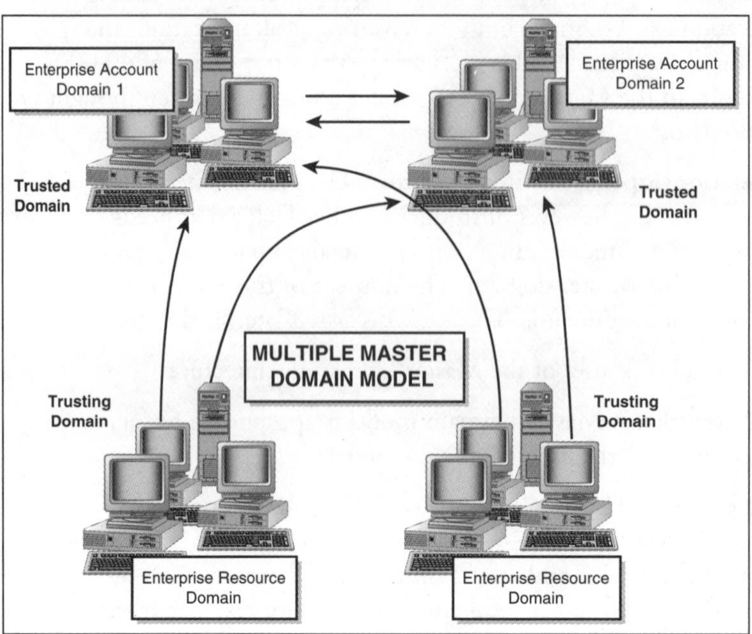

The following is a list of advantages of the Multiple Master Domain architecture:

- **Scalable.** This model will scale to support any size organization.
- **Centralized Security Management.** Because all user authentications occur from one of the Master domains, all user account security and resource access control are managed from a single point. This is contingent on the proper trust relationships being set up between the Master domains.
- **Local Management of Resources.** Just as the Master Domain model does, the Multiple Master Domain model allows for local administration of resource domains, while maintaining user management in the user domains.
- **Global Management of Resources.** As with the Master Domain model, through the use of Global groups in the Master domain, and Local groups in the resource domains, administrators in the Master domains can easily be configured to manage resources located in the resource domains.

- **Better Organization.** Resource domains can be used to organize resources logically. For example, users in the Sales Department might access servers and printers located in the Sales resource domain, whereas their user accounts reside in the Master domain.

The following is a list of disadvantages of the Multiple Master Domain architecture:

- **More Trusts.** Because each Master domain must have a two-way trust with any other Master domains, and each resource domain must trust each of the Master domains, trust relationships increase geometrically as the number of domains increases. For example, the two Master domains with three resource domains yields eight trust relationships. A single Master domain with three resource domains requires only three.
- **Complexity.** Because your users are no longer contained in a single SAM database, you must be careful to be aware of the location of each user's account, and of the relationships existing between all the users and groups.

The Multiple Master Domain model scales to support an organization of any size, so it should be used for networks that have outgrown the Master Domain model.

Complete Trust Domain Model

A Complete Trust Domain model is essentially a domain that is made up entirely of Master domains. That is, every domain contains users and resources. The local domain administrators, through the use of two-way trusts between domains, control access to resources.

This domain has fallen out of use as of late, due to some significant issues surrounding maintaining all the two-way trust relationships. *Figure 1.4* shows a Complete Trust Domain model.

FIGURE 1.4
An example of a Complete Trust Domain architecture.

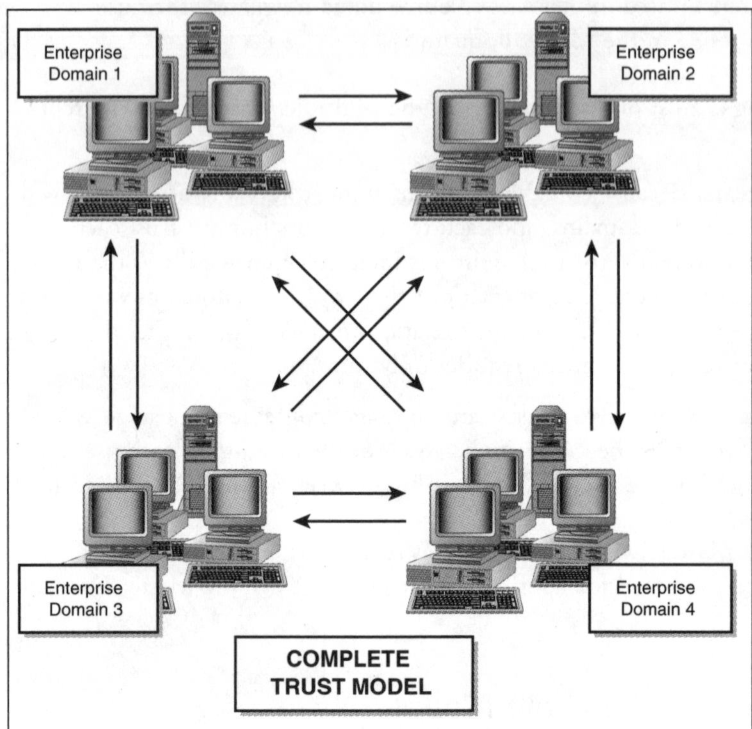

The following is a list of advantages of the Complete Trust Domain module architecture:

- **Scalable.** In theory, this model can be scaled to fit any size organization. In practice, however, the number of trust relationships can be prohibitive.
- **Departmental Control.** Each department retains control of its users and resources. Furthermore, no central MIS department is required.
- **Organization.** Because every department retains control of its own domain, users, groups, and resources, all remain in the local domain.

The following is a list of disadvantages of the Complete Trust Domain model architecture:

- **No Central Administration.** This is a very "anything goes" management model, and allows everyone to maintain his own users and resources. This also means that one department is very vulnerable to the configuration errors of other departments.

- **No Central Security.** Because this model requires that everyone trust everyone else, centralized security is not possible.
- **Trusts, Trusts, and More Trusts.** This model requires $n(n-1)$ trusts, where n is the number of domains. So for a 5 domain network, you would need 20 trust relationships. This can present a significant support issue, particularly when each department is responsible for maintaining its own trusts.

Never use this domain model! Even Microsoft has withdrawn its recommendations for utilizing this domain model, due to the amount of criticism it has gathered from the industry. Even so, take a close look at the advantages of this architecture because there is always the chance that a Complete Trust question might have snuck its way onto the exam.

Review of Domain Models

Because understanding the use of the appropriate domain model is critical to successfully passing the Enterprise exam, begin your review of the different directory services architectures by using some scenarios.

Scenario 1.1

Your company has 60,000 employees, broken up into four divisions, spread throughout the company. Each division has its own servers and printers, and you have a central IS organization that maintains user accounts and the domain design. What domain architecture should you use?

Required Results

- Use a Multiple Master Domain architecture. You should have at least two Master domains, with resource domains for each of the divisions to manage their resources.

Scenario 1.2

You are the owner of a small real estate office with 12 employees. Some are in the office all the time, while several travel with laptops. You don't have a dedicated administrator, so you are looking for a simple solution. What domain architecture should you use?

Required Results

- That was a trick question. You don't want or need a domain. Just configure everything to work in a workgroup.

Scenario 1.3

You work for a college with about 500 employees and 4,000 students. You have decided to deploy Windows NT. What domain architecture should you use?

Required Results

- Because this is a single campus, and the number of users and computers is well within the limits of a domain, a Single Domain architecture will work quite well.

Scenario 1.4

You work for the same college, but in this case each department pays for its own servers and printers, and wants to maintain control. What domain architecture should you deploy?

Required Results

- Use a Master Domain architecture. Your MIS department maintains the user accounts in the Master domain, and each department can have administration of its own resource domain.

Scenario 1.5

You are an administrator at corporate headquarters for a 30,000-user manufacturing corporation. Due to extremely nasty political infighting, none of the seven product lines can agree on a corporate domain structure, and none of them wants to give up administration to corporate headquarters, preferring to do their own thing. What domain architecture should you use?

Required Results

- For the exam, if asked, say Complete Trust. In the real world, however, either get some buy-in from senior management, force those divisions to give up control, and implement a Master or Multiple Master architecture, or find a new job. You don't ever want to be the person supporting a Complete Trust domain architecture, especially in a politically volatile environment.

Calculating the Size of the SAM (Security Accounts Manager) Database

Although it's very easy to understand that a Windows NT domain has a maximum size of 40,000 users, it's a little less clear what Microsoft means when it discusses the fact that the SAM database can be up to 40 MB. What exactly does that mean? In order to understand this a little better, take a look at how you can calculate the size of a SAM database.

First, there are four types of accounts contained in the SAM database:

- User
- Computer
- Local Group
- Global Group

Each of these accounts requires a certain amount of space in the SAM. Users and Computers have fixed sizes; each group needs space for the group itself and for each user in the group. Table 1.1 gives you the exact requirements.

TABLE 1.1

ACCOUNT TYPE SPACE REQUIREMENTS

Account Type	*Required Space*
User Account	1.0K
Computer Account	0.5K
Local Group Account	0.5K + 36 bytes per user
Global Group Account	0.5K + 12 bytes per user

Figure 1.5 shows a sample worksheet for calculating an account's size requirement.

FIGURE 1.5
Calculating the SAM database size.

Calculate each of the following, then total.

1.	Number of Users	____X	1.0K equals:	____
2.	Number of Computer Accounts	____X	0.5K equals:	____
3.	Number of Local Groups	____X	0.5K equals:	____
	Number of Members in Local Groups	____X	36 bytes equals:	____
4.	Number of Global Groups	____X	0.5K equals:	____
	Number of Members in Global Groups	____X	12 bytes equals:	____
Total:				____

If you will be doing a lot of capacity planning, this is an application that lends itself quite well to a spreadsheet. You can automatically calculate the database size by simply changing numbers.

Trust Relationships—Allowing Users to Access Resources in Different Domains

A trust relationship establishes a security relationship between two domains, allowing secure user authentication and resource access between two domains. If Domain A has a unique resource that Domain B users need to access, this access can be given through a trust relationship between Domains A and B. This allows the user to log on to the network once, and access resources on multiple domains, if necessary. Take a closer look at exactly how trusts work.

Simply put, a trust relationship is a one-way relationship consisting of a *trusted* and a *trusting* domain. Even a two-way trust, as described in the later section "Two-Way Trust Relationships," is really two one-way trusts, with each domain trusting the other in turn. It works as follows:

- A *trusted* domain allows another domain to share its SAM database. This domain's users can access resources in the trusting domain.
- A *trusting* domain can assign access and permissions to users and groups in the trusted domain.

Sounds simple, doesn't it? Unfortunately, trust relationships seem to be one of those things that you either understand immediately, or you really have to work to understand at all. I will attempt to give you a real-life example of a trust relationship. If this confuses you further, please ignore it and move on to the examples in the following sections. Sometimes this helps, sometimes not.

Suppose you have a resource—say it's a new car. In order for someone else to use the car, you need to give permission. Your neighbor across the street needs to use your car to get to the store. Because you *trust* your neighbor, you give him access to the car. You have *trusted* your neighbor with your resource. That makes you *trusting*, and him *trusted*. With luck, this example has helped.

It's important to remember that trust relationships can only be established between two Windows NT domains. Workgroups cannot participate in a trust relationship. In fact, trusts are actually made between the PDCs of each domain. Because a workgroup has no PDC, it cannot participate in a trust.

Now, the purpose of a trust relationship is to allow users to access resources in another domain. How exactly does that work? A trust relationship allows the administrator of the trusting domain to create Access Control Lists (ACLs) for a resource in a domain, and then use the ACLs to grant access to users in the trusted domain. This is done in almost the same manner as assigning access to local users, except that users from another domain include their domain as part of their user name in the trusting domain. One other feature of a trust is the ability of users in the trusted domain to log on to the domain from a workstation or computer in the trusting domain. This is known as *pass-through authentication* and is discussed in more detail later in the chapter.

One piece of advice for the exam: Use the scrap paper provided to diagram scenarios when they are given to you. Many times seeing the relationships can clarify any confusion surrounding a trusts question.

Trust relationships can be one-way between domains, or they can be two-way. Take a look at the simple, one-way case first.

One-way Trust Relationships

Figure 1.6 shows an example of a trust relationship that involves only two domains. Domain A is the trusted domain, and Domain B is the trusting domain. Notice the server located in Domain B. In order to give the user in Domain A access to the server, place the user in Domain A in a Local group in Domain B. Assign rights to the server to the Local group. You can also place a Global group from Domain A in the Local group in Domain B. {*Local and Global groups are discussed further in Chapter 3, "Managing Resources."*}

FIGURE 1.6
An example of a one-way trust.

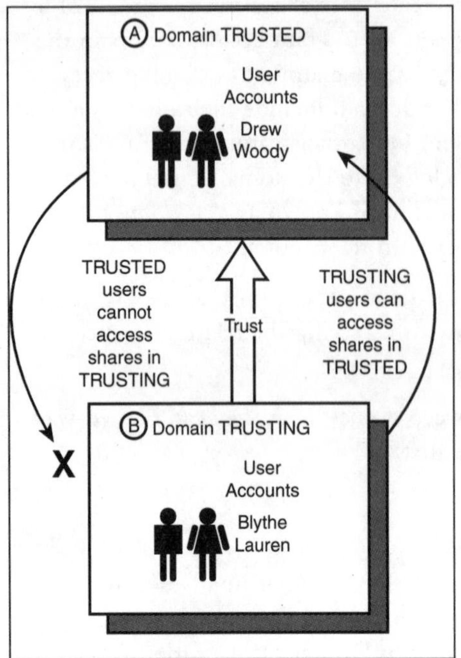

> **NOTE** Trust relationships are configured using User Manager for Domains. This is a two-step process in which the trusting domain must decide who to trust, and then the trusted domain must know who is trusting it. This relationship must be configured in both domains. It cannot be done from one domain.

Two-Way Trust Relationships

Figure 1.7 shows a two-way trust relationship. Two-way trusts require configuring two separate trust relationships. In a two-way trust, users in either domain can access resources in the other domain. Once again, users or Global groups from one domain can be placed in a Local group of the other, and that group can be granted permissions to local resources.

FIGURE 1.7
An example of a two-way trust.

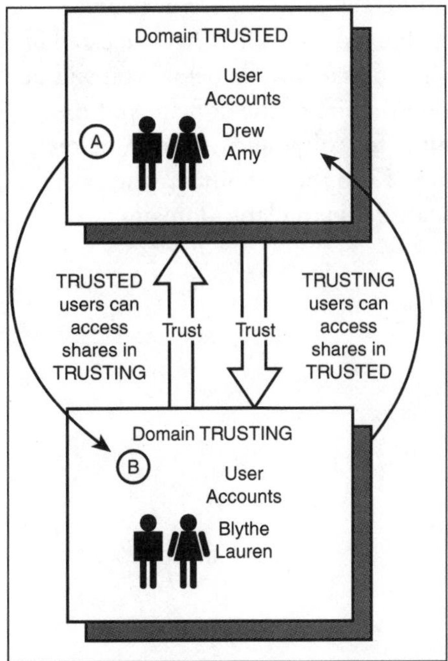

Pass-Through Authentication

Pass-through authentication must be taken into account when you are planning your domain architecture, for performance reasons. Pass-through authentication occurs at the following three points during Windows NT authentication:

- When you try to access a resource in a trusting domain, your domain (the trusted domain) must pass the authentication request to the trusting domain's domain controller to verify that you are allowed to access a resource.
- When you log on to a local domain from an NT Workstation or Server, the Net Logon service passes the authentication request to the domain controller for authentication.
- When you log on to the trusted domain from a trusting domain, the trusting domain must pass the authentication request on to the trusted domain's controller in order to be authenticated.

That's a very interesting bit of information for the true Windows NT fanatic, but it's tough to see why you need to be aware of this when you are planning your domain architecture. The key concept here is performance. If your authentication request is being passed to a domain controller that is located on the other side of a 56K WAN link, it's going to take a while before you will be authenticated to the domain. Depending on the size of the domain and the other traffic on the link, you could have time for coffee and a Danish before you are authenticated and can start working. Keep this in mind as you take the exam and, equally important, when you start designing large domains.

CHAPTER 2

Installation and Configuration

This chapter helps you prepare for the "Installation" sections of the Windows NT Server (Exam 70-067) and Windows NT Server Enterprise (Exam 70-068) exams. It is very easy to underestimate the importance of this section because it is very easy to install Windows NT on a server, right? You put in Disk 1, boot the system, and fill in the blanks. When you're done, you have a server. Unfortunately for anyone who needs to pass the exam, there is a little more to it than that. To help you understand all the facets of the installation, this chapter covers everything Microsoft considers important about installing Windows NT Server 4, in a variety of configurations. To start, take a look at what Microsoft expects you to know.

> **NOTE** You may notice that the number of objectives for the Server exam is significantly greater than for the Enterprise exam. That's a pretty good sign that you will see more Installation questions on the Server exam than on the Enterprise exam.

For Exam 70-067, the Windows NT Server Exam, Microsoft defines "Installation" objectives as follows:

- Install Windows NT Server to perform various server roles, including Primary Domain Controller (PDC), Backup Domain Controller (BDC), or as a Member server.

  For this objective, Microsoft wants you to understand the function of each of these types of server installations, when and why you might use them, and what it takes to install Windows NT to perform each function.

- Install Windows NT Server by using various methods, including CD-ROM, over-the-network. Also be familiar with the Network Client Administrator.

This objective is meant to ensure that you understand all the facets of installation methods. You never know when you will be asked to deploy 200 or 300 Windows NT Servers, and you don't want to put in Disk 1, boot the server, and follow the prompts 300 times. There are better ways to perform a multiple install, which will be discussed in this chapter.

- Configure protocols and protocol bindings for TCP/IP, NWLink IPX/SPX Compatible Transport, and NetBEUI.

  Recognizing that a server is not much use unless it's connected to a network, this objective requires you to understand the installation and configuration of some of the protocols that Microsoft supports.

- Configure network adapters. You should understand changing IRQ, IObase, and memory addresses, as well as configuring multiple adapters.

  This is one of the hardware objectives. You are expected to know what an IRQ is, what the IObase is, and how memory addresses are used. Finally, you should be aware of how to install multiple network adapters.

- Configure Windows NT Server core services, including Directory Replicator service, License Manager, and other services.

  Windows NT has a number of services that are loaded at installation. You are expected to know what they are, what they are used for, and how to configure them.

- Configure peripherals and devices, including communication devices, SCSI devices, tape device drivers, UPS devices and UPS service, mouse drivers, display drivers, and keyboard drivers.

  Another hardware objective. You are expected to know how to install, load drivers for, and configure a variety of system peripherals.

- Configure hard disks for allocating disk space capacity, providing redundancy, improving performance, providing security, and formatting.

  This contains all the implementations of disk storage strategies that were discussed in Chapter 1, "Planning." You must be familiar with the Disk Administrator utility for this section.

- Configure printers, including adding and configuring a printer, implementing a printer pool, and setting print priorities.

  With Windows NT's growing popularity as a file and print server, Microsoft wants to be sure you understand how to set up printing for the Windows NT environment.

- Configure a Windows NT Server computer for various types of client computers, including Windows NT Workstation, Microsoft Windows 95, and Microsoft MS-DOS.

A server is no good without clients to connect to it. This objective requires you to be able to configure Windows NT so clients can connect to it and use its services.

For Exam 70-068, the Windows NT Server Enterprise Exam, Microsoft defines "Installation" objectives as follows:

- Install Windows NT Server to perform various server roles, including Primary Domain Controller (PDC), Backup Domain Controller (BDC) and as a Member server.

  This is the same objective as for the Server exam. Be sure you understand the difference between the three types of servers, and what is different during the installation process.

- Configure protocols and protocol bindings, including TCP/IP, TCP/IP with DHCP and WINS, NWLink IPX/SPX Compatible Transport Protocol, DLC, and AppleTalk.

  While essentially the same as for the Server exam, this objective adds a few protocols.

- Configure Windows NT Server core services, including Directory Replicator and Computer Browser services.

  Another duplicate requirement with an additional service to discuss. Computer browsing in an Enterprise environment can be more challenging than in a small office, so this is very useful information for Enterprise exam takers.

- Configure hard disks for providing redundancy and improving performance.

  This objective has a slightly shorter list of drive requirements because a server in an Enterprise deployment tends to focus on only one of these two components.

- Configure printers, including adding and configuring a printer, implementing a printer pool, and setting print priorities.

  Because you still use printers in an Enterprise deployment, configuring them is a requirement for this exam as well.

- Configure a Windows NT Server computer for various types of clients, including Windows NT Workstation, Windows 95, and Macintosh.

  Pay attention to the addition of the Macintosh in the Enterprise exam. Some additional services must be set up to allow a Macintosh to connect to your Windows NT server.

This chapter covers the installation of Windows NT in depth, as well as the configuration of all the components that accept hardware with Windows NT loaded on it to create a production server, ready for use by end users. The discussions do not focus as heavily on the mechanics (flipping disks and filling in the blanks) as it does on the processes, mechanisms, and peripherals that make Windows NT the operating system of choice for so many users.

INSTALLING WINDOWS NT SERVER

The preceding sections discussed what you need to know, and why. Now you're ready to jump right into learning about the Windows NT installation process.

Hardware Requirements

One of the important parts of making sure you are successful in not only passing the exam, but in ensuring that your Windows NT installation is successful, is to be very familiar with the hardware requirements for Windows NT. It is important to keep in mind that these are minimum requirements. If you want more than a minimum of performance and capacity, it is strongly advised that you go with a more substantial hardware configuration. Also, make sure any of the components you are installing can be found on the Windows NT Hardware Compatibility List (HCL).

> **NOTE**
> One of the most important things to know before you start a Windows NT installation is whether the components you are using are on the *Hardware Compatibility List (HCL)*. This is a list of hardware components that Microsoft has certified as being fully compatible with Windows NT and are supported by Microsoft. There are a number of people in the industry who insist that they can build a server out of components that is *just as good* as a major vendor's server line. That may or may not be the case, but if you are working on a *built* system, it is a good idea to make sure the components are on the HCL. One other thing to remember: There is usually a bit of lag time between a product's release and when it hits the HCL. If this is a major server vendor, make sure that the vendor states whether the product is NT-compatible. If the vendor says it is, and you have a problem, you can always go back to the vendor for support.

Intel Platform

If you plan to install Windows NT Server on an Intel platform, the minimum hardware configuration needs to be as follows:

- *Processor*—Windows NT Server requires a minimum of a 32-bit x86 (a minimum Intel 80486-25DX) processor. Pentium or above is recommended for best performance.
- *RAM*—Windows NT requires a minimum of 12 MB of RAM in order to run.
- *Disk Space*—You need at least 124 MB of free space to install Windows NT.
- *Additional Hardware*—Windows NT also requires a 3.5"-floppy disk drive and a keyboard. It is also a good idea, but not required, to have a CD-ROM drive and a mouse or other pointing device.

Other Platforms

If you plan to install Windows NT Server on a RISC platform, the minimum hardware configuration needs to be as follows:

- *Processor*—You need a supported RISC–based microprocessor, such as the MIPS R4x00 or Digital Alpha Systems.
- *RAM*—Windows NT requires a minimum of 16 MB of RAM in order to run on a RISC platform.
- *Disk Space*—You need at least 158 MB of free space to install Windows NT on a RISC platform.
- *Additional Hardware*—Windows NT also requires a 3.5"-floppy disk drive and a keyboard. For a RISC system, a CD-ROM drive is required. A mouse or other pointing device is recommended, but not required.

Choosing a Server Role

Windows NT Server can fulfill one of three roles in your network. One thing you need to decide as part of the installation is what type of server you intend to install. Do you need a Primary Domain Controller, a Backup Domain Controller, or a Member server? Take a look at exactly what each of these is, and learn when you might select one over the other.

Primary Domain Controller

The Primary Domain Controller (PDC) is the main component of Microsoft's domain architecture. The PDC maintains the database of all the domain user accounts and provides authentication services to those users. It is important to remember there can be only one PDC in a domain, and it must be the first server installed in the domain. You cannot install a PDC into an existing domain.

Backup Domain Controller

The Backup Domain Controller (BDC) provides the function the name describes. It maintains a backup copy of the domain user account database, and can be used to authenticate users to the domain. This is only a read-only version of the database, however, and the PDC must be available for any changes to the user account database. If the PDC fails, the BDC can be promoted to PDC. In that event, any changes made to the database since the last time the BDC copied it are lost. A domain can have multiple BDCs.

> **NOTE** It's important to note that after a BDC is installed in a domain, it cannot be switched to be a BDC in another domain without being reinstalled.

Stand-Alone Server

A Stand-alone server (sometimes known as a *Member server*) is one that does not participate in domain authentication. A good example of this might be a dedicated application server. Because you don't want the overhead of domain authentication to affect the application, these servers are often Member servers.

Member servers can also be members of *workgroups*, and function in a peer-to-peer network with other Windows NT Member servers and workstations.

> **NOTE** A Member server cannot be promoted to either a BDC or PDC without a full reinstallation of the operating system. However, it can be moved from one domain to another without a reinstall.

Methods of Installation—Intel-Based Platform

Because the majority of Windows NT installations are performed on an Intel-based platform, the following step-by-step installation process assumes that's what you're using. Any significant differences existing between the Intel and non-Intel installations are highlighted accordingly. Go ahead and fire up that install.

Installing from the CD-ROM

In order to install Windows NT, you must run the appropriate version of the install program. For 16-bit operating systems, that is WINNT.EXE. For a 32-bit operating system (such as Windows NT Workstation), you need to run WINNT32.EXE. During the process, you are prompted for all the information you will need to complete the installation. The list that follows details the entire installation, from start to finish. After you've reviewed the process, you'll learn about some of the other features that you may need to configure in order to make the server useful in a production environment.

Scenario 2.1

Your manager has just handed you a box of Windows NT and is pointing at a server in the corner. His instructions are to install Windows NT and get it running.

Required Results

- Install Windows NT on the supplied hardware.

{*All the WINNT.EXE option switches are discussed later in the chapter, in the "WINNT(32).EXE Parameters" section.*}

1. The Windows NT installation process starts copying the source files to temporary directories on the hard drive of what will end up being your Windows NT server. These files are then used to complete the installation. After the copy is complete, the system starts looking for the installer's input as to how the system should be configured.
2. As soon as the reboot is complete, the system boots to the Welcome to Setup screen (see *Figure 2.1*). Microsoft refers to the process of installing Windows NT, as with its other products, as Setup. The Setup screen presents you with four options. Press Enter to continue the installation.

FIGURE 2.1
The Windows NT Server Setup welcome screen.

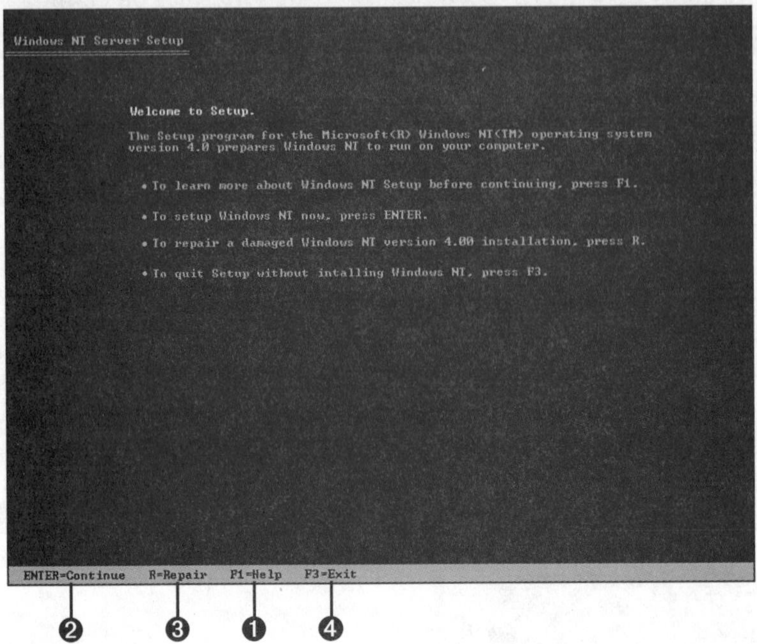

❶ Press F1 to enter a help screen that explains more about Setup.

❷ Press Enter to start Setup.

❸ Press R to repair a damaged installation, or perform an emergency repair.

❹ Press F3 to quit Setup.

{*Repairing a damaged installation is discussed in Chapter 6, "Troubleshooting."*}

> **NOTE**
> The F3 key is very handy if you forget to remove the CD-ROM from a machine with an autostarting CD-ROM drive. You will reboot the machine after the installation and find yourself right back at this screen. Just press F3 and remove the CD from the drive. Then reboot the system.

3. The Mass Storage Detection screen opens (see *Figure 2.2*). To have NT automatically detect your mass storage devices, press Enter. The installation program searches for any mass storage devices you have installed and displays any that it finds (see *Figure 2.3*).

FIGURE 2.2
The Mass Storage Detection screen.

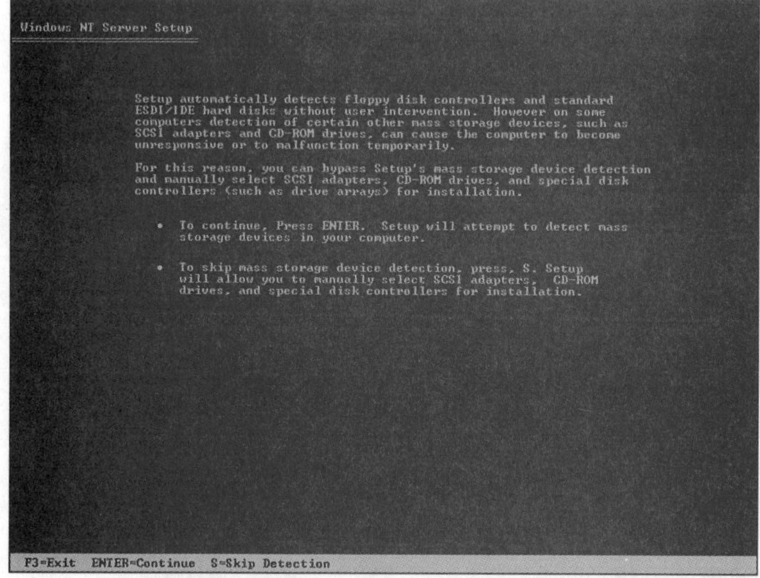

FIGURE 2.3
Detected mass storage devices are displayed.

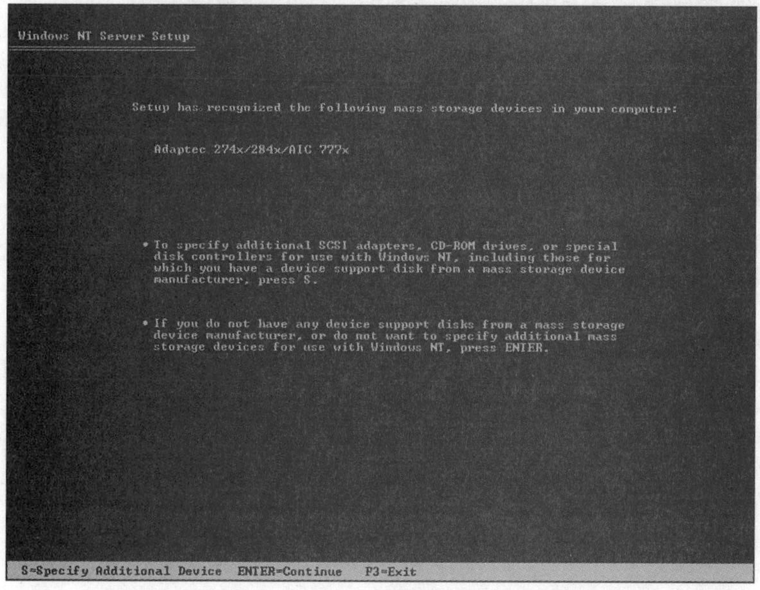

If any of the installed devices are not found, you can manually add them by pressing S for Specify Additional Device. Setup then presents a list of drivers for SCSI adapters. To load a driver, move through the list (using the up and down arrows) and press Enter to select the driver.

If the driver for your hardware is not listed, select Other and press Enter. Setup asks you for the driver disk from the hardware manufacturer. The driver you selected is added to the device list. If you need other drivers loaded, repeat this procedure.

When all the mass storage has been recognized, press Enter.

4. The next screen presents the Microsoft End-User License Agreement (EULA) (see *Figure 2.4*). Press the Page Down key to advance to the next screen, and then press F8 to indicate your agreement. It's a good idea to read this agreement at least once, just so you are aware of what you are agreeing to when you press the F8 key.

FIGURE 2.4
The Microsoft End-User License Agreement.

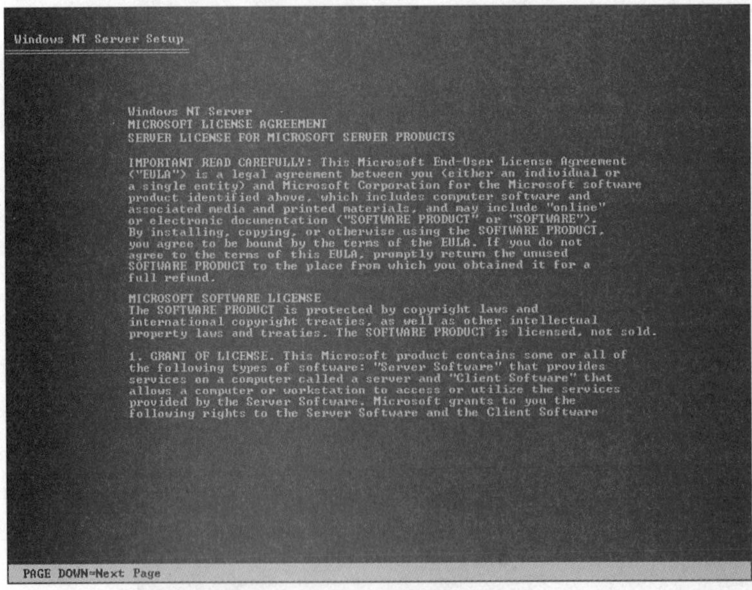

5. The next screen (see *Figure 2.5*) presents you with a summary of the hardware configuration Windows NT has auto-discovered.

FIGURE 2.5
Detected hardware and software components.

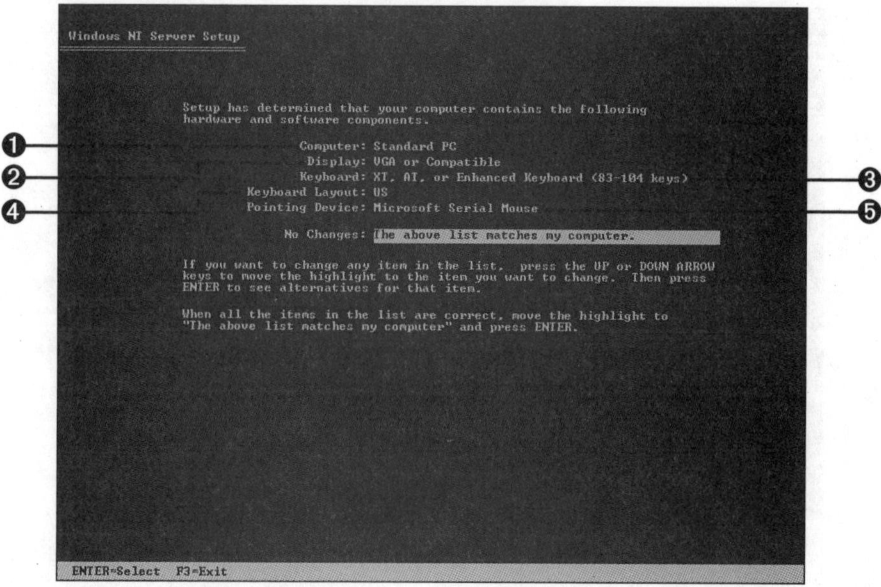

1. The type of PC that Windows NT thinks you are installing on. For most Intel installations, this reads Standard PC.
2. The type of monitor detected. Usually reads VGA or Compatible.
3. Usually displays XT, AT, or Enhanced Keyboard (83–104 keys).
4. In the United States, use US. If you are using a custom layout, or are installing in a different country, use the appropriate setting.
5. This indicates your mouse and usually reads Microsoft Serial Mouse.

To change any of these settings, use the up or down arrow to highlight the configuration to change, and change it to the appropriate setting. Press Enter to continue.

6. Setup shows a list of the hard drives on your server, along with any partitions on each of the drives. (see *Figure 2.6*) The first partition on the first drive is highlighted by default. At this point, you need to either select an existing partition, or create one to be used as the Windows NT system partition. The system partition is an important concept when deciding how to implement your disk redundancy, which is discussed in the "Allocating Disk Space Capacity" section of this chapter.

FIGURE 2.6

Hard drives and partitions available for the Windows NT installation.

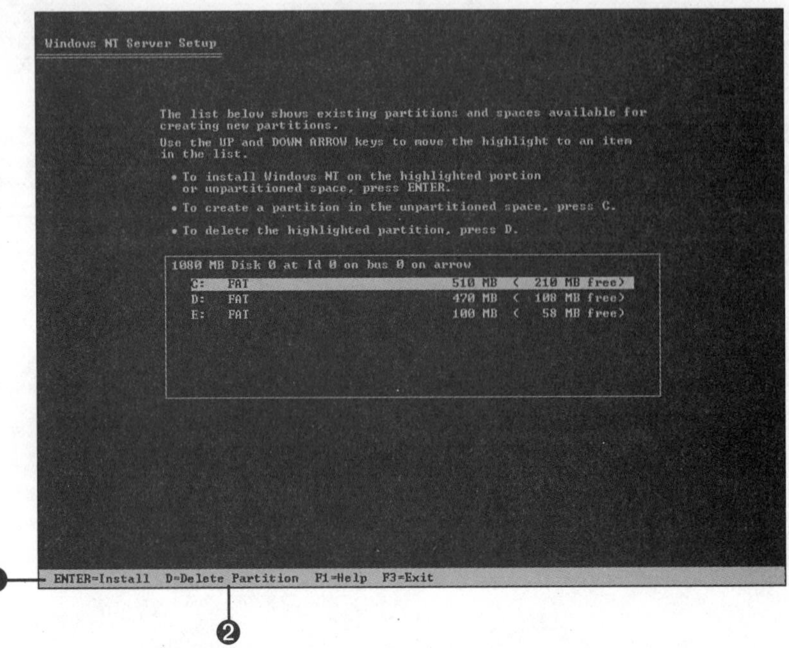

❶ Press ENTER to install.

❷ Press D to delete a partition.

> **NOTE** Before you install Windows NT, you might want or need to delete an existing partition. You can accomplish this by highlighting the partition (by pressing the arrow keys) and pressing the letter D. You are asked to confirm the deletion of the partition by pressing the letter L in the next screen. This is particularly useful for NTFS partitions, which can be difficult to delete with other operating systems' (DOS, OS/2, and so on) applications.

7. To create a partition, select any area labeled Unpartitioned space. When you're done, the option C=Create Partition appears at the bottom of the screen. Press C.

   This takes you to a new screen for creating a new partition. The minimum size for the new partition is 1 MB and the maximum size is the full size of the unpartitioned space, in megabytes.

In the box labeled Create Partition of Size (in MB), type in the size of the partition you want to create. Remember for Windows NT on an Intel platform, it must be at least 160 MB. Press Enter. You return to the original screen, but your new partition is now on the list.

8. Select an existing or newly created partition and press Enter. You can install on an existing FAT or NTFS partition, as long as there is adequate disk space, or you can select any unformatted space.

   The options you are given at this point vary depending whether you have selected an existing or unformatted partition.

9. If you are installing on an existing partition, you see four choices on the screen, as shown in *Figure 2.7*.

FIGURE 2.7
Selecting the files system for the installation drive.

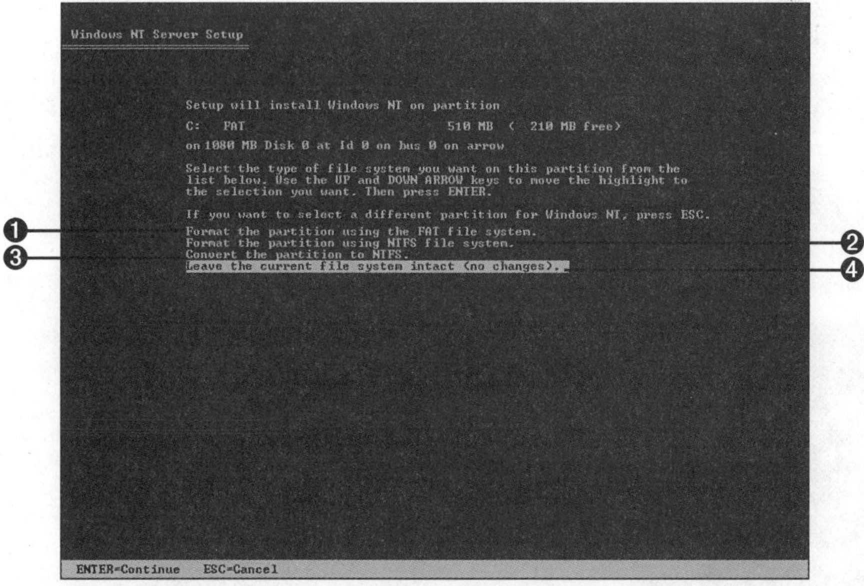

❶ Format the partition using the FAT file system.

❷ Format the partition using the NTFS file system.

❸ Convert the partition to NTFS. (This option is available if the partition is formatted with the FAT file system.)

❹ Leave the file system intact.

Select one of these options and press Enter. Choose the last option if there are files you need to preserve, or if you are upgrading or re-installing Windows NT.

> **NOTE** If you see a message indicating the file system is being formatted FAT and you selected NTFS, don't panic. NTFS partitions are first formatted with the FAT file system, and are then converted on the first boot of the server.

If you chose to install to a new partition in step 8, you have only the first two choices:

- Format the partition using the FAT file system.
- Format the partition using the NTFS file system.

10. After the partition has been formatted, you are prompted to specify a directory for Windows NT system files (see *Figure 2.8*).

    The default directory is `\WINNT` and resides on the partition you selected earlier. This directory is often be described as the `%systemroot%` directory. If you see `%systemroot%` anywhere in this book, or anywhere else, it generally refers to the `\WINNT` subdirectory.

FIGURE 2.8
The default installation directory.

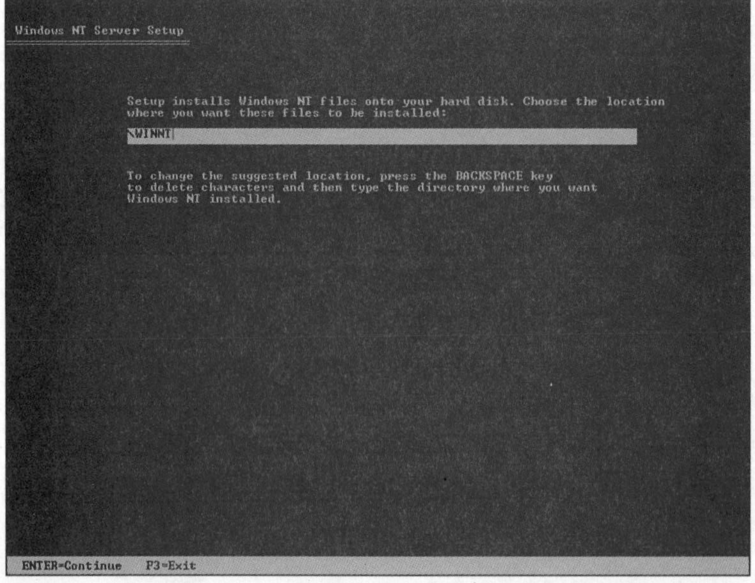

> **NOTE** If Windows NT is already installed on this system, you have the option of installing in the existing `%systemroot%` directory, or specifying a separate directory.

11. Next, Setup gives you the option of performing an exhaustive secondary examination of your hard disk (see *Figure* 2.9). Unless you are in a tremendous hurry, or you have already tested the drive, you should always perform this test. Be warned, however: This test can take quite a long time on systems with large hard drives. If you have a 4 GB drive, you might want to start the test and then run out for some lunch—and maybe a movie.

FIGURE 2.9
Choosing whether to perform an exhaustive test of the installation hard drive.

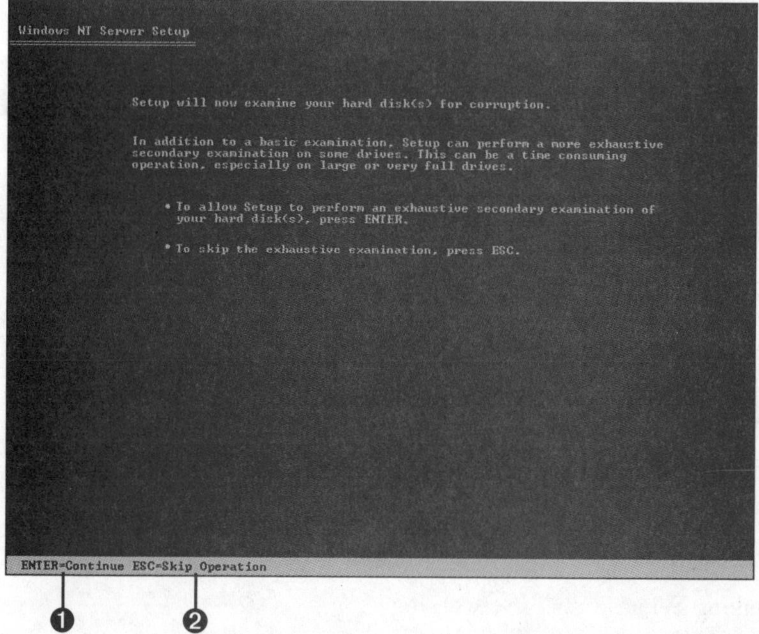

❶ Press Enter to begin the thorough examination.

❷ Press Esc to skip disk examination.

After the hard disks have been examined (or this step has been skipped), Setup copies files to the system partition.

If you are installing from floppy disks, you are prompted to change disks as needed.

12. When file copy is complete, you must reboot the computer (see *Figure 2.10*). Make sure the floppy drive is empty and press Enter.

FIGURE 2.10
Completing the initial phase of the installation.

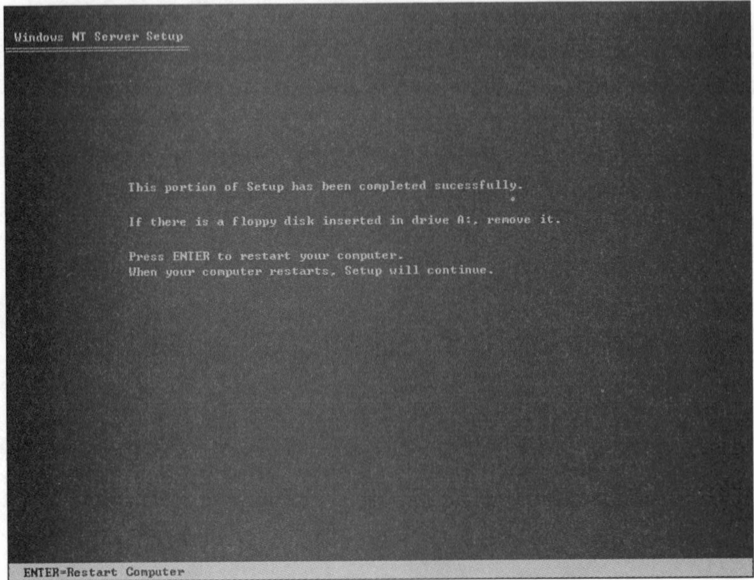

After the computer reboots, more files are copied to the system drive. These files allow you to complete the installation.

From this point on, the rest of the installation is in a GUI environment and is broken into three phases, which Windows NT is nice enough to display on the Windows NT Setup screen (see *Figure 2.11*). The three stages are as follows:

- Gathering information about your computer
- Installing Windows NT Networking
- Finishing Setup

FIGURE 2.11
The Windows NT Setup screen.

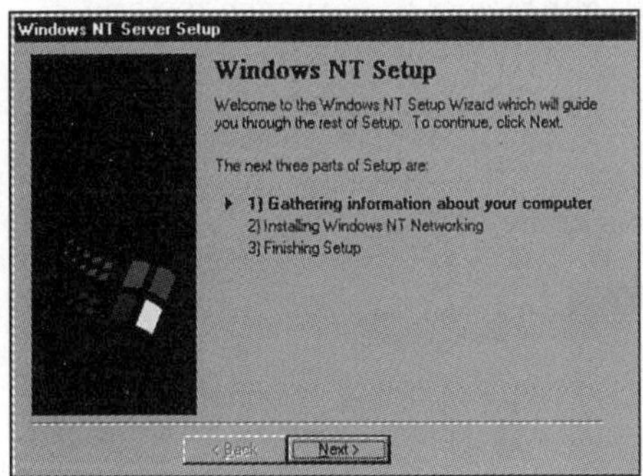

13. Click on Next to begin the "information gathering" portion of the installation.

> **NOTE** A nice feature of the GUI environment is the ability to back up if you have made a mistake. For most of the installation you can just click on the Back button at any point.

The Name and Organization screen is next (see *Figure 2.12*). On this screen you are prompted to enter the following:

- Name (This is a required field.)
- Organization (This is an optional field.)

14. Fill in the blanks appropriately and click Next to continue.

FIGURE 2.12
Entering your name and organization.

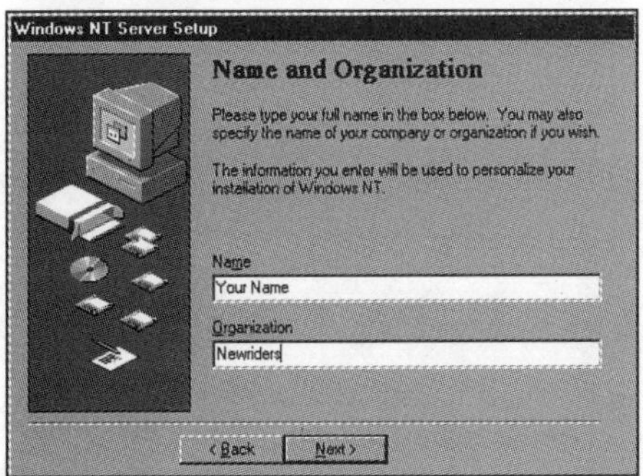

15. The Licensing Modes screen prompts you to select how the server will be licensed. You have two choices (see *Figure 2.13*). You might want to consult your Purchasing Department or your reseller to see which method offers the more advantageous pricing.

FIGURE 2.13
Selecting the licensing mode for the Windows NT Server.

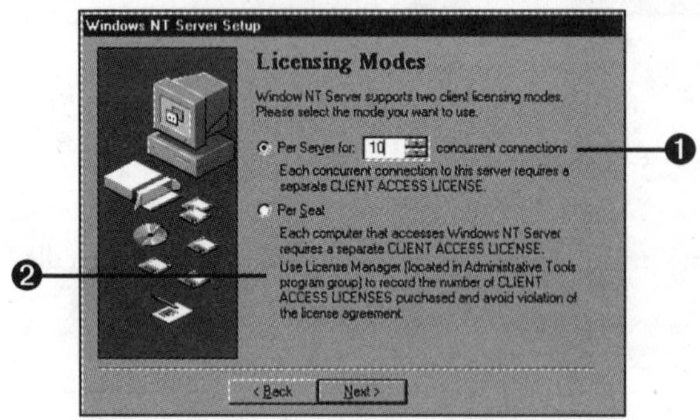

❶ Select Per Server if you want your licenses based on concurrent connections to this server. (For those of you familiar with Novell NetWare, this is how their licensing is handled.)

❷ Select Per Seat if you want your licenses based on the number of client computers on the network.

After carefully selecting a licensing mode, click Next to continue. {*We'll look at licensing in a little greater detail later in the chapter when we discuss Licensing Manager.*}

16. Next you see the Computer Name screen (see *Figure 2.14*). Each computer on a Windows NT network must have a unique name. This is an excellent reason for a global naming convention. Enter a name in the Name box and click on Next.

FIGURE 2.14
Entering the computer name.

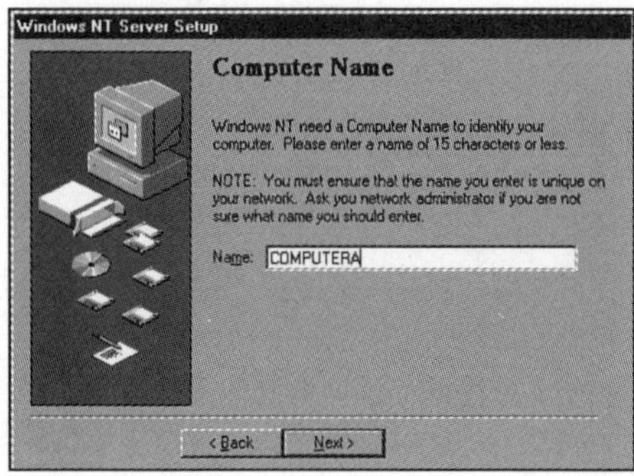

> **NOTE**
>
> Windows NT Server names can be up to 15 characters in length. They cannot contain the following characters:
>
> /\[]<>";:+=,*.|
>
> These are illegal characters.

> **NOTE**
>
> Just a quick tip on naming conventions. First, never underestimate the value of a naming convention on a large network. It ensures unique names and, if done correctly, can greatly assist in troubleshooting. Suppose you have an NT Server that is suddenly broadcasting its NetBIOS name every second, flooding your network with packets. If you are a large enterprise with loose IT controls over systems, and that administrator named her server *Diablo*, you have a problem. If, however, your IT control is a little tighter, and you require a *<first initial><last name>* naming convention for personal servers, and you suddenly see *CCROSBY* broadcasting over the network, you need only check the Corporate Directory to get Chris Crosby's extension, and solve the problem.

17. As discussed in the earlier "Choosing a Server Role" section, Windows NT Server can be installed as one of three types of server. Click on the option button next to your choice (see *Figure 2.15*). You should have decided before installation which of the following to choose:
    - Primary Domain Controller
    - Backup Domain Controller
    - Stand-Alone (Member) Server

FIGURE 2.15
Selecting the server role.

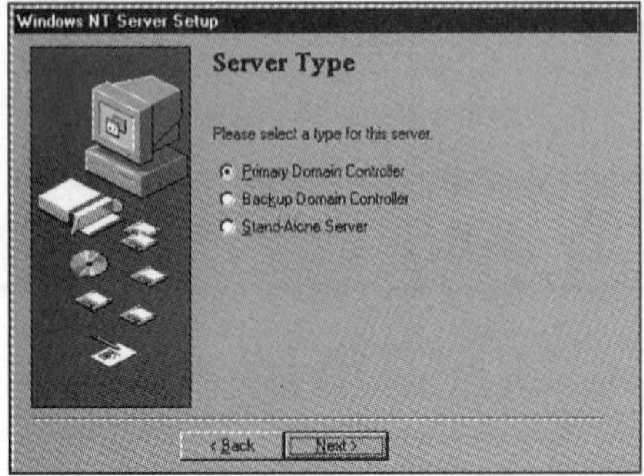

Click on Next to continue. (Because this is an exam preparation book, from here you'll learn about installing a PDC, which requires the largest amount of configuration.)

18. The next screen, Administrator Account, prompts you to specify a password for the Administrator account (see *Figure 2.16*). Notice that the screen indicates that the password can be up to 14 characters long. This account will have full administrative permissions for your domain. Specify your password by completing the following fields:
    - Password
    - Confirm Password

FIGURE 2.16
Entering the Administrator's password.

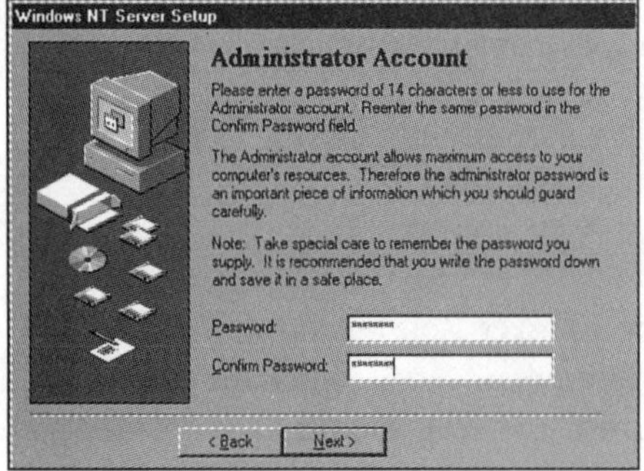

You must enter the same password in both fields. You can leave these fields blank, creating an Administrator account without a password, but in a production environment that is not advisable. Save the No Password option for the lab.

> **NOTE**
> Following installation, the Administrator account can be renamed. If you are concerned about security on your network, you should definitely do that. The other thing to do after you complete the installation is create an Administrator-equivalent account. This is in case you somehow find yourself locked out of the Administrator account.

If you selected Stand-Alone Server, you are asked for a user name and password for the server's administrative account. Click on Next to continue.

19. The Emergency Repair Disk screen appears (see *Figure 2.17*). Before you go any further, remember this sage advice: Always create an Emergency Repair Disk (ERD). Your ERD contains the hardware configuration information you need to recover the server if the server's system files are corrupt, preventing the server from booting.

FIGURE 2.17
Creating the Emergency Repair Disk.

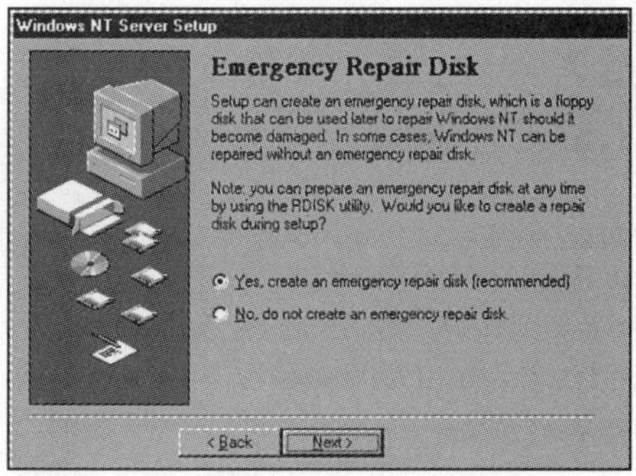

{*Use of the Emergency Repair Disk is covered in detail in Chapter 6, "Troubleshooting."*}

When Setup asks you if you want to create an Emergency Repair Disk, you should select Yes, Create an Emergency Repair Disk (Recommended) and click Next.

If you choose to skip the ERD at this time, select No, Do Not Create an Emergency Repair Disk. You can create an ERD after the install by using the RDISK utility.

20. The Select Components screen appears. It allows you to customize which components you will install. There are six categories of components (see *Figure 2.18*).

> **NOTE** If this is going to be a PDC in a production environment, you can probably skip Games, Multimedia, Microsoft Exchange, and some of the accessories. Will your users really need alternative mouse pointers or MS-Paint on your PDC? Select your options carefully.

FIGURE 2.18
Selecting the operating system components to be installed.

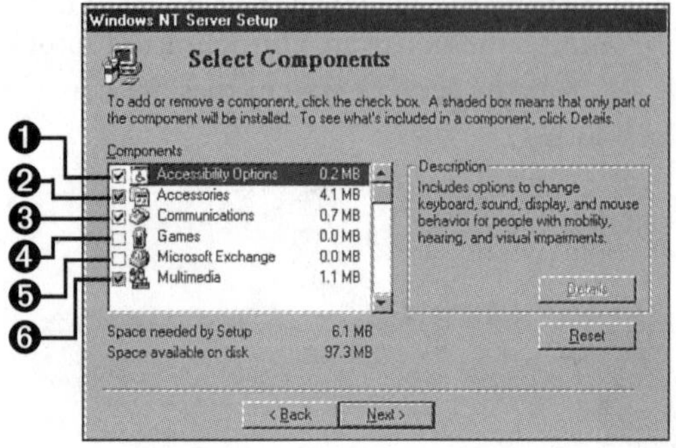

❶ *Accessibility Options*—These components are meant to make the computer easier to use by people with (per Microsoft) "mobility, hearing, or visual impairments." This component contains keyboard, mouse, sound, and display drivers, and utilities to customize the computing environment.

❷ *Accessories*—This component contains 13 optional accessories, such as the Calculator, Desktop Wallpaper, and Paint. Choose these components with care. There a number of utilities that might not belong on a server.

❸ *Communications*—This component contains the communications utilities including Chat, HyperTerminal (a modem communication program), and Phone Dialer. Depending on the function of the server, these could be useful.

FIGURE 2.18

❹ *Games*—Unless you spend a lot of late nights in the server room, avoid installing any of these components. None of these are installed by default.

❺ *Microsoft Exchange*—This component contains three messaging applications: Internet Mail, Microsoft Exchange (an integrated mail and messaging application), and Microsoft Mail (a mail client). (The Microsoft Exchange component is not the full Exchange application, which must be purchased separately.)

❻ *Multimedia*—This component contains a number of applications for playing sound and video clips. Generally, you can skip this for a server.

Any components that are not installed now can be installed after the Windows NT install is complete by going to the Add/Remove Programs applet in the Control Panel and clicking on the Windows NT Setup tab.

Choose Next when components have been selected. You have completed the "information gathering" portion of the installation.

21. Now you're back at the Windows NT Setup screen (see *Figure 2.19*), which shows that the installation is moving into the "Installing Windows NT Networking" portion of the installation. Click on Next to continue.

FIGURE 2.19
The Windows NT Setup screen before installing the networking components.

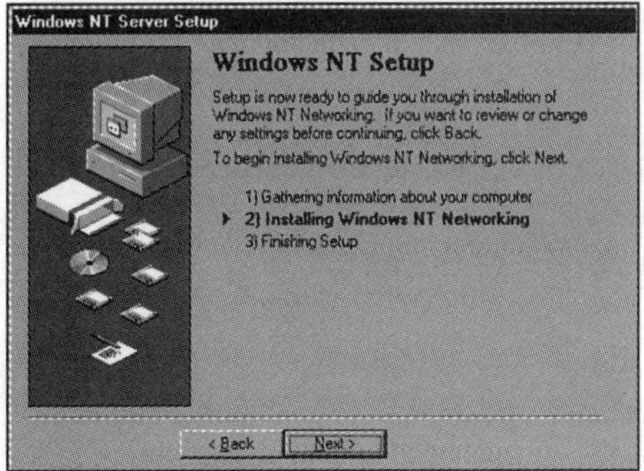

22. This screen (see *Figure 2.20*) asks you to specify how you are connected to the network.

FIGURE 2.20

Identifying how the server is connected to the network.

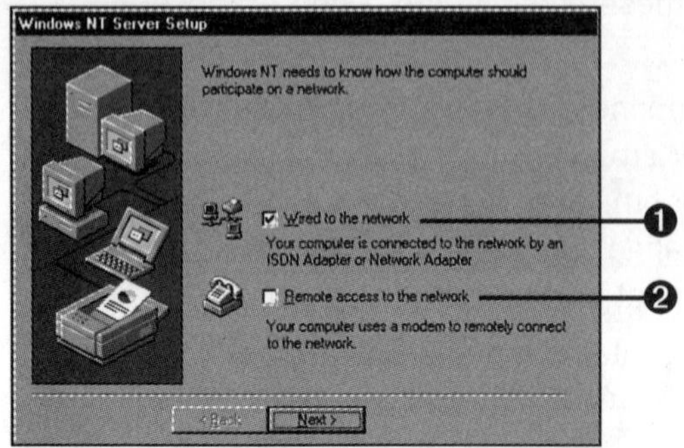

❶ This option indicates that your computer is wired directly to the network, via an ISDN Adapter or a Network Adapter.

❷ This option indicates that you connect to the network via modem. Selecting this option causes the installation to install Remote Access Server.

> **NOTE** For the exam, be aware that if you don't have a Network Adapter installed in your system, you can select the MC Loopback Adapter and simulate an installed adapter.

{*Remote Access Server is covered in depth in Chapter 4, "Connectivity."*}

You can check either, both, or neither of these options. If you choose none, the Setup program skips the network portion of the installation. This only works for a Stand-alone server. Domain Controllers require some sort of network connection to complete the installation.

Choose Next to continue.

23. The screen in *Figure 2.21* offers you the opportunity to install Internet Information Server (IIS). If you choose to install IIS, you must install TCP/IP as well. TCP/IP is installed by default.

FIGURE 2.21
You have the option of installing Internet Information Server at this point in the installation.

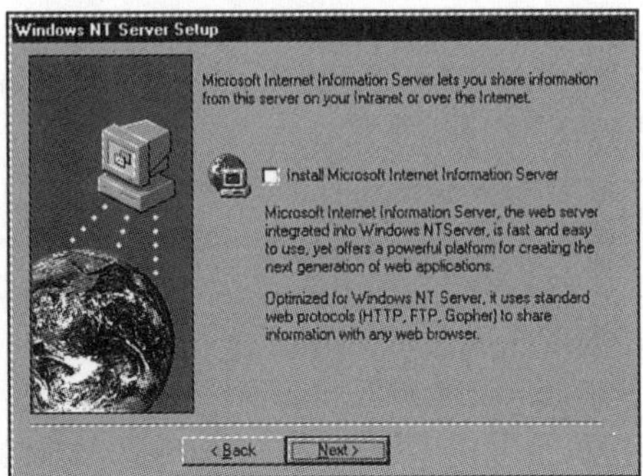

Click Next to continue.

{*IIS installation and configuration is covered in Chapter 4.*}

24. The Windows NT Server Setup has the ability to scan your computer, identify network cards, and determine their settings. This is very similar to the way it identified the Mass Storage Devices at the beginning of the installation. Click on the Start Search button to take advantage of this option. You will notice that after an adapter is found, this button changes to a Find Next button, shown in *Figure 2.22*. This is useful if you have multiple adapters in the system.

    If you use the automated scan, you are presented with three options after a card is found (see *Figure 2.22*).

FIGURE 2.22
Automatically detecting an installed adapter.

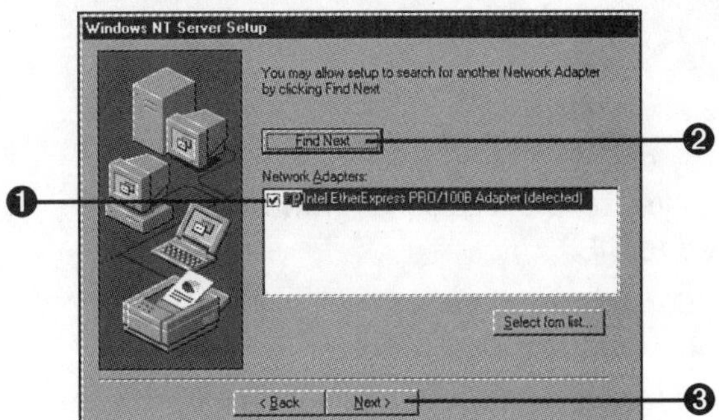

FIGURE 2.22 *cont.*

❶ Remove the check mark to ignore the adapter.

❷ Choose Find Next to find another card if more than one is installed. (If all your adapters are the same, don't use the Find Next button. All the adapters will run off the same driver.) It is only necessary to configure one card at this time.

❸ Choose Next to accept the entry and continue with the next installation step.

If the adapter discovery doesn't work, or you want to manually specify the adapter, click on Select from List This option skips the automatic detection. You can choose drivers from the window listing the card drivers bundled with Windows NT, or you can click on Have Disk to provide the drivers that came with the adapter.

After you select a network adapter, click Next to continue.

25. Now it's time to select the protocols to run. It is important to know which protocols you intend to run before you start the installation. Setup offers you four options at this point (see *Figure 2.23*).

FIGURE 2.23
Selecting the protocols to be installed.

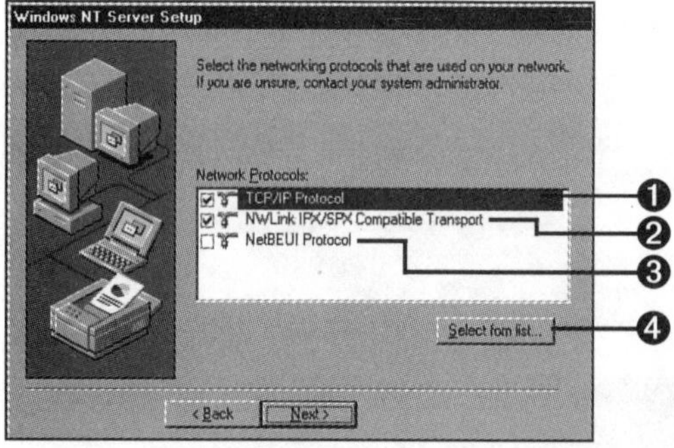

❶ This protocol is selected by default. The most popular protocol for networks these days, due to the explosive growth of the Internet, TCP/IP is required for IIS.

❷ This option is checked by default. If you have Novell servers on your network and would like your Windows NT server to interact with them in any way, you need this protocol. The immense popularity of Novell's NetWare operating system in the late '80s and early '90s got Novell's IPX protocol installed on a significant percentage of corporate networks.

FIGURE 2.23

❸ This option is not checked by default and is not required. Generally, this should only be enabled if necessary. NetBEUI, originally conceived of by IBM and used in the Microsoft/IBM collaboration on LAN Manager in the early '90s, is a non-routable, bandwidth-intensive protocol. Enable it only if you require NetBEUI compatibility with existing systems.

❹ If you want to install additional protocols, you can choose Select from List. From here you can choose the Have Disk option to install a protocol not included with Windows NT.

> **NOTE** One protocol that can be selected is DLC. This protocol is a HP-proprietary protocol that allows Windows NT to print directly to Hewlett-Packard printers that are connected directly to the network. In some cases, DLC can be used to connect to mainframes. This protocol is useful in small networks, but is not practical in environments in which there are many users printing to a small number of printers.

Select the protocols you would like to install, and click Next.

26. The next window (see *Figure 2.24*) lists the network services that will be installed. You cannot remove components at this time, but you can add others by choosing Select from List. Generally, the components selected are enough to complete the installation. You can always add services after the installation is complete.

FIGURE 2.24
Networking services that will be installed.

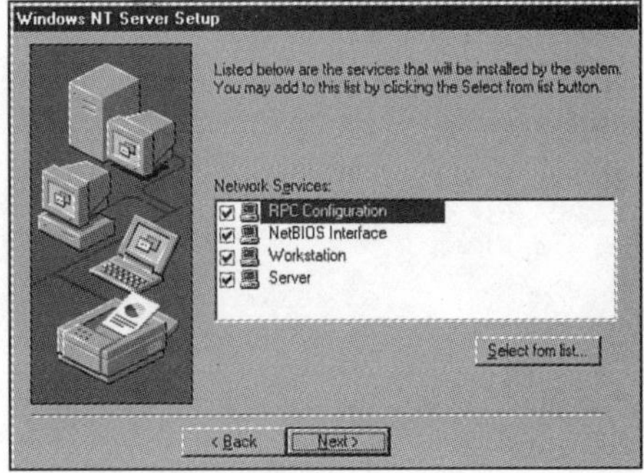

27. At this point, all the bindings have been completed based on your previous selections. You can now review the bindings that have been established (see *Figure 2.25*). A *binding* is the link from the network adapter, through the protocol to the service, forming a chain. In this step you can disable a binding by selecting it and choosing Disable.

FIGURE 2.25
Configuring the bind order for the network services.

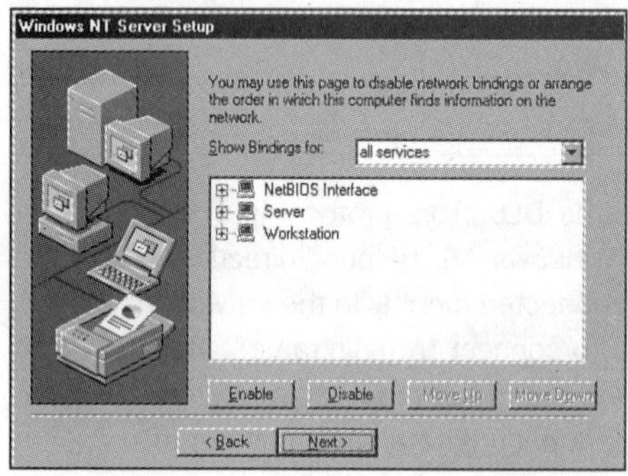

Choose Next to continue.

You have almost completed the installation. All required files are now copied to the computer.

28. The contents of the next screen window depend on the server type. There are three sets of possibilities, based on the three server types:
    - *Primary Domain Controller*—You will need to enter a computer name and a domain name (see *Figure 2.26*). If you have selected a unique name, the domain will be created. If you have inadvertently duplicated a domain name, the server will prompt you for another name.

FIGURE 2.26
Entering the domain name. The server name was entered previously.

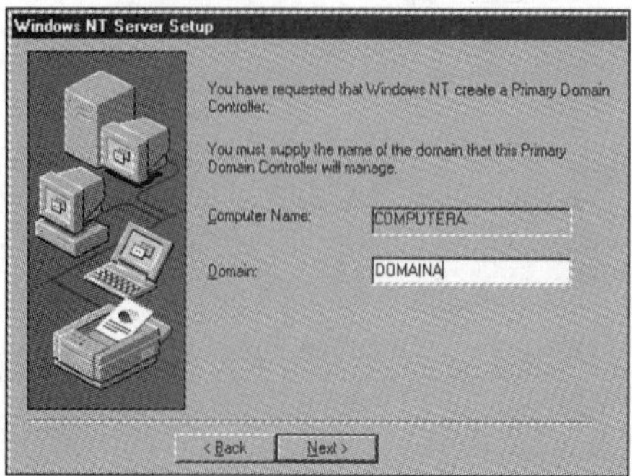

- *Backup Domain Controller*—You must provide a computer name, identify the domain in which the computer will reside, and provide the administrator name and password. The administrator name and password allow you to add this server to the domain you specify, where it will be configured as a BDC. If the user name and password you enter do not have administrator privileges in the domain, or the domain does not exist, the computer cannot be added.
- *Member Server*—You must provide a computer name, identify the domain in which the computer will reside, and provide the administrator name and password. If the user name and password you enter do not have administrator privileges in the domain, or the domain does not exist, the computer cannot be added. The domain name can also be a workgroup name, if the server will not be a member of a domain.

  There are two ways a Member server can be added to the domain. If you use the method described previously, an account for the computer is created in the domain when you provide the administrator user ID and password. You can also bring the server into the domain by creating a server account beforehand, and using that user ID and password to join the domain. {*Creating computer accounts is discussed in Chapter 3, "Managing Resources."*}

Choose Next to continue.

29. You should be able to see the light at the end of the tunnel. You have reached the "Finishing Setup" portion of the installation (see *Figure 2.27*). Choose Finish to continue. The server will be set up to run Windows NT based on your choices.

FIGURE 2.27
The Windows NT Setup windows now reflects that you are finishing Setup.

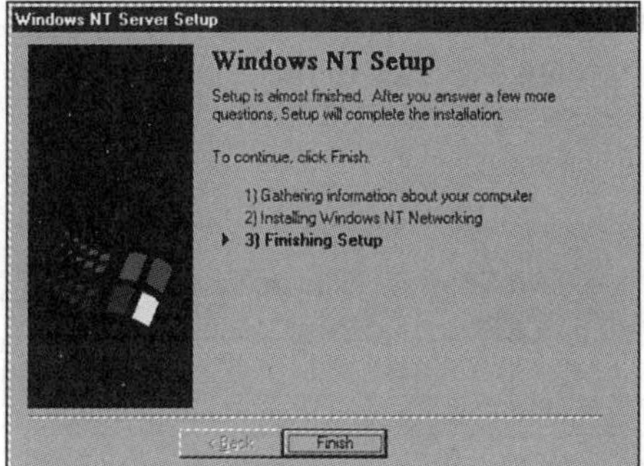

30. The last step takes place in the Date/Time Properties screen (see *Figure 2.28*). Choose Close to accept the settings.

FIGURE 2.28
Setting the Date and Time.

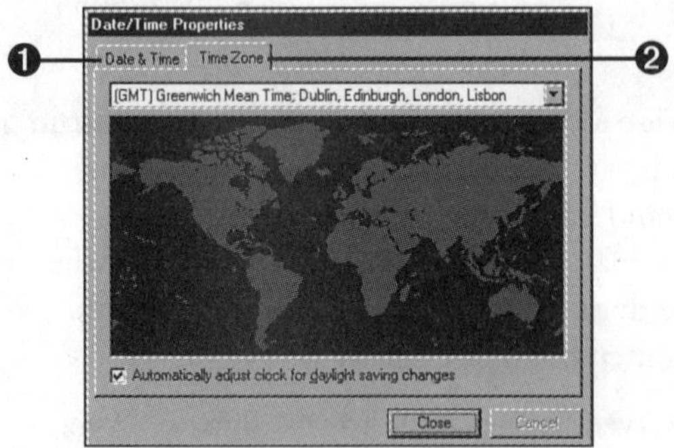

❶ Click on the Date & Time tab to set the system clock.

❷ Click on the Time Zone tab to pick your time zone. Choose a time zone by selecting it from the pull-down list. Be sure to check the box Automatically Adjust Clock for Daylight Saving Changes, if appropriate. This check box is deactivated for some time zone choices, such as Indiana (East).

Congratulations! Windows NT has been installed and you have completed the scenario.

Installing Over-the-Network

OK, you've looked at installing from a local CD-ROM. The nice thing about installing Windows NT Server is that the installation files don't even need to be on a local CD-ROM. They can quite easily reside on a shared CD-ROM out on the network or, if you have room on a network server, they could even reside on a network share. You just need to copy the files to the server, and share their drive.

> **NOTE** Before you copy the files, be sure you have Show All Files selected in Windows NT Explorer. The installation CD does contain hidden files.

{*Sharing directories is covered in Chapter 3, "Managing Resources."*}

Scenario 2.2

You are in the process of migrating some legacy servers to Windows NT. The hardware is up to the task in all respects, except the servers do not have CD-ROM drives. You still need to get Windows NT installed.

Required Results

- Install Windows NT on a server that does not have a CD-ROM drive.

The answer for this scenario is to install from the network. To complete this scenario, follow these steps:

1. Create a directory on the server to receive the master installation files.
2. Copy the appropriate directory or directories from the installation CD-ROM to the directory you created. For Intel-based servers, copy the `\I386` from the CD-ROM to the network directory.
3. Share the network directory.
4. Install MS-DOS on the computer that will be installing Windows NT Server. (You can perform network installations from Windows 95/98 or Windows NT Workstation as well.) Be sure the C: drive has sufficient free space to hold the temporary installation files.
5. Install the MS-DOS client software included with Windows NT. This process is detailed later in this chapter, in the "Network Client Administrator" section.
6. Restart the computer and log on to the network. Connect a drive letter to the share with the installation directory. Make the network share your current drive.
7. Change the directory into the directory that contains the installation files for your processor type. For an Intel-based computer, you would change the directory into the `I386` subdirectory.
8. Execute the command `winnt.exe /b` to begin installation. This starts the installation without requiring the floppy disks. For a more complete list of Windows NT parameters, see Table 2.1.
9. Follow the process detailed in the previous section, and Windows NT Server should install with no problem.

Congratulations! You have successfully installed Windows NT across the network.

WINNT(32).EXE Parameters

The WINNT.EXE or WINNT32.EXE performs an installation or upgrade of Windows NT 4.00. The command line has the following format:

```
Winnt(32) [/s:sourcepath] [/i:inf_file] [/t:drive_letter] [/x] [/b] [/ox]
[/u[:script] [/r:directory] [/e:command]
```

There are a number of parameters available for either of these applications. They are detailed in Table 2.1.

TABLE 2.1

WINNT(32) PARAMETERS

/s:sourcepath	Specifies the location of the Windows NT files. The default is /I386.
/i:inf_file	Specifies the filename (no path) of the setup information file. The default is DOSNET.INF. Setup information files are discussed in the "Unattended Installations" section of this chapter.
/t:drive_letter	Forces Setup to place temporary files on the specified drive. This can be very useful if you don't have enough space on your system drive for the install files and the temporary files. This option allows you to successfully install Windows NT on drives that might otherwise have too little free space.
/x	Prevents Setup from creating Setup boot floppies. Use this when you already have Setup boot floppies (from your administrator, for example) or when you are upgrading directly from a CD or from the network.
/b	Causes the boot files to be loaded on the system's hard drive rather than on floppy disks, so that floppy disks do not need to be loaded or removed by the user.
/ox	Specifies that Setup create boot floppies for CD-ROM installation. Very handy if you lose your boot floppies.
/u	Upgrades your previous version of Windows NT in unattended mode. All user settings are taken from the previous installation, requiring no user intervention during Setup.
/u:script	Similar to the /u parameter, but provides a script file for user settings, rather than using the settings from the previous installation. This parameter is discussed in the "Unattended Installation" section of this chapter.

WINNT(32) PARAMETERS

`/r:directory`	Installs an additional directory within the directory tree where the Windows NT files are installed. Use additional `/r` switches to install additional directories. Useful if you want to use this server as an install server for across-the-wire installations.
`/e:command`	Instructs Setup to execute a specific command after installation is complete. This isn't used a great deal, but could be used for a task such as mapping a drive and executing a batch file from the network, or sending a network message.
`/udf:filename`	This option allows you to specify a Uniqueness Database File (UDF), which allows you to customize the installation on a computer-by-computer basis–for example, if you want each machine to have a unique IP address. This parameter could also be used to assign a different IP address for an unattended installation.

Configuring for Multiboot

One of the very useful capabilities of Windows NT is that it can boot multiple operating systems. The best way to configure the system for multiboot is to be sure to install the system files to a different directory than the one in which the previous operating system resides. Windows NT Server can multiboot with Windows 95/98, Windows NT Workstation, and other copies of Windows NT Server. Keep in mind that applications you install in one OS will need to be reinstalled for use in the additional OS.

Uninstalling Windows NT Server

Uninstalling Windows NT is much less complicated than installing it. In fact, if you do it correctly you can uninstall Windows NT without losing your data files. You must reinstall any Windows NT applications, due to the Registry setting.

Scenario 2.3

You have upgraded to a new server, and would like to use the existing server as a Windows NT Workstation Administrator's workstation. Because all the applications and data are already on this hard drive, you'd like to preserve them for a while, just in case.

Required Results

- Remove Windows NT Server from the server without affecting the data.

To uninstall Windows NT, complete the following steps:

1. Boot the system to a different operating system. This can be done from the hard drive if this is a multiboot system, or from floppy disks if Windows NT is the sole OS on the system.
2. Delete the Windows NT `%systemroot%` directory.
3. Delete the swap file (`pagefile.sys`) from any of the partitions.
4. Remove the Hidden, System, and Read-Only attributes from the system files located in the root of the system partition. These files are as follows:

```
NTBOOTDD.SYS

NTLDR

BOOT.INI

BOOTSECT.DOS
```

5. Reboot the system. If you are multibooting the server, be sure to create a startup disk, just in case. If you have a problem, you may need to reinstall the OS system files, which can be done by running the command `SYS C:`.

Congratulations! Your data is intact and you're ready to install Windows NT Workstation.

Unattended Installations

Microsoft has a couple different utilities for helping to install and set up Windows NT in an unattended mode. There are two methods for installing Windows NT without manual intervention, listed in order.

unattend.txt File

The command for use with the `/u:` option for the Windows NT Setup program looks like this:

```
winnt[32] /u:<answer file> /s:<install source>
```

`<answer file>` is a file containing the answers to the questions that the Setup program asks the installer. `<install source>` is the location of the installation files.

The format of the file in general is as follows:

```
<<unattend.txt>>
[section1]
;
; Section contains keys and the corresponding
; values for those keys/parameters.
; keys and values are separated by "=" signs
; Values usually require double quotes "" around them
;
key = value
.
.
[section2]
key = value
.
.
```

> **NOTE**
> For complete information on the `unattend.txt` file, see Microsoft Knowledge Base Article PSS ID Number: Q155197

/UDF Option—The Uniqueness Database File

Another setup option is to use a Uniqueness Database File with the `/UDF` option. The UDF is a database of information with each machine to be installed identified by a *uniqueness ID*. This ID allows you to configure each server to be installed with machine-specific information.

> **NOTE**
> The Uniqueness Database File can be used in conjunction with the UNATTEND.TXT file (the /u option). What you can do is use the UDF to supply the unique information for the server's installation, while the UNATTEND.TCT file provides the parameters common to all the servers you will be installing.

SYSDIFF—Unattended Application Installations

Microsoft also has a utility for unattended installation of applications on a Windows NT Server.

Scenario 2.4

You have a dozen Windows NT Servers on which you need to install a proprietary management application. You want to do this without inserting the media in each machine.

Required Results

- Install your custom application in the easiest manner possible, while ensuring that the application runs.

To perform the unattended installation of an application or applications, do the following:

1. Install Windows NT Server and run `sysdiff /snap` to take a snapshot of the system. Microsoft refers to this as the *reference computer* and it needs to be of the same general hardware type as the destination computer's system.
2. Install the applications and run `sysdiff /diff` to create the difference file. The *difference file* is used to record the differences from the reference computer and the installed computer.
3. Run `sysdiff /apply` to apply the difference file to the new server.

   One other option for `sysdiff` is the ability to use the `/dump` option to save the difference file information to a file that you can read.

Your application has successfully installed your application without using the install media.

> NOTE
>
> Look for at least one question on unattended installations. Be familiar with the names of each type of file, and the order of the SYSDIFF commands.

CONFIGURE WINDOWS NT SERVER CORE SERVICES

Windows NT contains a number of services that can be (and sometimes must be) configured before they can be used, or for optimum performance. This section discusses a few of the more common services to be configured.

Server Service

The Server service responds to I/O requests from network clients and, if the client is authorized, responds with access to the requested resources. This is a service that can be optimized for its use of RAM. By default, Windows NT is configured to run with throughput maximized for file sharing (see *Figure 2.29*). As you can see, you can modify this service to do everything from minimizing memory use to maximizing network throughput.

FIGURE 2.29
Configuring the Server service for optimum memory use.

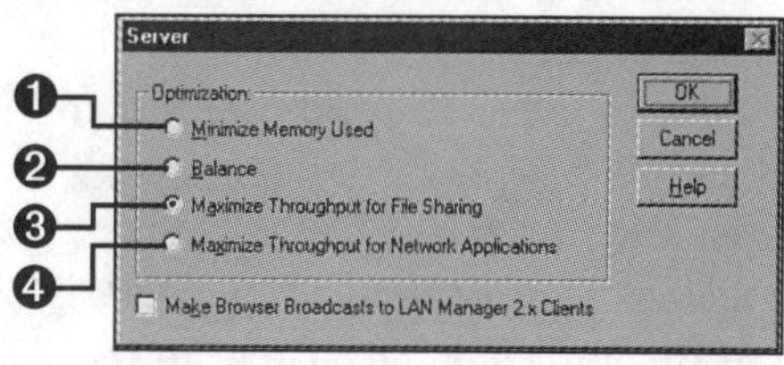

1. The Minimize Memory Used selection makes network performance as slow as possible, but conserves memory for the rest of the server's processing. If you have people running local applications and network processing is very low, this might be a good selection. This setting allows no more than 10 connections, and essentially renders the server as a workstation.
2. Balance is a good selection for a general-purpose server, which has some network traffic and some system processing. This setting allows 64 concurrent connections, and might be a member server in a workgroup or a domain.
3. Maximize Throughput for File Sharing is the default and is recommended for file and print servers. This setting takes heavier network use into account.
4. Maximize Throughput for Network Applications allocates the largest amount of memory possible for network usage, while limiting the amount of memory available for system use. This would be the setting for heavy client/server applications in which a large number of users will be accessing data on the server constantly.

Workstation Service

The Workstation service is the other aspect of the Server service. The Workstation service takes requests from the local workstation and redirects them to the network when network resources are requested. This service cannot be configured.

Computer Browser

Browsing is one of the cornerstones of Windows NT networking, and is also one of the more interesting implementations for finding network resources. In a Windows NT network, computers using broadcasts build a database of shared directories and printers that are available to users. The end user is then able to *browse* the Network Neighborhood and find the necessary resources. The interesting part of browsing is that when it works, it just *works.* Unlike DNS, WINS, or any of the other services that must be configured, network browsing works without any intervention. It is completely transparent to the user. However, for the purpose of the exams, you should know a little more about how browsing works. There are a number of different roles a computer on the network can play with regard to network browsing.

{*DNS and WINS are discussed in Chapter 4, "Connectivity."*}

The Master Browser

Every Windows NT domain must have a *master browser.* The master browser collects system announcements for the entire domain, across all the segments, and then provides that list to the entire domain. This list contains any machine that is broadcasting a resource to the network. These resources can be file shares, printers, and so on, and they are broadcast by the Server service, discussed previously.

If the PDC is active on a domain, it is the master browser. If the PDC is not available, then one of the BDCs picks up that duty. The interesting part is that the master browser in this case is elected. When the servers on the network detect the fact that there is not a master browser available, they start sending "Hey, I can be the master browser" packets to the network. An election takes place, using criteria like each server's role and load, and a new master browser is elected.

Backup Browsers

In an effort to help offload some of the overhead associated with being a master browser, new servers added to the network may become backup browsers. Windows NT computers does this by default. Backup browsers spread the load associated with browsing to a number of different machines across the network, improving response time and reducing the utilization of the PDC. After a backup browser is on the network, the master browser responds to browse requests with the location of the backup browsers. Backup browsers supply all the responses to browse requests.

Backup browsers check in every 15 minutes with the master browser to update their databases. That means it can take up to 15 minutes before a backup browser can update a browse database. (Wouldn't that 15-minute time make a great test question?)

When the master browser fails, it might be 15 minutes before backup browsers detect the failure. The first backup browser to detect the failure forces an election to select a new master browser.

Potential Browsers

Here is another excellent question: What operating systems have the potential to be browsers? A *potential browser* is a machine that can be a browser if necessary. Windows NT Server, Windows NT Workstation, and Windows 95/98 can all be browsers. They are weighted in that order. Therefore, if you have one Windows NT Workstation and a dozen Windows 95 PCs, the NT Workstation would become the master browser.

Non-browsers

A *non-browser* is a computer that cannot act as a master browser or a backup browser. MS-DOS or Novell NetWare are both examples of non-browsers.

Browser Elections

Three things are considered when electing a new master browser. These are listed in order of importance:

- *Operating system*—Windows NT Server gets a higher weight in the election than Windows NT Workstation. Windows NT Workstation gets a higher weight than Windows 95/98.
- *Operating system version*—Windows NT Server version 4.0 receives a higher weight then version 3.51. The same rule holds for NT Workstation and Windows 95/98.

- *Present role*—A Windows NT Workstation acting as a backup browser receives a higher weight that one that is a non-browser. The same holds true for the other operating systems.

> NOTE
>
> If you want to manually configure a Windows NT computer's capability for being a browser, you need to go to the Registry. Edit the `MaintainServerList` entry under the `HKEY_LOCAL_MACHINE\SYSTEM\CurrentControlSet\Services\Browser\Parameters` key. You can configure this entry three ways.
>
> If you set it to No, the computer will never be a browser.
>
> If you set it to Yes, the computer becomes a browser. At startup, the server tries to contact the master browser to get a current browse list. If it's successful, it becomes a backup browser. If it can't find the master browser, it forces a browser election, and can become the master browser. This is the default value for Windows NT Server computers.
>
> If you set it to Auto, the computer is a potential browser. Whether it becomes a browser depends on the number of existing browsers.

Directory Replicator

The Directory Replicator service is the engine that enables Windows NT Server to replicate files and directories throughout a domain. This is very useful for keeping things like login scripts, user profiles, custom help files, employee rosters, and other important files synchronized throughout an enterprise.

In order to use directory replication, you must configure an *export server* that maintains the original files and directories, and an *import server*, which receives the files.

Replication is a three-phase process:

1. The export server monitors the export directory periodically. When a change occurs, it notifies the import computer.
2. The import computer receives the call and connects to the export server.
3. The import computer then copies any changed files.

> **NOTE** A Windows NT Server can act as both an import server and export server if necessary. A Windows NT Workstation can perform import functions, but cannot be configured for export.

> **NOTE** For the exam, be sure to remember that although Windows NT does replicate files and directories, both are replicated by *directory.* You cannot replicate just a file. Windows NT does not allow that level of granularity.

Scenario 2.5

Your HR department has decided to put the employee listing on the network. This list is used to control access to the premises and permissions on the network, and determines who gets a paycheck. HR wants you to make sure that every office in the company has local access to the list, and that the list is updated every night after HR makes it changes.

Required Results

- Configure directory replication to distribute the file `employees.xls` to servers throughout the enterprise.

To configure directory replication, you must first start the Directory Replicator service.

{*Logon Scripts and User Profiles are covered in depth in Chapter 3.*}

Starting the Service

The first thing you need to do to configure directory replication is to start the service. Open the Control Panel and open the Services applet (see *Figure 2.30*).

FIGURE 2.30
Starting the Directory Replicator service.

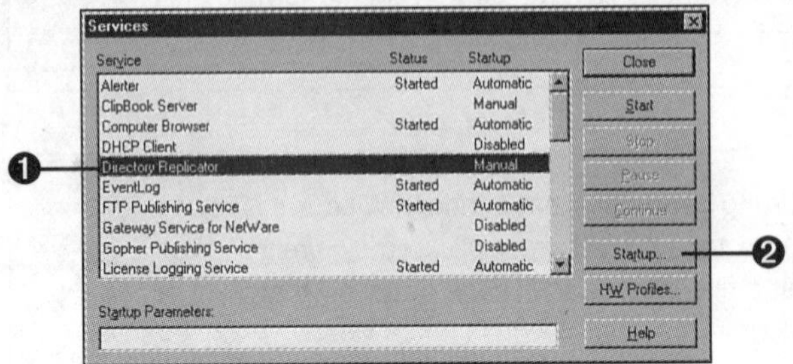

❶ Select the Directory Replicator service from the services listed. This service is set for manual startup by default.

❷ Click on the Startup button to configure the service. This opens the dialog box shown in *Figure 2.31*.

FIGURE 2.31
Configuring the startup parameters for the Directory Replicator service.

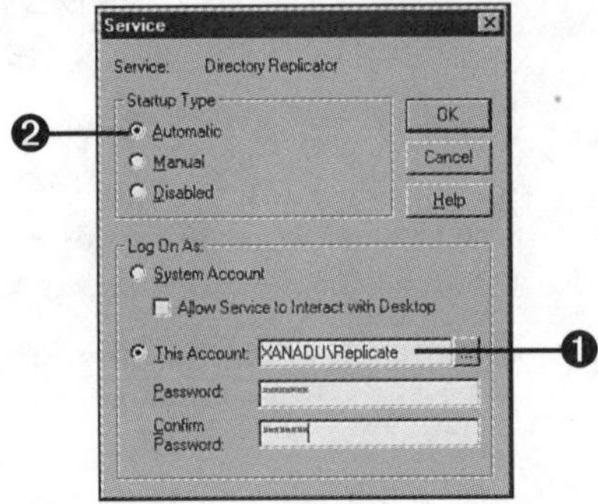

❶ The first thing you must do to create an account is fill in this blank. Use User Manager for Domains to create an account. This account needs to be in the Backup Operators or Replicator group. You can also use the system account, but it's generally a good idea to avoid that when possible.

❷ Set the Startup Type to Automatic to ensure the service will start whenever the server is rebooted. Click on OK when you're done.

When you assign an account to be used by the Directory Replicator service, it is granted the Log On As a Service right (see *Figure 2.32*). This right is required for the Directory Replicator service to start. Click on OK when that message appears, and then click Start (shown in *Figure 2.33*) to start the service the first time. Because the server is set to Automatic, it will start every time the server boots.

{*Creating users is covered in Chapter 3.*}

FIGURE 2.32
Note that the account you create is granted the Log On As A Service right.

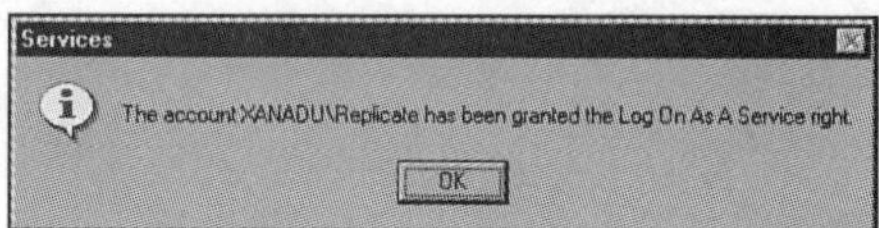

FIGURE 2.33
Click on Start to start the service after changing the Startup parameters.

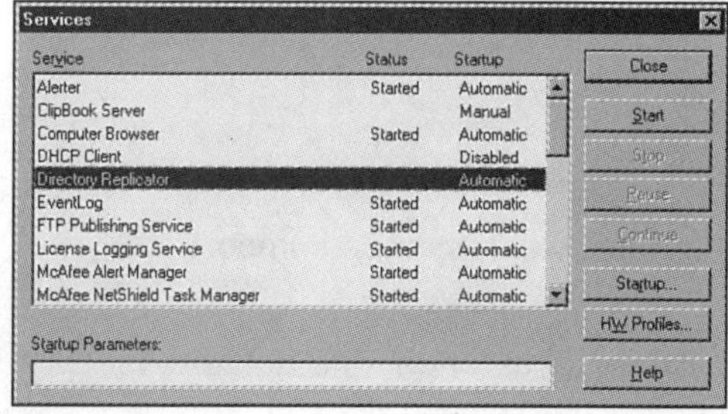

Repeat this process for any other server you want to receive the file updates.

Configuring the Replication

Now that the service is running, it's time to get replication configured. Open Server Manager from the Administrative Tools menu and double-click on your server from the list of servers. This opens the Properties dialog box shown in *Figure 2.34*.

FIGURE 2.34
Server Properties dialog box.

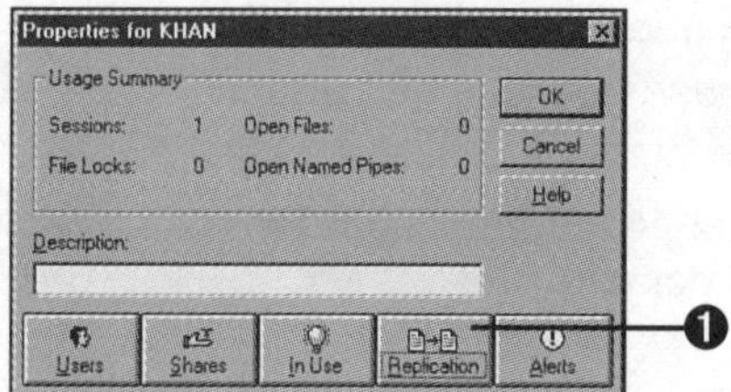

FIGURE 2.34 *cont.*

❶ Click on the Replication button to configure directory replication. This takes you to the Directory Replication dialog box shown in *Figure 2.35*.

{*Server Manager is covered in depth in Chapter 3.*}

FIGURE 2.35
Configuring directory replication.

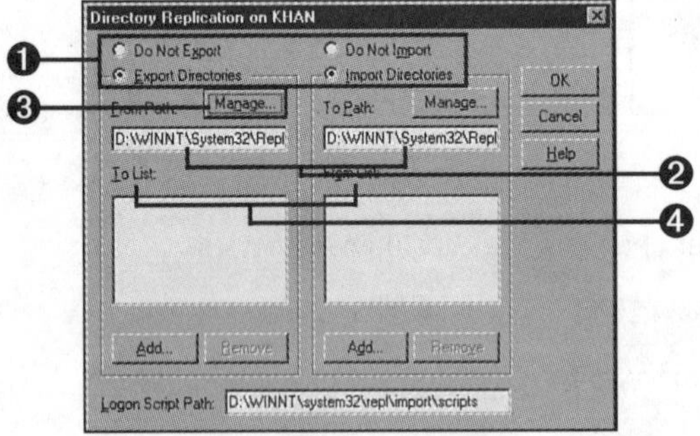

❶ Use these option buttons to enable the exporting and/or importing of directories.

❷ Here you can set the Import and Expert directories. The default for exporting is `<%systemroot%>\SYSTEM32\REPL\EXPORT`. The `SCRIPTS` directory is created by default under that directory for Logon Script replication. The default for import is `<%systemroot%>\SYSTEM32\REPL\IMPORT`. The same `SCRIPTS` directory is created by default here as well.

❸ Click on the Manage button to open the Manage Exported Directories dialog box, shown in *Figure 2.36*. From here, you can add subdirectories to be replicated. Take note that the `SCRIPTS` directory is enabled by default.

❹ In the To List and From List you configure which servers on the network your server will replicate to, or replicate from. The Select Domain dialog box (see *Figure 2.37*) shows how to select the server to replicate to. If this replication is to be between servers in different domains, you must use both the server and the domain names. If the To List is left blank, the server replicates to the local domain. If the From List is left blank, the server automatically imports from the local domain.

FIGURE 2.36
Managing replicated directories.

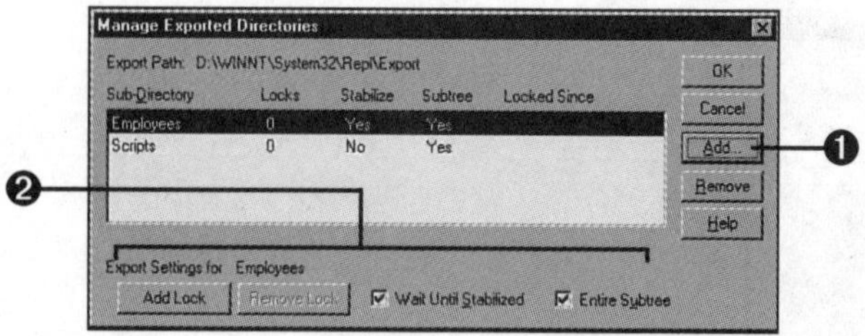

❶ Click on the Add button and enter the name of the directory you want to replicate. It must be under the export directory path.

❷ You can control the exporting of each directory individually. From here you can add *locks*, which prevent replication of the specific directory as well as make sure that replication copies the entire subtree. Finally, you can tell replication to wait until the changes have stabilized before replicating.

FIGURE 2.37
Managing replication servers.

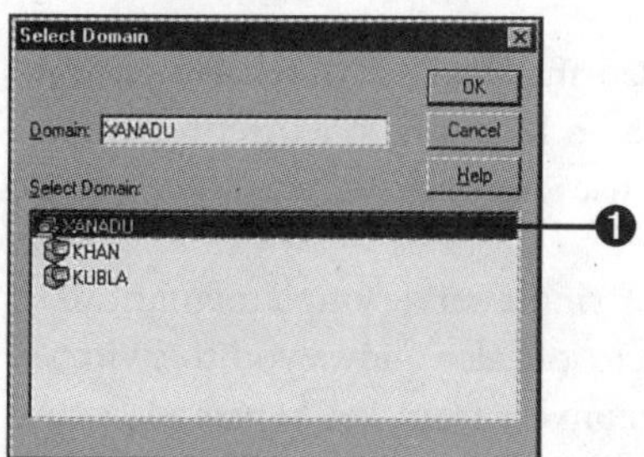

❶ Browse through the domain and find the import servers. As long as importing has been enabled on the computer selected, you have successfully configured replication.

License Manager

The License Manager allows you to manage how your server are licensed. In *Figure 2.38*, you can see how the server licenses look.

FIGURE 2.38
Choosing the Server Licensing mode.

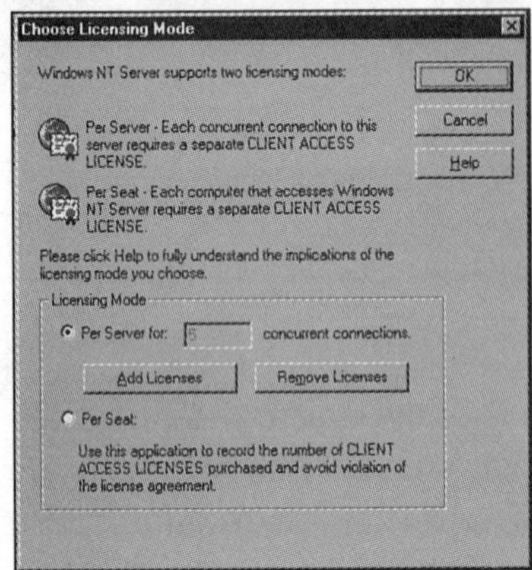

Microsoft allows two types of licensing for Windows NT Server:

- *Per Server*—This licensing limits the number of concurrent connections allowed on a server. For example, if you are licensed for 10 users, you might have 100 users on the network, but only 10 of them would be able to access the server at one time.
- *Per Seat*—When you move to Per Seat licensing, you are purchasing licenses for each client on the network. There is no limit on concurrent connections, but you must purchase separate licenses for each client.

Microsoft recommends Per Server licensing for single server implementations, and Per Seat licensing for anything larger. Microsoft also allows you to switch from Per Server to Per Seat, but not back. To convert from Per Server to Per Seat, open the Licensing applet in the Control Panel to access the Choose Licensing Mode dialog box (see *Figure 2.39*).

FIGURE 2.39
Converting licensing type from Per Server to Per Seat.

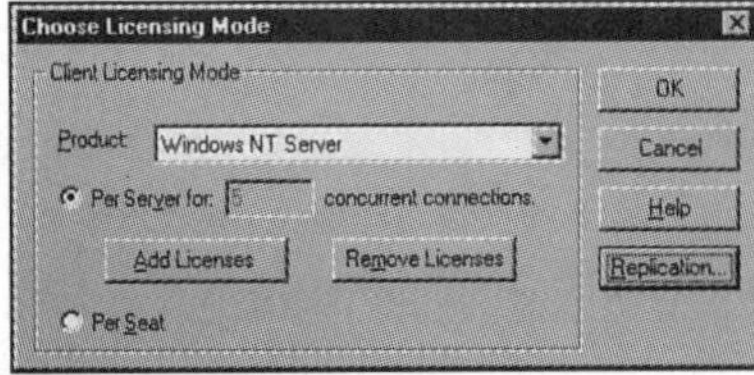

To change to Per Seat, just select the Per Seat option button.

If you click on the Replication button in the Choose Licensing Mode dialog box, you see the Replication Configuration dialog box (see *Figure 2.40*). Here you see another interesting feature of the Licensing applet: the ability to configure multiple licensing servers. You can configure a server or servers to maintain licensing for the domain. You can even configure replication between licensing servers. For the exam, be aware of these capabilities.

FIGURE 2.40
Configuring license replication.

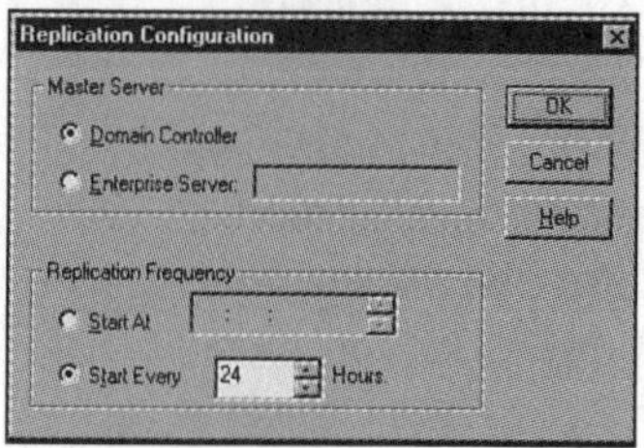

License Tracking

You've learned about using License Manager. Now turn your attention to license tracking. *License tracking* can be done on the local server, on a single domain, or across an entire organization. You configured single server licensing when you installed Windows NT.

In a domain environment, the PDC acts as the licensing server for the domain.

In an enterprise environment, where the company has determined that centralized license management makes sense, you can specify an enterprise licensing server that would be configured to keep a centralized database of all the licensing information for the enterprise. This server can be either a PDC for a domain or a dedicated licensing server. An *enterprise server* is the server that is replicated by multiple PDCs acting as license servers for their domains.

NETWORK CLIENT ADMINISTRATOR

The Network Client Administrator application allows you to create and share client files for DOS, Windows, and Windows for Workgroups. *Figure 2.41* shows the Network Client Administrator application. This is found in the Administrative Tools program group.

FIGURE 2.41
Network client administration.

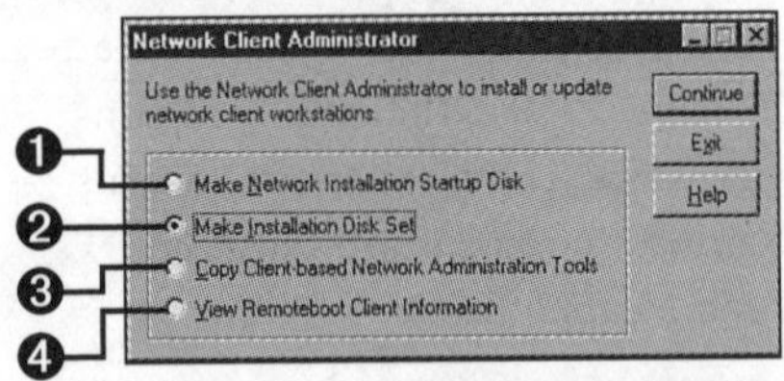

❶ Use this option to create a boot disk, which allows you to boot the client and automatically installs the Windows NT Client software. This option is available for DOS/Windows or Windows 95.

❷ Use this option to create installation disks for the following clients: Network Client v3.0 for MS-DOS and Windows; Remote Access v1.1a for MS-DOS; TCP/IP 32 for Windows for Workgroups 3.11; LAN Manager v2.2c for MS-DOS; or LAN Manager v2.2c for OS/2.

❸ Use this option to share the installation files for the client-based network administration tools on the Windows NT Server CD. You can also use this option to copy the installation files for the client-based network administration tools to a new directory on a server, and then share the files. Clients can then load the installation tools from the server, instead of requiring the Windows NT media.

❹ Use this option to view information about the Remoteboot service, which allows you to boot MS-DOS and Windows computers over the network. This is usually used in conjunction with diskless workstations.

The key to this application is it can be used to install the client files to the network, where any clients can access them via the network or installation disks can be created. *Figure 2.42* shows the configuration for sharing the files over the network.

FIGURE 2.42
Sharing the client files on the network.

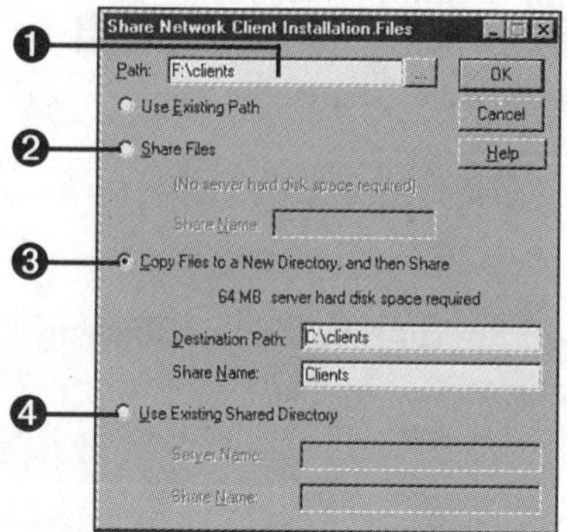

❶ Use the Path Window to identify the location of the client files.

❷ Use this option to configure the server to share the files from the installation media.

❸ Use this section to create a directory, copy the files, and share the directory.

❹ Use this section to select and configure an existing share you would like to use.

Figure 2.43 shows the important client files.

FIGURE 2.43
Creating client disks.

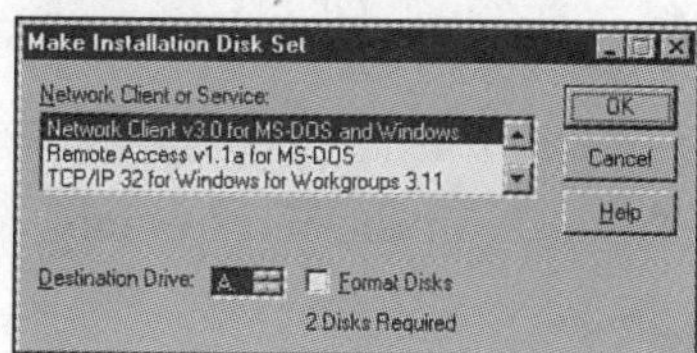

This is a very quick overview of the Network Client Administrator. The following sections describe what's involved for each client operating system.

Windows NT Workstation

Windows NT Workstation can access a Windows NT Server without the benefit of any special client installation.

Windows 95/98

Windows 95/98 ships with a Microsoft Client for Windows Networks. This can be installed from the operating system media, by going into the Control Panel, opening the Network applet, and adding the new client.

MS-DOS

MS-DOS computers can be added to the network by running the installation disks created with the Network Client Administrator.

Macintosh

To connect a Macintosh computer to a Windows NT Server, you must install the Services for Macintosh service.

Scenario 2.6

You have several managers who refuse to give up their Apple Macintosh computers even though your company has decided on an Intel processor/Windows NT standard. Because several of these managers are in fact VPs, you must give them access to your Windows NT server.

Required Results

- Configure Windows NT server connectivity for Macintosh clients.

Complete the following steps to install services for Macintosh:

1. Open the Network applet in the Control Panel. Click on the Services tab and select Add.
2. From the list of services, select Services for Macintosh.
3. Make sure you have the media available, and click OK.
4. After the files have copied, click Close to exit the Network applet.
5. You are asked to select a zone for the server to broadcast in. Alternatively, you can click on the Routing tab and make your server into a seed router for the AppleTalk network.
6. You are asked whether you want to reboot the server. Click OK; after the server has rebooted, it appears as an AppleTalk server on the AppleTalk network. Select it like a standard server, and you will be able to authenticate.

You have successfully completed another scenario. Congratulations!

NOTE

If you want to create a Macintosh volume, you must do it on an NTFS partition. The specifics of creating this partition are beyond the scope of this book, but for the exam you should be aware that it must be an NTFS volume.

CONFIGURING HARD DISKS FOR PERFORMANCE AND REDUNDANCY

Chapter 1, "Planning," discussed how to decide what disk configurations to implement when you install your Windows NT Server. In this section, you will learn how to implement the configurations discussed by using Windows NT's disk management utility: Disk Administrator.

NOTE

Whenever you make a change to your disk configuration, be sure to update your Emergency Repair Disk using the RDISK.EXE application. Disk Administrator also reminds you in case you forget.

Allocating Disk Space Capacity

There are three basic functions for allocating disk capacity: creating, formatting, and extending a partition. When you performed the installation of Windows NT, you had the opportunity to create a partition. In the following sections, you will learn to use Disk Administrator to create and format a partition, as well as to extend a partition to make it larger.

To open Disk Administrator, go to the Administrative Tools menu and select Disk Administrator. The first time you run Disk Administrator, it tells you that it hasn't been run before, and asks to write a signature to Drive 0. Click OK; you should see a display that looks a lot like the one in *Figure 2.44*. This is the Disk Configuration view of Disk Administrator. *Figure 2.45* shows the Volumes view of the application. To toggle between the two you can either select View from the menu bar or use the keystroke shortcuts: Ctrl+D for the Disk Configuration view and Ctrl+V for the Volumes view.

FIGURE 2.44
The Disk Administrator—Disk Configuration view.

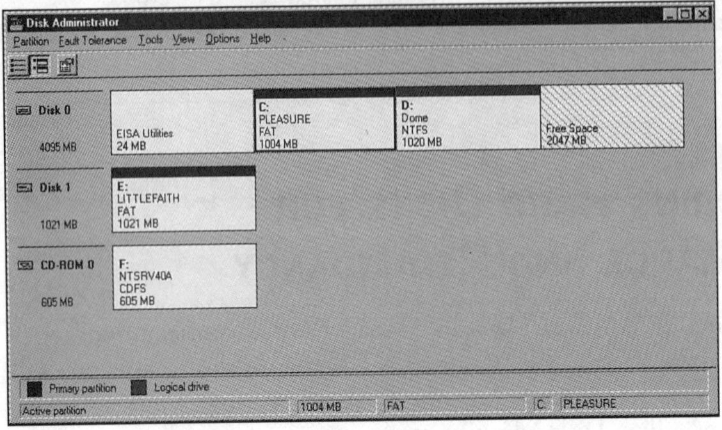

FIGURE 2.45
The Disk Administrator—Volumes view.

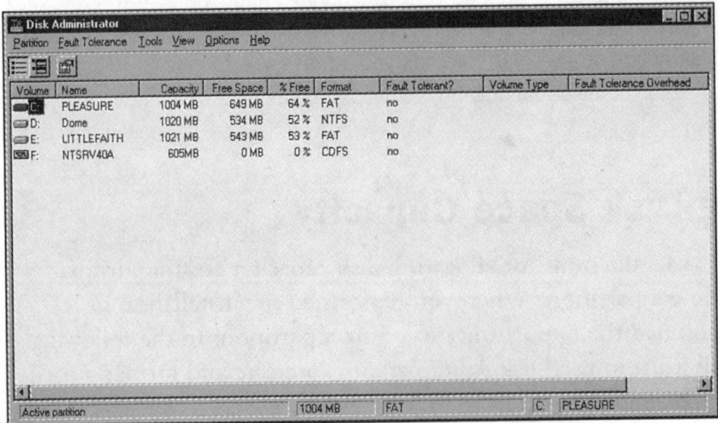

Creating a Partition

There must be one primary partition on the system that is set as the *active partition.* This is usually the partition with your system files on it. To set an active partition, select the drive, go to the Partition menu and select Mark Active. The selected drive becomes the boot drive.

Complete the following steps to create a partition:

1. Select a drive with some free space. Then go to the Partition menu and choose Create. *Figure 2.46* shows the Create Logical Drive window, which allows you to set the size of the partition. (You can also reach this

command by right clicking on the free space.) If this is the first partition to be created on the drive, it will be the primary partition for that drive. You can have as many as four primary partitions on a hard disk, unless there is an extended partition. If you have an extended partition on the disk, you can have a maximum of three primary partitions.

FIGURE 2.46
The Create Logical Drive window.

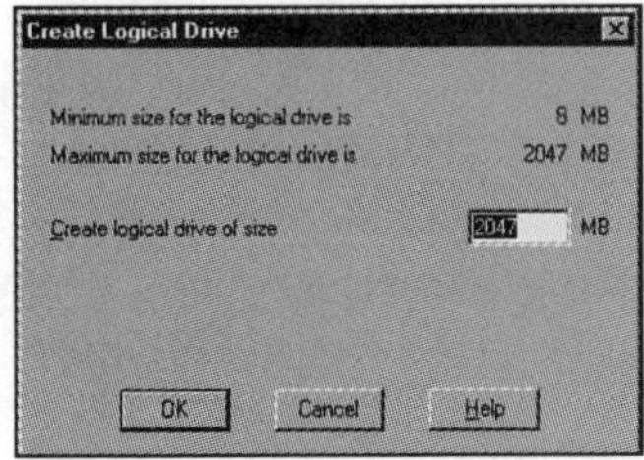

2. Set the size of drive you want to create and click OK.
3. To perform any further actions, you must make the changes permanent. Go to the Partition menu selection and select Commit Changes Now. Windows NT prompts you to confirm. Click on Yes.
4. Windows NT now reminds you to update your Emergency Repair Disk. Click OK again.

> **NOTE** If you have installed Windows NT on an extended partition, and you subsequently create a primary partition, you must modify the `boot.ini` if you want the server to boot correctly. This process is described in depth in Chapter 6, "Troubleshooting."

You have successfully created a partition. Now you need to format it in order for it to be useful.

Formatting a Partition

To format the partition, follow these steps:

1. Select the partition to be formatted. Be very careful to select the correct partition. It is very easy to inadvertently format the wrong partition—then you get a chance to test your disaster recovery procedures!

2. Go to the Tools menu and select Format. *Figure 2.47* shows the Format options window.

FIGURE 2.47
Formatting a partition.

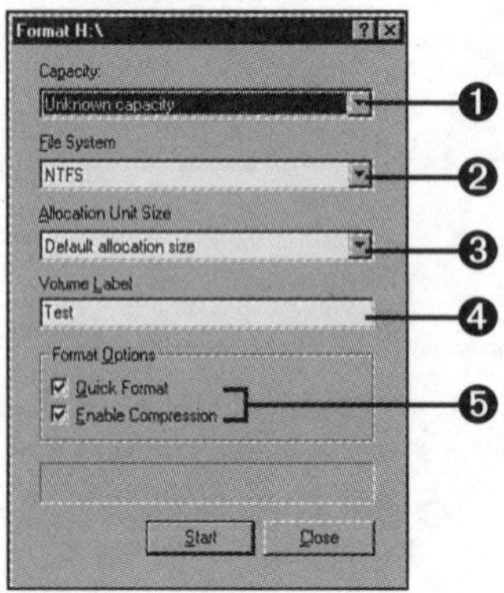

❶ The capacity of the drive shows up as unknown for an unformatted partition. If you are reformatting an existing partition, you should see the partition capacity in this box.

❷ The File System drop-down allows you to select the file system to format with. For hard drives, you can select NTFS or FAT. For a floppy disk, which cannot be formatted with NTFS, FAT is your only available choice.

❸ The Allocation Unit Size box allows you to determine the size of blocks to be used to store data on the partition. This specification is usually set at the default, but for application servers with specific storage requirements, you may want to change this size based on the vendor's recommendations.

❹ You can specify a name for the volume here.

❺ These check boxes allow you to select a quick format for partitions that have been formatted once, and also give you the choice of enabling compression.

3. In this window you can select the partition type (FAT or NTFS), the Allocation Unit Size, Capacity, and the Volume Label. You can also select the Quick Format option and the Enable Compression option. Click OK to format the drive. Windows NT warns you that you are about to destroy all the data on the drive, and prompts you to confirm. Click on OK to complete the format.

That is all there is to formatting a partition.

NOTE

Allocation Unit Size and Enable Compression are available only for NTFS formatting. FAT does not support these options.

{*NTFS and FAT are discussed in Chapter 1.*}

Extending a Partition

You've created and formatted a partition. Now what do you do if the volume you've created is too small? Well, if you have additional free space on the drive, or an additional drive, you can extend the partition.

Scenario 2.7

You have a Windows NT File and Print server set up for your office. A custom database application runs your business, and you have just run out of disk space. Your coworkers think you need to back up your data, upgrade all your drives, and then restore your data from the backup. You are convinced there is an easier way to do this, which won't involve restoring data. (Note, however, that you should always back up data before performing any operations like this.)

Required Results

- Add disk space for your database application without having to restore data.

Given the name of the section, you may have guessed that the answer is to extend the partition. First, you must either find some unused space on the drive or install an additional hard drive. Now that you have the free space, do the following to add the disk space:

1. Open Disk Administrator and click on the NTFS volume you want to extend.
2. While holding the Ctrl key, click on the free space you would like to add. Both the volume and the free space should now be selected.
3. Go to the Partition menu and select Extend Volume Set. This opens the Extend Volume Set dialog box, shown in *Figure 2.48*, which is very similar to the dialog box in which you selected the size of the original partition (refer to *Figure 2.46*). You can use all of the free space, or as little as 1 MB. Click on OK and the partition is extended to add the free space.

You've completed the scenario successfully!

NOTE Only NTFS volumes can be extended. If you want to extend a FAT partition, you must convert it to NTFS first. Also, you cannot extend the boot or system partition.

Whenever possible, try to plan for proper volume sizes, avoiding too many extended partitions. It becomes one more configuration that could potentially break.

FIGURE 2.48
Selecting the size of the extended partition.

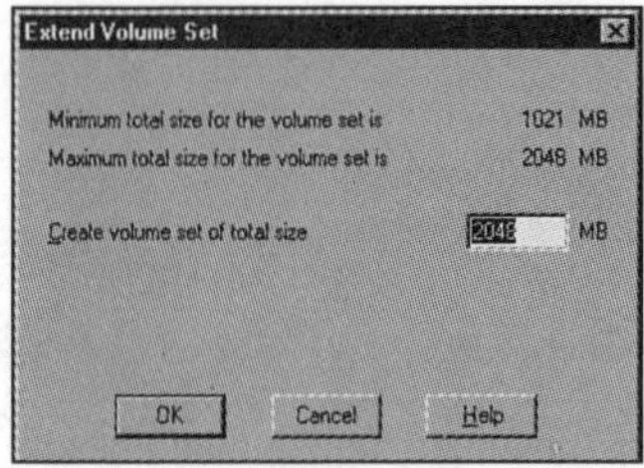

NOTE Although you can easily extend a partition, you cannot make a volume set smaller without deleting the data, creating the smaller partition, and then restoring the data.

Providing Redundancy

In a server environment, it can be a good idea to add some redundancy to your drive configurations. To this end, Windows NT offers a couple of configurations for providing fault-tolerance to your drive configurations.

NOTE Be sure to remember that your system and boot partitions (that is, the partitions that your system and boot files are on) cannot be part of a stripe set or a stripe set with parity. System and boot partitions can be mirrored, however. This process is described in the following section.

Creating a Mirror Set (RAID 1)

A mirror set implements RAID 1, in which you have two drives that are exact replicas. To implement a mirror set, complete the following steps:

1. Open Disk Administrator and click on the partition you want to mirror.
2. While holding the Ctrl key, click on an area of free space on a different drive you would like to mirror with. Both the volume and the free space should now be selected. Be very careful to select the drives in the correct order. Reversing the order will cause your drive with data to mirror the blank volume.
3. Choose Establish Mirror from the Fault Tolerance menu.
4. Select Commit Changes Now from the Partition menu to make the mirror set active. You are prompted to reboot the system. When the computer restarts, the drives will take a couple minutes (depending on the size) to synchronize.

{*Drive redundancy and RAID levels are discussed in depth in Chapter 1.*}

Creating a Stripe Set with Parity (RAID 5)

To create a stripe set with parity (RAID 5), you need at least three drives. Stripe sets are unlike mirrors in that mirror sets are created before saving data. If you have a drive with data on it and you would like to create a stripe set with parity for fault-tolerance, you must save your data, delete the partition, and create the stripe set. Then restore from the backup.

To create a stripe set with parity, complete the following steps:

1. Select an area of free space on a drive.
2. While holding the Ctrl key, select at least two but not more than 32 additional segments of free space. Each segment must be on a separate drive.
3. Choose Create Stripe Set with Parity from the Fault Tolerance menu.
4. In the Create Stripe Set with Parity dialog box, select the size of the stripe set. Disk Administrator shows all of the free space selected. Because each segment in a stripe set must be the same size, any space not used by the stripe set is spread evenly across all the drives. Select OK to create the set.
5. Select Commit Changes Now from the Partition Menu to make the stripe set active.
6. Select a segment and format it using the same method as formatting a partition, discussed earlier.

After the format is complete, the stripe set with parity is ready for data.

Improving Performance by Creating a Stripe Set

One additional configuration for a Windows NT Server is configuring the drives for performance. This is especially handy for servers with heavy I/O requirements, like database servers or an electronic commerce server. The highest performance disk configuration for Windows NT Server is a stripe set, without parity. This is because you have multiple read/write heads available for disk I/O, without the parity overhead of a stripe set with parity.

To create a stripe set, follow these steps:

1. Select an area of free space on a drive.
2. While holding the Ctrl key, select at least two but not more than 32 additional segments of free space. Each segment must be on a separate drive.
3. Choose Create Stripe Set from the Partition menu.
4. In the Create Stripe Set dialog box, select the size of the stripe set. Disk Administrator shows all of the free space selected. Because each segment in a stripe set must be the same size, any space not used by the stripe set is spread evenly across all the drives. Select OK to create the set.
5. Select Commit Changes Now from the Partition Menu to make the stripe set active.
6. Select a segment and format it using the same method as formatting a partition, discussed previously.

After the format is complete, the stripe set is ready for data.

Configuring Printers

One of the final pieces of installing Windows NT is installing and configuring a printer. But before looking at the steps to install, you need to be familiar with Microsoft's terminology and the printing architecture.

Windows NT Printing Architecture

Microsoft has some less than intuitive terminology it likes to use when discussing printing. This is very important to understand because if you don't understand the terminology, the architecture is almost unfathomable.

In Microsoft-speak, printing involves print devices and printers. Now to you and me, a printer is the thing you put paper and toner into, and retrieve your printouts from. To Microsoft, however, the actual hardware that prints your output on paper is a *print device. Printers*, in the Microsoft architecture, are instead the print drivers and other software that are loaded on a user's PC and communicate with the hardware print device. A *print server* actually provides the printer. In other words, a print server provides your software drivers. Finally, a job that is in a printer queue is referred to as a *document.*

One other concept that is important to understand is the spooler service. The *spooler service* is really a collection of device drivers and DLLs that provide Windows NT background print job processing by using background thread processing. The spooler passes data to the printer only when the printer is ready to receive more information, effectively managing the flow of printing from the print queue to the print device.

Take a look at how that breaks down from the user's PC to the paper printout.

The user prints from an application to a *printer* (the software driver.) The driver sends the *document* to a print queue on the server. When the *print device* (actual hardware device) is available, the queue sends the document to the print device, where it is transferred to paper (or whatever media.)

Adding and Configuring a Printer

If you remember that a printer is in fact the software component, you understand that when you install a printer, you are actually installing the drivers for your hardware.

Scenario 2.8

You have just received your first IBM 4019 laser printer and your manager wants it installed ASAP.

Required Results

- Successfully install the printer.

NOTE

To create a printer, you must be a member of one of the following groups: Administrators, Server Operators, or Print Operators.

To install a printer, follow these steps:

1. Connect the printer to one of your parallel ports.
2. Open the Printers icon in the Control Panel. You should see an icon for each printer that has been created on the server, as well as an icon for the Add Printer Wizard.
3. Because Microsoft has been nice enough to provide an Add Printer Wizard, double-click to open its dialog box.
4. Select the My Computer option button. This option indicates that the printer is physically attached to this computer. Click Next.
5. Specify the port your printer hardware is connected to. Click Next.
6. Select the appropriate driver for your printer. If your printer isn't listed, click on Have Disk to supply the vendor's drivers. Choose Next to continue.
7. Specify a printer name.
8. Configure the printer for sharing on the network. Select Shared so users will be permitted to access this printer through the network. You can also select which types of clients will be printing to this printer. It is important to know that Windows NT can provide drivers to other Windows NT computers. This prevents the need for loading drivers on each local machine. The server provides the drivers instead.

   Select a printer name for the share, and click Next. Remember, MS-DOS and Windows users can print only to printers named using the 8.3 DOS naming conventions. Choose Next to continue.

NOTE

If you are asked what you need to do if you have an Alpha or MIPS computer and you want it to print to a shared printer, the answer is to load the drivers for that machine. You will note in the Add Printer Wizard where you configure printer sharing, that Windows NT 4.0 is not listed as one of the additional drivers that needs to be loaded.

9. Next you are asked if you want to print a test page—click Yes and then click Finish. The drivers begin to copy.
10. The final step is to copy the drivers. You are prompted for the Windows 95 CD to load the Windows 95 drivers.

You have successfully installed your IBM printer.

Implementing a Printer Pool

If you have multiple print devices and you want to be able to print to all of them from a single printer, you can set up something called a *printer pool.* In order to set up a printer pool, the print devices must be connected directly to the same print server and the printer devices must be identical. This is so the configuration information can apply to all the print devices.

To create a printer pool, complete the following:

1. Connect two or more identical print devices to the server.
2. Add a printer for each device by using the steps detailed in the previous section.
3. Select the printer and select Properties from the File menu.
4. Select the Ports tab in the Properties dialog box, as shown in *Figure 2.49*.

FIGURE 2.49
Configuring a printer pool.

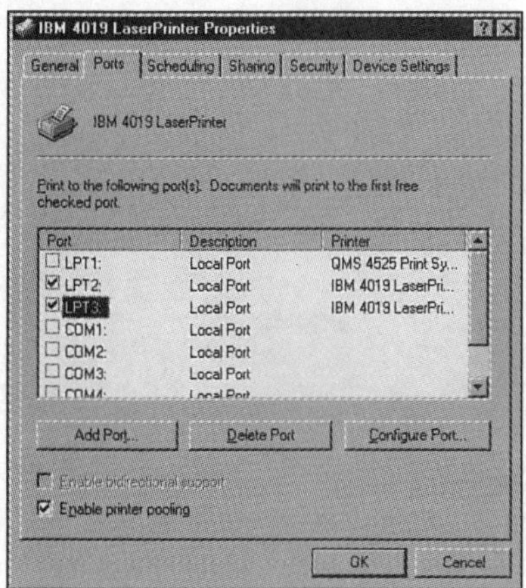

5. Click on the Enable Printer Pooling check box, and select as many ports as you would like to be included in the pool. Click OK.

Your printer pool is ready for printing.

Setting Print Priorities

After a document has reached the print queue, you can alter its priority by selecting the document, and selecting Properties from the Printer menu. This opens the dialog box shown in *Figure 2.50*. You can raise the priority from here, if you are an Administrator or a Printer Operator. This will move your job to the head of the queue.

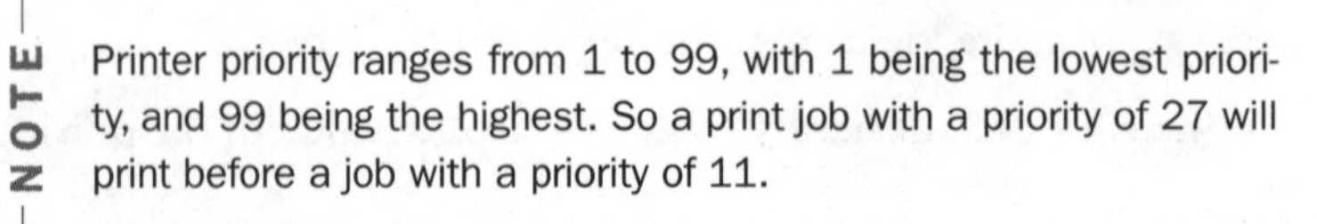

NOTE: Printer priority ranges from 1 to 99, with 1 being the lowest priority, and 99 being the highest. So a print job with a priority of 27 will print before a job with a priority of 11.

FIGURE 2.50
Changing a document's priority.

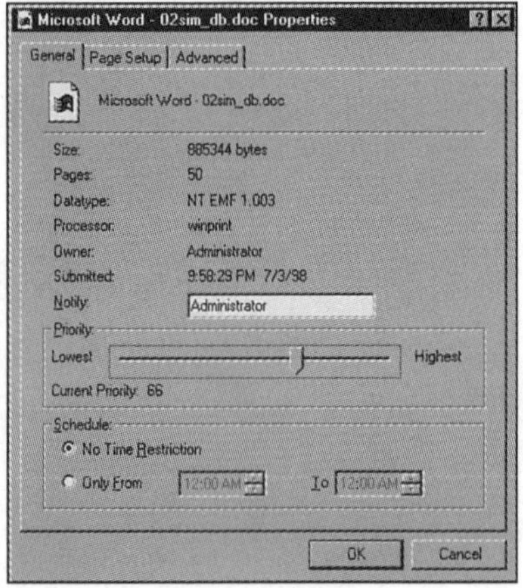

Alternatively, you may have a select group of users that needs to take priority on a printer. Suppose the accounting department needs to print end-of-week reports. Set up two print queues, and give each a different priority, as shown in the Scheduling tab in *Figure 2.51*.

FIGURE 2.51
Setting a printer's priority.

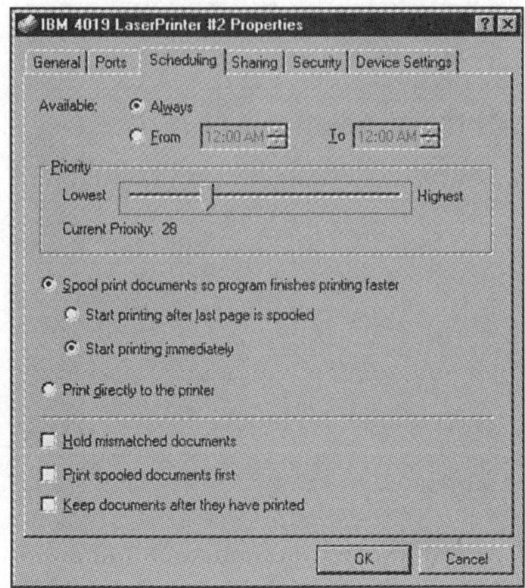

CONFIGURING PERIPHERALS AND DEVICES

There are a number of peripherals and devices that Windows NT supports. Understanding how to install and configure them is not only critical for the exams, but also for your ability to use Windows NT Server 4. Before you get too far into the devices, you must understand a few things:

- *IRQ*—Interrupt Request. A hardware interrupt used by a device to signal to the CPU that it needs CPU cycles.
- *IOBase*—The starting memory address reserved for a peripheral's drivers.
- *Memory Address*—The size of the memory needed by the peripheral.

The Devices applet in the Control Panel enables you to check the status of any of the installed device drivers, and how they should be loaded. Now take a look at installing some devices.

Installing a Modem

To install a modem, follow these steps:

1. Open the Modem applet in the Control Panel.
2. The Modem Wizard starts. You can ask Windows NT to find your modem, or select it yourself.

If Windows NT finds your modem, just click Next. If you asked NT to skip discovery, select the appropriate manufacturer and modem from the list, and click Next. You can also click on Have Disk if your modem is not on the list.

3. You are asked which port you want to install the modem on. Select the appropriate port and click Next.

The modem is installed.

Installing a SCSI Adapter

To install a SCSI adapter, follow these steps:

1. Open the SCSI Adapters applet in the Control Panel.
2. Click on the Drivers tab.
3. Click on Add. A list of drivers opens.
4. Select the appropriate manufacturer and adapter and click on OK.
5. Reboot the server when prompted.

Keep in mind that you do need to reboot the server after installing a SCSI adapter.

Installing a Tape Drive

To install a tape drive, follow these steps:

1. Open the Tape Drives applet in the Control Panel.
2. If your tape drive is not listed in the Device Window, click on Detect.
3. Click on the Drivers tab.
4. Click on Add. A list of tape devices opens.
5. Select the appropriate manufacturer and tape drive and click on OK.
6. Reboot the server when prompted.

Installing and Configuring a UPS with the UPS Service

Windows NT includes drivers that allow you to install and configure an Uninterruptible Power Supply (UPS) for a graceful shutdown of the system in case of a power outage. To install and configure the UPS, follow these instructions:

1. Connect the UPS to the building power.
2. Plug the server into the UPS.
3. Connect the UPS management port to one of the server's COM ports.
4. Open the UPS applet in the Control Panel.
5. Click on the Uninterruptible Power Supply Is Installed On check box and select the appropriate port (see *Figure 2.52*).

FIGURE 2.52
Configure the parameters for the UPS.

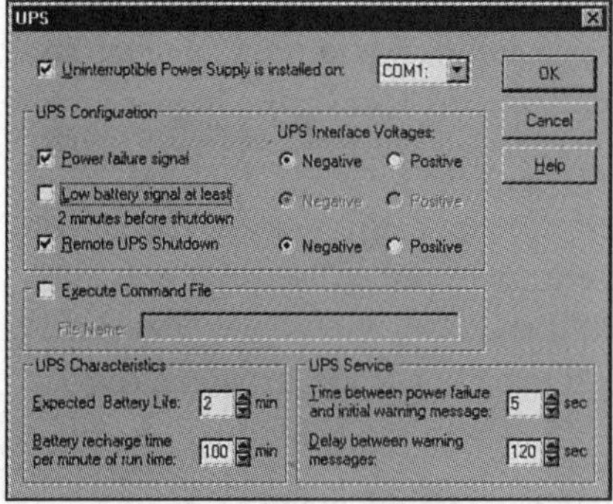

NOTE

Be sure to test your UPS. During startup, Windows NT sends a detection signal to each port in order to recognize hardware attached to that port. Unfortunately, some UPS units respond to the detection signal by turning off. If you have one of these UPSs, use the `/NoSerialMice` switch in the `Boot.ini` file to prevent Windows NT from sending this signal to the COM port that your UPS unit is connected to.

Other Devices

The final drivers to discuss may seem to be trivial, but they, in fact, can have the greatest impact on your day-to-day activities on the server. These directly affect the way you interact with the system.

Display Drivers

To configure your video display mode, use the following steps:

1. You can get to the Display Settings configuration in either of two ways. Right-click on the Desktop and select Properties, or open the Display applet in the Control Panel.
2. After you've gotten to the Display Properties dialog box, click on the Settings tab. Click on the Display Type button and confirm that the adapter is correct. If not, click on the Change button and select a different video adapter from the list. If your adapter is not on the list, use the Have Disk button to load the manufacturer's drivers.
3. Select the video display modes you want by setting appropriate values in the Color Palette, Desktop Area, Font Size, and Refresh Frequency fields. Check your monitor's documentation to ensure that you don't inadvertently damage the monitor. Some older monitors can't handle the higher refresh rates.
4. Choose Test. Setup displays a test pattern for the configuration you selected. After a few seconds, Windows NT returns to the old settings and asks "Did you see the test bit map properly?" If the display was how you wanted it, choose Yes to confirm the change. Then choose OK to make the change permanent.
5. After you are done setting up your display properties, click OK to exit.

Mouse Drivers

You can get to the Mouse settings by opening the Mouse applet (in the Control Panel). You are presented with four tabs for configuration:

- *Buttons*—From this tab you can configure the mouse buttons for either right- or left-handed operations, as well as set the double-click speed.
- *Pointers*—This tab allows you to either select a pointer scheme, or manually select your mouse pointer icons.

- *Motion*—In this tab, you can control the pointer speed and set the mouse pointer to snap to default, which takes the pointer to the default button in any application.
- *General*—This tab enables you to change the keyboard driver. Click on Change to select from a list of drivers, or to load the manufacturer's drivers with the Have Disk button.

Keyboard Drivers

You can get to the Keyboard settings by opening the Keyboard applet in the Control Panel. You are presented with three tabs for configuration:

- *Speed*—From this tab you can configure the Character Repeat and the Cursor Blink Rate.
- *Input Locales*—This tab enables you to configure the location for input. You can add or switch locales from this tab.
- *General*—This tab allows you to change the keyboard driver. Click on Change to select from a list of drivers or to load the manufacturer's drivers with the Have Disk button.

CHAPTER 3

Managing Resources

This chapter helps you get ready for the "Managing Resources" sections of the Windows NT Server (Exam 70-067) and Windows NT Server Enterprise (Exam 70-068) exams. This is one of the most critical chapters to be familiar with if you plan to pass either exam. It is also the chapter that covers the largest amount of information. Managing Resources describes everything from creating a user on your Windows NT Server to remotely managing your NT Server, and everything in between. Fortunately, Microsoft provides the following guidelines for prospective testers.

For Exam 70-067, the Windows NT Server Exam, Microsoft defines "Managing Resources" objectives as follows:

- Manage user and group accounts including managing Windows NT groups and user rights, administering account policies, auditing changes to the user account database, and creating and managing local, remote, and roaming user profiles. This also includes creating and managing system policies.

  This is the section of the exam that deals with all the activities surrounding user creation and management. Although you shouldn't expect to see a lot of questions about how to create a user, topics such as user profiles, auditing, and account policies are areas Microsoft feels are particularly important to a Microsoft Certified Professional (MCP).

- Administer remote servers from Windows 95 or Windows NT Workstation.

  Microsoft has tools available that allow you to administer servers from remote workstations. Because these tools are identical to the standard Windows NT management utilities, knowing which ones run on each platform, where to get them, and how they are installed is of more use than knowing the functionality of a particular utility. User Manager for Domains looks exactly the same whether it's running on a Domain Controller or the Windows NT Workstation on your desk.

- Manage disk resources including copying and moving files between file systems, creating and sharing resources, implementing permissions and security, and establishing file auditing.

  One of the cornerstones of the Windows NT Security model is the ability to control access to files on an NTFS (New Technology File System) partition. An understanding of how permissions are applied, especially during file operations, is important to an understanding of Windows NT security. Of equal importance is an understanding of how file sharing and sharing security work. Finally, you need to know how to determine what people are doing with the files. That means auditing. Because security is considered one of Windows NT's strengths, and also is very important to ensuring that an NT server or domain is set up correctly, this area is tested heavily.

For Exam 70-068, the Windows NT Server in the Enterprise Exam, Microsoft defines "Managing Resources" objectives as follows:

- Manage user and group accounts including managing Windows NT user accounts, user rights, groups, administering account policies, and auditing changes to the user account database.

  This objective expands on the objectives covered in the 70-067 exam by adding local and global groups to the objective. It still covers managing user accounts, and questions about this topic tend to be more domain-focused. Expect at least one question on granting resource access with local and global groups.

- Create and manage policies and profiles including local and roaming user policies, and system policies.

  Once again, this objective is very similar to the previous exam's objective. Being familiar with the different policy types and how to implement them in a domain environment with multiple domain controllers is a good idea for this exam.

- Administer remote servers from various types of client computers, including Windows 95 and Windows NT Workstation.

  Knowing where to get the remote administration utilities and how to install them are more important than the functionality of the actual utilities.

- Managing disk resources including creating and sharing resources, implementing permissions and security, and establishing file auditing.

This objective relates to the Windows NT security model. It is good to know how permissions work, particularly the sharing versus file permissions. It is also good to be aware of all the administrative tools from which you can configure file sharing.

This chapter covers the tasks you will need to understand in order to meet the exam objectives, and where possible, highlights sections that are covered heavily on one or both of the exams. This chapter discusses creating and managing users and groups, and makes you very familiar with the User Manager for Domains utility, which is where you perform most user-related activities. The chapter also covers the three types of profiles, and how to manage them. To complete your understanding of user environments, the chapter also delves into the System Policy Editor, and talks about how much control you have over a user's configuration while he is connected to the network. An in-depth look at the Server Manager utility and how to remotely manage your NT Servers from Windows NT Workstation and Windows 95 completes the server management portion of the chapter. The last utility covered is Disk Administrator; you look at how to set up and manage your hard disk resources. This is where the decisions regarding RAID levels and redundancy made during the pre-installation planning are implemented.

{*Planning your hard disk configuration and RAID levels is discussed in Chapter 1, "Planning."*}

Let's get started on the first "Managing Resources" scenario.

MANAGING USERS AND GROUPS

Managing Users and Groups is the cornerstone of a successful Windows NT network, and for that reason is also a highly tested area of the Windows NT exams. Using a variety of scenarios, this chapter covers the tasks related to managing users and groups in depth. You begin by adding a new user to your company. To complete the scenario, you look at creating the account, learn how to configure the account as if it were a new user in a department with specific access requirements, and then determine the things that can be done to manage his access to the network.

Managing Windows NT User Accounts

Before starting the simulation, there is one point you should keep in mind when dealing with user accounts in a Windows NT Domain. Each user account that you create is assigned a unique identifier, known as a Security ID (SID).

This is how Windows NT differentiates between individual users and groups. The practical side of this information is that after a user account is deleted, it is gone for good. It cannot be re-created, even if you create an account with the same name and attributes. Windows NT will not assign an account created with the same name or the same SID. This is important to understand because when the account is deleted, you lose all the permissions, file ownership, and any other specific rights granted the account. This is a topic that is usually good for at least one test question. Microsoft recommends that you disable accounts unless you are absolutely certain the employee is gone for good.

For example, suppose Dave Hatter has been with your company for 30 years, and is retiring next week. He is the manager and sole employee of the card-punch-programming department, which will finally be dissolved upon his retirement. When he leaves, should you delete or disable his account? This is one of the few cases (or one similar to this) in which Microsoft believes the account should be deleted. Now, if Dave were one of your Web developers, and you plan to replace him as soon as you can find another programmer, the answer is to disable the account. When the new developer starts, you can rename the account, give it a new password, and the new developer now has access to all of Dave's files, printers, and applications.

Scenario 3.1

You are the Network Administrator for Generic Recordings, Inc., a large recording studio located in Hollywood. Your company has just decided it needs to stop outsourcing its album cover designs, so it has created a Graphic Arts department. Your first graphic artist, Wayne Head, is starting on Monday and the studio manager wants to be sure he can hit the ground running. You need to give Wayne access to the system.

Required Results

- Grant Wayne access to your Windows NT Domain.

NOTE

One thing that is critical to being able to handle scenario-based exam questions is the ability to weed out all the extraneous material and concentrate on the objectives. It is often helpful to write down the important points on scratch paper as you read the question. Always read the question at least twice to be sure you understand all the objectives.

Creating a User Account with User Manager for Domains

The first step in creating a user is to open the User Manager for Domains application. Select User Manager for Domains from the Administrative Tools group. You see a User Manager window similar to *Figure 3.1*, where it is important to note that a number of default groups exist when you install Windows NT Server 4.0. From here, you create the new user (see *Figure 3.2*). You also need to assign a user name and password (see *Figure 3.3*).

If your account policy (discussed later in this section) permits blank passwords, you can create a new user by specifying only the name for the user. It is important to remember (in real life and in a test environment) that user names cannot contain the following characters: /\[]:;=,+*?<>

User names also have a 20-character length limitation. In real life, NT will tell you that you need to enter a valid user name if you use any unacceptable characters, and will not allow you to enter more than 20 characters in the "Username" field. (The test, unfortunately, is less forgiving.) Passwords are case sensitive and can be up to 14 characters in length.

NOTE

In order to create a user account in a domain, the Primary Domain Controller (PDC) must be available. The PDC hosts the Security Accounts Manager (SAM) database. All domain user accounts and Global groups for the domain are stored in that database. The Backup Domain Controllers (BDC) contain read-only replicas of the database, so although they can still conduct authentication to the domain when the PDC is unavailable, they cannot provide access to the SAM database without being promoted to a PDC. Promoting a BDC to a PDC is covered later in the chapter in the section "Server Management."

FIGURE 3.1
Default user accounts present in the User Manager window after the install.

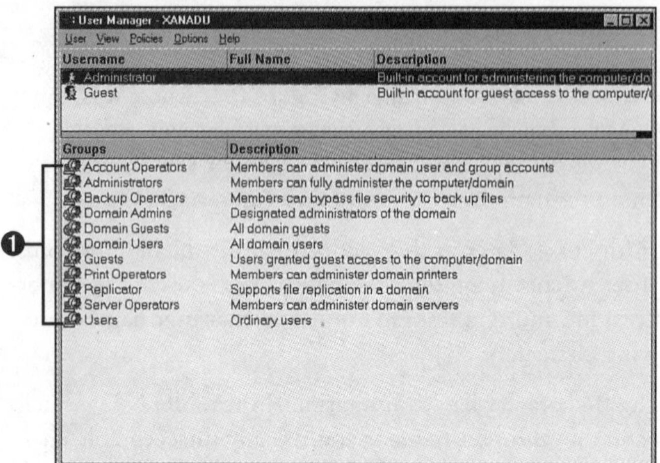

❶ It is important to note the Local Groups (heads over PC) and Global Groups (heads over globe).

> **NOTE**
>
> When you install Windows NT Server 4.0, the Guest account is disabled by default.

FIGURE 3.2
To create a new user, select New User from the User drop-down menu.

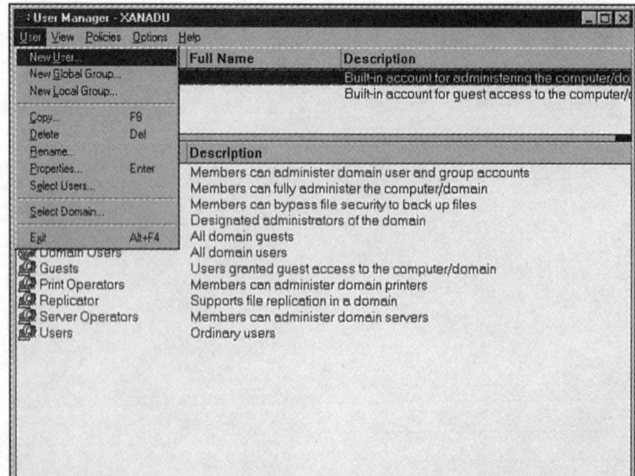

FIGURE 3.3
You must provide a Username and Password.

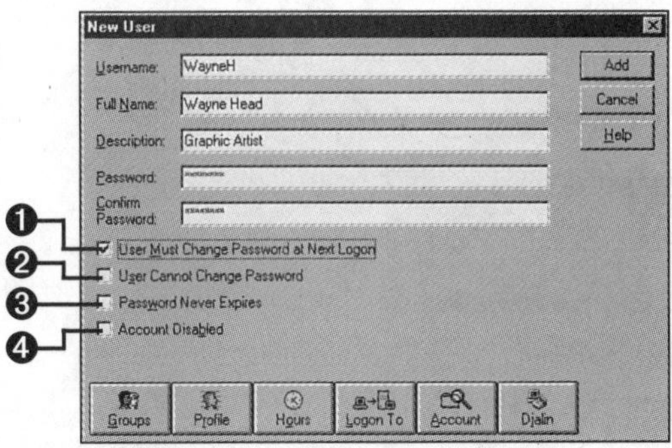

❶ User Must Change Password at Next Logon is selected by default whenever you create a new user, and is an excellent idea for day-to-day user account creation. If, on the other hand, it is required in the account policy that a user log on before changing his password, then this option is *unchecked* by default. Manually checking this box then prevents the user from logging on to the system at all. Your system will not produce any warning or error if both of these options are selected, so use care.

❷ User Cannot Change Password is useful for accounts that are shared by many people. Although it is generally a bad idea, you can also use this option in conjunction with a shared account, if you have a folder that many people use to drop or pick up copies of a report.

❸ The Administrator account has the Password Never Expires option selected by default. Any new accounts you create (unless you are copying the Administrator account) must have this option selected manually if you want to use it. In a production environment, this option should be used extremely sparingly because it bypasses any password security policies you may have in place.

❹ A check mark in the Account Disabled box causes the account to be disabled. A fairly obvious concept, but is stressed due to the uniqueness of SIDs; disabling an account is preferred to deleting it in the Microsoft user account model. Many companies using Windows NT will disable an account for a specified period of time (such as 30 or 60 days) before deleting it. This provides time for all account rights and permissions to be checked before an account is deleted. It is critical to understand that after an account has been deleted, it cannot be re-created. This topic will show up on at least one of your exams.

Congratulations. You have successfully met all the objectives for your first scenario (see *Figure 3.4*). Now it gets a bit more interesting.

FIGURE 3.4
The new user WayneH has been granted access to your Windows NT domain.

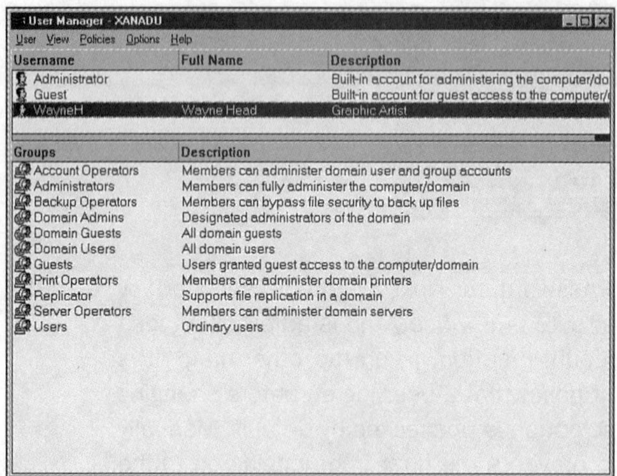

New User Options

There are a few other options available under the New User menu that are worth discussing:

- **Copy.** You can copy a user account or group. In the case of a user account, copying the account gives you all the attributes of the original except the Username, Full Name, and Password. All other account attributes, such as group membership, profile paths, time restrictions, and so on, are identical to those of the original account. The new account also gets a unique SID in the SAM database. When you copy a group, on the other hand, you copy the description and the group membership. You do not copy the rights of the original group. Groups also have unique SIDs in the SAM database, so your newly copied group also receives a unique SID.
- **Delete.** This allows you to delete a user or group (or multiples of either, by Ctrl-clicking on multiple users or multiple groups). When you attempt to delete a user or group, Windows NT reminds you that each account or group has a unique identifier, and that after it is deleted, it cannot be reclaimed or re-created.

- **Rename.** This is a fairly self-explanatory option—it allows you to rename a user or group. Many people recommend that you rename your Administrator account for security reasons.
- **Properties.** This opens the user or group properties page. You can see an example of a user account's properties page in *Figure 3.3*. Group properties can be seen later, in *Figure 3.6*.

> **NOTE** If you need to modify multiple users, you can select a range by first clicking the first user in the range, then hold the Shift key while selecting the last user in the range. To select multiple, non-contiguous users, again click the first user, but then hold the Ctrl key while selecting the other users you want to modify. Then open the Properties dialog as described above.

- **Select Users.** This allows you to select users based on group membership. This is not a function used a great deal because any modifications made to all the members of a group should be made to the group, not the individual users.
- **Select Domain.** As the title would indicate, this option allows you to select the domain you are administering.

> **NOTE** If you are feeling particularly unfriendly toward a would-be hacker, create a new account named Administrator with no rights to the system. Then monitor the new account. After the hacker breaks into the new Administrator account, he has no system access, but you can now track him down while he tries to figure out why he can't do anything. This can be a very frustrating experience for the person trying to get into your system.

Customizing Access

Now that you have created a new account, you will want to know how to modify and customize access privileges.

Scenario 3.2

Wayne can access the system, but now the boss wants to customize his access. Wayne needs access to the color printer, a profile (which we will cover later in the chapter), a logon script, and a home directory. The boss also wants Wayne restricted to system access from 6:00 AM to 6:00 PM. Finally, because Wayne may be doing some work from home, it would be nice if he had permission to access the network from home.

Required Results

- Grant Wayne access to the color printer.
- Configure Wayne's paths to his profile and home directory, and set up a logon script.
- Limit Wayne's access from 6:00 PM to 6:00 AM.

> **NOTE** Look closely at the third primary objective: You will notice a slightly different phrasing from the scenario. The scenario says to *grant* Wayne access to the system from 6:00 *AM* to 6:00 *PM*. The objective is to *limit* his access from 6:00 *PM* to 6:00 *AM*. I want to illustrate another reason that you need to read the scenarios and objectives very closely. Did you notice the difference when you read the scenario? Overlooking slight changes in phrasing could cost you points on an exam.

Required Results

- Configure Wayne's access so he can work from home.

To modify Wayne's account, either double-click on his user name, or select his account and go to User, Properties. Or finally, you can select his account and press the Enter key. All three methods open his user account properties. You should understand what each of the buttons on the bottom of the User Properties screen signifies (see *Figure 3.5*).

FIGURE 3.5
The User Properties screen.

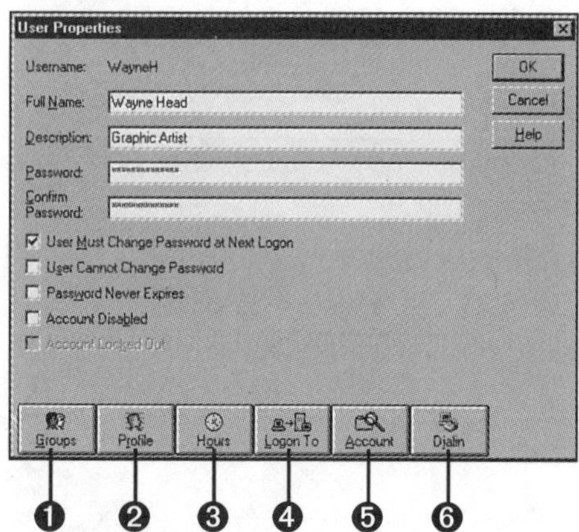

❶ The Groups button opens the Group Memberships screen (see *Figure 3.6*). From this screen you can add and remove a user from any of the groups. The concept of groups is usually good for several questions on the Enterprise exam.

❷ The Profile button opens the User Environment Profile screen (see *Figure 3.7*). We discuss the use of user profiles in the "Creating and Managing User Profiles" section of the chapter. This is also where you would set the user logon script. Logon scripts can be very useful for setting printer captures and drive mappings at logon time.

❸ The Hours button opens the Logon Hours screen (see *Figure 3.8*). This is where you can determine when a user can be connected to the server. When you look at setting account policies, you will see where you can determine what happens to a user when they are logged on and they reach the limit of their authorized access time. In the case of this scenario, this is where you will set Wayne's access times, which was one of our primary objectives.

❹ The Logon To button opens the Logon Workstations screen. This is where you can restrict a user's logon to certain machines. Because there is so little configuration that can be done on this screen, there is really nothing else to discuss. For the exams, you should be aware that this capability is available from within the user account properties, and that the workstations are

FIGURE 3.5 cont.

entered by NetBios name. If you try to use a MAC address or an IP address, it could prevent the user from logging on from *any* machine.

❺ The Account button opens the Account Information screen (see *Figure 3.9*). This option is discussed in the "Account Policies" section of the chapter.

❻ The Dialin button opens the Dialin Information screen (see *Figure 3.10*). This is where you will configure Wayne's account to allow dialin access to the system to complete our secondary objective.

{*You can find more information about the use of the Directory Replicator Service for distributing logon scripts in Chapter 2, "Installation and Configuration."*}

FIGURE 3.6

The Group Memberships screen is used to assign group membership for granting access to resources.

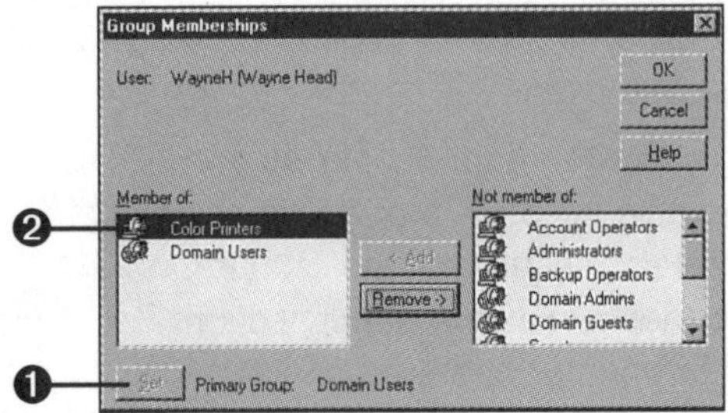

❶ The Set button gives you the ability to set a primary group. It should be mentioned that group membership can only be set to a Global group. The difference between Global and Local groups, and the functions of each type of group is discussed in the "Using Groups to Manage User Access Rights" section of the chapter.

❷ Wayne is now a member of the Color Printers group. To accomplish this, select the group you want to add the user to (in this case Color Printers) and click on Add. To remove a user, select a group in the Member Of box and click Remove. (As with most Windows applications, you can use Shift+click to select a range of groups to add, and Ctrl+click to select multiple groups from the list. While this is useful in theory, it can be dangerous in a production environment. It is very easy to inadvertently add a user to the wrong group. Use this feature with caution.)

In this scenario you need to add the newly created group Color Printers. This completes our first primary objective. For the purpose of this scenario, assume the group has the appropriate printer access.

{*Creating a group is discussed in the "Using Groups to Manage User Access Rights" section of the chapter.*}

{*Setting up and granting rights to printers is discussed in Chapter 2, "Installation and Configuration."*}

> **NOTE** Primary Groups are used only by users accessing the server through Services for Macintosh. When a Macintosh user creates a folder, the user's Primary Group is associated with the folder. Services for Macintosh are discussed in Chapter 2, "Installation and Configuration."

When you create users in a domain, they are automatically added to the Domain Users group. Unless you have a need for an unusually secure network, it is usually a good idea to leave users in this group. Many Global permissions are usually assigned using this group, and not taking advantage of this assignment can unnecessarily complicate your job as an administrator. Table 3.1 discusses the capabilities of each of the default groups.

TABLE 3.1

WINDOWS NT DEFAULT GROUPS

Group	*Group Use/Capabilities*
Domain Users—Global Group	Contains all the users in the domain. It is generally used to assign permissions to common printers, directories, and file shares. Access to any global domain resource should be granted using this group.
Domain Admins—Global Group	With luck, this is the group that is reading this book. Domain Admins has total control over all the domain resources. Be very careful when adding members to this group.
Domain Guests—Global Group	Domain Guests is a fairly innocuous group with no capabilities by default.

cont.

TABLE 3.1 *Cont.*

WINDOWS NT DEFAULT GROUPS

Account Operators—Local Group	Useful if you want to delegate the ability to manage Users and Groups. Anyone in this group has that ability.
Administrators—Local Group	Can manage the computer/domain. This is a group to which you should be cautious about adding members.
Backup Operators—Local Group	These users can perform system backups. This group of users is useful for delegating responsibilities to—in this case, responsibility for backing up computers, locally or in the domain.
Guests—Local Group	A fairly unused group. It has no rights to the domain by default.
Print Operators—Local Group	Group for your print managers.
Replicator—Local Group	Group used for replication in the domain.
Server Operators—Local Group	Group used to delegate server administrative tasks to a group of administrators.
Users—Local Group	Contains all the users.

Many training guides have long discussions regarding these groups, including extensive tables listing all the permissions for each group. This book does not cover these groups in that detail for two reasons. First, on any of the exams I have taken, I have never seen a question on the exact permissions of any of these groups. Exam questions do not tend to be that granular. Second, and in some cases more important, in the two-and-a-half years I have been working with Windows NT systems, I have never needed to modify or even investigate the permissions for any default group. My advice would be to know the function of each group, and use them as intended. Modify the default groups at your own risk. For the exams, you should be generally familiar with which groups have what capabilities.

In this scenario, you have given Wayne a profile located on the primary domain controller, a logon script, and a home directory that is also on the primary domain controller.

FIGURE 3.7

From this screen you can really start to customize a user's account. You can assign a user profile, a logon script, and a home directory.

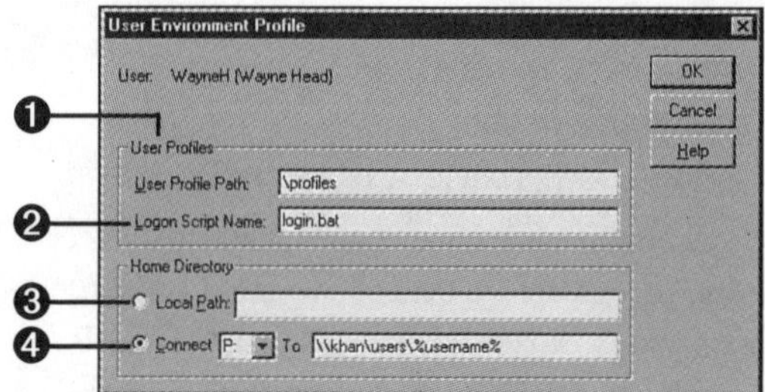

❶ User Profile Path specifies the location of the user's roaming or mandatory profile. If you are connecting to the domain from a Windows NT 3.x machine, be sure to include the profile name.

❷ Logon Script Name is used to specify the name of a user's logon script. Logon scripts are very useful for mapping drives and printers using the Net Use command. Logon scripts are stored in the <server_name>\<winnt_root>\SYSTEM32\REPL\IMPORT\SCRIPTS subdirectory of the domain controller and can be replicated utilizing the Directory Replicator service.

❸ Local Path is used if you want the user's home directory to reside on the local workstation. Unless there is some very good reason not to store the users files on the network, where they can be backed up and managed, this field is usually left blank in favor of a network home directory.

❹ The Connect option button allows you to specify a network drive as the user's home directory by specifying a fully distinguished Universal Naming Convention (UNC) path. This is the best method for providing a home directory because it allows a user to store files on a network server where the network administrator can maintain them. In the case of a drive failure on the network, backup copies, RAID arrays, hot spare servers, and clustering technologies can all help keep those files available. In many cases of workstation hard drive failure, those files are lost. It is important to note that the %username% variable can be used to automatically connect to a directory with a name of username. (That was a really awkward way to say that in our example, Wayne's home directory would end up being named WayneH.) Windows NT automatically creates this directory as long as the preceding directory structure exists. In our scenario,

FIGURE 3.7 *Cont.*

that means the Users directory must be created before creating home directories if you want the home directories to be created automatically. You must also manually share the Users subdirectory if you want people to have access to their home directories. Windows NT does not do this automatically.

This scenario uses a small network for the simulations, so the PDC is the file server. In a production setting, this is probably not a valid configuration except in small environments. Generally home directories should be located on servers dedicated to file sharing. The last thing you want on your PDC (or BDC) is someone making a *backup* copy of his or her computer to your PDC and filling the disk. After you fill the available disk space on a domain controller, you can expect it to be unstable. This is a particularly bad situation in a production environment.

> **NOTE** If your network has both Windows NT and Windows 95 workstations, keep in mind that they cannot use the same profiles. The Windows 95 profiles are not discussed in this book; neither should the Windows NT profiles discussed in this book be applied to Windows 95 clients.

> **NOTE** If you are using mandatory user profiles and the server that is storing the user profile is unavailable, the user will be unable to access the domain. Microsoft may question you on this point regarding user profiles.

{*Roaming and mandatory are covered in the "Creating and Managing User Profiles" section of this chapter.*}

{*The Directory Replicator service is covered in Chapter 2, "Installation and Configuration."*}

> **NOTE** On a non-test-related topic, it is generally an excellent idea to have a naming convention for selecting the drive letters, for not only the home directory, but for any drives mapped in the logon script as well. Some conventions commonly used are H: for the home directory, M: for a mail share (if necessary), and G: (group) for any common directories. Other conventions include using P: (personal directory) for the home directory, as seen in *Figure 3.7*.

NOTE

> The Universal Naming Convention (UNC) is a Microsoft standard method for identifying network resources. The UNC begins with a double slash (\\). This tells the system that a UNC will follow. The server name appears next. Then the path to the shared resource you want to specify follows, separated by single slashes .
>
> For example, suppose you have a directory named Doom. It is located on the Development server and is located under the Games share. The UNC for this directory would appear as follows:
>
> \\Development\Games\Doom
>
> UNCs are not case sensitive.

This completes the second primary objective. Now you learn how to restrict Wayne's system access.

In *Figure 3.8*'s simulation you should note that Wayne's access from midnight until 6:00 AM has already been removed and now 6:00 PM until midnight is selected. The interface is relatively straightforward. Click on Allow to allow domain access, and on Disallow to prevent access. Hours are broken down to the hour, and also by the day of the week. The blue line indicates that a user has system access during an indicated hour.

FIGURE 3.8

The Logon Hours screen is used for one thing: to determine when users can be on the system.

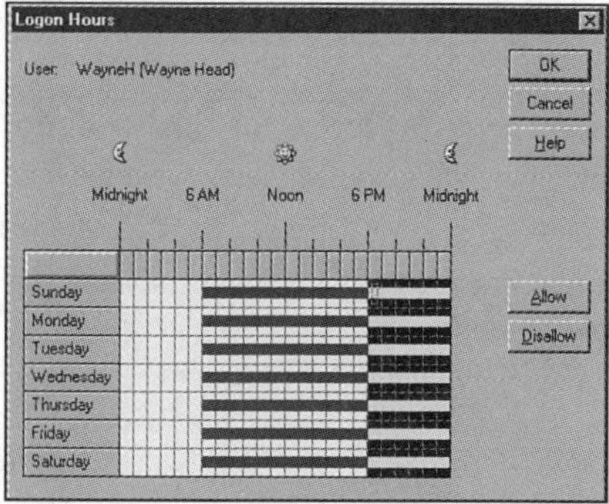

It is a good idea to control system access whenever possible. If you have administrative users who are never on the system except during business hours, limit their access to that time frame. It is better to have too much security on your network than not enough.

You have just completed the final primary objective.

Figure 3.9 provides one further capability that is very important in a Windows NT network. From this screen you have the ability to set an expiration date on an account. This is a terrific feature if you use a short-term temporary help, or high school or college co-op students. Suppose you have five college students who will be co-oping with your company for the summer. You know they'll be starting on June 1, and leaving for school on August 31. From this screen you have the ability to automatically expire their account on 08/31/98. This saves you the problem of putting "Disable co-op accounts" on your calendar for three months hence, and ensures that your network remains secure should you forget. In this business, in 90 days you could have a completely different job, and your replacement may not even be aware the co-ops are leaving.

FIGURE 3.9
The Account Information screen can be useful but is not actually pertinent to this scenario.

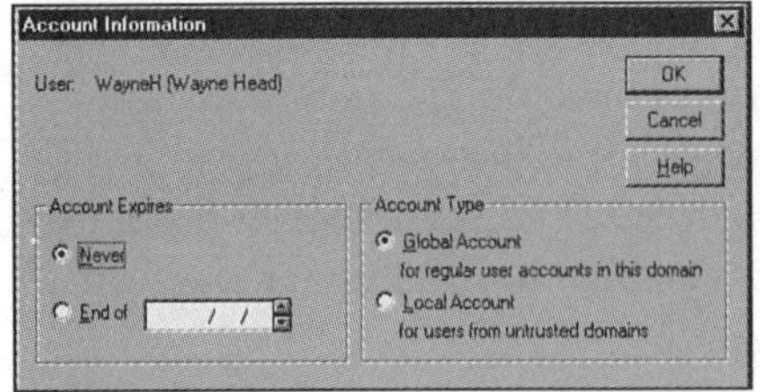

> **NOTE** Account Type can be used to create accounts for users who are in untrusted domains. Most accounts you encounter will be Global, which is the default.

You have one final objective to cover. The secondary objective for this scenario is to grant Wayne remote access to the system.

FIGURE 3.10
Check the Grant Dialin Permission to User check box.

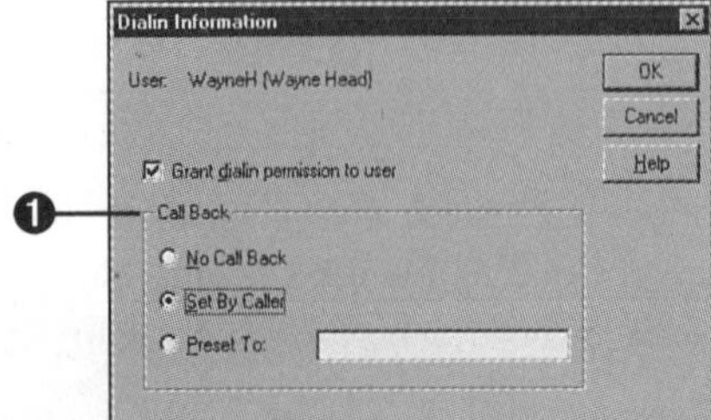

FIGURE 3.10 *Cont.*

❶ Callback is an additional security feature that deserves a brief discussion. To prevent anyone from attempting to access your network via RAS, you can require that the server call the end user back. The user must be dialing from a preset number or must provide the number from which he is calling. If the user provides a number, it is logged and can be traced should an unauthorized individual access the network from that account. It is a good idea to use callback whenever possible.

Although this feature allows Wayne the permission to dial in to the server, unless Remote Access Service (RAS) is set up, this is a useless permission.

{*Remote Access Service is covered in Chapter 4, "Connectivity."*}

> **NOTE**
>
> You might also want to use callback if you have a user who does a lot of traveling. Allow the user to specify a callback number, and then the server will initiate the call back to the user and allow her to access the system after the modems connect. The advantage here lies in how the long distance is charged. A standard long-distance rate from the phone on your desk (or from a RAS server) is an order of magnitude cheaper than a traveling user can access with a phone card or a hotel long-distance line. You would be surprised how quickly the savings can add up if you have a lot of traveling users.

You have accomplished the three primary objectives and the secondary objective for this scenario. Congratulations. Now it's time to look at configuring account policies, the basis for account security.

Defining Account Policies

So far you have looked at creating and configuring a user account. The next step is to examine how to set up an account policy for any of the accounts on the system. When you make a change to the account policies, you are making a change to all the accounts on the system. Account policies define how passwords are handled, as well as what to do when a user enters the wrong password for an account. The following scenario walks you through setting up an account policy for Generic Records.

Scenario 3.3

The head of security at Generic Records has noticed more and more people using the internal computer network. Because she is unfamiliar with computer technology, she has been reading some mailing lists and has checked out a few hacker books at the library. She wants you to set some password policies. She wants people to be required to change their passwords every 90 days, and she'd like the account to shut down for half an hour if someone enters the wrong password five consecutive times. She would like all passwords to be at least eight characters long, and if you can figure out how to do it, she would also like users to have to choose a unique password for at least 10 passwords.

Required Results

- Set the Windows NT Account Policy to force a password change every 90 days.
- Set an Intruder Lockout for five bad attempts, with a 30-minute lockout timer.
- Set a Minimum Password Length of eight characters.

Required Results

- Configure the Account Policy to require at least 10 unique passwords.

Before getting into the scenario, there are a few general rules of thumb for setting up an account policy. If your company has no concerns for security, setting everything to 0 (disabled) is perfectly acceptable. In that type of environment, minimum password lengths and intruder lockouts can just get in the way. For a medium-security environment, using the parameters discussed in the scenario would probably be appropriate. For a high-security environment, however, you might lengthen the minimum password length, set the intruder lockout to indefinite duration, and require 45 unique passwords instead of just 10. Finally, set the policy so passwords expire every 30 days (see *Figure 3.11*). This configuration could be a little more inconvenient for your legitimate end users, but is the best configuration for your network's security posture.

FIGURE 3.11
Account Policy configured for the scenario.

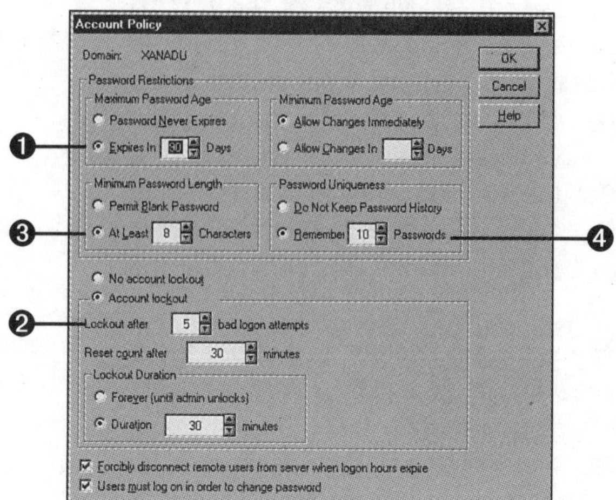

❶ To accomplish the first objective, set the Maximum Password Age to 90 days. This can be done by selecting the Expires In box and typing 90, or using the spin box to set the age to 90. The age can be anywhere from no password expiration (a very dangerous setting from a security perspective) to 999 days.

❷ To accomplish the second primary objective, set the maximum number of bad logon attempts to 5 with a lockout of 30 minutes. It's important to note that you can also set a Reset Count time, although that is not a requirement of this scenario. These three parameters specify that if there are five bad logon attempts within 30 minutes, the account is locked for 30 minutes before anyone can log on. This is an important concept, not only from an administration standpoint, but also from a testing perspective. It's not unusual to see a locked account question on one of the NT Server exams. You can set the number of bad logon attempts from 1 to 999, the reset count time from one minute to 99999 minutes, and the lockout duration from one minute to 99999 minutes, or to Forever, which requires an administrative reset.

❸ The third objective deals with password length, which is set in the Minimum Password Length section of the dialog box. This length can vary from Permit Blank Password, to a minimum of 14 characters. Set it to 8 characters for the scenario.

FIGURE 3.11 *Cont.*

❹ The secondary objective is to require 10 unique passwords. Suppose you're a user's password is *love* (one of the top 10 passwords used) and the password aging policy has expired the password; it's time for the user to set a new password. If you haven't specified a number of unique passwords, the user can set his new password to *love*, which defeats the purpose of a password aging policy. Set the Remember spin box to 10 to require the user to provide 10 consecutive unique passwords before he can reuse one. Congratulations! This completes the objectives for the scenario.

❺ The Minimum Password Age setting is another side of password aging. You have already set a maximum age that requires users to change their passwords after a certain time. The Minimum Password Age prevents users from changing their passwords for a certain period of time. Although it is not used a lot, this setting, which varies from 1 to 999 days, or to allow immediately, can be used to prevent users from setting all 10 unique passwords as soon as the time to change passwords arrives. Sometimes a user is so enamored with his password he will go to such extreme lengths to retain the same password.

❻ There are two check boxes at the bottom of the screen. The first, Forcibly Disconnect Remote Users from Server when Logon Hours Expire does essentially what it says. If you are logged on and your logon hours expire, you will be warned to log off. If you don't, you will be disconnected. Users MUST Log On to Change Password can be dangerous if used in conjunction with the User Must Change Password at Next Logon parameter in the account properties. It is possible to inadvertently lock a user out of the network by enabling both of these policies.

At a glance, the Reset Count time and Lockout Duration may look very similar. The Reset Count time is the amount of time after the first bad logon attempt that the system will wait before resetting the Bad Logon count to 0. Lockout Duration is the amount of time for which the account will be locked before anyone can logon, even with the correct password.

It's important to remember that after a password has expired, a user will not be able to logon. There is no grace period. If the user's password has expired, an administrator must reset it.

Creating a Group to Manage User Accounts

You've done quite a bit of work creating and configuring a user account. Now it's time to take a look at groups. Groups as a concept are very easy to understand. If you have ever attended a trade show, you picked up your name badge at a booth marked A-G, H-N, O-U, and so on. The trade show organizer is using the alphabet to *group* attendees for easier management of the distribution of name badges and show materials.

Windows NT uses groups in a similar fashion, but instead of organizing users alphabetically (at least in most cases), groups in Windows NT are used to organize users who need access to the same resources. For example, suppose there is a very expensive color printer in the graphics department of your company. It costs one dollar per page to print a document. You could manually grant rights to the printer to the 25 graphic designers in the department. The down side to this is you have to remember who all those people are. When Wayne gets promoted out of the graphics department to head up the new "Year 2000" project, you must remember to remove his access to the printer. That should be no big deal—after all, it's easy to remove a user from the printer's access list, right? But suppose there are actually five graphics printers, eight servers, and 24 file shares that the graphics department uses in its day to day activities. That's a little more complicated. The easy solution is to create a Graphics Department group, place all the graphic designers in it, and then grant group rights to the printer and whatever other resources the department needs access to. When Wayne gets promoted, you just move him from the GraphicsDepartment global group to the Y2K global group.

Scenario 3.4

The new graphic arts department has proven to be an excellent investment for your recording studio. Album sales are through the roof, and hiring designers is cheaper than outsourcing. The company just hired three new graphic artists, and the boss has asked you to give them access to all the resources Wayne has access to. He would like you to do it in the easiest possible manner.

Required Results

- Give the new graphic artists access to resources.

Required Results

- Do it the easy way.

To create a group, go to User, New Local Group (see *Figure 3.12*). Note that this example uses Local Groups because we are in a single domain model for simulations. In a multiple-domain network, you would probably set up a Local Group for the file share access, and a Global Group to organize the users. See the next section for an explanation of Local versus Global groups.

FIGURE 3.12
Creating a new local group.

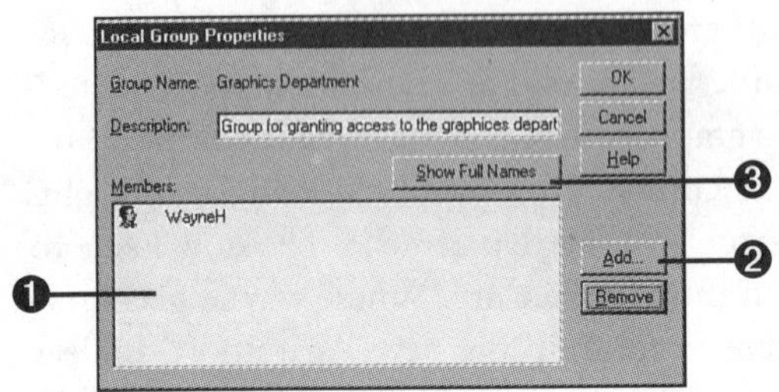

1. WayneH is already a member of the group Graphics Department because his user name was selected when the group was created. If you know whom you want in a group, you can use the Windows Ctrl+click to select all the members. When you create the group, they will be added automatically.
2. To add users to a group, click on the Add button. This opens the Add Users and Groups dialog box with all the Global Groups and user names (see *Figure 3.13*). There are no Local groups shown in the box because Local groups cannot be added to other Local groups. The exam usually has a question about adding Global groups to Local groups, so be sure you understand the difference between the two.
3. The Show Full Names button appends the Full Name field to the username to make it easier to keep track of whom you are working with. In many instances, naming conventions can make it problematic to keep track of "who's who." To alleviate many similar issues, it is also important to ensure that you complete the Full Name field when creating your accounts on a production network. A little extra work up front can save you a lot of time figuring out who is who down the road.

FIGURE 3.13
Users and groups that can be added.

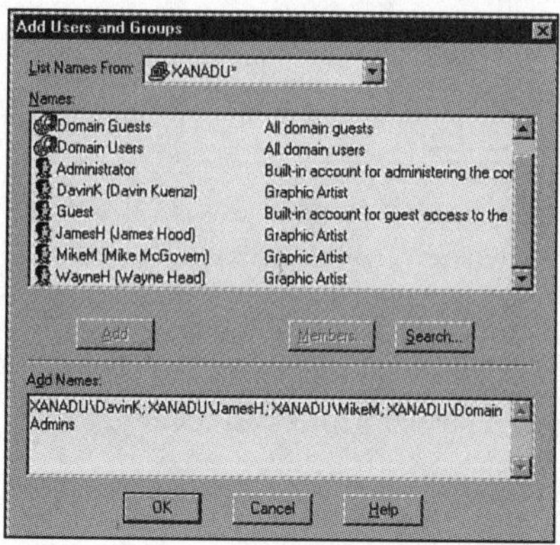

Local vs. Global Groups

The difference between Local and Global groups was touched on briefly in the preceding Printer Access scenario. This is a critical concept in the Windows NT user management model, and is highly tested. You can usually expect to see at least one related question on both the server and the enterprise exams. Simply put, Local groups are used to organize access to resources. Global groups are used to organize users. This can be one of the more difficult user management concepts to understand, so take a look at another scenario.

Scenario 3.5

The same fictional record company has a regional domain network with domains for the North, South, East, and West regions of the U.S. There are multiple sales offices in each region, each with its own sales director. Hollywood is your corporate headquarters, and every Monday the CEO wants a report of the preceding week's sales from the sales director of each office location. For simplicity's sake, the IT department has decided that the easiest way for the directors to get their reports to the CEO is to save their reports on a secure share on a server in Hollywood. Assume proper trust relationships in this scenario. Chapter 1, "Planning," discusses planning your trust relationships.

Here's how you would accomplish this:

1. Ensure that each of your sales directors has a user account in his or her domain.

cont.

Scenario 3.5 cont.

2. Create a Global group called Sales Directors in each of the domains. Because groups cannot span domains, you must duplicate Global groups for each domain in which they will have members.
3. Create a Local group in the East domain called Sales Reports. Grant this group access to the share on which you want the reports stored.
4. Place the Global group Sales Directors in the Sales Reports Local group.

It is critical to remember that you can only place global groups in local groups, and not the reverse. This is a favorite concept for test questions.

Managing System Policies with System Policy Editor

You have successfully set up a user on the network by creating a user account, and you've used a group to manage the access that users have to system resources. Now it's time to talk about how you can control the users capabilities on the network, and even on their local systems.

The System Policy Editor is an administrator's dream, and potentially an exam-takers nightmare. The reason for both is the amount of functionality this tool has.

The following scenario uses a very simple example of the System Policy Editor's capabilities for the purpose of simulating the creation of a System Policy. Before taking the test, it is an excellent idea to get in and familiarize yourself with the System Policy Editor, including the large number of settings you can control.

One thing to keep in mind, especially for the exam, is that the System Policy Editor can be used to set Windows 95 policies as well as Windows NT policies. The Windows NT policies are stored in the file `NTConfig.pol`. Any policy files have a .pol extension.

To enable System Policies, create this file using the System Policy Editor (a sample policy will be created in the following scenario) and save it to the `\(winnt_root)\System32\Repl\Import\Scripts` folder of the Primary Domain Controller. This is also shared as the `\\PDCServerName\netlogon` directory, and is used to store system policies, login scripts, and user profiles, which are discussed in the next section of this chapter.

When the computer or user logs onto the network, the system looks in this directory for a policy file. If there is no specific policy defined for the user or computer logging on, then the default policies are in effect.

> **NOTE**
>
> For Windows 95 policies, store the file as Config.pol. Windows NT policies should be stored as NTConfig.pol. Don't just save the template twice. Windows 95 policies must use a different template than Windows NT policies. Templates are added under the Options, Policy Templates dialog box.

It is important to realize in the background as you set System Policies, a number of modifications are being made to the Registry of the target computer. One of the functions the System Policy Editor can perform is Registry editing. Because the scope of Microsoft's testing requirements refers specifically to *System Policies*, this book does not discuss using System Policy Editor as a Registry editor. However, you should be aware that that the System Policy Editor can perform that function, in some cases better than typical Registry editors.

Scenario 3.6

The Generic Records graphics department has designed a new logo background for use on all corporate computers. You have been tasked with setting this as the default wallpaper, and ensuring that the end users cannot change it.

Required Results

- Set generic.bmp as the default wallpaper for all your users, and ensure that they can't change it.

The first thing you need to do is go to the Administrative Tools group and open the System Policy Editor. If you have not created any policies, you see a dialog box like that in *Figure 3.14*.

FIGURE 3.14
The System Policy Editor before any policies have been created.

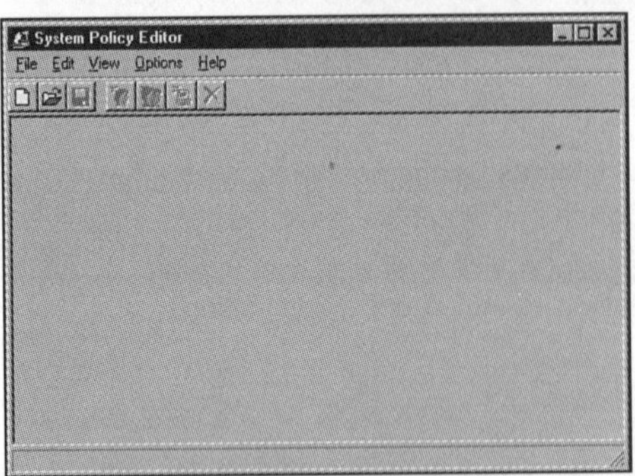

Select File, New Policy. This yields a more useful dialog box, shown in *Figure 3.15*. The two objects shown are the Default User and Default Computer. These policies are in effect for any users, groups, or computers not covered by a specific policy. Be careful when modifying these policies. You could inadvertently affect users you didn't mean to. Whenever possible, assign policies to specific groups of users, as opposed to making global changes to these default policies. It is generally a good idea to set global policies using global groups, like Domain Users. This is illustrated by the scenario.

FIGURE 3.15
The Default Computer and Default User policies. In the absence of a user or computer-specific policy, these policies are in effect for all users.

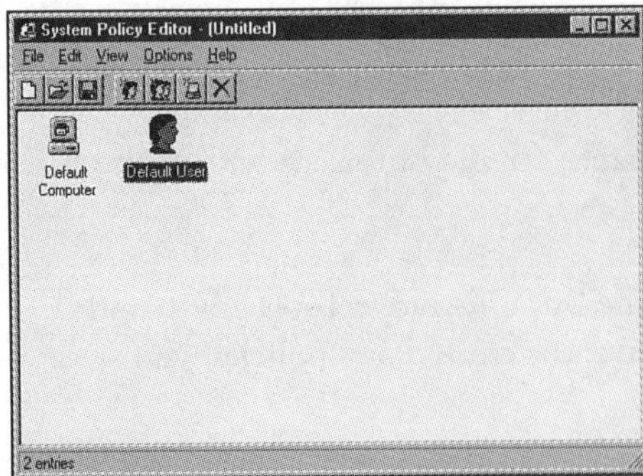

Some common user settings are as follows:

- **Controlling Display properties.** In environments in which computers are shared, or in applications like an Intranet that is designed to be viewed at a specific display size, this can be a fairly common configuration. You can also control the tabs that are available for the Display properties under the Control Panel.

- **Restricting access to the operating system shell.** In tightly controlled environments like Call Centers or Manufacturing Floors, where every machine needs to have the same configuration, access to the shell can be restricted. This includes options like access to the Run command, DOS Prompt, the Shutdown command and most other system commands. Another place this is very useful is in the academic arena, where the object is to keep a standard configuration on lab machines, and keep the students out of areas they don't belong.
- **System access.** You can disable access to the Registry. If you plan to use profiles, it is often a good idea to enable this just to keep beginners from poking around in the Registry.

Some common machine settings are as follows:

- **System.** This allows you to configure SNMP for all the machines in your domain. If you are using a network management platform, this can be very useful. It also allows you to control access to the Run command for that machine, as opposed to controlling access by user, as detailed above.
- Under Windows NT Network, you can control whether the hidden administrative shares are created on a server or workstation. In a highly secure environment, you should disable the creation of those shares unless absolutely necessary because anyone who knows anything about Windows NT knows there is a `Netlogon$` share created automatically. One caveat, however: Don't disable this function on domain controllers. Those shares are needed so that people can log on.
- **Windows NT System/Logon.** This section allows you to configure logon banners, and determine whether a user is able to shut down the machine without logging on. If you have a strict security policy, these are important features.

Figures 3.16 and 3.17 give you an idea as to the number of options you can control for the computers in your domain as well as the users in your domain. If you work in a very control-oriented environment, a good working knowledge of this tool is invaluable. To complete the scenario, you must add the group Domain Users to the System Policy Editor. Click on the Add a Group icon, and select the Domain Users group by clicking on the Browse button.

FIGURE 3.16
The available options for a computer policy.

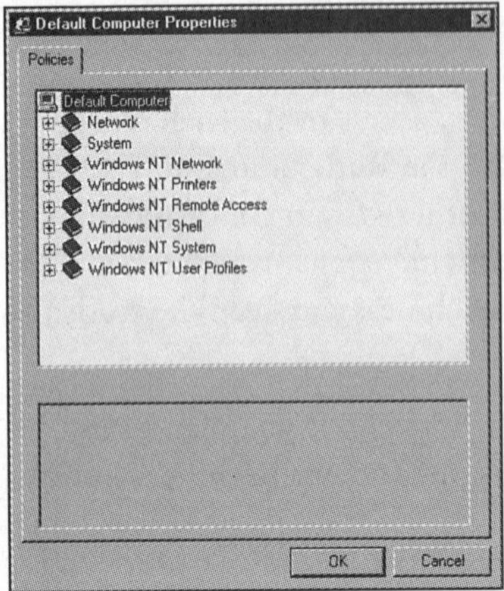

FIGURE 3.17
The available options for a user policy.

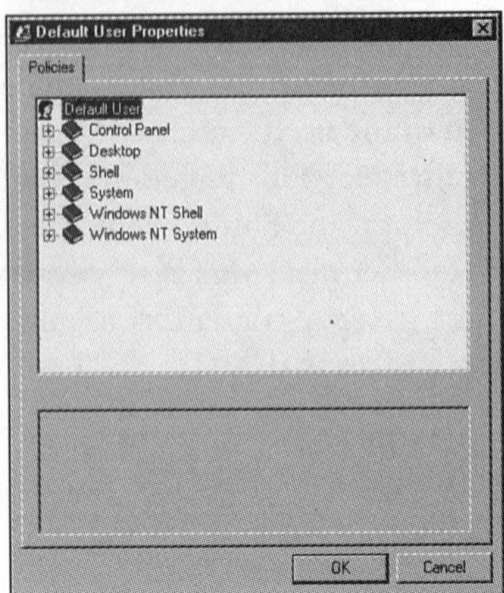

For this scenario, you could modify the Default User policy. This simulation will add a new policy to illustrate the process (see *Figure 3.18*). It is important to remember that any changes made to the Default User or Default Computer apply to any user or computer not explicitly covered in a different policy.

FIGURE 3.18
System Policy Editor after adding a policy for the Domain Users group.

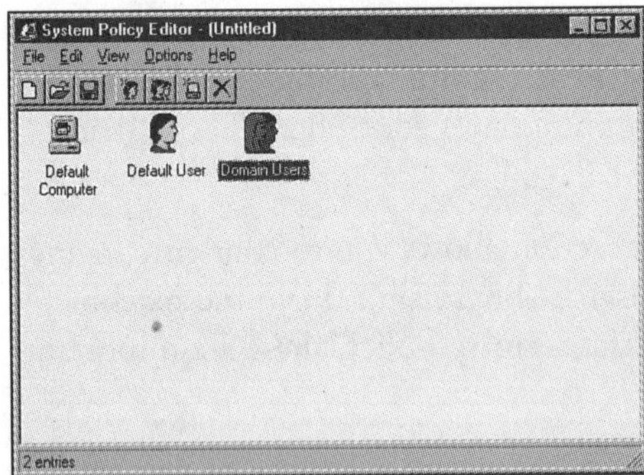

Double-click the Domain Users icon or select Edit, Properties with the Domain Users icon selected to open the policy as shown in *Figure 3.19*.

FIGURE 3.19
The Domain Users group policy options.

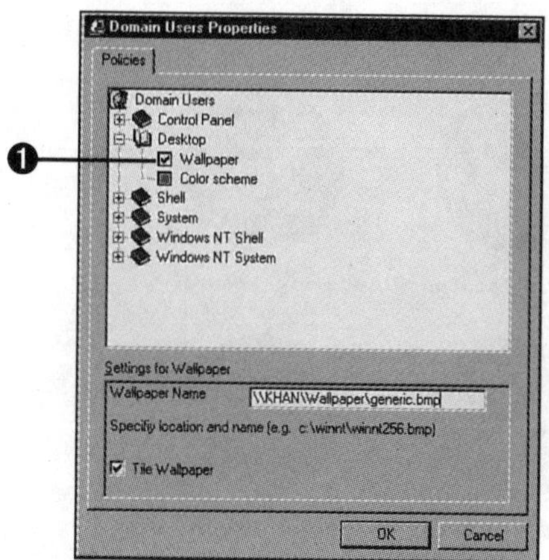

❶ This check box appears in one of three states. When you first open a policy, all the boxes are gray, indicating that whatever setting is enabled in the user's Registry remains in effect. A white, or blank, box indicates if there is any Registry setting in the user's Registry that will not be implemented. The checked box, as shown in *Figure 3.19*, indicates that the setting is mandatory for the user, group, or computer the policy is configured for.

> **NOTE** In *Figure 3.19*, the wallpaper file you are configuring is stored on a network file share. You could also put a physical path on the system, such as `C:\WINNT\`, but that would force you to place a copy of the `generic.bmp` file on each computer.

After logging out and logging on again, the computer sports the Generic Records logo bitmap, as evidenced in *Figure 3.20*.

FIGURE 3.20
The Generic Records logo is set to the system background.

Congratulations. You have successfully set a background for all your users. Whenever they log on to the network, this background is automatically set. Although this is a trivial example of the power of the System Policy Editor, some experimentation with the tool can yield a wealth of configuration options. For the exam, be aware of the capabilities of the tool, and also be aware that the application modifies the Registry in order to make these changes. Also remember that the file for NT machines is `NTConfig.pol`, and for Windows 95 it is the `Config.pol`. These files are stored on the `NETLOGON` share on the domain controller.

Creating and Managing User Profiles

The complement to the System Policy Editor is the User Profile. Although the System Policy Editor allows you to modify a user's or computer's Registry settings, a User Profile contains all the information about the user's operating environment. Whenever a user logs on to a Windows NT computer, a Local User Profile is created. This profile includes a set of directories and a portion of the Registry. The directory structure is located under the `<winnt_root>\profiles` subdirectory (see *Figure 3.21*) and contains information such as what appears on the Start Menu, what destinations appear in the Send To menu when you right-click on a file, and essentially everything else about the user's configuration.

FIGURE 3.21
User Profile directories.

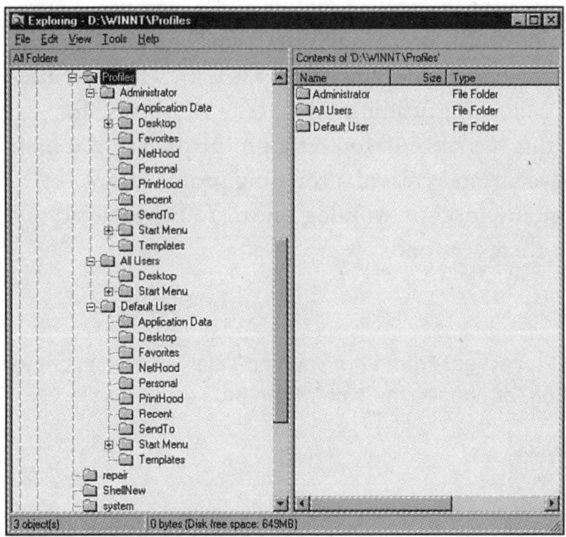

Anything in the All Users directory is assigned to any user logging on to the system. The user's Registry information is contained in a file named `NTUSER.DAT`, which can be found in the user's directory under the `<winnt_root>\profiles` directory. This is a nice feature, but suppose you have users traveling from workstation to workstation and want to keep the same settings? You could go from machine to machine and make sure they are all in sync, but it would be easier to implement a roaming profile.

Scenario 3.7

You are still the network administrator for Generic Records. Your boss has decided that you are going to be the traveling administrator, driving from site to site to support the five local studios in Los Angeles. You have just spent the last year configuring your machine with all the shortcuts and administrative tools you could possibly need to do your job. You want to maintain those settings as you travel from site to site. All the sites are in the same domain.

Required Results

- Set up the network so you have the same configuration wherever you go on the network.

First, you must create a profile. Fortunately that is as easy as logging on to the system. After you have logged on, go to the Control Panel and open up the System applet. Click on the User Profiles tab (see *Figure 3.22*). You will notice that Administrator has a roaming profile and DaveB has a local profile. In order to create a roaming profile, you must specify a profile path when the user ID is created. See the section "Managing Windows NT User Accounts" for details. Here's the best part of this scenario: If you set a profile path in the first scenario in the chapter, you have already created a roaming profile and will have the same configuration on any machine you log on to. You completed the scenario before you even knew there was one.

FIGURE 3.22

The User Profiles tab of System Properties. From here you can delete a profile, copy a profile so it is in another location, or change the type of the profile.

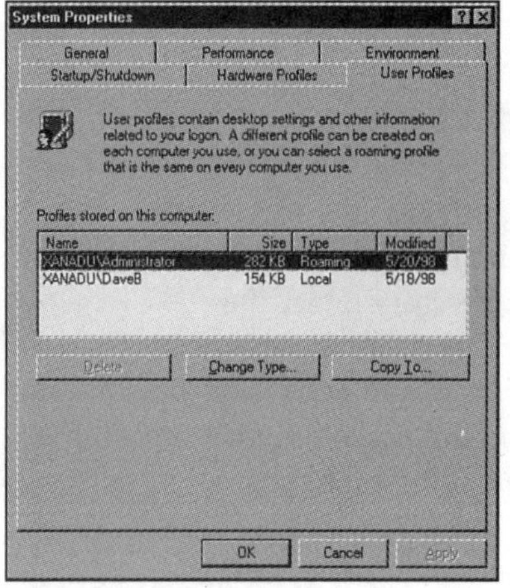

There are two things to note in *Figure 3.23*. First, you can change a roaming profile to a local one. You might use this option if you have a user who changes jobs so she does not move from machine to machine. Second, the Use Cached Profile on Slow Link check box is very handy if your profile is stored across a WAN link. You will take a performance hit the first time you log on because the profile needs to be loaded, but subsequent logons will use a cached copy of the profile.

FIGURE 3.23
Changing a profile type.

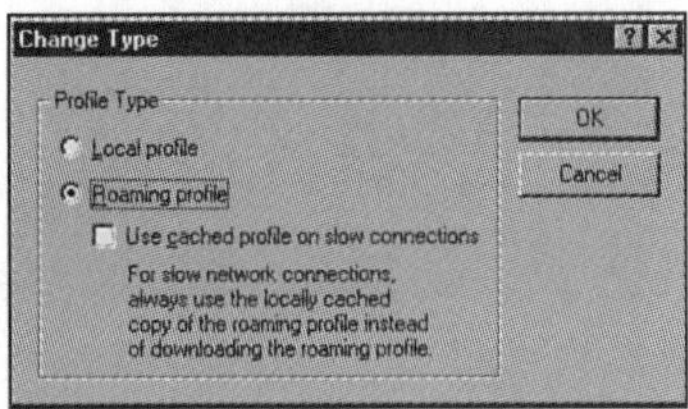

> **NOTE** While the Change Type button makes it look as though you can click on it to change a local profile into a roaming profile, it doesn't work that way. You can change a roaming profile into a local one, but to make a local into a roaming profile, you must set the profile path.

Along with local and roaming profiles, *mandatory* is the third type of profile. If you are using a mandatory profile, any changes a user makes to his environment are discarded. Many people aren't too sure how to make a profile mandatory, and how you use them. It is actually very easy. Change the `NTUSER.DAT` file in the user's roaming profile directory to `NTUSER.MAN`. This makes the file read only, and converts the profile from roaming to mandatory.

If the server storing the roaming profile is down, the user is still able to log on using a local profile. If the profile is mandatory and the server is unavailable, however, the user is unable to log on. (You might have noticed that this note appears twice in this chapter. This is a very testable topic, and although it is usually appears in only one question, it is an easy one to miss.)

SERVER MANAGEMENT

Another very important part of managing resources in a Windows NT network is server management. Windows NT gives you a number of tools to manage your servers. Although many of them are local utilities such as Control Panel, an application that allows you to do most of your server management is Server Manager. Server Manager gives you the ability to manage the workstations and servers in your domain, including viewing connected users, file shares, and resources in use, and configuring directory replication. You can also create file shares, stop sharing files, and view, start, and stop services. The final major feature of Server Manager is the ability to manage the PDCs and BDCs in the domain. You can promote a BDC in the event of a PDC failure, and synchronize all the domain controllers in the domain to make sure the databases match. Finally, you can select the domain, workgroup, or computer to manage. This is a very powerful application for an administrator, and as such, contains many testable features.

> **NOTE**
>
> One fact to get out of the way right away is that you cannot *demote* a PDC unless there are two PDCs in the domain. The only way to change a PDC into a BDC under ordinary circumstances is to promote one of the domain's BDCs to primary. This is commonly missed on exam questions because the ability to promote almost implies the ability to demote, when in fact you will almost never see the Demote option unless your PDC has crashed.

Before the scenarios start, take a quick look at the Server Manager Application. *Figure 3.24* shows the opening screen of the Server Manager Application.

FIGURE 3.24
The Server Manager application.

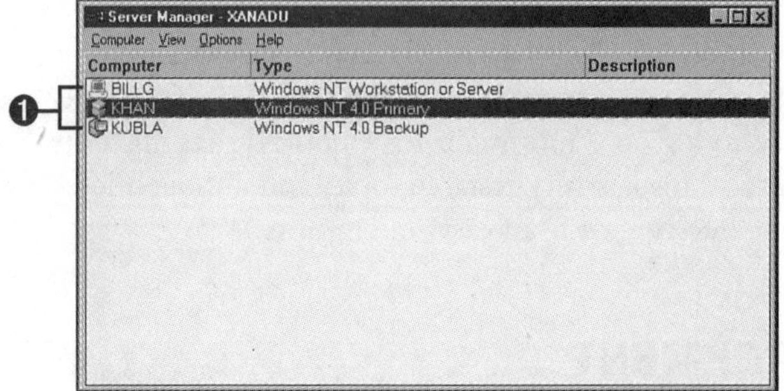

❶ Notice that there are three different machine types listed in Server Manager. The first, BILLG, is a Windows NT Workstation, designated as such by its PC icon. This icon is dimmed because that machine is not presently on the network. Any machine not

FIGURE 3.24 *Cont.*

reachable is displayed in the same fashion. The second, KHAN, is the Primary Domain Controller, signified by the "Windows NT 4.0 Primary" comment. Finally, KUBLA is the Backup Domain Controller, signified by the "Windows NT 4.0 Backup" comment.

Promoting a BDC

Now take a look at some of the functions you can perform with Server Manager in the following scenarios, beginning with promoting a BDC.

Scenario 3.8

Your Primary Domain Controller just suffered a RAID controller failure and is out of commission. Users are able to authenticate to the network, but the new controller will not be in for 48 hours, and you need to be able to modify user accounts in the interim.

Required Results

- Regain the ability to modify user accounts.

To promote a BDC to a PDC, select a BDC from the Server Manager view window, and go to Computer, Promote to Primary Domain Controller. This generates the message in *Figure 3.25*. In *Figure 3.26*, you can see one of the messages you receive while the promotion takes place. A variety of messages concerning the NetLogon process, the different servers, and the successful completion or the failure of the process are displayed in this window. Note in *Figure 3.27* that the icons and descriptions have changed for the controllers. That is all it takes to promote a BDC. One thing to be aware of, however, is that when the failed PDC comes up, it does not know there is another PDC on the network, so it tries to resume its duties as the PDC. In this event, a new selection appears under the Computer menu. You are now able to select Demote to Backup Domain Controller. This works only if the PDC is a duplicate.

FIGURE 3.25
Using Server Manager to Promote a BDC to a PDC.

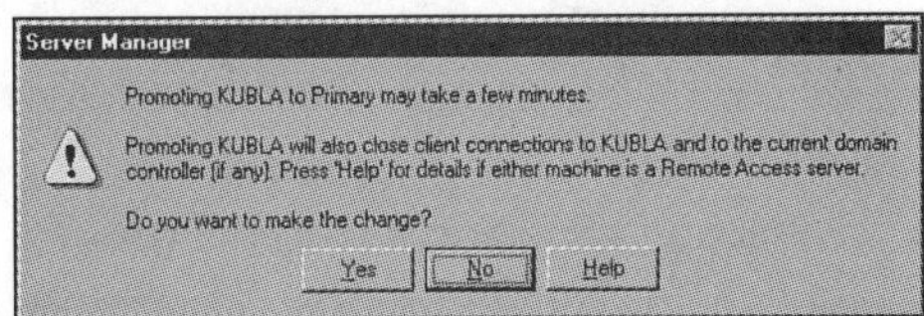

FIGURE 3.26
The Promotion Process.

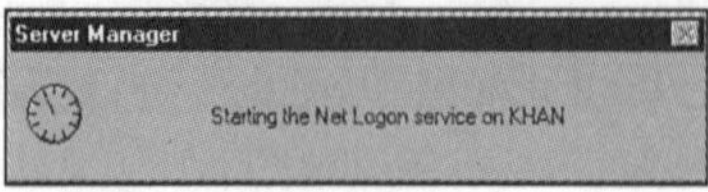

FIGURE 3.27
The promotion process is complete and the roles have been reversed.

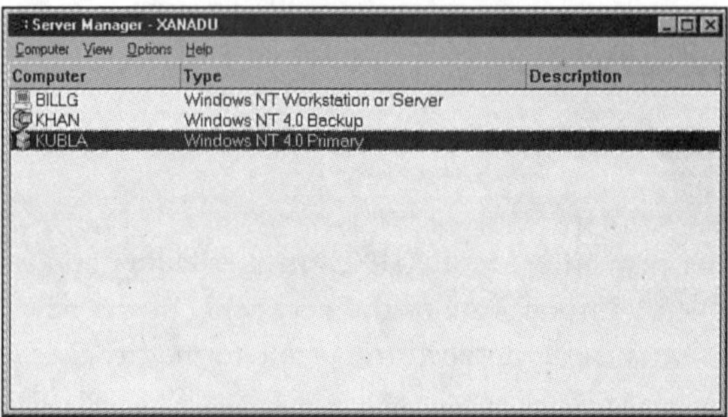

Synchronizing the Domain

Synchronizing the domain is a very easy process, although in a large domain it can take quite a while to touch all the domain controllers. Even worse, the only way you can tell if the synchronization is complete is to check the event log on each domain controller in the domain. This can be a difficult task in a large environment.

Scenario 3.9

Generic Recordings has a sales office in Honolulu, Hawaii, that was struck by a storm last week. After being without power for eight days, the office has finally gotten power restored. You have made a number of changes to the SAM database while their office was off the network, including some that affect their local users. You would like to force the updates to the local Backup Domain Controller (BDC) so they are in effect as soon as possible.

Required Results

- Place a current copy of the SAM database on the Honolulu BDC.

To start the process of synchronization, select the PDC and go to the Computer, Synchronize Entire Domain. This action generates a message (shown in *Figure 3.28*) requesting your verification of the resynchronization. The Server

Manager message tells you where to check to determine whether synchronization was successful (see *Figure 3.29*). When you check the event log in the Event Viewer (see *Figure 3.30*) you can read the event detail description.

FIGURE 3.28
The synchronization warning message.

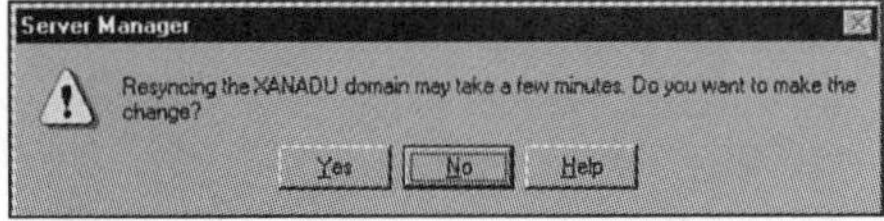

FIGURE 3.29
This message tells you where to look to see if the synchronization was successful.

FIGURE 3.30
The entry in Event Viewer indicating the synchronization was successful. This information is found in the System Log.

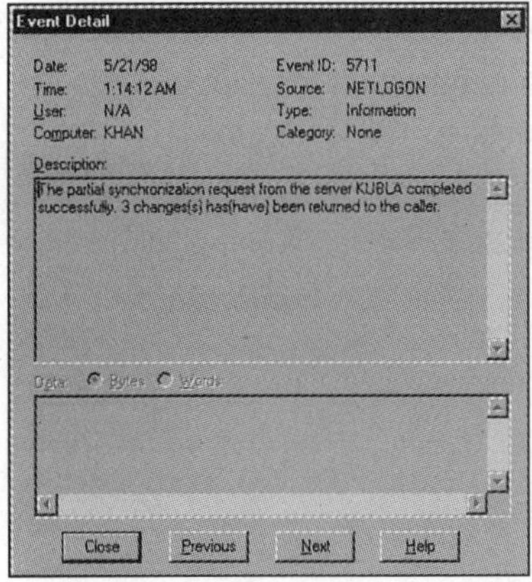

{*Event Viewer is covered in more detail in Chapter 6, "Troubleshooting."*}

There are a few other features that need to be discussed before we move on. In *Figure 3.31*, note the result of opening a server's properties dialog box, which can be viewed by double-clicking the server, or going to Computer, Properties.

FIGURE 3.31
Properties for the Domain Controller KHAN.

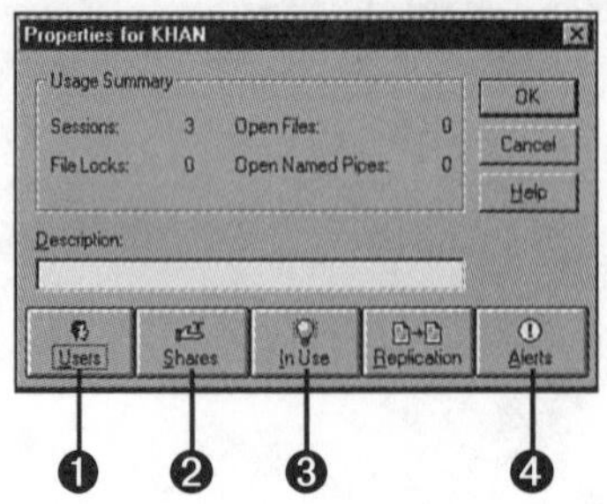

❶ The Users button opens up the dialog box in *Figure 3.32*, and allows you to see who is connected to the server, and what resources they are using. From here you can disconnect users, either one at a time, or all of them.

❷ The Shares button opens the Shared Resources dialog box. This shows you the file shares for the computer, and who is connected to them, as shown in *Figure 3.33*. You can disconnect users from shares from this dialog box.

❸ The In Use button opens the Open Resources dialog box. In *Figure 3.34*, you will see that administrator is reading the `D:\WINNT` directory, and has `NOTEPAD.EXE` open.

❹ The Alerts button allows you to configure a destination for alerts. This allows you to forward any server alerts to a management server, or to the administrator's workstation.

{*Directory Replication is covered in Chapter 2, Installation and Configuration."*}

FIGURE 3.32
The Users dialog box.

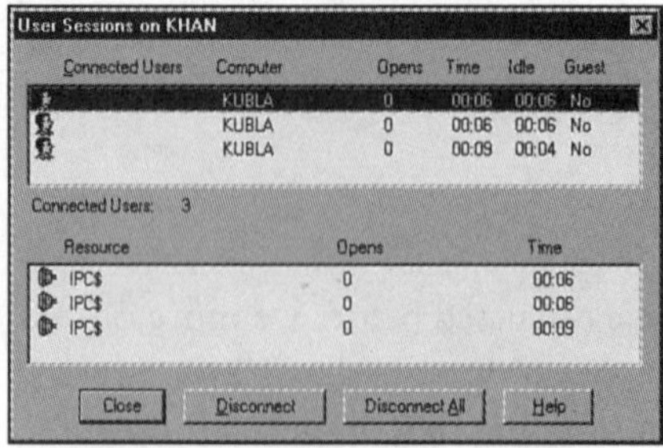

FIGURE 3.33
The Shared Resources dialog box. The administrative shares can be distinguished by the $ at the end. This makes them hidden shares. Creating shares is discussed later in the chapter, in the "File Sharing" section.

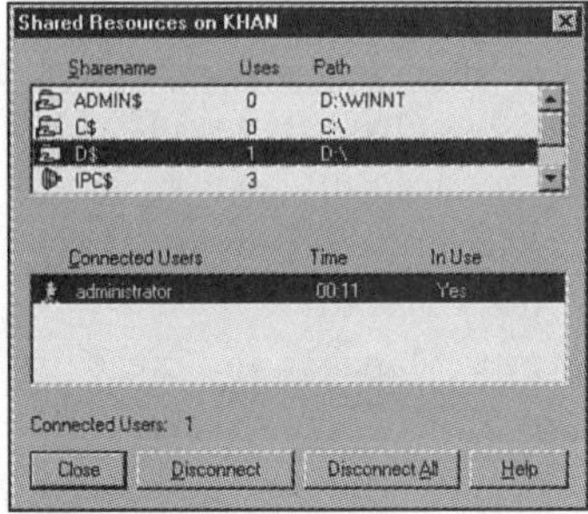

FIGURE 3.34
The Open Resources dialog box. In this example, administrator is running `NOTEPAD.EXE` from the `D:\WINNT` subdirectory. You can disconnect users from resources from this dialog box.

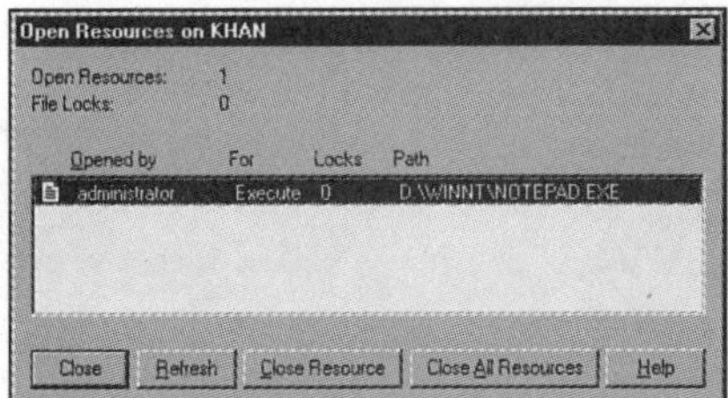

There are a few other functions of Server Manager that can pop up on an exam. The first is the ability to manage services. By selecting Computer, Services, you can view, start, stop, and manage any of the services running on the server, as shown in *Figure 3.35*. You have the same functionality here that you would from the Services applet under the Control Panel.

FIGURE 3.35
The Services available on the selected computer.

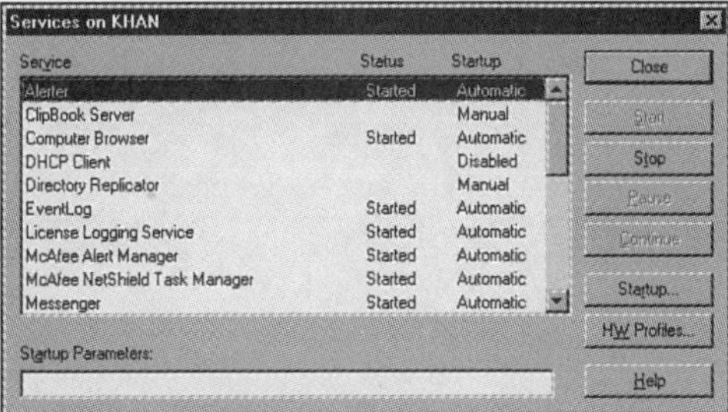

Another important feature is the ability to share directories, which is covered later in the chapter in the "Sharing" section.

Domain Accounts

The final feature of Server Manager to be discussed is the concept of domain accounts. Any Windows NT computer that is going to connect to a domain must have an account in that domain. This is not a user account such as you would use to log on to the network, but is a unique account to allow the computer to be a member of the domain. You can add your computer to the domain either of two ways. The first is to go into Server Manager and create a Domain account for the machine, as shown in *Figure 3.36*. To get to this screen, select Computer, Add to Domain. *Figure 3.37* shows the new computer, BOBT. It is dimmed because the computer hasn't joined the domain yet, and isn't available. A second method is to have an administrator user ID and password when installing Windows NT on the machine. At that time you are asked if you want to create >an account in the domain.

To delete a computer from the domain, you can go to Computer, Remove from Domain, or you can select the computer and press the Delete key.

FIGURE 3.36
Adding the computer BOBT to the domain.

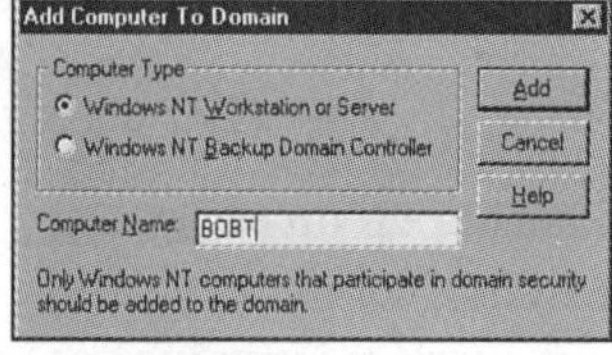

FIGURE 3.37
The domain after BOBT has been added.

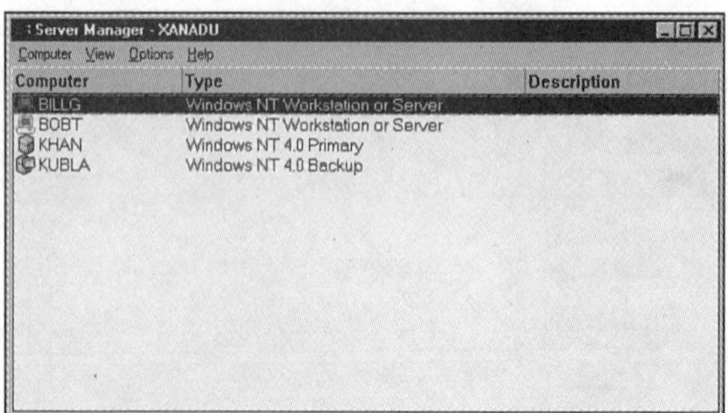

Remote Server Administration

One of the largest challenges in managing a Windows NT domain is managing it remotely. As a general rule, there is no PDC or BDC under the administrator's desk, and many people, including the author for quite a while, believe that all administration must happen from a domain controller. Fortunately Microsoft recognized the inherent difficulties in managing a network from a domain controller, and it has made a number of remote management tools available to Windows NT administrators.

With the Remote Administration Tools for Windows NT, it is possible to perform domain management from a Windows NT or a Windows 95 workstation. These tools ship on the Windows NT Server CD-ROM. As part of its "take everything to the Web" strategy, Microsoft also offers a Web-based management utility as part of the Windows NT Server Resource Kit. This utility can be purchased or is bundled in Microsoft's TechNet support CDs. The following sections discuss the different capabilities of each version, because they are all slightly different.

Remote Administration for Windows NT

The Remote Administration Tools can be installed on a Windows NT Workstation or Windows NT Member Server, and includes the following utilities:

- User Manager for Domains
- Server Manager
- System Policy Editor
- DHCP Manager
- Remote Access Admin
- WINS Manager
- Remote Boot Manager

{*DHCP Manager and Remote Access Admin will be discussed in Chapter 4, "Connectivity."*}

In order to install the Remote Administration Tools under Windows NT Workstation or on a Windows NT Member Server, go to the subdirectory and execute SETUP.BAT. This copies all the necessary files for the administration tools, and makes the necessary Registry changes. Although SETUP.BAT installs the files, you must create icons manually for each tool. The setup procedure does not do that for you.

NOTE

Event Viewer on an NT Workstation or NT Member Server can be used to view remote logs by default. This differs from Windows 95, in which a version of the Event Viewer must be installed as part of the remote tools.

EXAM TIP

For the exam, be familiar with the tools available under Windows NT. They differ from the Windows 95 and Web-based tools, and asking what functions can be accomplished from a given platform is a common exam question. Another possible test question asks which platforms can run a specific application. For instance, you might be asked which platforms can run Server Manager.

Windows 95 Tools

The Remote Administration Tools can be installed on a Windows 95 workstation and includes the following utilities:

- User Manager for Domains
- Server Manager
- Event Viewer

Windows 95 Explorer can be used to manage NTFS permissions, file sharing, and print permissions due to installed extensions to the application. Keep in mind that these are extensions only. The application is not replaced. Also keep in mind that servers running File and Print Services for NetWare can be managed from the Windows 95 machine.

To install the Remote Administration Tools under Windows 95, follow these steps:

1. Insert the Windows NT Server CD in your CD-ROM drive.
2. Open the Control Panel, and then open the Add/Remove Applications applet.
3. Click on the Windows Setup tab, and then click on the Have Disk button.
4. The correct path is `<cd-rom drive letter>:\CLIENTS\SRVTOOLS\WIN95`. This is where the `SRVTOOLS.INF` file needed for the install is located.

5. Select Windows NT Server Tools and click Install. You will need 3 MB of hard drive space to complete the installation.
6. Manually add the directory `C:\SRVTOOLS` to the `AUTOEXEC.BAT` file so Windows 95 can locate the proper DLLs for the applications to run.

> **NOTE** Whenever a user tries to use one of the management tools, they are prompted for a user ID and password. This ensures that they are authorized to run the utility.

EXAM TIP

For the exam, be familiar with the tools available under Windows 95. They differ from the Windows NT and Web-based tools, and asking what functions can be accomplished from a given platform is a popular exam question. Windows 95 has a significantly reduced set of capabilities. Be aware of this. Another possible test question asks which platforms can run a specific application. For instance, you may be asked which platforms can run User Manager for Domains.

Web-based Tools

Web-based tools are a new type of management for Microsoft in the Windows NT arena. They are installed on each server to be managed, and require a running Web service in order to be accessed. To install the Web-based management on your domain controller, follow these steps:

1. Insert the Windows NT Server Resource Kit CD-ROM into the domain controller (primary or secondary) to be managed. The Autorun screen opens automatically; select the Web Administration link.

> **NOTE** In keeping with Microsoft's new direction, the Resource Kit is a Web-based application. Service Pack 3 and TechNet have also moved to this model.

2. Select Install Now.
3. Next comes the ubiquitous Microsoft License Agreement. Read it and click Yes to agree.
4. Click on Continue.
5. When the installation is complete, click on Exit to Windows. You now see the Web Administration `README` file.

6. Close the `README` file when you are done, and the installation is complete. To access the Web Tools, open Internet Explorer and go to `http://<domain server name>/ntadmin/ntadmin.htm`. From there you will be able to manage the following:

   - Manage users and groups.
   - Manage domain accounts.
   - Manage shared directories, including their permissions.
   - Manage NTFS permissions.
   - Manage printers.
   - View the event logs.
   - Start, stop, and configure services. Be careful not to inadvertently stop the Web publishing service, which would remove your access to the Web Administration Tools.
   - Manage active session. This is similar to the functionality of Server Manager, where you can disconnect users if necessary.
   - View the server configuration and performance metrics.

For the exam, you should be familiar with the capabilities of Web-based administration. They differ from the Windows NT and Windows 95 tools, and asking what functions can be accomplished from any given platform is a common question. This is especially critical with the Web-based tools because they have the functionality of several utilities, all from a common HTML interface. Another possible test question asks which platforms can run a specific application or perform a specific function. For instance, you may be asked which platforms can add users. (Although you can add users by utilizing the Web-based tools, you do it through an HTML interface rather than through User Manager for Domains.)

AUDITING THE SYSTEM

The word *audit* often brings to mind armies of IRS accountants poking into every detail of your finances, looking for something amiss. Windows NT Auditing enables you to do essentially the same thing, except that instead of your finances, you are watching every detail of your server and domain looking for something amiss. Windows NT Auditing can give you information about user activities such as logons and logouts, directory and file activities such as copies and deletes, and printing activities such as who tried to print, manage, or delete a print job. All this information is logged in the Security Log, which can be viewed with Event Viewer. In the following scenario you will revisit your old friends at Generic Recordings, where the new Director of Network Security is a little concerned about the lax security procedures on the production network. She is very interested to learn what is going on.

{*Event Viewer is covered in more detail in Chapter 6, "Troubleshooting."*}

Auditing the File System

Before you start auditing directory access, you need to understand a little about how Windows NT performs Directory and File auditing.

Scenario 3.10

Amy Gagnon, the new director of security, is concerned about who is accessing the HR records on the production file server. She has asked you to audit who is accessing the HR directory, and find out who is opening the salaries spreadsheet.

Required Results

- Audit who is accessing the HR directory.
- Audit who is opening the SALARIES.XLS file.

Windows NT Auditing assumes that you want to audit for a specific group of users, and as such, requires you to determine who you are going to audit, what events you want to audit, and if you want the audit policy applied to subdirectories. To start auditing directory and file activities, you must open Windows NT Explorer. Right-click on the directory you want to audit, and select the Security tab. From there, click on the Audit button. *Figure 3.38* shows the Auditing screen, without any auditing configured. *Figure 3.39* demonstrates how to add a user or group to be audited, and *Figure 3.40* shows the results.

For testing purposes, pay close attention to what can be audited on files and directories, and where you go to configure auditing. *Figure 3.41* shows the results of the audit on file access. Although overuse of this capability can rapidly render the information almost unusable due to the sheer volume of events, if used carefully Auditing can be a very valuable tool for keeping track of what's going on with your servers.

FIGURE 3.38
Configuring auditing for the HR directory, before the configuration.

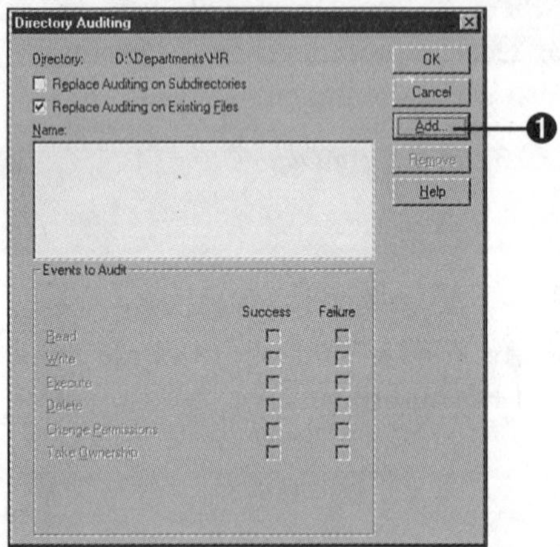

1 To add a group to be audited, click on Add. Selecting an existing audited user or group and clicking Remove will remove that user or group from the list of audited accounts.

FIGURE 3.39
Adding the group Everyone to be audited. This is very similar to the interface you use to add users to groups.

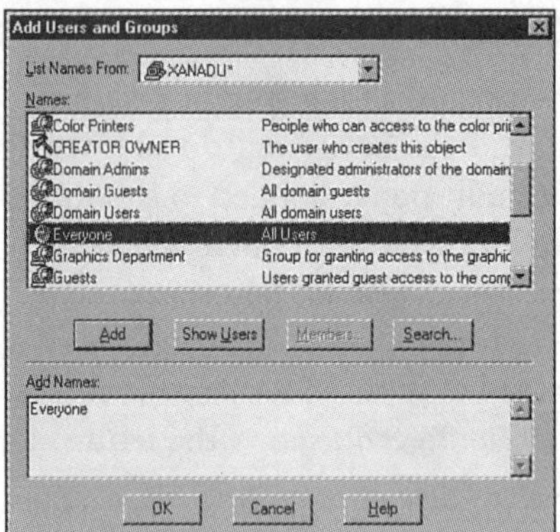

> **NOTE** The group Everyone is a special system group used by Windows NT for any activity that requires all the users on the system. The group Everyone is granted permission to file shares by default, enabling anyone to access the share. This group cannot be deleted or modified. When in doubt, avoid using this group to grant permission to an object. From a security perspective, as well as from an administrative perspective, it makes more sense to grant rights to things based on groups that you can control.

FIGURE 3.40
The group Everyone is now being audited for all access to the HR directory. By configuring the auditing for Read success, you have actually accomplished both objectives.

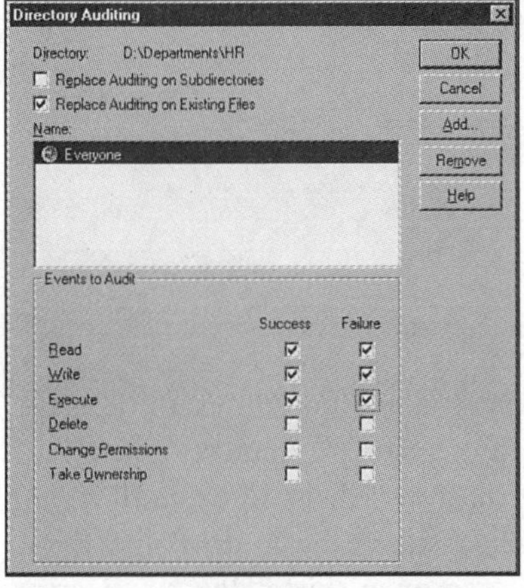

FIGURE 3.41
Event Viewer shows the successful access of the `Salaries.xls` by the Administrator account. Event Viewer can be opened by going to Administrative Tools, Event Viewer. Double-click on the event to see the Event Detail window.

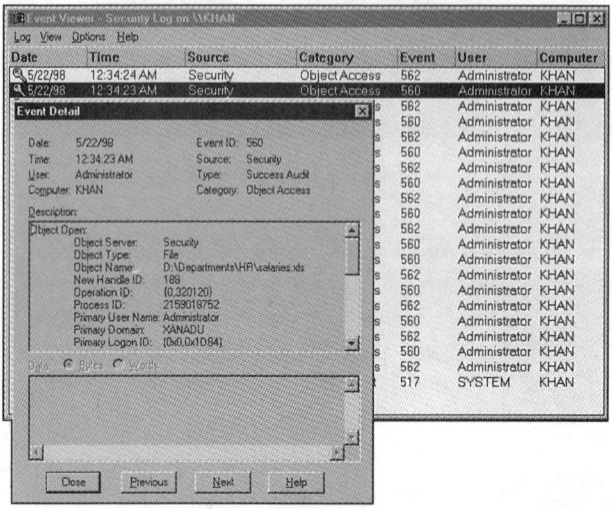

Auditing User Activity

Because auditing on each of these events is very similar, and you examine the results in Event Viewer for each, there aren't any scenarios for auditing user activity. For the exam, it is important for you to know what can be audited, and where you go to set the auditing. *Figure 3.42* shows the Audit Policy dialog box from User Manager for Domains. You can open this dialog by selecting Policies, Audit. Once again, for the exam, pay attention to what can be audited, and where you go to configure user access auditing.

FIGURE 3.42
Auditing user activities with a User Audit Policy. This is configured in User Manager for Domains.

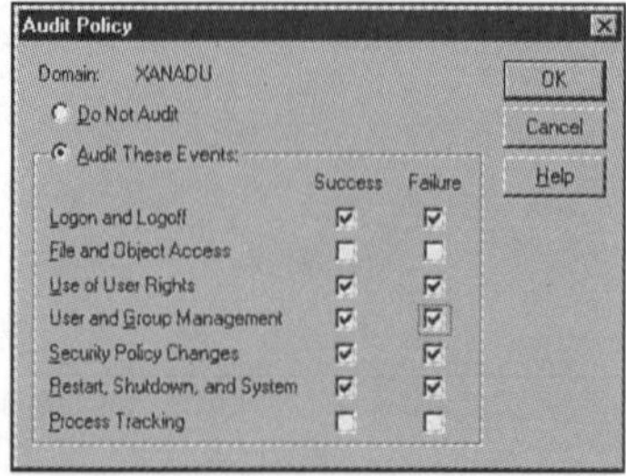

Auditing Printing Events

Printer auditing is very similar to the preceding two types of auditing. To access the Audit Policy for a printer, open the printer's properties. Click on the Security tab, and then click on the Auditing button to see the Printer Auditing dialog box (see *Figure 3.43*).

FIGURE 3.43
Auditing printer activities with a Printer Audit Policy.

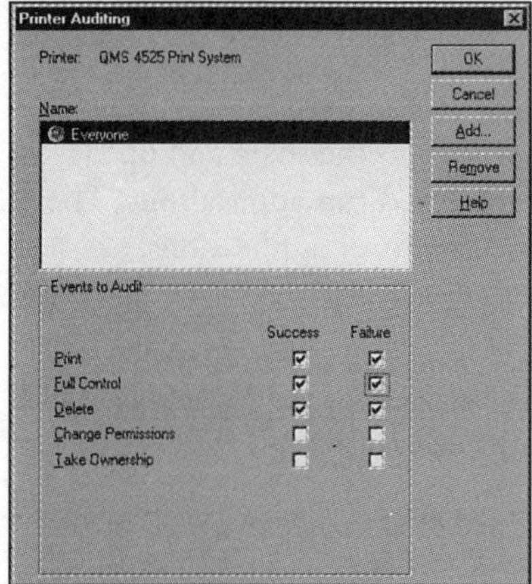

That finishes up the topic of auditing. Although this is an incredibly powerful feature of the operating system, its lack of general use in most networks frequently makes it the most powerful *unused* feature of the operating system. Expect one or two auditing questions on the Windows NT Server exam.

MANAGING DISK RESOURCES

This chapter has spent a great deal of time discussing how to use users, groups, and administrative utilities to manage whom can access your network and your servers. The final portion of controlling access is controlling what can be accessed after the user is connected. This means controlling access to disk resources such as files and directories.

There are two ways to access a file on a Windows NT server. First, you can attach to the server and access files across the network. This is known as accessing a *shared resource.* An administrator controls access to a shared resource by setting the *share permissions.*

The other way to access a file is to log on to the server directly. If you have the proper access, you can log on to the server from the console and access the files directly from the hard drive. To control this type of access, you must use *file system permissions.*

Before discussing exactly how to create a share, it is important to be familiar with the four types of access security. This is critical not only from an exam perspective, but from a career perspective as well. The first time you accidentally share HR's salary files and make them accessible by the group Everyone, you will be looking for a new career.

There are four explicit share permissions that you can grant to a group on a file share. They are as follows:

- **Read.** This permission enables a user to connect to the share and open documents. It also allows the user to copy files and run applications. The user cannot change or delete any of the documents or applications.
- **Change.** This permission allows a user to connect to the server and open documents. The user can also change files, create and delete files and directories, and copy files and run programs. This permission does not allow the user to change the permissions that affect other users.
- **Full Control.** A user with Full Control access to a share can do all of the things listed in the two preceding permissions, as well as modify share permissions that affect other users. Do not grant this right lightly. Unless the user is an administrator, Read or Change permissions should be more than adequate.
- **No Access.** This right revokes all the rights granted to a user. When you look at determining effective rights, you should note that the No Access right supercedes any other permissions granted to a user. A user with No Access permission to a share cannot connect to the share, nor do any of the other things listed in the previous rights.

Determining Effective Access Rights

Access rights, with the exception of No Access, are *additive.* If a user has explicit Read access to a file share, and belongs to a group with Full Control access, the user's effective rights to the directory are Full Control. The other side of that is that if the user has explicit Full Control permission, and belongs to a group with the No Access permission, the No Access permission would be effective. No other permission overrides a No Access permission.

Sharing Files

This section provides two scenarios. They are very similar, but illustrate the two methods for sharing files. For the exam, you should be aware that you can manage file sharing through Server Manager, which will be used in the second example. Microsoft likes to be sure you know all the ways to accomplish a task, so you will probably see a reference to this on one of the two exams.

Scenario 3.11

The boss has come to you and requested that you share the Graphics directory on the network. He would like it to be accessible to the graphics department only.

Required Results

- Make the Graphics directory available on the network.
- Ensure that only the graphics department has access to the files through the share.

In this scenario, use Server Manager to share the directory. Complete the following steps:

1. Open Server Manager, highlight the server and open the Properties dialog box. Refer to the Server Management section of this chapter for more information about this process.
2. Click on the Share button, and then click on Add. This opens the New Share dialog box, shown in *Figure 3.44*.
3. Enter the directory path and click OK.

You just completed the first primary objective. But what about restricting access? Double-click on the share to open its Properties dialog box and click on Permissions. Add the Graphics Department group with Full Control permission. Now remove the group Everyone. You have successfully completed the scenario. The Graphics directory is on the network, accessible by only the graphics department.

FIGURE 3.44
Sharing a directory using Server Manager.

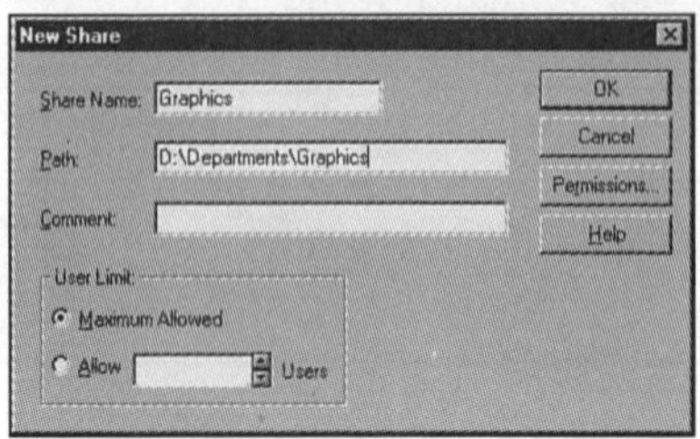

Scenario 3.12

The boss is back at your desk. Now he wants you to share the Recording directory for everyone in the company. He would like everyone to be able to try out the new digital recordings in this directory.

Required Results

- Make the Recording directory available on the network.
- Ensure that everyone has access to the files through the share.

The method of sharing to be used in this scenario is the Windows NT Explorer method.

Complete the following steps:

1. Highlight the directory, right-click it, and select Properties to open the Recording Properties dialog box.
2. Click on the Sharing tab.
3. Click on the Shared As option and name the Share Name in the text box.
4. Click on the Permissions button to see the Access Through Share Permissions dialog box shown in *Figure 3.46*.

Here you can add or remove users from the share permissions. In this case, because all the users are supposed to have access, leaving the Everyone group enabled with Full Control accomplishes the second primary objective.

FIGURE 3.45

The Recording Properties dialog box.

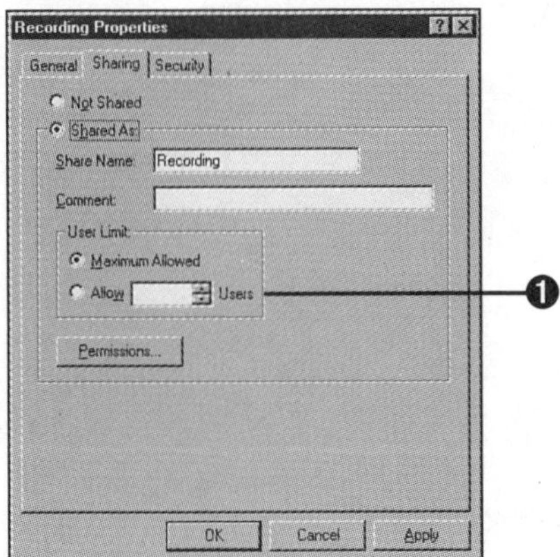

❶ You can configure the number of concurrent connections allowed to the share through this section.

FIGURE 3.46

Configuring the users who have access to this directory. In this case, the group Everyone has Full Control of the share, which is the default.

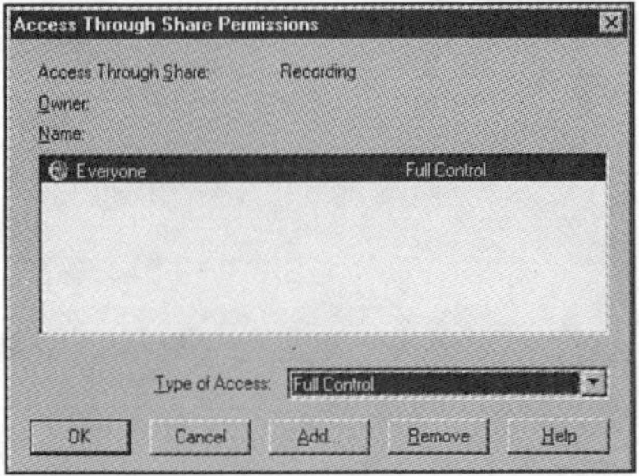

CHAPTER 4

Connectivity

This chapter helps you prepare for the "Connectivity" sections of the Windows NT Server (Exam 70-067) and Windows NT Server Enterprise (Exam 70-068) exams. This is an important chapter because the 70-067 and 70-068 exams have very different objectives, which are detailed below. This chapter covers NT connectivity from applications to protocols, and discusses Novell NetWare interoperability at length. This chapter is also an excellent primer for those who haven't dealt a great deal with connectivity. Networking is arguably the fastest growing segment of the computer industry, with applications such as the Internet, Virtual Private Networking, and Wide Area Networks growing exponentially. This chapter is a great place to study for the exams and get a simulated hands-on look at networking.

For Exam 70-067, the Windows NT Server Exam, Microsoft defines "Managing Resources" objectives as follows:

- Configure Windows NT Server for interoperability with NetWare servers by using Gateway Service for NetWare (GSNW) and the Migration Tool for NetWare.

  This objective deals entirely with providing interoperability with and migration from Novell NetWare. Novell NetWare is considered the other leading Network Operating System available on the market today, and has a large installed base. This objective is meant to ensure that the prospective MCP is very familiar with the applications Windows NT provides to install Windows NT into a Novell environment. This is a heavily tested topic on the 70-067 exam.

- Install and configure Remote Access Service (RAS), including configuring RAS communications, protocols, and security. Also configuring Dial-Up Networking clients.

  One of the most powerful features of Windows NT has always been the fact that Remote Access Services are a part of the core operating system.

Not only is remote access is one of the largest issues in the industry, but RAS has differentiated Windows NT from other operating systems. This is another topic that Microsoft asks questions about on both exams.

For Exam 70-068, the Windows NT Server in the Enterprise Exam, Microsoft defines "Managing Resources" objectives as follows:

- Configure Windows NT Server for interoperability with NetWare servers by using Gateway Service for NetWare (GSNW) and the Migration Tool for NetWare.

  This is the same objective as shown for the Server exam. Although the Enterprise exam asks questions about NetWare interoperability, it doesn't focus on this objective as heavily as does the Server exam. If you are familiar enough with this objective to answer the questions on 70-067, you should have no problems with this objective on the 70-068 exam.

- Install and configure multi-protocol routing to make Windows NT an Internet router, a BOOTP/DHCP Relay Agent, and an IPX router.

  One of the features that Windows NT offers as part of its networking and connectivity features is its ability to act as a router. In the real world, this means you can save the cost of a hardware router by adding the correct services to your Windows NT server. For the purposes of the exam, you should be familiar with some of the more common routing services that Windows NT can provide.

- Install and configure Internet Information Server.

  It is easy to see that the Internet is the fastest growing network in history. As the Internet grows in size and popularity, Windows NT is growing in popularity as the platform of choice for people offering Internet services. This objective covers Microsoft's solution for web, FTP, and Gopher services. The two facets of this application to concentrate on are web and FTP. Gopher, while once enjoying quite a bit of popularity, has been supplanted by index servers and search engines. You will not see any questions about Gopher on this exam.

- Install and configure Internet services such as World Wide Web, DNS, and Intranet.

  This objective is meant to demonstrate NT's capabilities in the booming Internet and Intranet server part of the industry. World Wide Web, DNS, and Intranet are all services that Windows NT can provide out of the box, and you should be familiar with how Windows NT delivers each of the services.

- Install and configure Remote Access Service (RAS), including configuring RAS communications, protocols, and security.

  This is essentially the same objective as on the 70-067 exam, without the dial-up networking requirement. As mentioned earlier, RAS has long been used to differentiate Windows NT from its competition, and you can expect to see a few RAS questions on each exam.

This chapter covers the tasks you will need to understand in order to meet the exam objectives and, where possible, highlights sections that are covered heavily on one or both of the exams. This chapter discusses Windows NT connectivity in depth, including TCP/IP and IPX protocols and routing, Novell NetWare interoperability, Internet services, and finally, Remote Access Services. This discussion also covers installing and configuring Microsoft's Internet Information Server (IIS) 3.0, and touches on the DNS service for NT. This chapter begins its discussion of networking with NetBEUI, Microsoft's contribution to the protocol mix.

NetBEUI

NetBEUI (NetBIOS Extended User Interface) is Microsoft's native protocol. The functionality of the protocol is discussed in Chapter 1, "Planning," in the "Selecting the Appropriate Protocol" section. Here, the focus is on the installation of the protocol.

Complete the following steps to install NetBEUI:

1. Open the Network applet in Control Panel.
2. Click on the Protocols tab.
3. Click on `Add`.
4. Select NetBEUI.

You are prompted for the location of the media, and then the protocol loads. You must reboot the server after the installation completes.

NetBEUI is a self-tuning protocol, so there are no configuration options to look at. It is possible to modify NetBEUI's characteristics by editing the Registry. The parameters for NetBEUI are contained in the `HKEY_LOCAL_MACHINE\SYSTEM\CurrentControlSet\Services\Nbf\Parameters` section of the Registry. If you absolutely need to modify these parameters, refer to the Windows NT Resource Kits or Microsoft TechNet for full details.

TCP/IP

These days it is almost impossible to work in the computer industry, or even be a casual computer user, without having to know what TCP/IP (Transmission Control Protocol/Internet Protocol) is. From using DNS to access your favorite web site by name, to those obscure 12-digit numbers that show up from time to time, people are often exposed to TCP/IP without even realizing it. A painfully frequent question in bulletin boards, in message groups, and on Help Desks is "What is my IP address, and why do I need it?" Because you'll need to know the answers in order to pass these exams, now is a great time to answer those questions, as well as any others Microsoft might want to ask you.

NOTE

TCP/IP Discussion

Before getting too far into this chapter, it is important for you to realize that this is not an in-depth discussion of the TCP/IP protocol. That discussion can fill book after book, and would go well beyond the scope of the NT Server exams. This discussion concentrates on the high points of the protocol, such as addressing and subnet masks, and then gets right into the services Microsoft supplies with Windows NT to take advantage of TCP/IP.

No discussion of TCP/IP these days can start without mentioning that TCP/IP is the protocol on which the Internet is based. Originally designed for the Department of Defense in the 1970s, TCP/IP's open nature, rich feature set, and reliability made it the natural selection for the Department of Defense's national network, which eventually grew into what we all know as the Internet. With the explosive growth of the Internet in the last several years, TCP/IP has become the ubiquitous protocol, becoming far more widely used than a number of competitive, proprietary protocols such as IPX, SNA, and others. Enough history—now take a look at the mechanics of TCP/IP.

Addressing

Back in the '70s when the idea of connecting computers throughout the country was still just a concept, the architects of TCP/IP needed a method for identifying or *addressing* each of the machines to be connected. The solution they agreed on uses *IP addresses*. If you've ever surfed the Internet, you've undoubtedly seen an address like 206.117.45.9. That is the address of the host computer. The method for representing these addresses is known as *dotted decimal notation*.

> **NOTE** In a TCP/IP network, every device is considered a host. So, technically speaking, your desktop PC becomes a host as soon as you give it an IP address.

Dotted Decimal Notation

What exactly is an IP address? Technically, an IP address is a 32-bit binary number. Although your PC understands this perfectly, for you to remember that you need to go to http://10111101111100101011110111110010 in order to check your horoscope on the Web would rapidly drive you insane. Back when the protocol was being written, it was decided to break this up into a more user-friendly format. Take a look at how the following binary number becomes the more familiar dotted decimal number:

```
11000000101010001001000100011011
```

> **NOTE** For any of you not familiar with binary numbers, think of the 0s and 1s as positions on a light switch. If the value is 0, then that position is off, and is not counted. If it's 1, then it's on, and that position is counted.

First, break the preceding binary number into 4 sections. These are known as *octets,* because they are each 8 bits long:

```
11000000.10101000.10010001.00011011
```

Each of these octets is then converted to a decimal number. Each place in the octet represents a power of 2. See the following table to understand how the number 10101000 breaks down:

Binary Digit	*Decimal Value*	*Result*
0	0 X 2^0	0
0	0 X 2^1	0
0	0 X 2^2	0
1	1 X 2^3	8
0	0 X 2^4 (16)	0
1	1 X 2^5 (32)	32
0	0 X 2^6 (64)	0
1	1 X 27 (128)	128
	Total:	168

Using the information given in the preceding table as a guide, the example binary number (`11000000.10101000.10010001.00011011`) is converted to the following:

```
192.168.145.27
```

If you don't feel the urge to calculate these numbers by hand, open Windows Calculator in the Accessories group, and set it to Scientific under the View menu. You can use this calculator to perform these conversions for you.

The "Installing and Configuring Additional Services" section of this chapter discusses DNS (Domain Name Service), a global hierarchical directory service that allows you to use intuitive aliases for the still relatively arcane IP addresses.

Address Classes

Now that you know where these addresses come from, you should be aware of how they are broken up. An IP address consists of two pieces of information:

- The *netid*, which is the numeric identifier for the network the host is attached to.
- The *hostid*, which is the portion of the IP address that identifies the host on the network.

The IP addresses that you have probably seen are broken into three *classes*: A, B, and C. There are some other classes that have been reserved for research purposes, but they are not covered on the NT exams. This chapter focuses on the first three.

> **NOTE** Whenever you are dealing with IP addresses, it is important to remember that addresses ending with 0 or 255 are not valid host addresses. 0 denotes the address of the network, and 255 is the broadcast address for the network. For example, 144.45.5.0 indicates the 144.45.5.x network, and 144.45.5.255 is the address for any broadcast messages.

Before we get into the specific classes, however, you should know a little about how IP address classes are determined. IP addresses are divided into classes depending on how many bits make up the netid and how many make up the hostid. If there are a small number of netid bits, and a large number of hostid bits, you can have a few networks with lots of hosts per network. If there are a large number of netid bits and a small number of hostid bits, you can have a large number of networks with to a small number of hosts on each network. Now apply this information to the three aforementioned address classes:

- Class A network addresses have the following format:

  0NNNNNNN.HHHHHHHH.HHHHHHHH.HHHHHHHH

  N is part of the netid, and H is part of the hostid. This class of address ranges from 1.0.0.0 to 126.255.255.255. There are 126 Class A addresses, each supporting 16,777,214 hosts. Networks 0 and 127 are reserved for special uses.

- Class B network addresses have the following format:

  10NNNNNN.NNNNNNNN.HHHHHHHH.HHHHHHHH

  N is part of the netid, and H is part of the hostid. This class of address ranges from 128.0.0.0 to 191.255.255.255. There are 16,384 Class B addresses, each supporting 65,534 hosts.

- Class C network addresses have the following format:

  110NNNNN.NNNNNNNN.NNNNNNNN.HHHHHHHH

  N is part of the netid, and H is part of the hostid. This class of address ranges from 192.0.0.0 to 223.255.255.255. There are 2,097,152 Class C addresses, each supporting 254 hosts.

> **NOTE** You may have heard that because of the unexpected growth of the Internet, there is a crisis in available IP addresses. This is absolutely correct, and there is a new version of IP known as IPV6 (IP version 6), which addresses this issue. However, NT has yet to adopt the new IP version, so IPV6 is not addressed on the exam.

Subnet Masks

All right, now that you understand how IP addresses are calculated, what their makeup is, and what class a particular address falls in, there's only one piece of the puzzle left before moving on to some scenarios: subnet masks.

But before you can understand subnets or subnet masks, you need to understand what an IP network is. An *IP network* is a contiguous network segment in which all the hosts have the same netid. That means for a Class A network, you could have more than 16 million hosts on a single network, without any routers. Even a 65,000-host Class B network is a bit daunting. So, the designers of TCP/IP included the concept of subnets. A *subnet* is a network segment that uses a subset of addresses from an IP address range.

Now, the concept of subnet masks and creating subnets is arguably one of the most difficult to grasp for people just starting out with TCP/IP networks. The good news is Microsoft does not test on the concept of variable-length subnetting. Just be familiar with the fact that, by default, the subnet mask for a Class A network is 255.0.0.0, for a Class B network is 255.255.0.0, and for a Class C network is 255.255.255.0. But for the real world, it's a good idea to be able to break a big network into smaller pieces. That's what you use subnet masks for.

A subnet mask is used to mask the netid portion of the IP address, telling any devices on the network where the hostid portion of the address begins. You might be thinking that the class of the address should tell the network devices where the hostid portion of the address begins. Very true—by default. But, as we discussed above, sometimes you need to split large networks into smaller ones for more efficient address usage. That's where subnetting comes in.

Subnetting a network allows you to borrow some of the hostid bits and use them to create more networks, with fewer hosts. This practice can be used to assign Class A and Class B IP addresses more efficiently. The mechanism for this is much simpler than it might sound. A *subnet mask* is a binary number consisting of 0s and 1s, just like an IP address. In the case of a subnet mask, however, 1s are used to denote the netid portion of an address, and 0s to denote the hostid portion of the address. Take a look at the following scenario.

Scenario 4.1

The corporate network manager has just assigned a portion of the Class B address 154.44.0.0 to your division. You have been assigned the addresses 154.44.1.0 through 154.44.75.255. Your division consists of 70 offices scattered throughout the country, most of them with 150 to 200 employees. You need to divide this in the most efficient manner, allowing for growth in each office.

Required Results

- Efficiently divide your Class B addresses for use over your division's Wide Area Network.

Begin the scenario by converting your address range to a binary number:

154.44.1.0

This converts to the following binary number:

10011010.00101100.00000001.00000000

Now you know that the Class B address you've been assigned gives you just one network, and you need 70. How do you divide up the addresses? Subnet the address to a Class C-style address. Set a mask with all 1s in the first three octets, and the rest set to 0s for the hosts:

Address: 10011010.00101100.00000001.00000000

Subnet Mask: 11111111.11111111.11111111.00000000

In dotted decimal notation the address would look like this:

Address: 154.44.1.0

Subnet Mask: 255.255.255.0

This yields a block of addresses with a 24-bit netid, and an 8-bit host ID, yielding 75 networks, each with 254 hosts, which accomplishes the primary objective.

NOTE For the exams, just be aware that the default subnet mask for a Class A network is 255.0.0.0, for a Class B network is 255.255.0.0, and for a Class C is 255.255.255.0. Variable-length subnet masks, which were just described, do not usually turn up on the exams. It is a very important concept for IP networking, however.

You might also wonder where to go to get an IP address range. IP addresses that are used on the Internet are known as *registered addresses.* This means that the addresses have been registered with the Internet Network Information Center (InterNIC) and no one else connected to the Internet will be using them. Today, you will generally get your addresses from your Internet Service Provider (ISP). The ISP generally has gotten a large block of addresses from the InterNIC, or perhaps even from their ISP, if they are a smaller provider.

NOTE If you are not connecting to the Internet (known as a *private network*), there are three address ranges that have been set aside for exactly that use. They are as follows:

Class A—10.0.0.0—10.255.255.255

Class B—172.16.0.0—172.31.255.255

Class C—192.168.0.0—192.168.255.255

So far, this chapter has discussed a lot of the theory behind TCP/IP networking. Now take a look at a scenario that illustrates the installation of TCP/IP on an NT Server.

Installation and Configuration

First, understand this background information. For any of the following scenarios, use the following information as given:

IP Network: 10.1.15.0

IP Address: 10.1.15.75

Subnet Mask: 255.255.255.0

There will be more information for later scenarios.

Scenario 4.2

Your management team has decided that Generic Recordings needs an Intranet server. The server was ordered, and arrived with Windows NT Server installed, but doesn't have TCP/IP installed. You need to install it now.

Required Results

- Install TCP/IP on your Intranet server, using the information provided previously.

First, open the Networking applet in the Control Panel. You can reach the same screen by right-clicking the Network Neighborhood icon on the desktop and selecting Properties. This opens the Network screen, shown in *Figure 4.1*.

The Network applet allows you to add, remove, or configure protocols, adapters, and Windows NT services. You can also change domains or rename the computer, and examine or modify the protocol/adapter bindings from this applet.

FIGURE 4.1
This is where you will do all your network installations and a large number of the configurations.

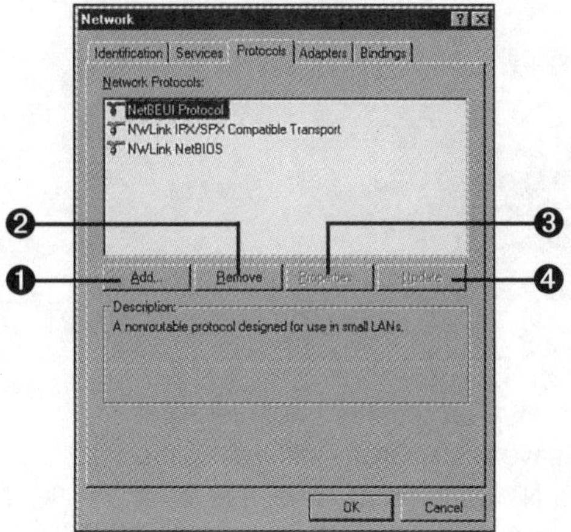

1. The Add button is used to add protocols to the system.
2. The Remove button does pretty much what it says: It is used to remove protocols. If you remove a protocol, the system also removes any additional protocols that may rely on the protocol being removed. For example, if you remove the NWLink IPX/SPX Compatible Transport protocol while the NWLink NetBIOS protocol is installed, both are removed. NWLink NetBIOS will not work without NWLink IPX/SPX Compatible Transport installed.
3. The Properties button, which is grayed out in the example, is used to open configuration screens for protocols that are configurable. You will look at those screens in depth as you work through the following scenarios.
4. The update button is used to update the drivers for a protocol. This isn't used very often, if at all, because Windows NT Service Packs are usually used to update drivers.

Click on the Add button to see a list of protocols that are available (see *Figure 4.2*). Select TCP/IP Protocol and click OK. This starts the installation of TCP/IP, and the first question the system prompts you with is shown in *Figure 4.3*. Click No in response to this question for the purposes of this scenario.

FIGURE 4.2
For this scenario, you would select TCP/IP and then OK.

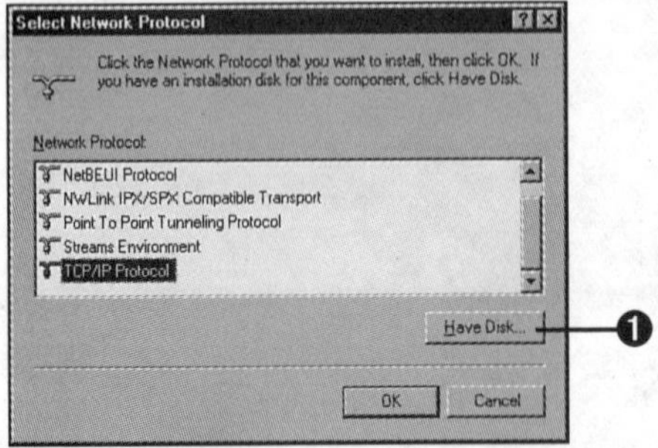

❶ If for some reason you need to install a protocol not bundled with Windows NT, you can click on the Have Disk button and install the drivers from floppy disk. Windows NT bundles most of the most commonly used protocols, so this button is not used a great deal.

FIGURE 4.3
The first question Windows NT asks is whether your network has any DHCP (Dynamic Host Control Protocol) servers, if you want to use them. For this scenario, select No. DHCP is discussed in the next section.

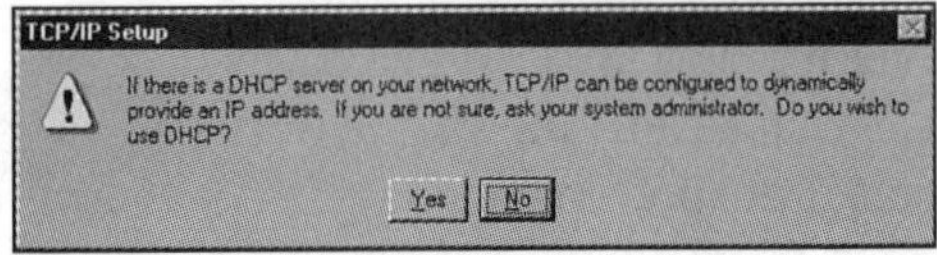

You are notified that Windows NT Setup needs to copy some files (see *Figure 4.4*). You are prompted to verify the default location of the files. Click Continue. When the file copying is complete, the Properties dialog box shown in *Figure 4.5* appears, and allows you to configure the TCP/IP properties.

FIGURE 4.4
The ubiquitous NT "Tell me where your installation files are" message.

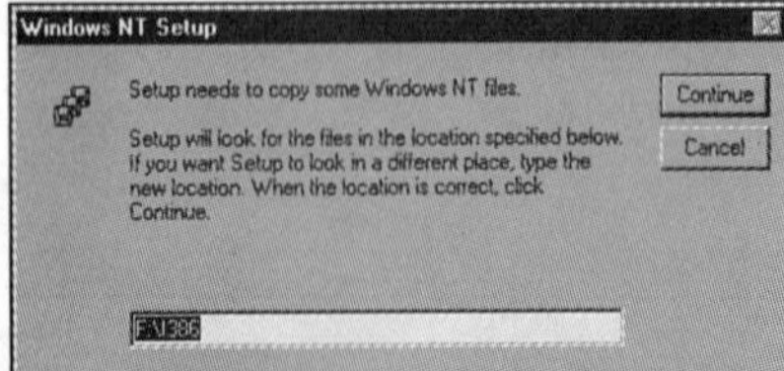

FIGURE 4.5

The TCP/IP Properties screen allows you to configure the TCP/IP properties.

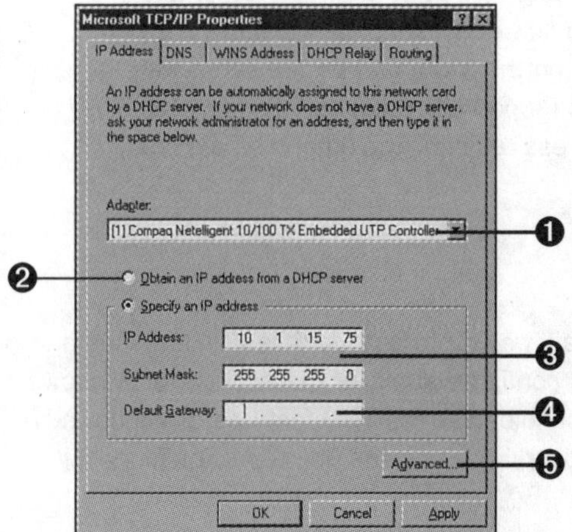

❶ The Adapter pull-down list shows you the adapter you are setting parameters for. The information set on this screen differs according to adapter. Some of the information under the other tabs is applied to all the adapters in the system. These other tabs are discussed in the next section. If you have multiple adapters in your system, you should see all of them listed in this pull-down list.

❷ The Obtain an IP Address from a DHCP Server button is used if you have a DHCP (Dynamic Host Control Protocol) server on the network. This server is used to dynamically allocate IP addresses over the network, and is discussed in greater detail in the next section.

❸ The IP Address and Subnet Mask fields are used to set the address parameters as discussed previously. These are the minimum parameters needed to configure TCP/IP on your system.

❹ Default Gateway indicates a network router, and is used so the workstation can send data to machines on other network segments. IP routers are discussed in the "Multiprotocol Routing" section.

❺ Click the Advanced button to open the Advanced IP Addressing dialog box, shown in *Figure 4.6*.

NOTE

The TCP/IP Properties window is the most important screen for getting familiar with what you can and cannot do with the TCP/IP protocol with Windows NT. *You are now entering a highly testable area.* Many of the TCP/IP questions on the exam can be answered with information garnered from this Properties dialog box. For this scenario, you work with the IP Address tab only. The other tabs are covered in the next section.

FIGURE 4.6
The Advanced IP Addressing dialog box allows you to set multiple IP addresses and gateways on a single adapter, as well as configure some of the aspects of Windows NT's Virtual Private Networking (VPN) technologies. The VPN features of Windows NT are discussed in the "Virtual Private Networking using the Point-to-Point Tunneling Protocol" section, later in the chapter.

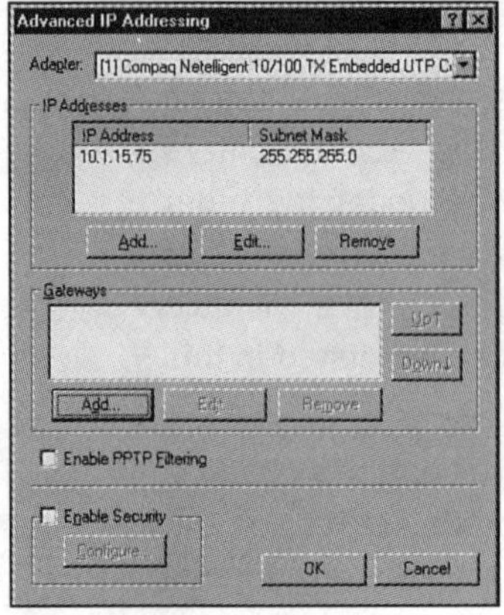

EXAM TIP

Adding a protocol forces you to reboot the server.

You have successfully completed the scenario. The TCP/IP Protocol has been added to the list of network protocols (see *Figure 4.7*).

FIGURE 4.7
The Protocols tab now shows TCP/IP as an installed protocol.

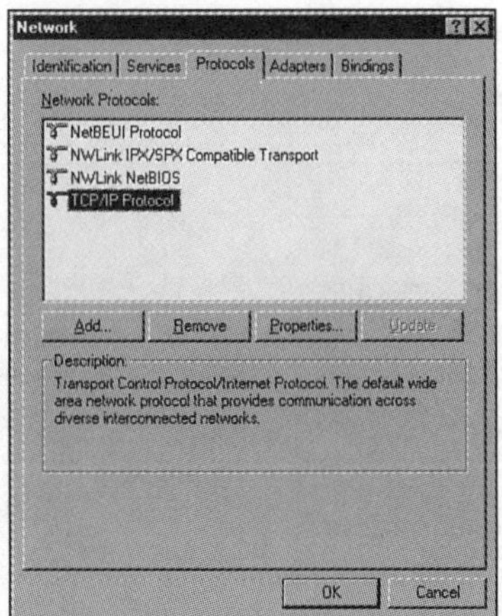

Installing and Configuring Additional Services

Before you get too far into this chapter, it is important to keep in mind that for these exams the requirements are to know what each service is for, and how to configure the server to take advantage of the service. This book does not cover installing and configuring Windows NT 4.0 as a DNS server, but does discuss what DNS is, and how to configure your Windows NT 4 server to take advantage of it. At this point, check out another scenario for an excellent way to examine these services. These services are discussed in depth as the scenario progresses. As you did in the previous section, please make the following assumptions:

IP Network: 10.1.15.0

IP Address: 10.1.15.75

Subnet Mask: 255.255.255.0

IP Router: 10.1.15.254

Primary DNS Server: 10.1.25.1

Secondary DNS Server: 10.1.35.1

Domain Name: Generic.com

Primary WINS Server: 10.1.25.2

Secondary WINS Server: 10.1.35.2

EXAM TIP

The IP Router is necessary for the WINS objective. IP Routing is discussed in the "Multiprotocol Routing" section of the chapter.

Scenario 4.3

You have successfully installed TCP/IP on your soon-to-be web server. Now you need to complete the installation so the server can take advantage of the other IP services on the network. You must be able to link to two existing systems: `mail.generic.com` and `info.generic.com`, but you don't have the IP addresses, and you would like to browse servers that are not on your local network segment. See *Figure 4.8* for the scenario environment.

FIGURE 4.8
Network diagram for scenario.

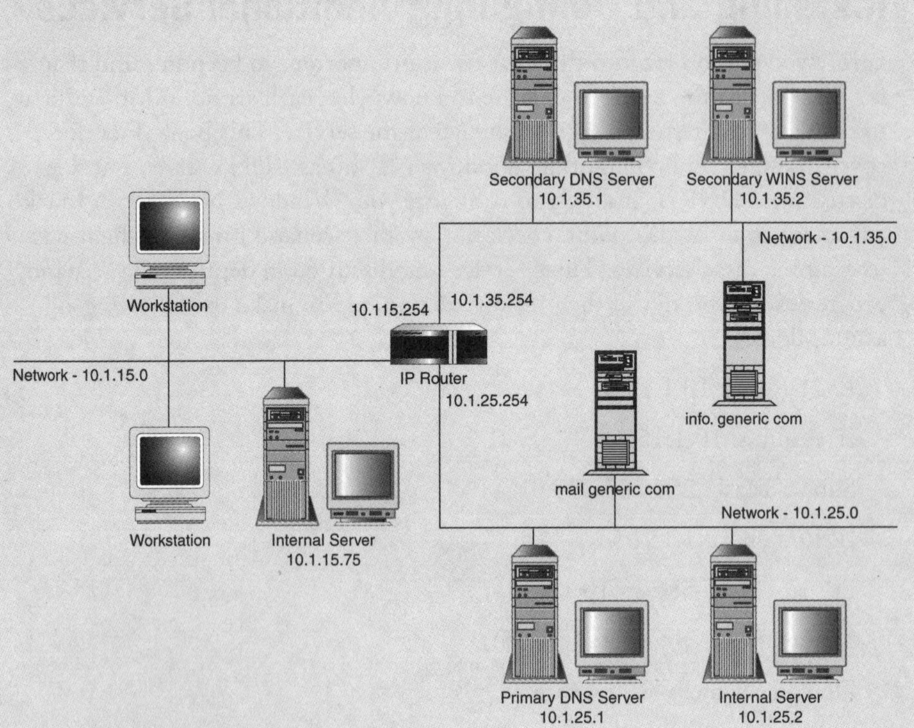

cont.

Scenario 4.3 cont.

Primary Objectives:

- Configure the server to access the production mail and information servers by name.
- Configure the server so it can browse NT servers on other network segments.
- Configure the server to access systems on other network segments.

To get started on this scenario, you must get back into the Network applet of the Control Panel. Click on the Protocols tab, and select TCP/IP. Either double-click on TCP/IP or click on the Properties button to open the TCP/IP Properties dialog box. Clicking on the DNS tab yields *Figure 4.10*, which appears later in the chapter.

Understanding DNS

Before you set up DNS, you need to understand what exactly DNS is. The Domain Name Service is a service used on the Internet for resolving host names to IP addresses. Suppose you want to order a copy of this book to give to your best friend at the office. You need to go out to the Macmillan Computer Publishing web site and order it. Which do you think is easier to remember: `http://www.mcp.com` or `http://204.95.236.226`? Most people would say `www.mcp.com`, and the Internet community recognized this as they were building the original architecture. And DNS was born.

> **NOTE** One thing you may notice as you work with DNS is that it can be identified as an acronym for Domain Name Service and Domain Name System. Both are accurate. Microsoft refers to DNS as a *system*. The Internet community generally refers to it a *service*. In an exam, assume either is fine.

DNS is a hierarchical database containing names and addresses for IP networks and hosts, and is generally represented as a tree. Because it is hierarchical, the same host name can exist in the database as long as the duplicate names are located in different branches of the tree. In *Figure 4.9*, you see a portion of the

DNS architecture that contains the Generic Recordings network. Note `<root>` at the top of the tree. This appears because DNS was based around the UNIX file system, which also starts at the `<root>` of the directory.

FIGURE 4.9
DNS domain architecture for Generic.com.

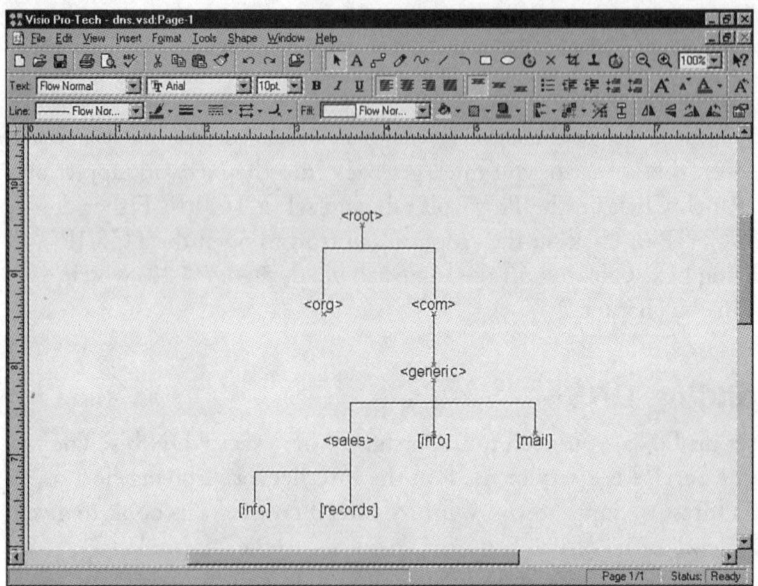

Starting at the bottom of the tree (the mail server), and tracing up to the root, you get a domain name of `mail.generic.com`. This is known as the *fully qualified domain name* because it identifies exactly where in the DNS tree this server is located. Note that there are two info servers in the example. One would have the fully qualified domain name of `info.generic.com`, whereas the other would be `info.sales.generic.com`. This book could spend another 100 pages discussing DNS, but because that level of detail won't appear on the exams, instead refocuses on the scenario. In the Microsoft TCP/IP Properties dialog box, click on the DNS tab (see *Figure 4.10*).

NOTE

You can duplicate the function of a DNS server by setting up a local `HOSTS` file. This file contains entries in an `<ip address> <host name>` format. For the scenario, `info.generic.com` could be placed in the `hosts` file in the following manner:

```
10.1.35.100     info.generic.com
```

The `HOSTS` file can be found in the `\%systemroot%\system32\drivers\etc` subdirectory.

FIGURE 4.10
Configuring the server to use Domain Name System (DNS).

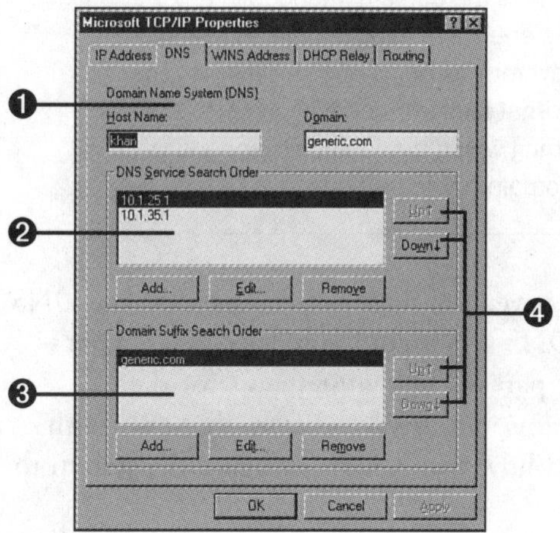

1. The Host Name and Domain fields are optional for using DNS. When you configure the Host Name option, NT sets the host name to your computer name, but it doesn't need to be. The domain should be set to your network's domain. For this scenario, set the host name to **Khan**, and the domain to **generic.com**.
2. The DNS service Search Order determines in what order the system will query the DNS servers on your network. In this scenario, the server queries the primary DSN server first, then the secondary. Fill in the addresses specified in the scenario assumptions.
3. The Domain Suffix Search Order is similar to the DNS service Search Order; however, instead of telling the system from which server to request information, it tells the system which domain to look in first. Enter **generic.com**.
4. The Up and Down buttons to the right of the Domain Suffix Search Order and DNS Service Search Order windows perform exactly the function they imply. They allow you to change the order in which the servers or domains are searched. They will be grayed out unless you have multiple DNS servers on your network.

> **NOTE**
>
> A quick note on filling in the domain name: This causes the system to assume that this domain name is the domain intended in any situations where a domain name is specified. For example, in this scenario you are configuring the system to point at the `generic.com` domain. If you were to open Internet Explorer and type **`http://info`** in the address bar, the DNS setting would automatically append the `generic.com` because of the domain name setting.

That completes the first primary objective. You have not yet installed the DNS service on the system, or gotten the DNS server configured, however. That's because the actual DNS service is not part of the requirements for the Windows NT Server or Enterprise exams. You need to be familiar only with what functionality DNS provides, and how you would configure the system to use it as a client.

To complete the next objective, click on the WINS Address tab of the Properties dialog box (see *Figure 4.11.*) Configuring the server to use WINS is similar to setting up DNS. In fact, DNS and WINS have very similar functions. The Microsoft WINS server maintains a list of NetBIOS computer names and IP addresses that the server learns through the NetBIOS protocol, which is encapsulated in a TCP/IP packet. Essentially, the servers and workstations advertise their names and addresses and the WINS server maintains them in a database. Because these broadcast packets are not routable, a WINS server must be present in order to browse to the server by the name in your Network Neighborhood. (This isn't entirely true: You can duplicate this function by using a local LMHOSTS file, but those would need to be set up on a workstation-by-workstation basis—not practical in an enterprise environment.) One powerful feature of a WINS server is the fact that it can replicate its database to other WINS servers. If you configure it correctly, you can ensure that every NT server on your network is browseable just by properly deploying WINS servers.

> **NOTE**
>
> As with DNS, it is important to understand that configuring Windows NT as a WINS server is beyond the scope of this book. This exercise deals only with configuring the server as a WINS client.

FIGURE 4.11
Configuring the server to use Windows Internet Name Server (WINS).

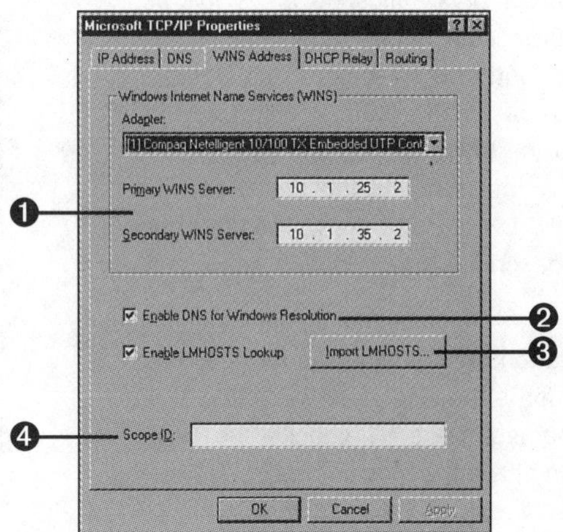

❶ In the Primary and Secondary WINS Server boxes, you enter the IP addresses of the servers. These servers can be located anywhere on the network, on the same segment as the server, or across a WAN link. Try to keep this traffic from crossing WAN links wherever possible. It can be bandwidth intensive, depending on your activities.

❷ The Enable DNS for Windows Resolution check box allows your DNS server to act as a WINS server. If the server you are trying to access is in the DNS database, Windows NT looks to the DNS server for an IP address.

❸ The Enable LMHOSTS Lookup check box allows Windows NT to look to the local LMHOSTS file in addition to checking the WINS server configured previously. An LMHOSTS file is the WINS version of a HOSTS file, described earlier. In the LMHOSTS file, you put the IP address and name of the host you want to be able to browse to. When you try to connect to the server, either through the Network Neighborhood or by using a command line NET USE statement, the server looks to the LMHOSTS file for an address. The Import LMHOSTS button allows you to browse for the existing file, in case it's not in the `\%systemroot%\system32\drivers\etc` subdirectory (the default).

❹ The Scope ID field is almost never used, and does not appear on any exams. It is used to divide up a NetBIOS network into different groups.

> **NOTE**
>
> Name-to-address resolution can happen in one of six places. Prior to WINS being installed, the order of significance is as follows. Windows NT performs a local broadcast to see if the machine it's looking for is on the local segment. Then it looks in its NetBIOS name cache, which is a cache of all the names it has already resolved once. Next it looks to the WINS server. The HOSTS file is checked next. If the machine name is not in the HOSTS file, the LMHOSTS file is checked. Finally, DNS is checked. The final two checks have to be enabled, as described in conjunction with *Figure 4.10*.
>
> After WINS is installed, the order changes. Windows NT checks to see if the machine **it's looking for** is the local machine name, then check **its** cache of remote names. Next NT checks the WINS Server. If the WINS server doesn't have the machine name, **NT** tries broadcasting. If that still doesn't resolve the machine name, NT checks the LMHOSTS file. Then **it** looks in the HOSTS file and then finally at DNS.

That completes the second primary objective. The interesting thing is that you haven't gotten the computer to talk beyond its segment yet. That's the third objective, and is shown in the IP Address tab (see *Figure 4.12*).

This is probably not the way you would do set up TCP/IP in a real world situation, but for the purposes of illustration, this scenario is deliberately out of sequence. Remember when you take the exam that just because the order of events is not the way you would do it in a real environment, that doesn't mean it's wrong. When you are dealing with one of the new situational questions, read the question and the answer very carefully. Be sure you understand exactly what Microsoft is asking for, and exactly what the answer or solution says.

FIGURE 4.12
Configuring the server to work in a routed environment.

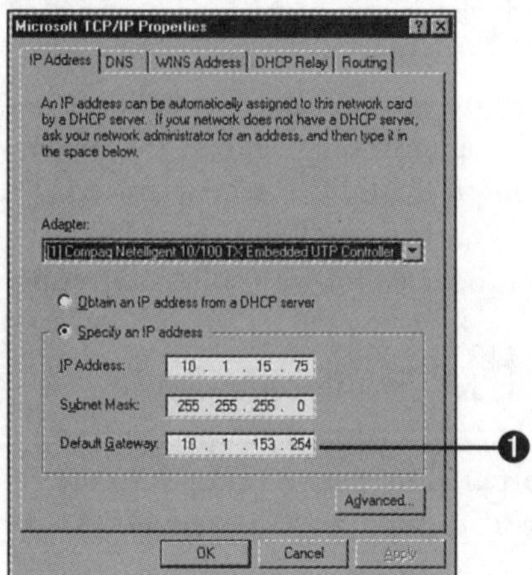

1 This screen shouldn't look too new. It's the same screen you skipped the Gateway field on in the last scenario. Fill in the field as shown in the figure, and you have successfully completed the scenario. What you have done is told Windows NT where to find the next hop to get off the network. In large networks you could have two or three routers on the same segment, each allowing you a path to another segment. At that point, it is important to check with your network support staff regarding how the server should be configured.

Dynamic Host Control Protocol

Dynamic Host Control Protocol (DHCP) is the successor to the BOOTP protocol. BOOTP was the first protocol in the TCP/IP suite that allowed a central server to dynamically allocate IP addresses on a network. Although BOOTP worked, there were some limitations. DHCP defines a method for dynamically allocating IP addresses on a network segment, while addressing the shortcomings of the BOOTP protocol.

Don't be surprised if you run across a BOOTP implementation out in the business world. It was used extensively in some places, and when it works, people are hesitant to remove it. For the sake of the exam, just be aware what it is and what it is used for.

Now, why would you use DHCP? Take a look at a mini-scenario to explore those uses. Suppose you have decided to add TCP/IP to your network and you have 250 end users. Your objective is to get a unique IP address assigned to each workstation. You could go to each workstation and manually assign an IP address, and then come up with a spreadsheet or database to track the IPs that have been assigned, what's still available, and who is using which address, in case there's a problem. Keep in mind that you would need to set the subnet mask, default gateway, and DNS information on each machine, as well. Or you could configure each machine to use DHCP for addressing, and set the subnet mask, default gateway, and DNS information on the DHCP server, instead. Then, when TCP/IP is installed on each workstation, you'll just select Use DHCP, and when the system reboots, it's on the network with valid addressing and network information.

DHCP is used extensively in larger networks, as well as in networks with a large mobile population and a limited number of IP addresses. Imagine being able to walk into any office in a national corporation, plug a laptop into the network, and be on the network ready to work as soon as the system boots.

> **NOTE** If you are a security specialist, the idea that anyone with access to your building could also get network access just by plugging in a PC must be a frightening concept. It should be. In networks that utilize DHCP, it is important to keep the network physically secure from hackers, and use tools to ensure that the wrong people aren't on your network.

Additional Utilities and Applications

You have installed TCP/IP, you are using DNS, WINS, and you can get packets to other segments. You're even familiar with DHCP, and why you might want to use it. Now what? Well, Windows NT bundles several applications and utilities to help you take advantage of the TCP/IP protocols. If you are familiar with UNIX, you will find that most of these are just NT versions of familiar UNIX utilities.

The following are TCP/IP applications and utilities:

- **Ping**—Ping.exe uses a protocol from the TCP/IP suite of protocols called ICMP (Internet Control Message Protocol) to determine if a device is responding to IP.

  In our scenario, if you were to type **`ping 10.1.15.254`** and press enter at a command prompt, you would get the following result:

```
Pinging 10.1.15.254 with 32 bytes of data:Reply
from 10.1.15.254: bytes=32 time<10ms TTL=128Reply
from 10.1.15.254: bytes=32 time<10ms TTL=128Reply
from 10.1.15.254: bytes=32 time<10ms TTL=128Reply
from 10.1.15.254: bytes=32 time<10ms TTL=128
```

This shows that the router is alive and responding. This can also be done by using the DNS name of a device. Ping has a number of other options that can be pulled up by typing **ping** with no options specified.

- **Tracert**—Tracert.exe uses the same ICMP protocol not only to determine if a device is active, but also to determine the path the packets take, by having each intermediate device respond. This is particularly useful in a large network in which you are trying to determine where delays or outages are between one device and another. Like ping, tracert has a number of options that can be displayed by typing **tracert** with no options selected.
- **Netstat**—Netstat.exe, although not used a great deal in day-to-day support, provides a great way to see what's going on with your TCP/IP packets. It can show you what your active connections are, as well as provide you with a number of statistics. Type **Netstat /?** for the full list of options.
- **Ipconfig**—The Ipconfig utility can tell you everything you need to know about your system's TCP/IP configuration. It can also be used in conjunctionwith DHCP to release or renew dynamic IP addresses. It comes with a number of optionsthat you can display by typing **ipconfig /?**. You will find that this utility becomes very useful if you need to know your MAC address, driver version, or IP address.
- **FTP**—One of the TCP/IP applications Windows NT includes is FTP.exe. FTP uses the File Transfer Protocol to send and receive files across a TCP/IP-based network. FTP was one of the anchors of the Internet before the ability to use browsers was even a concept. Today you will probably find yourself downloading patches, new driver versions, or, in some cases, new versions of applications. FTP can also be used for dropping log files and configuration files on vendor FTP sites when you are having a problem. To open the FTP application, open a DOS window (Start, Programs, Command Prompt), type **FTP**, and press Enter. This gives you an ftp> prompt. If you type a **?** and press Enter, you will get a list of options. The standard usage is as follows:

```
ftp <ip address> or <DNS name> and hit enter.
```

- **Telnet**—Telnet.exe is a GUI-based terminal emulatorthat allows you to connect to a command prompt on a system running a telnet process. This was the other major application on the Internet during the "BB" (Before Browsers) era. Telnet is still utilized heavily for accessing legacy application on UNIX, AS/400, and mainframe applications. It is also very handy for testing whether a system is listening on a specific port, because you can specify what port to connect on. This is useful for testing TCP/IP port-specific applications, to see if you can establish a connection.

- **Internet Explorer**—If you've ever surfed the Internet, you've used either Internet Explorer or one of its competitors. Browsers allow you to graphically navigate a server by reading the HTML (HyperText Markup Language) scripts, Java applets, Active Server Pages, and so on.

Internet Information Server (IIS) 3.0.

Every time you load a web page or download a file, you are accessing server processes running on some sort of application server. The process can be a web server process, an FTP process, or any of a growing number of other processes that serve up information. Microsoft generously provides IIS 3.0 free of charge as their application for running a web server on Windows NT.

Scenario 4.4

Your boss is still looking for that Intranet server. You have successfully networked the server, but now you need to make it available via the Web. In addition, the Help Desk would like to use the same server for people to download patches. You need to install IIS 3.0 and configure the services that will be running.

Primary Objectives:

- Install IIS 3.0.
- Configure the WWW service.
- Configure the FTP service.

In order to install IIS 3.0, you must first install IIS 2.0. Open the Network applet in the Control Panel, and click on the Services tab. This yields the Network dialog box, shown in *Figure 4.13*.

> **NOTE** You have to install IIS 2.0 first because IIS 3.0 is an upgrade bundled as part of Windows NT Server Service Pack 3. In order to successfully upgrade, IIS 2.0 must already be installed.

FIGURE 4.13
Adding the IIS 2.0 service to Window NT via the Services tab of Network Properties.

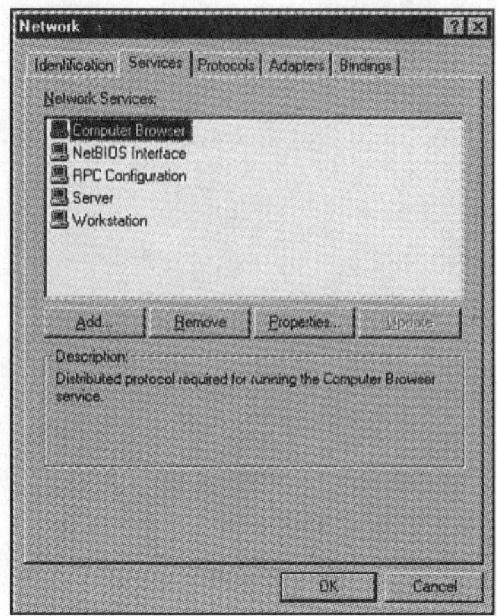

Click on the Add button to see a list of services, as shown in the Select Network Service dialog box (see *Figure 4.14*).

FIGURE 4.14
Selecting the IIS 2.0 service for installation.

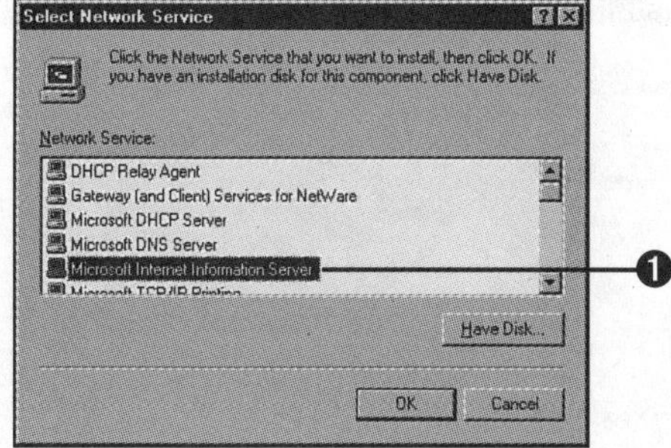

❶ Select the Microsoft Internet Information Server service and click OK. You will be prompted for the Windows NT Server disk for those files.

In *Figure 4.15*, you will notice that there is no version listed. This is version 2.0. By the time this scenario is complete, you will have upgraded to IIS 3.0. You should also note that this is where you can add services to Windows NT. You will return to this in the "Novell NetWare Connectivity" section of this chapter, to install some of the NetWare services.

> **NOTE** If you work in an environment in which media is hard to keep track of, it is a good idea to copy the i386 subdirectory from the CD to one of the hard drives. Saving a copy of the latest service pack is also a good idea.

FIGURE 4.15
Files from the Windows NT Server CD are needed for the IIS 2.0 install.

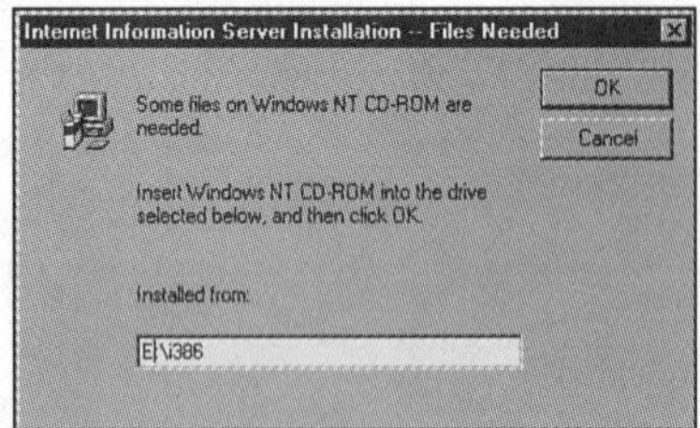

After the CD is in the drive, click OK. This opens the IIS 2.0 Setup, shown in *Figure 4.16*.

FIGURE 4.16
The IIS 2.0 Installation Setup. Pay attention to the warning regarding having other applications running while performing the installation. They can cause problems.

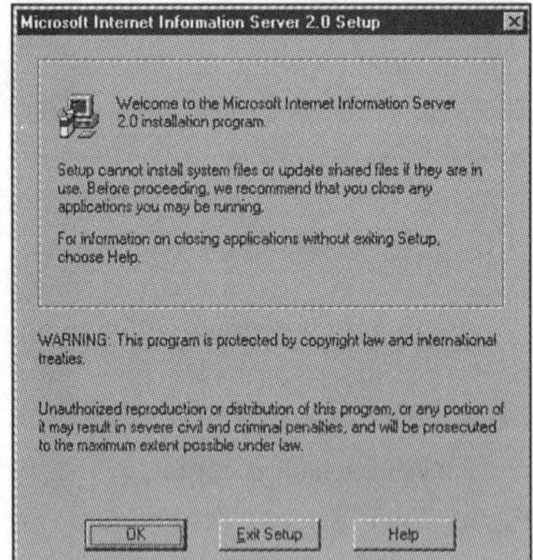

This is a standard Microsoft Setup screen. Take note of the copyright information, then click OK to start the installation. The screen shown in *Figure 4.17* appears.

FIGURE 4.17
Selecting the features of IIS 2.0 to install.

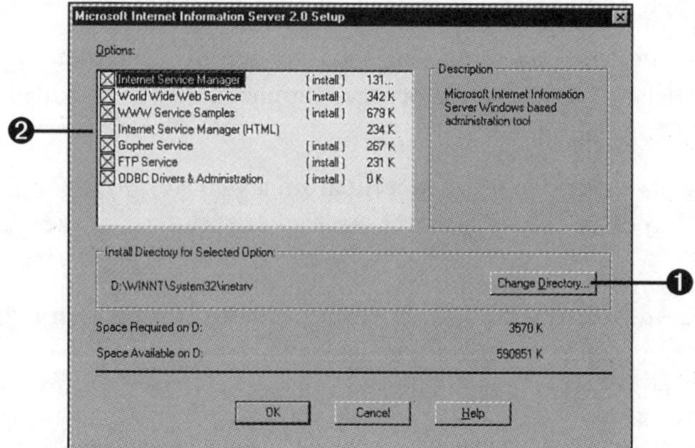

❶ As in any Microsoft application, the Change Directory button allows you to control where the files are installed. In some cases it's a good idea to install the IIS files on a separate volume from the server files, or data files. That's an additional protection against inadvertently making something important or confidential available on the WWW.

❷ There are a number of different services and applications you can install as part of IIS. If you neglect to install something you need, IIS leaves a copy of the `setup.exe` file in the `%SystemRoot%\System32\inetsrv\` directory. Running this setup program will allow you to install, reinstall or remove components from IIS.

The components you can install are as follows:

- **Internet Service Manager**—This is the application you will use to configure any of the installed services. In this scenario, you will look at the WWW and FTP service.
- **World Wide Web Service**—The service for serving Internet browser viewable files.
- **WWW Service Samples**—An entire sample web page, including the HTML code, graphics, links, and even on online form. If you already know exactly what you are going to do with your site, or are very familiar with web development, you probably don't need to install these files.

- **Internet Service Manager (HTML)**—An HTML version of the Internet Service Manager. Because the functionality of both is the same, we will not be installing this application.
- **Gopher Service**—Once the best way to navigate the pre-GUI Internet, Gopher has been relegated to the world of legacy applications. It's included in IIS for backward compatibility.
- **FTP Service**—If you've ever downloaded a file from a web site, you've probably used FTP to do it. We look at this service in depth later in the scenario.
- **ODBC Drivers & Administration**—These drivers are for storing your log files in an ODBC-compliant database for analysis. They are beyond the scope of the exam, and thus are not discussed in detail.

After you've selected the services you would like to install, click OK. The next screen you see asks where you want the information published (see *Figure 4.18*).

FIGURE 4.18
Setting the publishing directories for IIS 2.0.

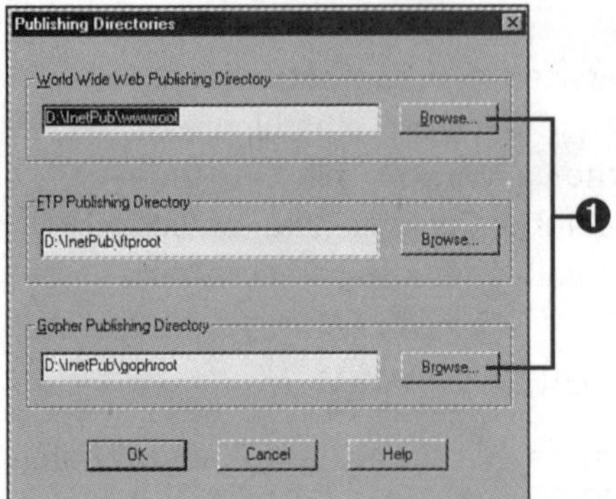

1 In *Figure 4.17*, you had the ability to decide where the IIS files would be stored. In this window you can decide where files you want to make available to the network are stored. Once again, it is often a good idea to install these on a volume separate from that on which important system or data files are kept. Click on OK to begin installing the files. For security and performance, it is a good idea to install this application on an NTFS partition. To protect the security of your accounts database, you should probably use a stand-alone server for this application.

The installation process requests whether it is okay to create the directories for the files you want published. Click Yes to each; the installation begins copying files.

To upgrade to IIS 3.0, you must apply Service Pack 3. This Service Pack can be downloaded from Microsoft, or can be ordered on CD. To install from CD, complete the following steps:

1. The CD should autoload in a browser window. Read down the screen until you reach the Install Service Pack 3 line.
2. Read and accept the licensing information.
3. Determine whether you want to create an uninstall directory. If you respond Yes, you'll be asked to specify a directory.
4. The installation begins copying files. If any of the files on the server are newer than the service pack's files, you are asked whether you want to keep the existing files.
5. When the installation completes the file copying, you are prompted to reboot the server. When the server comes back up, you will be running IIS 3.0.

After the installation of IIS, you will notice that a new group called Microsoft Internet Server (Common) has been created in the Programs menu. In that group, select Internet Service Manager to open the management application. You have completed the first primary objective. Now you can configure the different services. Notice in User Manager for Domains a new user ID, with the format of `IUSR_<server name>`. This is used for anonymous logins.

> **NOTE** Any of the activities denoted by a button can be performed either by double-clicking on the appropriate service, or using the standard Windows menu commands.

Configuring the WWW Service

As a general rule when setting up an Intranet server, the first thing you will want to configure is the web server component. This will complete the second objective of this scenario.

To configure the WWW Service, select the WWW service running on the local server (in this case Khan) and click on the Properties button (see *Figure 4.19*).

This opens the WWW Service Properties for the server, on the Service tab (see *Figure 4.20*).

FIGURE 4.19
Internet Service Manager can be used to manage multiple IIS servers.

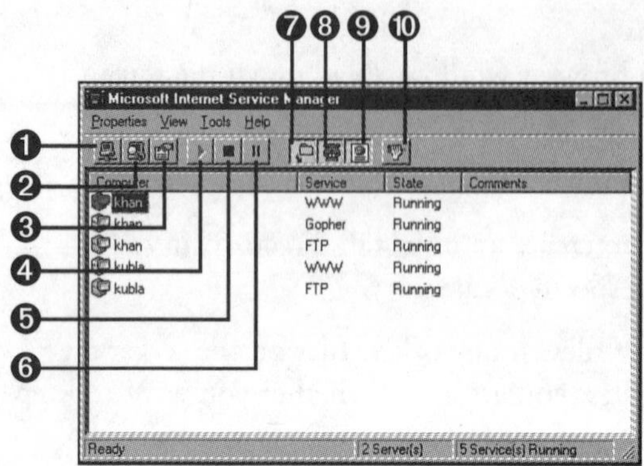

❶ Connect to a Server allows an administrator to manage multiple machines or remote machines.

❷ Find Internet Servers will go out and search the network for IIS servers. This is useful if you don't know the name of the server you need to connect to.

❸ Properties opens the properties of any service. We examine these in depth in this scenario.

❹ Play will start a stopped service.

❺ Stop will stop a running service.

❻ Pause will pause a running service, or allow a paused service to continue running.

❼ View FTP Servers is useful if you have a large number of servers and you want to work on just FTP services. Clicking this button shows only FTP servers.

❽ View Gopher Servers is useful if you have a large number of servers and you want to work on just Gopher services. Clicking this button shows only Gopher servers.

❾ View WWW Servers is useful if you have a large number of servers and you want to work on just WWW services. Clicking this button shows only WWW servers.

❿ Key Manager opens the Key Manager application, which deals with digital keys.

FIGURE 4.20
WWW Service Properties—the Service tab.

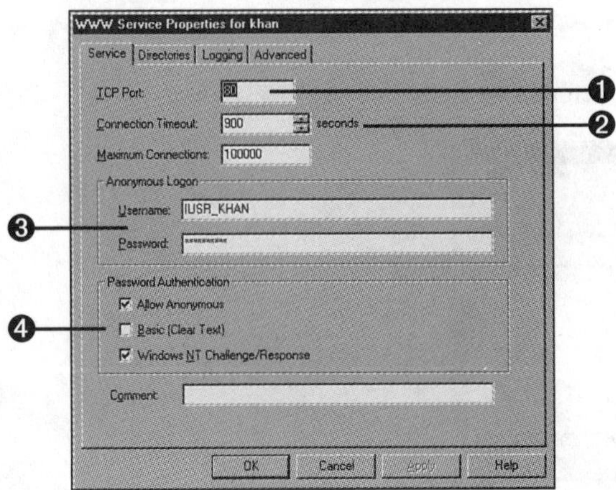

❶ The TCP port is the IP port the server is listening on for WWW requests. If you change this port, users trying to reach your server must manually enter the port as well as the address. As a general rule, redirecting this port is a bad idea.

❷ The Connection Timeout and Maximum Connections fields are both parameters dealing with the actual connection to the server. As a general rule, these shouldn't need to be changed, unless you are on a very slow network, or are providing services to a very small population of users.

❸ These fields set the user ID and password to be used for accessing the web server anonymously. Unless you are running a secure web site that requires people to login, leave these fields alone. Also, if you change the password for this ID, you must also reset the password in User Manager for Domains. That does not happen automatically.

❹ These check boxes set the security requirements for connecting to the server. As a general rule, the defaults work great for a standard web server. If you try to select the Basic (Clear Test) method of authentication, Windows NT warns that it's a bad idea because your passwords will travel across the network unencrypted. Deselecting Allow Anonymous requires that anyone connecting to the server authenticate to the server using Windows NT ID and password.

The next step in configuring this service involves the directory parameters. Click the Directories tab (see *Figure 4.21*).

FIGURE 4.21
WWW Service Properties—the Directories tab.

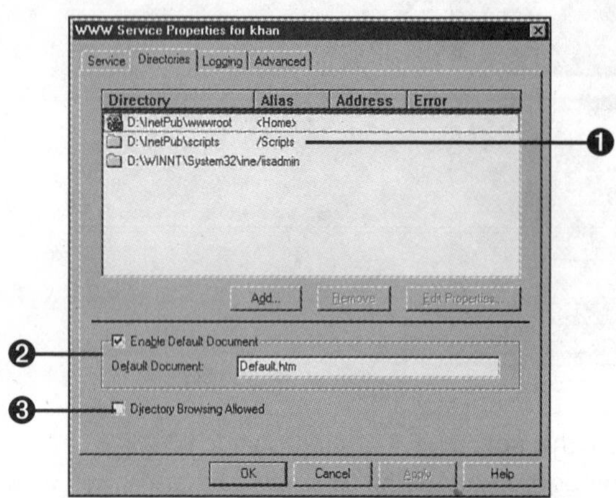

1. From this screen you can set up which directories on the server are available to users connecting to the web page. Each of the aliases becomes a directory off the root of the web server. Suppose you created a alias called Proposals for your sales department, and it mapped to the directory `D:\SALES\PROPOSALS`. You would access that directory from a browser by going to `http://<web_server_name>/proposals`. Clicking on the Add button creates new directories. One interesting feature of IIS is the ability to create *virtual servers.* When you add a new directory, you have the option of associating an IP address with it. This gives you the ability to have multiple web servers running on the same server. To maintain good security, be sure to place all your data on NTFS partitions with security configured appropriately.

2. The Enable Default Document field gives you the ability to specify which document will be opened when the server is accessed. For example, when you go to your favorite web server, you type in something like **`http://www.myfavoritewebsite.com`**. What actually loads is `http://www.myfavoritewebsite.com/<default document>`. This is usually `default.htm` or `index.htm`.

FIGURE 4.21 *Cont.*

❸ The Directory Browsing Allowed check box allows people to view files in your directories if enabled. This is generally left blank because giving the ability to browse directories can be a security problem.

Figure 4.22 shows the Logging tab, where you complete the next step in configuring this service: the logging parameters.

FIGURE 4.22
WWW Service Properties—the Logging tab.

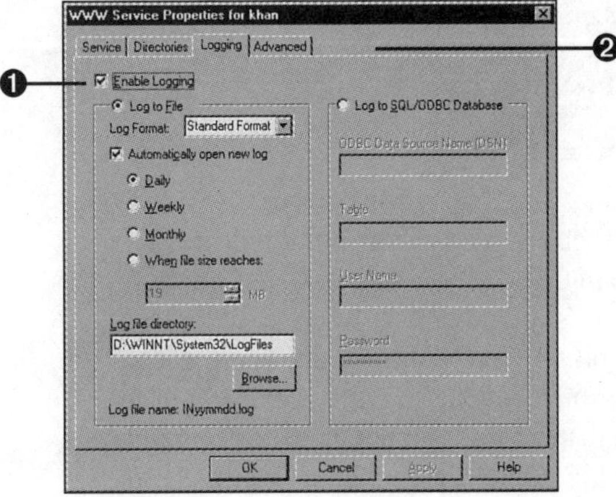

❶ From this screen you can configure the format, time interval, and location of your log. One thing to keep in mind is that log files remain on the server unless you manually delete them. If you have a busy server, these can become fairly large and gobble up your disk space.

❷ If you had installed the ODBC drivers, these would be valid options that would allow you to select a database server for logging, instead of your local server.

Figure 4.23 shows the Advanced tab, where you complete the next step in configuring this service: the access parameters.

FIGURE 4.23
WWW Service Properties—the Advanced tab.

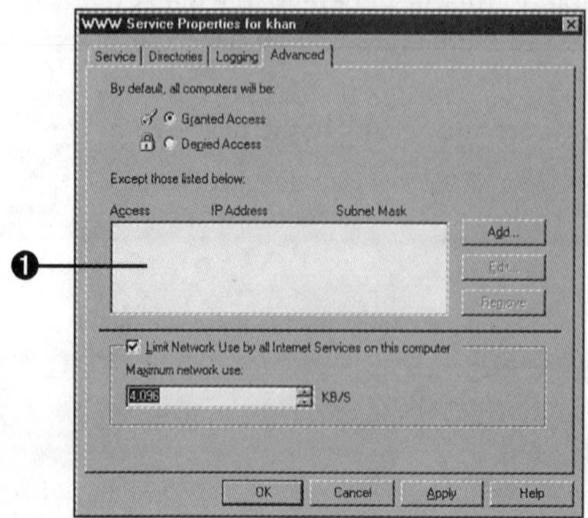

❶ This tab allows you to restrict server access with either a grant or a deny capability. One limitation is the fact that you are controlling access by IP address. If someone who doesn't have access changes his IP address to one that is allowed, he can obtain server access. For this reason, you very seldom utilize this box. You can also limit the total amount of network bandwidth that can be used by the Web IIS processes. This is useful if your web server is a multi-purpose server, and you don't want all the resources used by IIS.

You have successfully completed the second objective. The WWW Service is ready to use. Now take a look at the FTP Service.

Configuring the FTP Service

You've already configured most of the FTP Service. Well, not really—but with two exceptions, the FTP Service is identical to the WWW Service, which you *have* already configured. The first exception can be seen *Figure 4.24*.

FIGURE 4.24
FTP Service Properties—the Service tab.

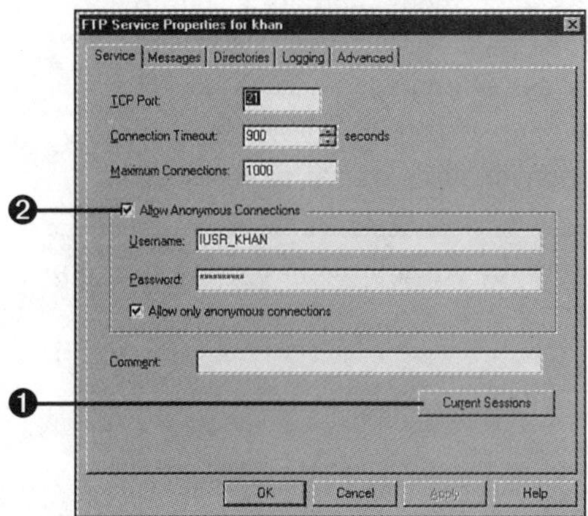

❶ The Current Sessions button was not present in the WWW Service configuration. Click on it to reveal the users who are connected to the system (see *Figure 4.25*).

❷ The Allow Only Anonymous Connections button prevents all your users from accessing the FTP server by using their user IDs and passwords. Anonymous (using the `IUSR_<server_name>` user ID) is the only way to access the system.

FIGURE 4.25
Current FTP Session Connections.

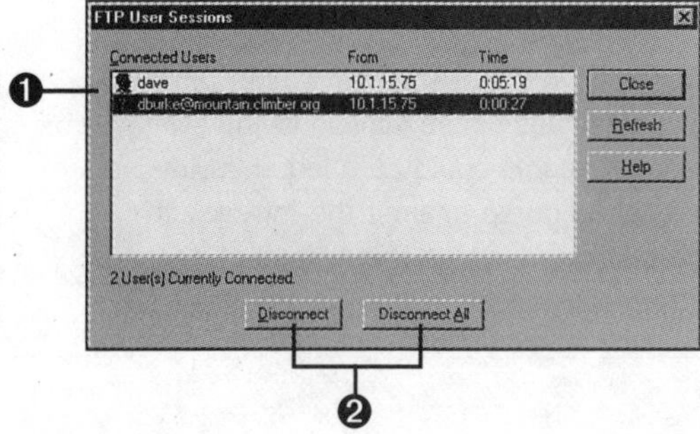

FIGURE 4.25 *Cont.*

❶ The format of this is pretty interesting. If you have anonymous FTP enabled, users can log in as Anonymous, and are asked to use their email addresses as their passwords. These users are identified in this screen by their e-mail addresses. Windows NT User IDs identify users who authenticate to the system.

❷ These buttons allow you to disconnect a single user, or all users.

The second thing that differentiates the WWW Service and the FTP Service is the Messages tab. *Figure 4.26* illustrates the possibilities of this tab and completes the final objective for this scenario.

FIGURE 4.26
FTP Service Properties—the Messages tab.

> **NOTE** A word of caution with messages: If your message says "Welcome to my FTP server" and there is an unauthorized access to the system, it is possible that the word Welcome could be ruled an invitation and you could have no legal recourse against the intruder. If you want only people who are supposed to use the system on the system, say so. Better safe than sorry.

Configuring the Gopher Service

There was a time when Gopher was the way to navigate the Internet and search for documents. With Gopher you could link computers and file systems with hierarchical links. However, with the introduction of the World Wide

Web and search engines, Gopher is now considered a legacy technology, and is only included with IIS 3.0 for backward compatibility.

> **NOTE** Some things to watch for on the exam: Be sure you are aware of what each service provides, particularly WWW and FTP. If you get a question on an exam about the Gopher service, just know that it exists for compatibility, and it was for text-based Internet navigation. Most of the questions are of the "You need to do this <fill in the task>. Which part of IIS do you use?" type.

MULTIPROTOCOL ROUTING

In this section you will become familiar with what routers are, some of the functions they perform, and what Windows NT can provide if you use it as a router. Microsoft provides a very robust routing engine in Windows NT server, allowing for static and dynamic routing (discussed later), multiple protocol routing, and remote access routing, which is discussed in the "Remote Access Services" section of this chapter. Although they are not generally used in large national or international Wide Area Networks, Windows NT servers make excellent routers for smaller networks, as well as for networks that need to connect to the Internet.

> **NOTE** You may notice there are not a lot of scenarios in this section. In fact, there aren't any! This is a section of the exam that doesn't lend itself to the scenario-style questions. The questions you will see on an exam will tend to be very straightforward, and will test your knowledge of the basics.

Function of a Router

What is the function of a router? The basic answer is that a *router* routes packets from one place to another. (You probably could have figured that out from the name.)

What routers are good at is breaking up a network into manageable pieces. Routers are used to connect multiple LANs to form WANs, or to break up your LAN into more usable pieces. Routers can provide traffic management by keeping packets destined for the local network on the local network, and can also connect dissimilar network topologies, such as ethernet and token ring.

A router works by looking at a packet's address and determining its destination. The router then checks its routing table for directions to the next *hop* towards the packet's destination. If the packet is destined for the local network, the router delivers it. If it is destined for a remote network the router has a route to, it forwards the packet to the next hop along that path. If the router cannot reach the packets final destination, it will drop the packet.

For example, in *Figure 4.27* you can see how this works. Suppose Larry sends a message to Shemp—the message never leaves the local segment. If Larry sends the same message to Moe, however, when the message reaches the router, the router forwards the message on to Moe's PC. The final instance involves Larry sending a message to Groucho. Because Groucho doesn't have a computer on this network, the router discards the packet.

FIGURE 4.27
Sample routed network.

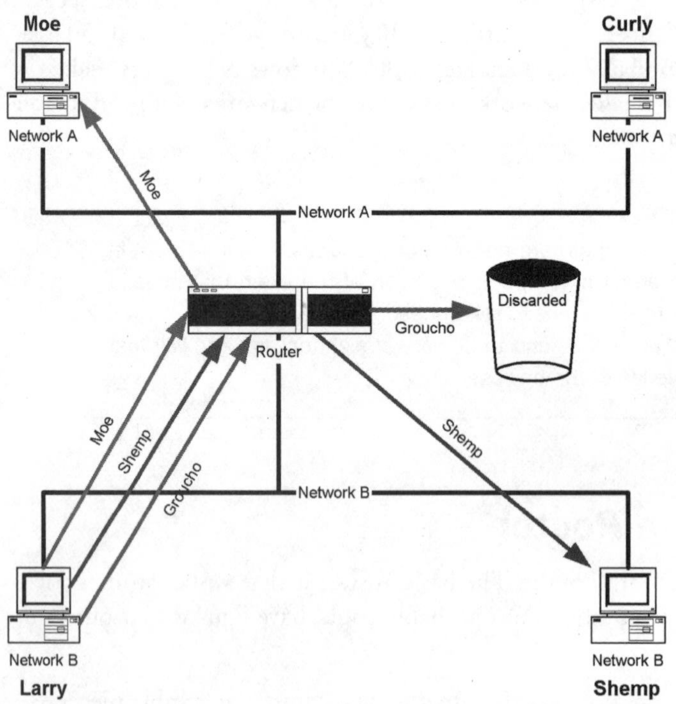

TCP/IP Routing

Understanding TCP/IP routing is one of the hottest skills on the job market today, due to the huge growth of the Internet. Competing protocols like IPX or AppleTalk are rapidly being lost in the rush to get everyone connected to the Net. There are a variety of protocols available for routing TCP/IP packets. For the exam, you should understand two methods for routing TCP/IP: Static routing and dynamic routing using the Routing Information Protocol (RIP). For the 70-067 and 70-068 exams, be familiar with how IP routing works. The really tough TCP/IP questions appear on the TCP/IP exam.

TCP/IP Static Routing—the Route Command

Enabling IP routing is very easy. Open the Network applet in the Control Panel. Go to Protocols and open the TCP/IP Properties and select the Routing tab. Click on the Enable IP Forwarding check box, shown in *Figure 4.28*, and you have just turned your server into a TCP/IP router. You must have two Network Interface Cards to start routing packets. Each NIC is connected to a different TCP/IP network. To add routes manually, you must utilize the `route` command. *Figure 4.29* lists all the parameters for the `route` command.

FIGURE 4.28
Enabling TCP/IP routing with Windows NT.

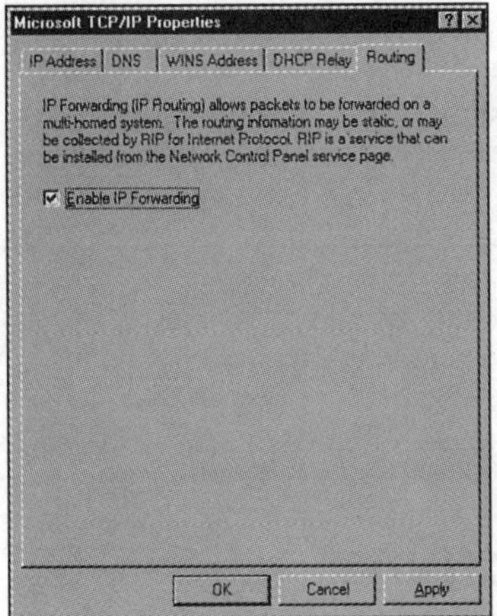

FIGURE 4.29
The Windows NT `route` command.

```
Command Prompt

D:\users>route

Manipulates network routing tables.

ROUTE [-f] [command [destination] [MASK netmask] [gateway] [METRIC metric]]

  -f           Clears the routing tables of all gateway entries.  If this is
               used in conjunction with one of the commands, the tables are
               cleared prior to running the command.

  -p           When used with the ADD command, makes a route persistent across
               boots of the system. By default, routes are not preserved
               when the system is restarted. When used with the PRINT command,
               displays the list of registered persistent routes. Ignored for
               all other commands, which always affect the appropriate
               persistent routes.

  command      Specifies one of four commands
                 PRINT     Prints a route
                 ADD       Adds a route
                 DELETE    Deletes a route
                 CHANGE    Modifies an existing route

  destination  Specifies the host.

  MASK         If the MASK keyword is present, the next parameter is
               interpreted as the netmask parameter.

  netmask      If provided, specifies a sub-net mask value to be associated
               with this route entry.  If not specified, it defaults to
               255.255.255.255.

  gateway      Specifies gateway.

  METRIC       specifies the metric/cost for the destination

All symbolic names used for destination are looked up in the network database
file NETWORKS. The symbolic names for gateway are looked up in the host name
database file HOSTS.
If the command is print or delete, wildcards may be used for the destination
and gateway, or the gateway argument may be omitted.

D:\users>_
```

TCP/IP Dynamic Routing—Installing RIP for Internet Protocol

This is a pretty straightforward installation. As you did for the IIS Service, open the Network applet in the Control Panel. Select the Services tab, and click on Add. Select RIP for Internet Protocol and click OK. You are prompted for the Windows NT media, and the service installs. Your server is now a dynamic IP router.

> **NOTE**
> Whenever you install a Network Service like this, be sure to re-apply the latest Service Pack when you are done.

NOVELL NETWARE CONNECTIVITY

Before getting too far into this section, it's important to point out that this is a topic that is heavily tested on, especially on exam 70-067 (Windows NT Server). Be very aware of exactly what capabilities each of these utilities have. NetWare interoperability is a very important feature of Windows NT server, and can assist you immensely if you are working in a mixed NetWare/Windows

NT environment. This section discusses the two basic components of NetWare integration: Gateway Services for NetWare, and the Migration Tool for NetWare.

NOTE

The following sections discuss a number of different services and utilities for accessing NetWare resources. If you have a client/server application running on a NetWare server, the only thing you need to load to access it is the NWLink IPX/SPX Compatible Transport protocol. This protocol gives the client portion of the application access to the NetWare server, and allows the application to function.

Installing and Configuring Gateway (and Client) Services for NetWare

If you are going to be putting a Windows NT server into a Novell NetWare environment and you want to make the NT server talk to the legacy Novell systems, you must install *Gateway Services for NetWare (GSNW)*. GSNW allows your server to talk to the NetWare servers (2.x, 3.x, and 4.x) and can allow you to do some very useful things to integrate the two operating systems. Take a look at the following scenario to really get a feel for how GSNW works.

Scenario 4.5

You need to install a Windows NT Server into your Novell NetWare network. You must be able to see NetWare 3.x and 4.x servers for activities such as file and print services. Because you are planning to migrate to Windows NT in the near future, you would also like to use this server to ease the migration by providing NetWare server access to the newly migrated Windows NT clients.

Primary Objectives:

- Integrate your Windows NT Server into the NetWare network.
- Provide access to the legacy NetWare servers for new Windows NT clients.

Installing NWLink IPX/SPX Compatible Transport

The first thing you need to do in order to establish connectivity in a Novell NetWare environment is load Windows NT's NWLink IPX/SPX Compatible Transport. In Chapter 1, "Planning," IPX/SPX is discussed as the protocol Novell created when it first started selling network operating systems. Novell has released some TCP/IP connectivity applications to allow users to connect to their servers by using TCP/IP. Because these are proprietary TCP/IP stacks, you will probably need IPX/SPX until the release of Novell NetWare 5, which promises to deliver native TCP/IP connectivity. Installing NWLink IPX/SPX Compatible Transport is almost identical to installing TCP/IP (or any other protocol), so you should begin with a quick review of the installation before jumping into the configuration of the protocol.

Complete the following steps to install NWLink IPX/SPX Compatible Transport:

- Open the Network applet in Control Panel.
- Click on the Protocols tab.
- Click on Add.
- Select NWLink IPX/SPX Compatible Transport.

You are prompted for the location of the media, and then the protocol loads. You will need to reboot the server after the installation completes.

After the installation is complete, notice that two protocols have actually been installed. In addition to the NWLink IPX/SPX Compatible Transport, which you should have expected, there is also a NWLink NetBIOS protocol. This protocol is used to allow NetBIOS packets to be forwarded.

Before moving on to the services, take a moment to look at a few settings for the NWLink IPX/SPX Compatible Transport protocol. First, you have the ability to set an Internal IPX number, which is a hexadecimal number that is necessary if you plan to run IPX routing or File and Print Services for NetWare. Both are discussed later.

You can also set the Frame Type Detection to Auto or Manual. Use the Auto selection on networks in which there is only one frame type in use. If you are running multiple frame types, you should select Manual and select the frame type from the list of available types. The following are the NWLink IPX/SPX Compatible Transport Frame Types:

- **802.2**—One of two frame types used by the IPX protocol, this frame type is the default for NetWare 3.12 and 4.x servers.

- **802.3**—The other frame type usually associated with IPX, this is the default for Novell NetWare 2.x or 3.x servers (through 3.11). .
- **Ethernet_II**—This frame type is used by NetWare servers running the TCP/IP protocol.
- **Ethernet_SNAP**—This frame type is used by NetWare servers running the AppleTalk protocol.

The application for integrating a Windows NT Server into a NetWare environment is Gateway Services for NetWare (GSNW). This service is installed by opening the Network applet in the Control Panel, going to the Services tab, and selecting Gateway (and client) Services for NetWare. After the installation is complete, you must reboot the server. After the server is backed up, it's time to configure the service.

> **NOTE**
> If NWLink is not already installed, Gateway Services for NetWare installs it automatically.

Open the Control Panel (see *Figure 4.30*). Checking to make sure there is a new applet for Gateway Services is a good way to ensure it is installed correctly. Then, open the GSNW applet. This yields the dialog box shown in *Figure 4.31*.

FIGURE 4.30

Installing Gateway (and Client) Services for NetWare adds a GSNW icon to the Control Panel.

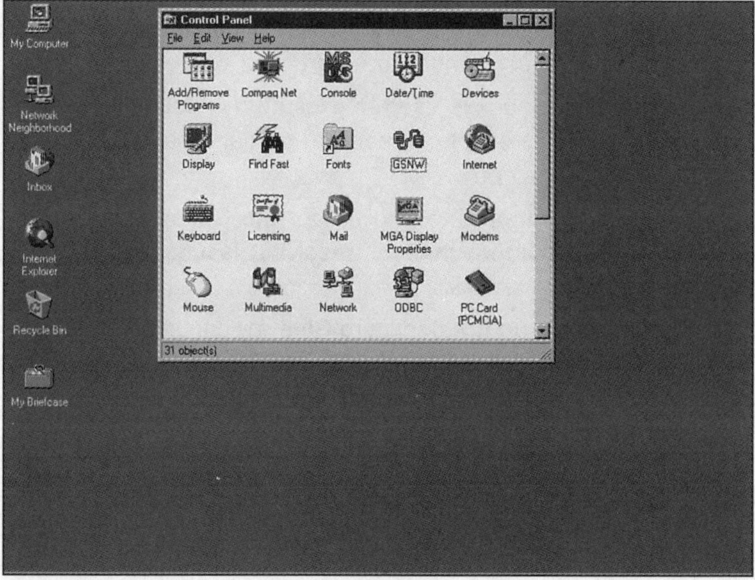

FIGURE 4.31
Configuring the Novell login parameters for GSNW.

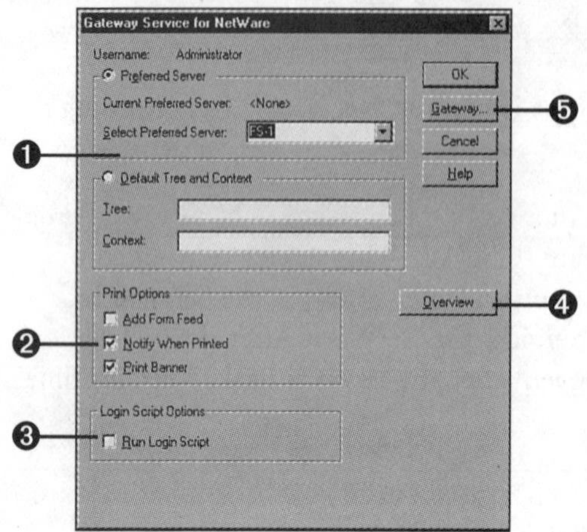

❶ These boxes allow you to select whether you will be logging into a NetWare 3.x server using bindery authentication or logging into a Novell Directory Services (NDS) tree. For a 3.x server, enter the name of the server in the select Preferred Server box; for NDS enter the name of the tree, and the fully delimited context. Because this isn't a book on NetWare integration, any further differences between NetWare 3.x and 4.x are not discussed.

❷ Here you set your printing options for the connection. As you can see, these are fairly standard options. In order to conserve paper, you may want to consider disabling banner printing, especially if a small number of users print to a particular printer.

❸ The Run Login Script check box is used to execute the NetWare login script. NetWare's login script can perform similar functions to the Windows NT logon script.

❹ The Overview button opens up the Help file for the GSNW service. This can be a good resource for resolving issues and increasing your familiarity with GSNW.

❺ The Gateway button opens up the Configure Gateway dialog box, shown in *Figure 4.32*. This dialog box lets you configure the second piece of GSNW: the ability to make NetWare resources available to Windows NT users.

NOTE

Although you are undoubtedly accustomed to a Windows NT logon, Novell NetWare uses a slightly different terminology. You *log on* to a Windows NT domain. You *log in* to a Novell NDS tree.

FIGURE 4.32
Configuring the gateway and sharing capabilities of Gateway Services.

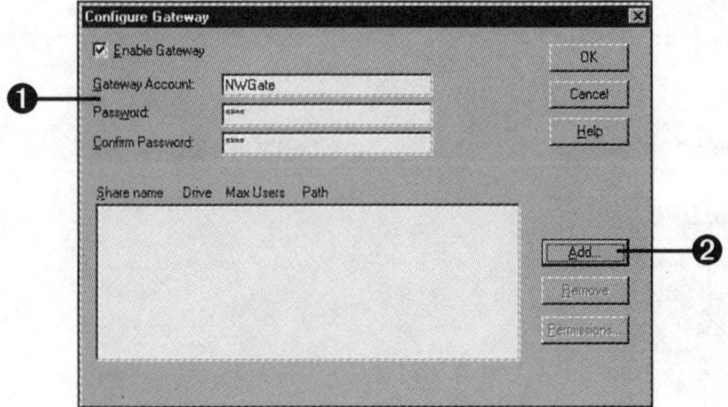

1. To configure the gateway, first you need to select the Enable Gateway check box. You then enter the appropriate gateway sccount and password information.
2. Click on the Add button to open the New Share dialog box, shown in *Figure 4.33*, which allows you to enter directories to be shared from this gateway server. To the end user, these will look like normal Windows NT shares.

There is one piece of work that needs to be completed on the NetWare side before this account will work. Create a group called NTGATEWAY. In this group place the user ID you will be using to access NetWare resources. This user ID must exist in either the NetWare bindery (3.x servers) or in NDS. Make sure the NTGATEWAY group has the proper permissions to access the resources you want to share. After the NT side of the process is set up, the gateway server will be able to share any resources the NTGATEWAY group has to share. Because you are using a group to assign permissions, you must keep in mind that you cannot restrict an individual user's access to a share. Any directories or files shared via GSNW are group accounts because anyone that can access the shares on the gateway server has the same rights as any other user.

NOTE

Technically, use of GSNW could be considered a violation of Novell's licensing agreement for Novell NetWare. Because all the Windows domain clients are accessing NetWare resources via the GSNW connection, GSNW is only using a single login connection. The flip side of this is that the shared connection can make accessing the server a long and painful event. For this reason Microsoft recommends using this for migration purposes only. This is not a great long-term solution.

FIGURE 4.33
Adding a Novell directory to be shared through Gateway Services for NetWare.

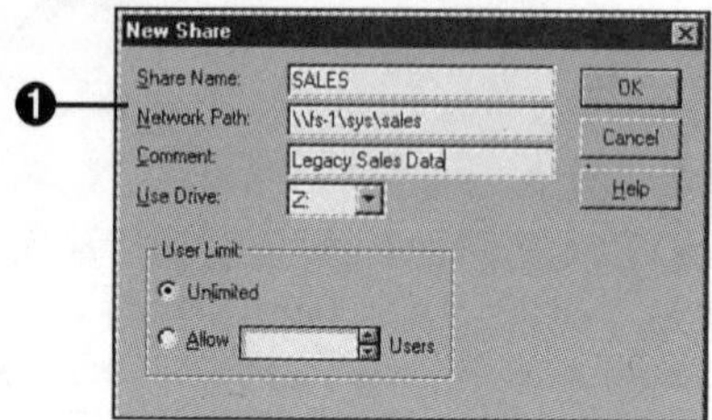

1. You may notice that this is very similar to setting up a Windows NT share, except that you cannot set the access permissions. Access permissions are determined by the rights the NTGATEWAY account has for that resource. Network paths should be entered using the standard Windows NT UNC pathname, in the format of `\\<server_name>\volume_name\directory_name`.

Using the Migration Tool for NetWare

If you have ever used the GSNW to supply access to a NetWare server, you recognize that it is a stop gap measure at best. Performance is sluggish, security is non-existent, and there is a lot more support overhead caused by supporting two platforms, plus the GSNW configuration. So if you are presented with a situation where it's time to get rid of that gateway server and get everything moved from NetWare to Windows NT, use the Migration Tool for NetWare, which can be found under the Administrative Tools program group.

Before you use the Migration Tool for NetWare, you should be aware of some requirements for the server running the migration utility. This list makes excellent material for test questions, particularly on the Windows NT Server exam.

The following are migration preconditions:

- Volumes that will be receiving the migrated data from the NetWare server must be on an NTFS partition. This is so the NetWare rights can be successfully migrated.
- The Gateway Service for NetWare must be installed on the server to provide access to the NetWare server.
- The NWLink protocol (IPX) must be installed on the gateway server.

To take a look at the migration utility, go to the Administrative Tools program group and select Migration Tool for NetWare. It opens to the blank screen shown in *Figure 4.34*.

FIGURE 4.34
The Migration Utility for NetWare opening screen.

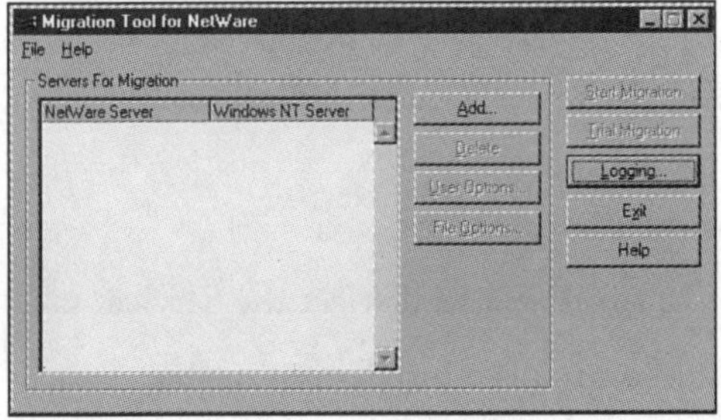

Rather than spend a great deal of time going over every facet of this utility, you should focus on the important features of the application. This is the test material you will probably see presented on the exam.

The Migration Utility for NetWare allows you to migrate users, groups, and data from a NetWare server to a Windows NT server. Keep in mind that although you can set new passwords for users during the migration, you will not be able to migrate the passwords, due to Novell's security. Passwords are not even accessible to Novell upgrades in some cases. You also have the ability to migrate just data, if you have already created users in your Windows NT domain.

One important feature of the Migration Utility is the ability to run a trial migration. Following a trial migration, you can examine the errors and correct them before running the real migration.

Finally, you have the ability to determine how Novell's Supervisor rights are handled during the migration. Supervisor rights can be transferred directly, or you can have those users added to the Administrators Group during the migration.

File and Print Services for NetWare (FPNW)

So far you've looked at integrating Windows NT into a NetWare environment using Gateway (and Client) Services for NetWare, and migrating from Novell NetWare to Windows NT using the migration utility. Suppose you want to make your Windows NT server available to Novell NetWare clients without loading the Windows NT client? Load File and Print Services for NetWare (FPNW).

FPNW is an emulator that makes a Windows NT server appear to be a NetWare 3.x (*not* NetWare 4.x) server to Novell NetWare client software. One interesting thing to remember about FPNW is that is does *not* ship with NT, and must be obtained separately.

FPNW installs two components: the FPNW service and the Administrative Tools. As a general rule, the FPNW service is installed on the Primary Domain Controller, and the Administrative Tools are installed on Backup Domain Controller. After these two components are installed, the Windows NT server appears to be a NetWare server to any of the Novell Clients, from the monolithic IPX/NETx, to the DOS VLMs. The NT server also appears as a NetWare server to any of the new 32-bit clients released by Novell for Windows 95/98 or even Windows NT.

In order to install FPNW, do the following:

1. Open the Network applet in the Control Panel, and select the Services tab.
2. Click on the Have Disk button and point at the installation media. (FPNW is not one of the services bundled with Windows NT. You must purchase it and have the media ready.)
3. Select a directory for the installation when prompted. Because this directory will appear to Novell clients as the server's SYS volume, Microsoft recommends this directory be on an NTFS volume. NTFS provides the greatest security, and provides similar security to that found under NetWare.
4. The installation prompts you for a server name, which the Windows NT server will announce to the Novell clients. By default, this name is `<server_name>FPNW`.
5. Reboot the system. FPNW is installed.

> **NOTE** The installation process creates the standard Novell directory structure, with the `LOGIN`, `MAIL`, `PUBLIC`, and `SYSTEM` directories. The installation also provides NT versions of common Novell utilities like CAPTURE, SLIST, MAP, and so on. The process also creates a Supervisor account, which is placed in the Administrator's group.

To create users for the FPNW server, use the FPNW applet in the Control Panel. If you open a user with User Manager for Domains, you will notice a new option at the bottom of the properties screen. FPNW adds a Maintain NetWare Compatible Logon check box. Check this box to allow a user to use the FPNW server.

NOTE

Directory Services Manager for NetWare (DSMN) is another add-on service you can purchase from Microsoft. In short, DSMN with Windows NT Server allows an administrator to centrally manage a mixed Windows NT and NetWare environment with the Windows NT Directory Services. DSMN copies the NetWare user accounts to the Windows NT Directory Service and then propagates any changes back to the NetWare server. All the accounts are managed from a single interface, using a standard Windows NT utility.

Client Services for NetWare (CSNW)

Now that you know how to make your Windows NT Server accessible to Novell NetWare clients, you should learn how to give your Windows NT Workstations access to Novell NetWare servers. This is accomplished by loading Client Services for NetWare (CSNW).

CSNW is a service that ships with Windows NT Workstation and when installed, gives a Windows NT Workstation access to Novell NetWare 2.x, 3.x, and 4.x server resources. The 4.x servers can be running in bindery emulation mode or in NDS mode.

Installing CSNW is done in the same manner as all the other services discussed thus far. Open the Network applet, go to the Services tab, select the Client Services for NetWare service and let the installation complete. You must reboot the workstation when the install is complete. When the workstation comes back up, you will notice a CSNW icon in the Control Panel. Opening this applet gives you the ability to configure the same information as or the Gateway Services discussed previously, with the exception of the Gateway button and associated parameters (refer to *Figure 4.31*).

Installing RIP for NWLink IPX/SPX Compatible Transport

Installing RIP for NwLink is identical to the installation of RIP for Internet Protocol detailed previously. The one configurable component for RIP for IPX is control over whether encapsulated NetBIOS packets will be propagated by the routing service. Packet propagation by the routing service can eat up a lot of bandwidth depending on how the network is configured. Be very careful when enabling NetBIOS propagation on a production network.

Installing and Configuring Remote Access Server (RAS)

The final topic in this chapter is the Remote Access Server, which is Windows NT's answer to remote network access. One of the key features that separates Windows NT from some of its competitors is its ability to serve as a remote access service out of the box. Because this is a key difference, you can expect to see some Remote Access Server questions on the exams. To successfully answer these questions, you'll need a solid understanding of Remote Access Server. {*Before you can install and configure RAS, you must have a modem installed. Modem installation is covered in Chapter 2, "Installation and Configuration."*}

Understanding Remote Access Server (RAS)

Remote Access Server (RAS) is Windows NT's answer to remote access services. A component of Microsoft's operating systems since Windows for Workgroups 3.11, RAS is used for inbound and outbound remote access. RAS servers are used quite frequently as dialup Internet routers for small offices to connect to the Internet or as dial-in servers providing LAN access to remote users. Some of the features RAS adds to Windows NT's capabilities include the following:

- Support for asynchronous protocols like Serial Line Interface Protocol (SLIP), the Point-to-Point Protocol (PPP), and Microsoft RAS Protocol. RAS also supports the Point-to-Point Tunneling Protocol (PPTP), an extension of the PPP protocol used for secure, encrypted network access.
- Support for a large number of clients. RAS can support MS-DOS, Windows, Windows for Workgroups, Windows NT, and even LAN Manager RAS. With support for PPP, Windows NT RAS can also support any PPP-compatible client dialing into an NT RAS server.

- Support for a number of different media connections, including ISDN, X.25, phone lines (with modems), and null modem cables. RAS also supports the aggregating features of the multilink protocol, which allows multiple modem connections to be aggregated into a single logical connection, affording additional bandwidth.
- Support for multiple protocols, including TCP/IP (including DHCP), IPX, and NetBEUI. RAS can also be configured to restrict access to the RAS server, or to allow access to the entire network.

RAS Protocols

When discussing Remote Access Server protocols, you should divide the protocols into two types. First, you have the dialup protocols: Serial Line Interface Protocol (SLIP), Point-to-Point Protocol (PPP), and Microsoft RAS protocol. RAS also supports the TCP/IP, NetBEUI, and IPX network protocols.

SLIP

SLIP is an older dialup protocol, createdin the mid '80s. This has been the standard protocol for TCP/IP networks, and is used heavily in UNIX environments, but has rapidly been replaced by PPP due to SLIP's lack of features. One of the limitations of SLIP is that it only supports TCP/IP, whereas PPP also supports IPX and NetBEUI. SLIP's encryption capabilities are also much less robust than those of PPP. For example, SLIP cannot encrypt the logon information, which means that the user ID and password for a SLIP session are transmitted as clear text. This protocol also will not work with DHCP, which means that each remote IP address must be assigned and maintained manually. This adds significantly to the support overhead associated with the protocol.

PPP

Point-to-Point Protocol is the new standard for remote access communications for a number of reasons. First, PPP enjoys almost ubiquitous acceptance in the business community. All major networking vendors support PPP on their dial-in access servers, and it is also the asynchronous protocol of choice when connecting to most Internet Service Providers (ISPs). The fact that PPP is protocol independent makes it very popular with people who need to provide IPX or NetBEUI connectivity. PPP also supports AppleTalk and DECnet.

PPP offers much more robust error checking (SLIP offered none) and authentication features. PPP uses checksums to verify packet integrity. A *checksum* is a value that is generated by adding the binary value of each character in a packet and then sending the result with the packet. When the packet arrives, the receiving machine performs the same calculation and if the result doesn't match, the packet is rejected and must be resent. In the authentication arena, PPP supports the following methods, known as the PPP Control Protocols:

- Password Authentication Protocol (PAP)
- Challenge Handshake Authentication Protocol (CHAP)
- Shiva Password Authentication Protocol (SPAP)

Microsoft RAS Protocol

Microsoft RAS Protocol is a legacy Microsoft protocol used to support the older versions of RAS used in Windows NT 3.51 and Windows for Workgroups. The major drawback of this protocol is the fact that it requires NetBEUI and NetBIOS in order to function. Protocols such as TCP/IP and IPX are then supported via a gateway function, instead of natively. Unless you have legacy clients, this is a good protocol to skip.

Network Protocols

Microsoft's RAS supports the following network protocols natively:

- TCP/IP
- NetBEUI
- IPX

With additional software, RAS will also support AppleTalk and DECNet.

Remote Access Connection Methods

Remote Access Server offers five methods of access to the network:

- **Modem**—Remote Access Server can be accessed via a standard modem and analog phone line.
- **ISDN**—Integrated Services Digital Network is a high-speed digital service available in some parts of the country. Running at speeds of up to 128 KBPS, ISDN can be an excellent solution for a remote office. Availability in some areas of the country is limited.

- **X.25 PAD**—A connection to a packet-switched network. This is a legacy technology used less and less. X.25 can be accessed either directly or via dialup.

> NOTE
>
> In order to use X.25, you must have an additional piece of equipment known as a *Packet Assembler Disassembler (PAD)*. This is used in conjunction with the X.25 switched network and is used to break packets into characters to be sent across the X.25 network. At the other end, another PAD reassembles the characters into packets and forwards them to the destination machine.

- **Null Modem cable**—Two machines can be connected using a null modem cable. Excellent for lab exercises, this is of limited use in a production environment.
- **Virtual Private Network**—With the use of the Point-to-Point Tunneling Protocol, a Windows NT RAS server can offer network access via an encrypted Virtual Private Network. PPTP is discussed in greater detail later.

> NOTE
>
> One new feature for Remote Access Server is the Multilink capability. In short, *Multilink* allows you to aggregate a modem pool into what appears to the end user as a single connection. This can be an inexpensive solution to provide more bandwidth without expensive ISDN lines.

Remote Access Security Mechanisms

One question you might see on the exams asks about the types of security that Remote Access Server provides. The following are RAS security mechanisms:

- **Callback**—RAS can be configured to call back a dial-in user to ensure that he is at the correct telephone number when he dials in. This is often used to save on toll calls—it's less expensive for the server to call the end user than it is for a traveling user to call from a hotel.
- **Encryption**—Remote Access Server can encrypt logon data, and even all data if necessary.

- **Auditing**—As with everything else in Windows NT, you can audit any user activity on the RAS server.
- **PPTP**—You can configure the server in conjunction with RAS to accept only PPTP packets for increased security.
- **Third Party Authentication**—If domain authentication is inadequate, a third party security server can be used instead.

Installing RAS

Now that you've learned all the nuts and bolts information on how RAS works, and what protocols it will support, it's time get into the meat of it, and look at another scenario.

Scenario 4.6

Your company has decided that the best way to maximize your sales department's productivity is to get the salespeople out of the office and calling on customers. So your entire sales force just had their offices closed, and they are now all mobile users. Now it's up to you to give them access to the company's data, intranet, and email services.

Required Results

- Grant your mobile users access to the company's network resources using Windows NT Server.

You've probably guessed that the best option for this is to install and configure Windows NT's Remote Access Server.

> **NOTE** This scenario assumes you have already installed and configured your modem.

{*Installing a modem is covered in the "Installing a Modem" section of Chapter 2.*}

The first step is to install the service, which is accomplished in the same way as the other services you installed in this chapter.

Open the Network applet under the Control Panel, and select the Services tab. Select Remote Access Service and click OK. The Add RAS Device dialog appears (see *Figure 4.35*). Provide the Windows NT media, and the files will be copied. After the files are copied, the installation takes you right into the RAS configuration, as shown in *Figure 4.36*.

FIGURE 4.35
Selecting the RAS Device.

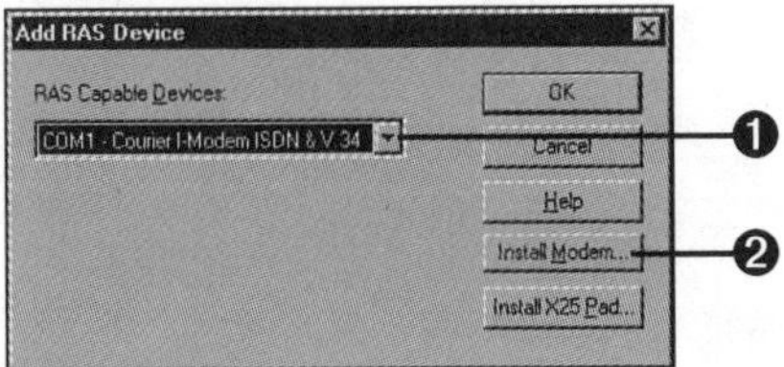

❶ The RAS Capable Devices drop down box is used to select the RAS device to be utilized for the inbound (or outbound) connectivity. If there is a single RAS device installed, it will be the item listed in the drop down box. Otherwise, you can select the device you want to configure. RAS can use multiple devices. For this scenario, use the one device.

❷ If you have a modem that you have just added, you can use the Install Modem button to start the Install New Modem Wizard. The Install X.25 Pad works in a similar fashion, although you will seldom use that button. Modems are much more common than X.25 Pads as RAS devices. Click OK to continue.

FIGURE 4.36
The Remote Access Setup screen.

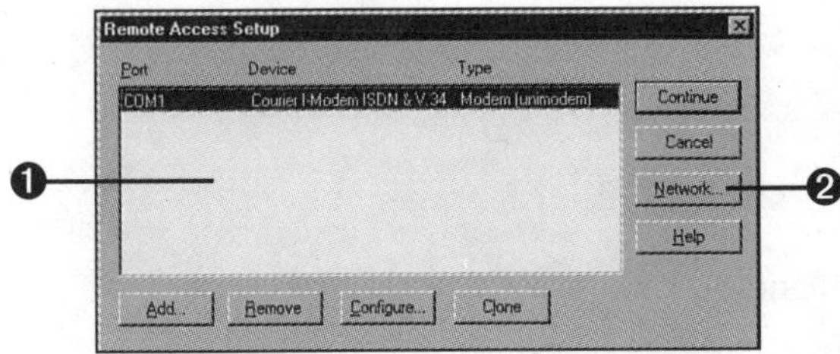

❶ The Add and Remove buttons do pretty much what you would expect. The Configure button opens the Configure Port Usage dialog box, shown in *Figure 4.37*. The Clone button is used to duplicate a RAS Device configuration. Click on Continue to proceed with the installation.

❷ The Network Button allows you to configure the network protocols. Clicking on this button opens the Network Configuration dialog box, shown in *Figure 4.38*.

> **NOTE**
>
> Each RAS Device can have a completely separate configuration. Some can be configured for Dial Out, Receive, or both.

FIGURE 4.37
Configuring the Port Usage for the RAS Device.

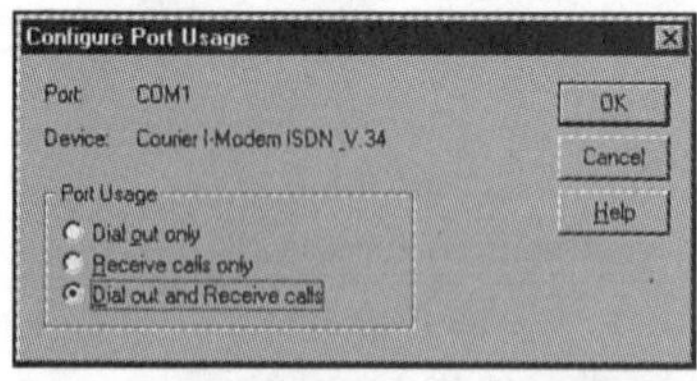

FIGURE 4.38
The Network Configuration dialog box.

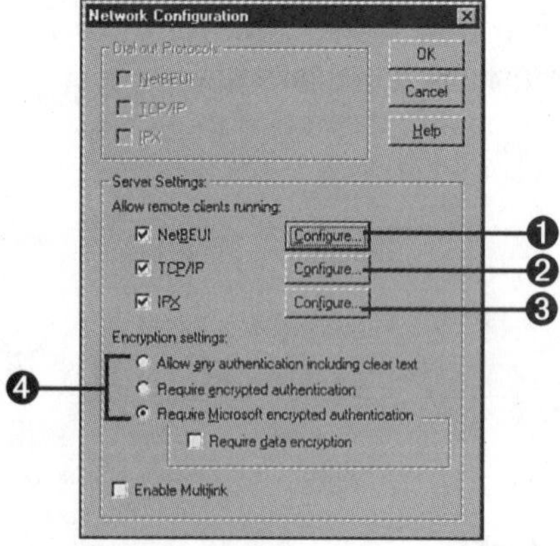

1. The NetBEUI settings configuration window is opened by clicking on this button (see *Figure 4.39*).
2. The TCP/IP settings configuration window is opened by clicking on this button (see *Figure 4.40*).
3. The IPX settings configuration window is opened by clicking on this button (see *Figure 4.41*).
4. These option buttons allow you to set the level of encryption used for the connection.

FIGURE 4.39
The NetBEUI routing configuration screen.

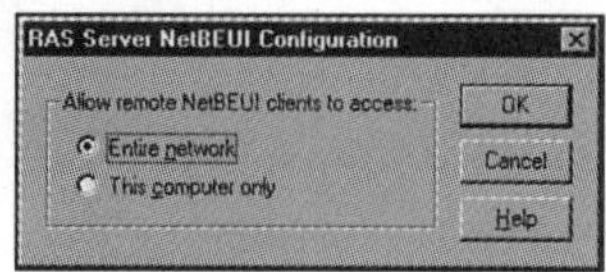

> **NOTE** For each protocol you have available, you are asked for configuration information. For NetBEUI, you'll be asked if the remote user should be using only the dial-up server, or can access the entire network.

FIGURE 4.40
Configuring TCP/IP RAS protocol.

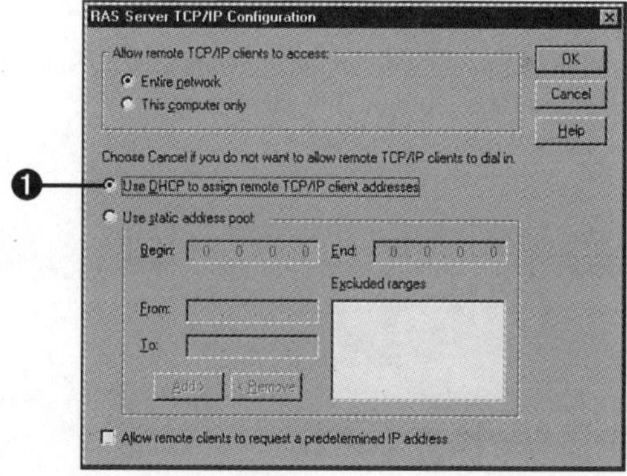

1. You can configure DCHP within this screen. After DCHP is activated, remote users can set their machines for DHCP and they will still be able to access the server, but not the network. Note that you can also allow the users to use their own TCP/IP address.

FIGURE 4.41
Configuring the IPX RAS protocol.

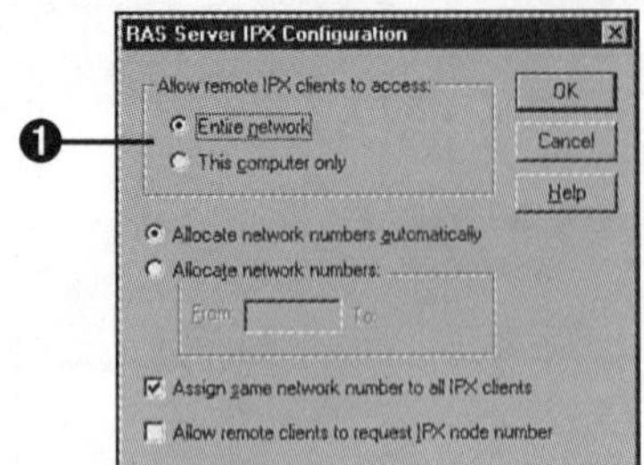

1 Again, you can configure where the user can go with routing. With IPX, you also have a number of options for configuring the IPX network numbers for the client. The defaults generally work for most environments.

> **NOTE** Note that loading the Remote Access Server also adds the RIP for IPX routing service to the system. That's so that IPX clients can access their networks through the IPX routes.

You're halfway through the primary objective. RAS is installed, so now you must configure it.

Configuring and Administering RAS

To configure RAS access, you can go to one of two places. Chapter 3 discussed creating a user with User Manager for Domains. One of the parameters you configured during the scenario is to enable Remote Access. Select that check box to enable access.

The other way to configure the Remote Access Server is to use the Remote Access Admin. This allows you to enable users for dial in, as well as see who is connected. After you have enabled the users, you have completed the primary objective for this scenario.

Dial Up Networking

Dial Up Networking (DUN) is Windows NT's version of a dialup client. Windows 95/98 uses a similar mechanism for its Internet (and other types) of PPP connections. It's a very simple mechanism that allows you to set a phone number and location, and also allows you to create a phonebook for multiple places to dial. This is the client component of the Remote Access Service. I have not seen any questions on this for either of the NT Server exams, although because configuring dial-up networking clients is an objective, we have covered it briefly here.

Virtual Private Networking Using the Point-to-Point Tunneling Protocol

Point to Point Protocol (PPTP), a secure form of the PPP protocol discussed previously, is Microsoft's answer to the rapidly growing segment of the market known as Virtual Private Networking (VPN). A *VPN* allows a network node or a segment to connect to another network across a public network (like the Internet), while still providing the same level of security (or almost the same) as a private WAN connection would. The security is provided by using strong encryption technology to keep snooping eyes out.

The main advantage to using technology like this is cost. If you have a branch office that is connected to the Internet, and your office is also connected to the Internet, it is significantly cheaper to implement a PPTP solution using the existing connection than it is to pay for a dedicated line. You are, however, subject to any Internet congestion, outages, and routing issues. Some of the major frame-relay vendors are setting up private/public networks, which allow companies to use VPNs on a shared network. It would be a network restricted to customers paying for the service, and would run entirely on the vendor's network backbone, so there is an added measure of control, security, and reliability.

One interesting facet of PPTP that separates it from a lot of the VPN competition is the fact that is "protocol neutral." Many VPN solutions are restricted to passing IP traffic only. Because PPTP is an offshoot of PPP, Microsoft is able to safely send TCP/IP, IPX, or NetBEUI across the virtual connection.

That is probably as clear as mud if you are not familiar with how VPNs can be used. Take a look at the following VPN scenario for a feel for how VPNs are used in the real world.

Scenario 4.7

You have just been tasked with the job of providing the company's 200 sales representatives with access to the production network. The company doesn't want to spend the big money for a 1-800-number dial-in solution, but has agreed to provide dialup Internet accounts to all the sales representatives.

Required Results

- Give the sales representatives access to the network using the Internet dialup accounts, while not compromising security.

Required Results

- It would be nice if you could use your Windows NT domain user accounts and passwords to authenticate the users.

You get one guess as to what the answer is. You guessed it—use PPTP. You won't find a long simulation for this because you've already done most of what this requires earlier in the chapter. What your users will do to connect to the network is as follows:

1. Install the latest PPTP client software, available from Microsoft.
2. Connect to the Internet using the dialup account.
3. Load the PPTP client software, and make a connection to the company's PPTP server.
4. When prompted, enter their user ID and password.
5. When authentication is complete, the users' PCs operate as extensions of the production network. All their data to anything on the corporate network is encrypted by the PPTP protocol, and remains secure.

You have successfully completed both objectives. There are a number of ways that this could be implemented, and a number of client configurations that are involved as well. But they are well beyond the scope of this exam. This scenario is intended to illustrate the uses for PPTP as a VPN technology, not as a "how-to" primer to complete the installation.

CHAPTER 5

Monitoring and Optimization

This chapter helps you prepare for the "Monitoring and Optimization" sections of the Windows NT Server (Exam 70-067) and Windows NT Server Enterprise (Exam 70-068) exams. You'll see monitoring and optimization questions on both exams because being able to tell when a server is reaching its capacity is a critical skill in Windows NT support. On the Enterprise exam you will also need to be familiar with monitoring the network, which is an important skill in an enterprise environment.

For Exam 70-067, the Windows NT Server Exam, Microsoft defines "Monitoring and Optimization" objectives as follows:

- Monitor performance of various functions by using Performance Monitor, including Processor, Memory, Disk, and Network.

  For this objective, you need to be familiar with how to use Performance Monitor to monitor the performance of the major components of the server hardware.

- Identify performance bottlenecks.

After you're able to monitor the preceding components, you need to be sure you know how to identify bottlenecks with the same components.

For Exam 70-068, the Windows NT Server in the Enterprise Exam, Microsoft defines "Monitoring and Optimization" objectives as follows:

- Establish a baseline for measuring system performance by creating a database of measurement data.

  If you plan to monitor the performance of a system, you need to be able to set a baseline. When you have a problem with the system, you can compare the results against the baseline. Without a baseline, you cannot determine what's changed.

- Monitor performance of various functions by using Performance Monitor, including Processor, Memory, Disk, and Network.

  As in the 70-67 exam, you need to be familiar with how to use Performance Monitor to monitor the performance of the major components of the server hardware.

- Monitor network traffic by using Network Monitor. Tasks include collecting, presenting, and filtering data.

  The Enterprise exam takes performance monitoring to its next level, that of network monitoring.

- Identify performance bottlenecks.

  Once again, you need to be sure you know how to identify bottlenecks with the system components.

- Optimize performance for controlling network traffic or controlling server load.

  Finally, you need to know how to tune the operating system in order to optimize the server for its tasks. For a web server, where most of the activity is occurring across the network, you might want to optimize for network activity. For a calculation-intensive application server, controlling server load might be more appropriate.

This chapter covers monitoring and optimization of the Windows NT network operating system. It discusses baselining the system—the how and the why. This chapter talks about using Performance Monitor to monitor and report on the system statistics, including Disk, Memory, Processor, and Network. It also talks about using Network Monitor to monitor network statistics. This chapter covers some of the other tools you can use to monitor the system's health, and concludes with how to best optimize Windows NT's performance for specific activities. However, before you get ahead of yourself, you should first focus on why you should monitor Windows NT.

SYSTEM MONITORING

One of the key concepts this chapter discusses is system monitoring. It is relatively easy to set up a Windows NT server and get users connected to it. Oddly enough, most administrators do not spend every day installing Windows NT servers. A large part of their job, beyond user management and support, is maintaining the server. It's very easy to just say an administrator maintains the server, but what does that mean? In large part, it means that an administrator must be proactive, and monitor the server. An administrator should be the first person to know when the server is almost out of disk space, when processor utilization is spiking to 100% at 11:00 every morning, or if the network is being flooded with errors from a failing ethernet adapter. In this section you'll look at some of the tools you can use to perform these functions. In addition, this chapter presents all the information you'll need to pass this section of the Windows NT exams.

Resources to Monitor

Before we start looking at scenarios, briefly look at the four resources you should be monitoring:

- Processor
- Memory
- Disk
- Network

These resources are discussed in the following sections.

Processor

The processor can be considered the heart of the system. Processor performance is critical to everything the system does, and making sure the processor is not being overutilized is one of the first things to check when you have a server that appears to be running slowly.

Windows NT supports *symmetric multiprocessing*, which means you can have multiple CPUs processing system requests. Windows NT can have up to 32 processors. If you have a *multithreaded application*, you can even have different application threads being processed by different CPUs. Windows NT's monitoring utilities allow you to monitor each individual processor, as well as some aggregate statistics.

Memory

There are two sorts of memory to be monitored in a Windows NT server:

- *Random Access Memory (RAM)*. The physical memory in the server.
- *Virtual Memory*. The cache memory for the system's pagefile. The pagefile is used to store information from RAM when RAM is full.

A general rule of thumb for memory in a server is to put in as much as you can afford. (There are very few applications that function poorly with too *much* memory.) Memory tends to be the first place you find bottlenecks because many of today's applications are extremely memory intensive.

One thing that can affect the performance of virtual memory is the location of the pagefile. If you place the pagefile on a slow hard drive, system performance will be slow. If you either spread the pagefile across multiple hard drives, or place it on a striped disk array, you will see better performance for your virtual memory. Microsoft also recommends that you place the pagefile on a hard drive separate from the system files, if possible. If that drive is also on a separate controller, you should get even better pagefile performance. {*For more information on RAID arrays, see Chapter 1, "Planning."*}

Disk

> **NOTE** In order to monitor disk statistics, you must issue the command `diskperf -y`. You will need to reboot the server. After you are done monitoring, be sure to turn off disk monitoring with `diskperf -n`. This feature does add some overhead to the system.

Disk performance can be one of the most complicated areas of performance monitoring and optimization. That's because hard drives are generally the slowest component on the system. Compared to RAM, disk access is an order of magnitude slower. There are also a number of other things that impact disk performance:

- Drive type
- Controller type
- Number of controllers/disks
- Type of disk usage

Drive Type

The measure of a hard drive is always taken in access time. A year ago a 10-millisecond access time was considered fast, whereas 2- to 3-millisecond drives are now becoming increasingly common. IDE drives are usually slower than SCSI drives, and there are a number of different types of SCSI formats. SCSI-1, SCSI-2, Fast SCSI-2, and SCSI-3 are the common SCSI formats for hard drives.

A few metrics that are gaining popularity are the revolutions per minute (RPM), and the maximum data transfer rate. It is becoming more common to see the RPMs listed as part of the drive description. The key to drive types is to match the drive technology to the rest of the system. You wouldn't run a slow SCSI-1 drive on a SCSI-3 controller—it would slow the entire system down.

Controller Type

There are a number of different controllers available on the market today, at a variety of transfer speeds. Table 5.1 lists some of the common controller types.

TABLE 5.1

COMMON DISK CONTROLLER TYPES

Drive Type	*Maximum Transfer Rate*
IDE	Approx. 2.5 MB/sec
EIDE	Approx. 16.6 MB/sec
SCSI-1	Approx. 4.0 MB/sec
SCSI-2	Approx. 5.0 MB/sec
Fast SCSI-2	Approx. 10.0 MB/sec
Fast Wide SCSI	Approx. 20.0 MB/sec
Ultra2 SCSI / SCSI-3	Approx. 40.0 MB/sec
Wide Ultra2 SCSI	Approx. 80.0 MB/sec

Another thing to consider about controllers is whether they support RAID. A RAID-5 (Disk striping with parity) controller is of much higher performance than a standard hard drive, due to the additional read/write heads in the additional drives. Also, a hardware RAID implementation is much faster than a Windows NT software implementation because the processing associated with maintaining the array is offloaded to the controller's processor, and removed from the operating system and the CPU.

Number of Controllers/Disks

Another factor when considering disk controllers and performance is the number of drive controllers installed. The more disk controllers you have installed, the more aggregate throughput you have available to the system. If you can get 5 MB per second from one SCSI-2 controller, you can get up to 10 MB per second with two SCSI-2 controllers. There is certainly a point of diminished returns, especially when you begin to reach the throughput levels of the system bus, but in a lot of cases an additional controller can significantly improve performance.

Additional hard drives can also improve performance. Each hard drive on the system adds an additional read/write head to disk operations. As discussed in Chapter 1, disk striping (multiple drives in a single array) is the highest performance drive configuration because of the array's capability to perform concurrent reads and writes. Therefore, if you have four drives in an array, theoretically you can move four times as much data written to or read from the hard drives. As with the controllers, there is a point of diminished returns, but additional drives can certainly improve system performance.

The highest performance disk controllers are *bus mastering* controllers. Bus mastering controllers have an onboard processor that handles interrupt requests. This offloads the disk-processing overhead from the system processor. These controllers also transfer data directly to memory. When the CPU is available, it processes the data directly from memory. This reduces the number of interrupts the CPU must handle.

Disk Usage

When we say *disk usage*, what we are really saying is the use of the server. In other words, a database server with a large number of records affects disk performance more heavily than a file and print server, in which users are simply storing word processing documents and printing memos. The size of database records or files being stored can also affect performance. If you are designing a high-end database server, you should be looking at the fastest drives possible, preferably in a hardware RAID configuration, and with multiple controllers, if possible.

For single processor servers, Microsoft recommends using a SCSI-2 controller as the minimum.

Network

The final piece of the performance puzzle is the network. Just as with the disk performance, there are a number of factors to take into account when you assess network performance. The most significant factors include the following:

- Network adapter type
- Number of adapters
- Number of protocols
- Additional network services
- Amount of traffic
- Network infrastructure

These factors are discussed in the following sections.

Network Adapter Type

This might be obvious, but it is important to remember that an Arcnet adapter, which runs at 2 MB/sec., offers slower performance then a Gigabit Ethernet connection, which offers 1 GB/sec. throughput. Between these two extremes are 10 MB Ethernet, 100 MB Ethernet, 4 MB Token Ring, 16 MB Token Ring, and even 100 MB Arcnet, if you can still find the adapters. The media that a network interface card offers are very important to performance metrics. The speed of the adapter affects the server's network performance.

The bus type of the adapter is also important to performance calculations. An 8-bit ISA adapter is significantly slower than a 64-bit PCI adapter. A good rule of thumb for this is to try to use PCI adapters whenever possible. If you have an EISA bus, try to use 32-bit cards. With ISA, you are limited to 16-bit cards, but that is still better than an 8-bit card: You have twice as wide a data path to the CPU and the other components.

Network adapters are also available with their own processors. This is a useful feature because it offloads a lot of the traffic processing from the system CPU, and leaves it on the network adapter. In a high-traffic environment in which the server is forced to process a large number of packets, a processor on the network adapter can be the difference between a functional server and a paperweight with hard drives.

Number of Adapters

This factor can actually be a double-edged sword. Just as with the disk controllers discussed previously, additional network interface cards can provide additional throughput to the system. On the other hand, if the additional cards are being used in conjunction with routing activities, the additional processing required by the routing function (covered in the "Additional Network Services" section of the chapter) could negate the advantage of multiple cards.

Suppose you have a Windows NT Application server in an environment with two separate networks. If you put two cards in the server, with one on each network, users on either network would be able to reach the server without being forced to cross a router, which can add *latency* (additional time) to the connection.

Now take the same configuration, but with the Windows NT server acting as the router between segments, instead of using a separate router. In order for Windows NT to act as a router, you generally need to load a routing protocol service. In many instances, you need to load them for TCP/IP and IPX. These services use system resources. Now every packet that must be routed generates an interrupt on the card that receives it. The routing function must then check the packet to determine the best route, and forward it if necessary. If it is forwarded to the other network, it must go out the other ethernet adapter, where it generates yet another interrupt. These interrupts, and the buffers used to store the packets as they are analyzed, impact system performance, and in many instances can balance or negate the advantage of the two network adapters.

Number of Protocols

This is an easy one. Just remember that protocol equals overhead. For every protocol the system is using, additional system resources must be dedicated to communications. For example, if you have IPX and TCP/IP loaded on the system, the system must advertise itself for both protocols. If you add things like network browsing or the Workstation and Server services, to name a few, the overhead can become substantial.

Whenever possible, try to limit the number of protocols used by the system. If you can't limit the protocols, try to disable any unneeded services using both protocols.

Additional Network Services

Services like routing, DNS, DHCP, WINS, and others all add overhead to the network processing. As with the additional protocols, any additional network services add overhead to the system. Whenever possible, limit the number of additional services running on a server. As an example, every Windows NT server in your enterprise does not need to be a DNS server.

Be especially careful when you are using your server as a LAN or WAN router. Not only does this use add a lot of overhead to your server, but software routing is also generally less efficient than a hardware implementation. This can induce latency in network communications.

Amount of Network Traffic

There are two ways to look at network traffic and its impact on performance. First, a highly congested network gives the appearance of slow server performance because the congestion requires many packet rebroadcasts.

The second issue with a highly congested network is the fact that the server needs to process all those packets. While network interface cards are available with on-board processors, which can significantly reduce the load on the server CPU, you must be aware of what your traffic levels should normally be, what sort of card you have, and what the impact of the traffic will be on the server. Large amounts of traffic directed to the server can even cause the server to stop running. If you are familiar with Internet connectivity, you may have heard of something called a Denial of Service (DoS) attack, which hackers often use to try to shut down a server or network. This can be accomplished in a number of ways, but most involve arranging for the server to be attacked with huge amounts of traffic, so it is either swamped under the traffic, or crashes entirely.

Network Infrastructure

The final piece of the network puzzle is not really part of the server at all, but can have a significant impact on the server's performance. What does this mean to an administrator? Well, be aware of where you routers are. Know what path users must take in order to access the server. If you are running an application server for the accounting department, make sure it's not six network hops away from the users. Also, be aware that older routers don't handle traffic as efficiently as newer ones. Switches generally yield a faster network response time than a hub or router-based Local Area Network. You also need to know how the routers are configured. Do your routers forward NetBios traffic? If so, they can add to the broadcast traffic on your network. Are the switches on your network Layer 2 or Layer 3? Although this is not a section that is intended to teach you everything you need to know about networking, it's a good thing to become familiar with networking as you progress in your career.

Now that you've covered the basics of what to look for, take a look at how to monitor the critical pieces of your Windows NT server.

Performance Monitor

The major application for monitoring performance is Performance Monitor, which can be found in the Administrator Tools program group. Performance Monitor collects data about system resources and then presents them in a graphical format for interpretation by an administrator. Performance Monitor can be used for a number of tasks, including the following:

- *Establishing System Baselines.* Establishing baselines, as you see in the next section, is a critical ability to master if you truly want to be able to monitor the system. If you don't know how the system performs when things are running normally, you will be at a severe disadvantage when you start looking for bottlenecks on a misbehaving system.
- *Identifying Bottlenecks.* After you've established your system baseline, you can monitor it periodically to find out whether you are approaching bottlenecks on any of the system's components. This is a particularly useful task when you are trying to justify upgrades to the system. Management loves to see facts when justifying spending several thousand dollars on upgrades.

- *Monitoring Resource Usage over a Period of Time.* Not only can you do spot checks from time to time to identify bottlenecks, but you can also run Performance Monitor to see how resources are utilized over a period of time. This is especially useful when you are performing trend analysis or capacity planning. For example, suppose you are monitoring memory usage. If you watch the monitor, you will notice that the amount of available RAM is reduced as you install more applications. Before this becomes an issue, you can see the trend and upgrade the server memory before it becomes an emergency.
- *Performing Capacity Planning.* With Performance Monitor, you can collect information with set parameters, and by altering the parameters, you can determine future resource requirements. For example, if you have 10 typical users connecting to a web server, you can take the data related to their system usage and determine the requirements (approximately, of course) for 1,000 users. This type of proactive capacity planning is something that many organizations lack these days, and is a very useful skill for any administrator.
- *Troubleshooting.* Performance Monitor can provide valuable information if you are having problems with the system. Performance Monitor can quickly identify abnormal resource utilization, and can help reduce the time needed to track down problems with a system that is having problems.

All of these things are critical to your ability to effectively administer a Windows NT server. There is nothing more embarrassing than going to management with a rush purchase order for another hard disk because the database has suddenly filled the volume and you weren't expecting or prepared for it.

Before you get to the scenarios, take a look at some of Windows NT's definitions for monitoring resources on the system.

Understanding Performance Monitor Information and Terminology

It's important to understand how Performance Monitor organizes its information. When you are monitoring a system, you are really monitoring the behavior of its *objects.* What exactly does that mean? Windows NT uses objects to identify system resources. The Processor, Disk, Network, and so on, are all objects. *Objects* can represent processes, sections of shared memory, and physical devices. Performance Monitor then uses these objects to organize the counters. Each object has its own set of *counters* for gathering statistical information. Some objects and counters are standard on all NT systems, whereas others are either application- or process-specific. SQL Server has a unique set of objects and counters that are only available on a system with SQL loaded on it.

Another interesting fact about what Performance Monitor can monitor is that each object can appear multiple times. For example, if you have a system with four processors in it, each processor will have its own set of counters. Memory and Server, however, are two objects that cannot have multiple instances because you can have only one instance of each in a single server.

One other piece of the puzzle is the concept of threads. From Performance Monitor's perspective, *threads* exist as objects within processes. These objects then execute program instructions. Only applications have threads. Threads allow concurrent operations within a process and enable one process to simultaneously execute different parts of its program on different processors. This is where the concept of a multi-threaded application comes from. In Performance Monitor, each thread on a system shows up as an instance for the Thread object type and is associated with its parent process.

Now that you understand the terminology of system performance monitoring, take a look at a scenario on how to go about doing it.

> **NOTE**
>
> If you have an administrator account on a server or in the domain, you can also remotely monitor other Windows NT servers by selecting them in the browse list. In cases in which you want to be extremely accurate in your measurements, it's a good idea to monitor the server remotely. Performance Monitor, while designed to use few resources, does add overhead to whatever system it is running on. This can alter the information you obtain from the system.

Scenario 5.1

You've just installed an IIS-based Web server, and management wants to be sure that the server is up to the task. They've asked you to monitor the system performance and determine whether the system needs to be upgraded as usage climbs.

Required Results

- Before you can learn anything about the server's performance, you have to set a baseline. For this scenario, we'll just baseline processor utilization.
- After you've gotten your baseline, you need to monitor memory usage, processor utilization, disk usage, and network utilization.
- Configure a log file in which to store data for review. This is kind of a trick objective, because it is the same as baselining the system, the first objective. *Baselining* is just the act of storing information prior to having server problems, so that when you have a problem, you have some information to go back and look at to tell what's changed.

cont.

Scenario 5.1 cont.

- Configure a report on the important parameters of each resource that you are monitoring.

Required Results

- Now that you are monitoring all these functions, you'd really like to generate an alert any time that the processor utilization exceeds 80%.

Begin the scenario by looking at baselining the system.

> **NOTE** For the purpose of this scenario, you will be picking parameters for the illustration of Performance Monitor's capabilities. You should consider what parameters affect your server, and implement monitoring for them appropriately. Don't assume that because you see a parameter monitored in this scenario that it will be appropriate for your situation.

There are a number of ways to establish a baseline, depending on your requirements. Take an overview of an easy way to establish a baseline before you follow along in a scenario:

1. From the Log View of Performance Monitor, click on the + sign and add any of the metrics you need to monitor. It is very important to realize that baselining a system can vary widely from system to system. You might want to refer to the "Resource Monitoring" section of this chapter for some ideas about what to baseline.
2. After you have added all the items you want to monitor, click on the Options icon. This opens the Log Options dialog box. Decide where you want to store this information, give the log a name (baseline plus the date is always a good idea) and click on Start Log. You'll notice that the button then becomes Stop Log. This is what appears when the log is running.
3. Let this log run for at least 24 hours. If you have the disk space, and you think system use is heavier on certain days of the week, let it run for a week. When you feel you have collected enough data, go back to the Log View in Performance Monitor and open the Options dialog box as you did in step 2. Click on the Stop Log button.
4. Review the information in the log so you are aware of what your baseline looks like, and then keep the file for later comparisons.

These steps take care of two objectives for the price of one. Now take a look at how to do real-time monitoring of the system:

1. To perform real-time monitoring, go to the Chart View of Performance Monitor, shown in *Figure 5.1*.
2. Click on the + sign to open the Add to Chart dialog box shown in *Figure 5.2*. Add a counter for each of the objects discussed. Click Add after you add each counter.
3. You just finished your second objective. Performance Monitor is monitoring the parameters you have selected. Now you need to analyze the results of those parameters. That's the tricky part. You will find more information about what these parameters indicate in the "Monitoring System Resources" section of the chapter.

That completes three of the primary objectives. Now take a look at getting the secondary objective finished, and then wrap up the scenario with the final objective.

Baselining the System

Before you start monitoring any server, you need to establish the baseline. To start this process, open to Performance Monitor in the Administrative Tools program group. You will see the Chart View of Performance Monitor in *Figure 5.1*.

FIGURE 5.1

The Chart View of Performance Monitor is used to show the ongoing results of any resources being monitored.

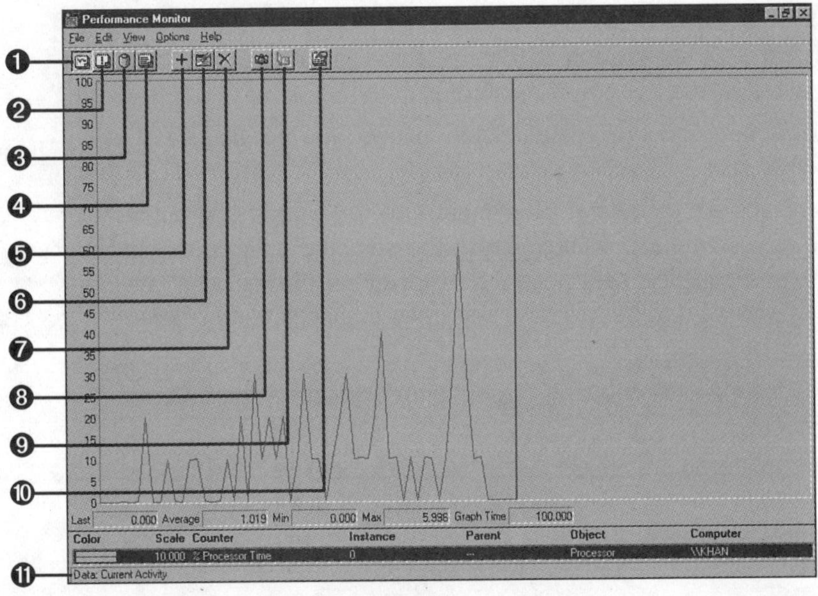

FIGURE 5.1 *Cont.*

❶ The View a Chart button brings up the Chart View displayed in this figure. You can also reach this view by going to the View menu, and selecting Chart, or by typing Ctrl + C. If you are moving from view to view, this brings you back to the active chart.

❷ The View the Alerts button is used to view any alerts generated by Performance Monitor. (You will learn how alerts can be configured later in the scenario.) You can also reach this view by going to View, Alert, or you can type Ctrl + A. You can configure an alert on any of the things that you can chart.

❸ The View Output Log File Status button is used to configure and check the status of a log file you have configured to store server statistics for later review. This is a great way to store statistics for your baseline. You can also reach this view by going to View, Log, or you can type Ctrl + L.

❹ The View Report Data button allows you to view and configure reports on the statistics that Performance Monitor is gathering. You can also reach this view by going to View, Reports, or you can type Ctrl + R.

❺ Clicking on the + sign opens the Add to Chart dialog box, where you can add another counter to the Chart View.

❻ The Modify button opens a dialog box displaying the properties for an existing counter. You can modify existing settings as needed. For multiple counters, you can select the counter you want to modify from the list at the bottom of the screen.

❼ Click the Delete button to delete whatever counter you have selected at the bottom of the screen.

❽ The Update counter data button allows you to update the counter data.

❾ The Place a Commented Bookmark into the Output Log button allows you to place a comment at the selected point in the log file. This can be useful if you plan to review the log at a later point and want to be able to quickly find a specific time or event in the log.

❿ The Options button opens the options for each of the different views.

⓫ The monitored counters section of the screen contains the list of counters being monitored. If you need to delete or modify a counter, you select it here.

Clicking the Modify button on the Performance Monitor screen will open a dialog box similar to that shown in *Figure 5.2*.

FIGURE 5.2
Adding a counter to the running chart.

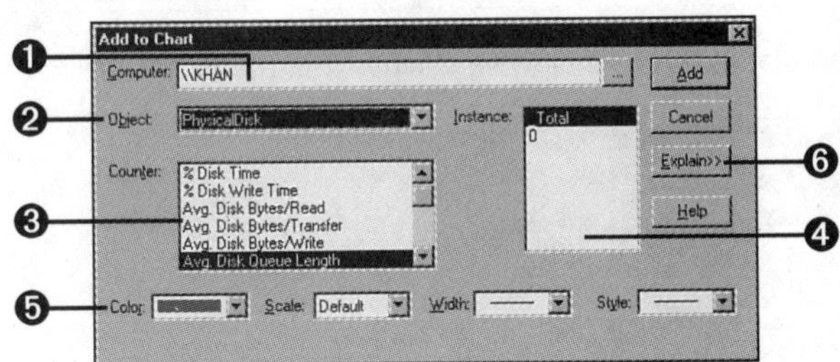

❶ The Computer window allows you to specify which computer the counter is monitoring. The Browse button (...) enables you to browse the network for the system you want to monitor.

❷ The Object pull-down box allows you to select the object you want to monitor. For the scenario, you should add counters for the processor, disk, network, and memory objects. After selecting the appropriate counters (dependent on what you are trying to monitor) click on Add each time and you have completed one of your primary objectives.

❸ The Counter list contains all the counters available for monitoring the object you have selected.

❹ The Instance box is used in only two cases. First, if the counter you are monitoring benefits from a total, you will see one instance for the actual activity of the counter, and another for the total. The other time you will see multiple instances is when there are multiples of the object being charted. For example, a quad-processor system would have four instances for the processor object's counters. Each processor can be monitored separately.

❺ These four windows (Color, Scale, Width, and Style) allow you to customize the appearance of the line for the counter being charted. You can change the color, style, the numeric scale, and the width of the line. Be careful not to select the same color for two different counters. It can be very confusing.

❻ The Explain button is every administrator's favorite feature of Performance Monitor. It gives you a thumbnail definition of the selected counter.

Click on the Explain button (refer to *Figure 5.2*) to see a thumbnail explanation of a selected counter (see *Figure 5.3*). Prior to the exam, it's not a bad idea to read through some of the explanations of the counters, just so you have a better feel for what Performance Monitor is doing for you on the system.

FIGURE 5.3
The Explain button expands the dialog box to include a Counter Definition.

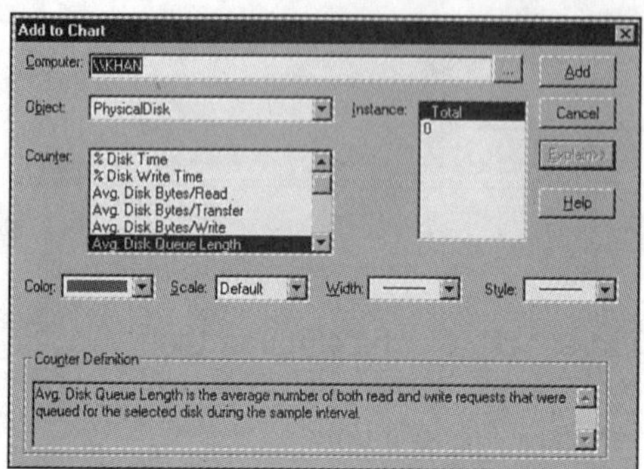

Click on the Options button (refer to *Figure 5.1*) in the Chart view to use the Chart Options dialog box (shown in *Figure 5.4*) to customize the look and feel of the running Chart. You can add grid lines, change the update interval, and change the type of graph displayed.

FIGURE 5.4
The Chart Options dialog box.

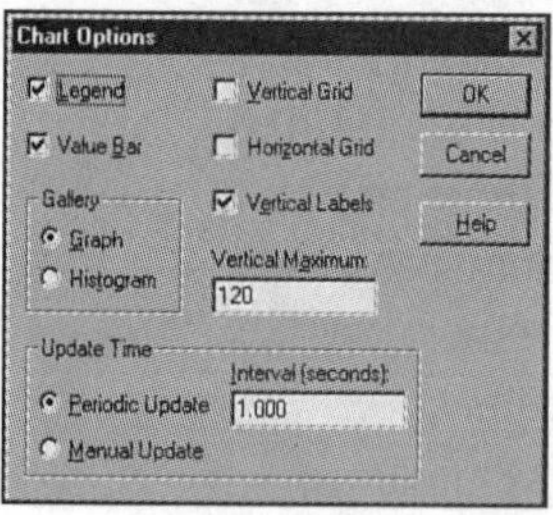

Alert View

Click the View the Alerts button to view any alerts generated by Performance Monitor. The view in *Figure 5.5* is used to show the results of any configured alerts.

This is where we will finish the scenario by configuring an alert. To set up an alert, do the following:

1. To configure an alert, open Performance Monitor, and switch to the Alert View (see *Figure 5.5*).
2. Click on the + sign to add an alert. This opens the Add to Alert dialog box, shown in *Figure 5.6*.
3. Make sure the Object is Processor, and select the %Processor Time counter.
4. In the Alert If box, enter 80%, and select the Over option button.
5. Click on Add and you have completed the secondary objective. One more to go!

FIGURE 5.5
The Alert View of Performance Monitor.

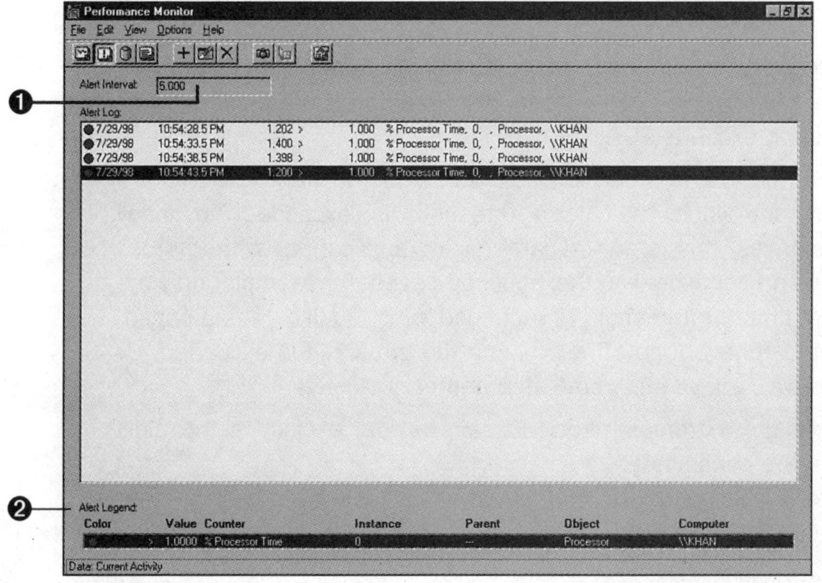

❶ The Alert Interval indicates the amount of time between Performance Monitor system checks. In this scenario, Performance Monitor is checking the system every five minutes to see if the alarm threshold has been exceeded. This interval can be modified by clicking on the Options button.

❷ The Alert Legend shows you the parameters of any alerts you have configured on the system. If you need to delete or modify an alert, you can select it here and click on the appropriate button.

When in the Alert View, you can click on the + button to add an alert (see *Figure 5.6*) or the Options button to view the alert options (see *Figure 5.7*).

FIGURE 5.6
Adding an alert to the Alert View.

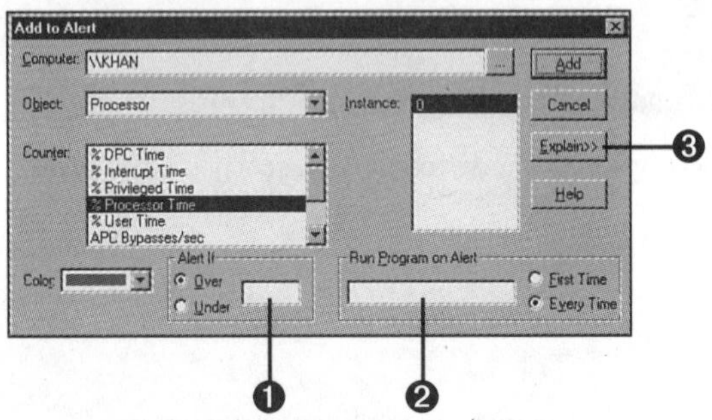

❶ The Alert If section allows you to set the threshold for the alert. For example, you can set the alert to alarm if the processor utilization exceeds 90%.

❷ The Run Program on Alert box is used if you want to execute a program when the alarm threshold is exceeded. In many instances, this is a third-party paging application. With this box you can configure whether you'll be paged (for example) only the first time the threshold is exceeded, or if you like getting paged, you can have it go off every time the threshold is exceeded. By the way, you've just completed another objective.

❸ Note the extremely useful Explain button, explaining the alert you are configuring.

FIGURE 5.7
The Alert Options dialog box.

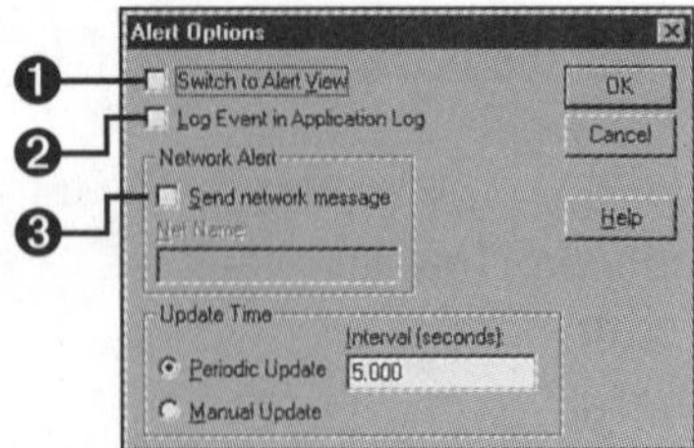

FIGURE 5.7 *cont.*

❶ The Switch to Alert View check box causes Performance Monitor to switch to the Alert View as soon as a threshold is exceeded. This saves you needing to switch to the screen when you investigate the alert.

❷ You can have Performance Monitor alerts logged in the Event Log.

❸ You can configure Performance Monitor to send a network message when an alert exceeds its threshold. Just specify a Network Name for the server to receive the alert.

Log View

The View Output Log File Status button is used to configure and check the status of a log file in Performance Monitor. The Log View in *Figure 5.8* is used to show you the objects being stored to the log for review later.

FIGURE 5.8

The Log View of Performance Monitor.

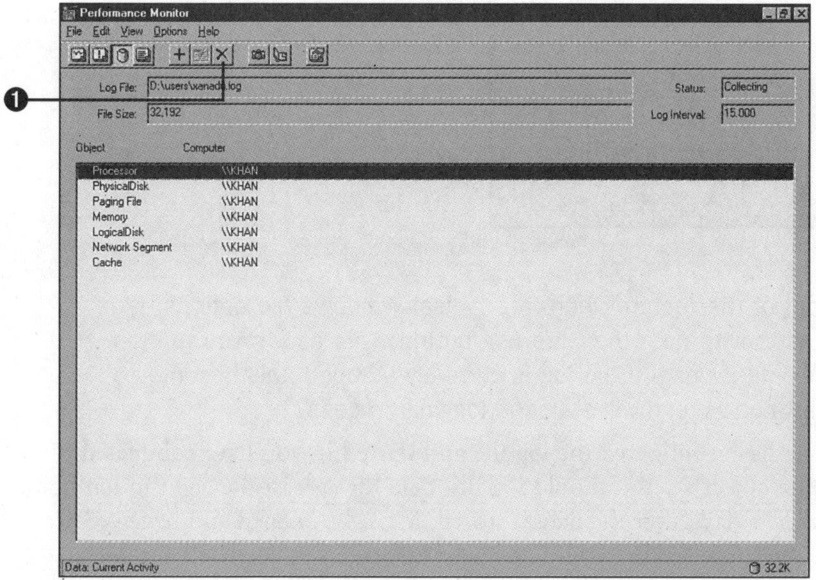

❶ Clicking on the X deletes the selected counter.

Adding an object to be logged is very straightforward: Just select the object you would like to add to the log, and click on the Add button (see *Figure 5.9*). Clicking the Options button opens the Log Options dialog box (see *Figure*

5.10). From here, you can modify the options associated with the log file you are building.

FIGURE 5.9
The Add to Log dialog box allows you to add objects to the log you are accumulating.

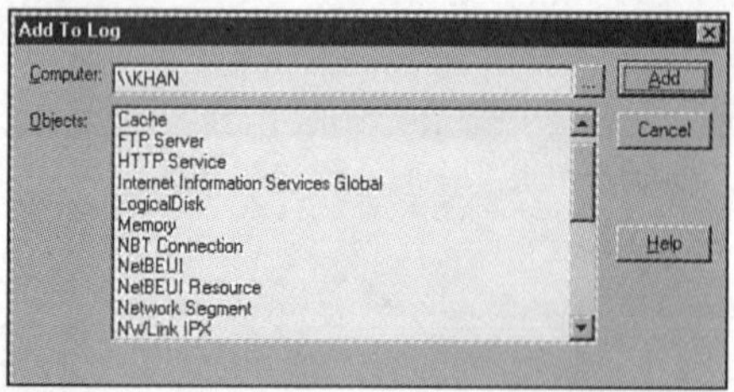

FIGURE 5.10
Setting the Log Options.

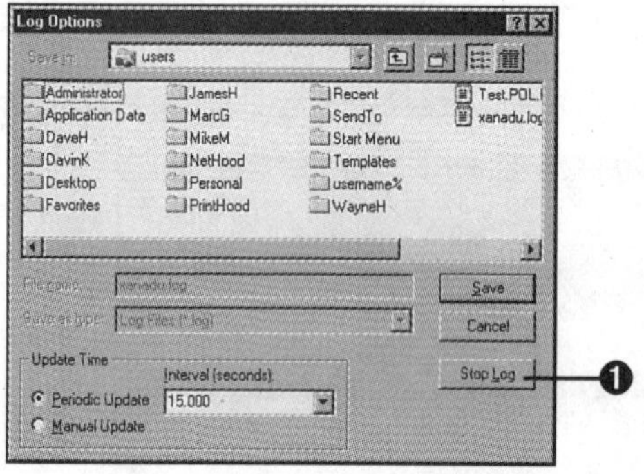

1. Most of the features here are typical Windows file options. It's important to note the Stop Log button. This allows you to stop the data logging. If the log is currently stopped, this becomes a Start button, and will start the logging process.

After you have configured the log file and started it, you have completed the baselining objective. You should log this data for at least the eight to ten hours of a business day. After the data is stored, it can be opened and reviewed at your leisure for checking your baseline statistics. Even better, if you do experience a problem, you have the ability to pull up this file and look to see what's changed since you set up the original Performance Monitor sessions.

Report View

The Report View of the Performance Monitor (see *Figure 5.11*) is used to configure reports based on a configurable list of objects and counters.

The final objective in this scenario is to generate a report. To generate a report, follow these steps:

1. Open the Report View of Performance Monitor, shown in *Figure 5.11*.
2. To add a counter to be reported on, click on the + sign. This opens *Figure 5.12*, the Add to Report dialog box. Select the counter you want to add to the report and click on Add.
3. Once you have added the counters you want to report on, you have successfully completed the final objective, and the scenario. Congratulations.

FIGURE 5.11
The Report View of Performance Monitor.

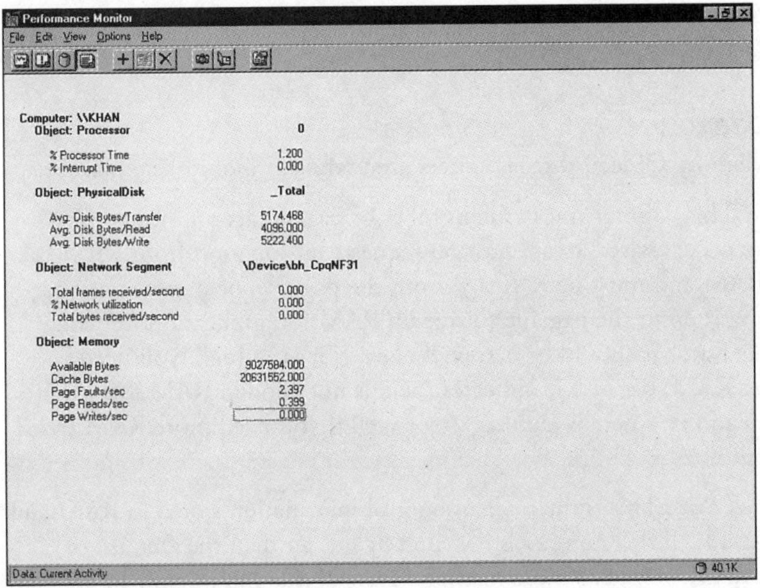

FIGURE 5.12
The Add to Report dialog box.

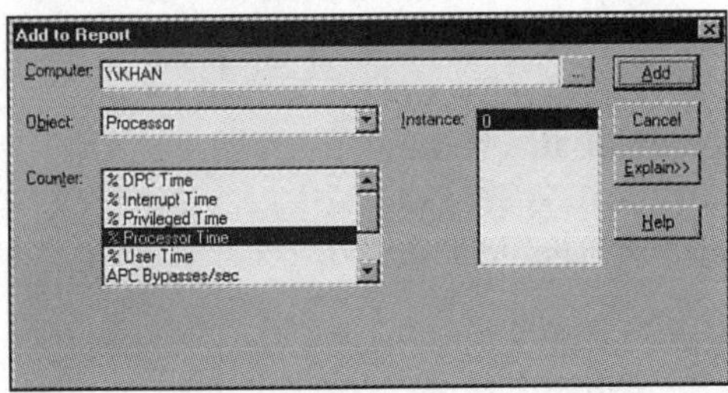

Clicking the Options button opens the Report Options dialog box (shown in *Figure 5.13*), in which you can choose a periodic or manual update.

FIGURE 5.13
The Report Options dialog box.

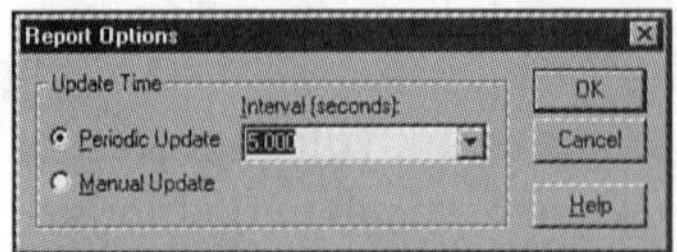

Monitor System Resources

Now that you have an idea of how to use the Performance Monitor application to gather information, you need to understand some of the ways to use the information.

Memory Usage

Under the Memory Object, three counters are useful for monitoring memory:

- *Pages/Sec.* This counter tracks the number of page faults on the system. A *page fault* occurs when an application requests information from RAM that isn't in RAM and must be retrieved from the pagefile, or if information must be written to the pagefile to free up RAM for application information. This number should be extremely low. If it's too high, you need to add more RAM, because it indicates there is not enough RAM to support the applications. There is another way to tell if you need more RAM based on this number.
- *Committed Bytes.* This is the total amount of information stored in RAM and in the pagefile. If this number is consistently greater than the amount of installed RAM, you need more memory. The pagefile should only be written to as a last resort for the application. Any disk I/0 is significantly slower than retrieving information from RAM, and can seriously affect performance.
- *Commit Limit.* This counter can be used to fine-tune the size of your pagefile. This counter tracks the amount of space remaining in the pagefile before it will need to be extended. When Windows NT is forced to automatically extend the size of the pagefile, it affects the performance of the system. Disk I/O, as mentioned previously, is very slow. By keeping track of this counter, you can make sure your pagefile is the correct size.

In many cases, the answer to memory issues is to add more RAM. The other piece of the memory puzzle is the pagefile. Microsoft's general rule for the pagefile is to take the amount of RAM in the system and make the pagefile the same size. That gives you the minimum for the pagefile. Set the maximum based on your requirements, or as a percentage of available diskspace.

Processor Utilization

Under the Processor object, there are four important counters to keep an eye on:

- *%Processor Time.* This counter tracks the total processor utilization. It's a bit too general to tell you precisely where the problem is, but it can give you a good idea that you're having utilization problems.
- *%User Time.* This tells you the amount of processor time that is being used by applications. If you have an application that is using a large amount of processing resources, it will show up here.
- *%Privileged Time.* This is the amount of utilization the Windows NT operating system (the Kernel) is using. If you have a system service that is using too much processor, this counter will tell you.
- *Interrupts/Sec.* This counter keeps track of the number of hardware interrupts the CPU is servicing. Your baseline is very useful if you think this is where the problem lies. It's tough to determine a good number for your processor to deal with. If you go back to your baseline, you'll be able to see if the number has risen significantly.

If you identify a processor issue, the best course of action is to upgrade the processor, or in the case of systems that support symmetric multiprocessing, you can add additional CPUs.

Disk Usage

Two different Performance Monitor objects relate to monitoring disk activity:

- The *PhysicalDisk* object counters track the activities related to the actual disk drive as a whole. If you are trying to balance disk activity, the PhysicalDisk counters can be used to see how the hardware drives in the system are being used. If you have one disk with very high usage, and another drive that is barely being used, you might want to look at moving an application or the pagefile to the underused disk.

- The *LogicalDisk* object deals with the partitions on the physical hard drive. These counters are useful for determining which partition is generating all the usage of the PhysicalDisk.

Disk Counters are virtually identical for both objects. Four counters are particularly useful for determining how well your drives are performing:

> **NOTE**
> Remember, if you want to get results for the disk counters, you need to go to a DOS prompt and type **`diskperf -y`**. This enables performance tracking for the hard drives.

- *%Disk Time.* This counter tracks the percentage of time the disk spent performing I/O processes. Consistently high values here indicate a heavily used drive. Moving files/applications that generate a lot of disk I/O to a different physical disk can help address this issue. Moving the pagefile is also a frequent solution to this problem.
- *Current Disk Queue Length.* This counter tracks the number of pending I/O write requests. If this number is consistently more than 2 or 3, you have a heavily utilized disk, and you should look into a faster drive, or offloading some of the load.
- *Disk Bytes/sec.* This counter shows you the data transfer rate for data onto and off the drive. The higher the number, the more efficient the drive's performance. Consistently low numbers could indicate a need for an upgrade. Degradation of this number over time could indicate a future drive failure.
- *Avg. Disk Bytes/Transfer.* This is very similar to the previous counter. The higher the number, the more efficient data transfers to and from the drive are.

If you have concerns about drive performance, you should do a couple things. First, move high-use applications (such as the pagefile) to less utilized drives. Next, you can look into implementing a striped array instead of single drives. Finally, you can upgrade to faster drives. You should also remember that the drive controller can be a bottleneck and may need to be upgraded.

Network Utilization

Network utilization is a bit trickier an object to try to measure. For example, if you have a very high Frames/sec counter, is it good? Well, it does indicate that you are processing many frames through the system. For a hard drive, a high amount of processing I/O is a good thing. But what if the reason the Frames/sec counter is high is that there is a network adapter on the network that is flooding the network with invalid broadcast traffic? Then that high I/O is actually a bad thing, because it indicates the network is broken.

If you identify a network bottleneck on the system, there are a couple things you can do. You can buy a faster network adapter, or you could install additional network adapters. You can also look into upgrading your network infrastructure. Removing unused services and protocols will also contribute to your network efficiency, due to the lower system overhead.

> **NOTE**
> You will be able to monitor TCP/IP counters only if you have the SNMP service installed.

Network Monitor

Network Monitor is to network performance as Performance Monitor is to your system performance monitoring. If you suspect there is a problem on the network, Network Monitor is the utility to help you find it.

> **NOTE**
> Keep in mind that the version of Network Monitor that ships with Windows NT can only monitor traffic to and from the system. If you need additional network monitoring, Microsoft recommends you use the version that ships with Microsoft's Systems Management Server.

You will use a scenario that presents a possible network issue, by monitoring performance, looking for bottlenecks, and then doing a packet analysis. But before you learn how to use Network Monitor, you must install it. Complete the following steps to install the Network Monitor:

1. Open the Network applet in the Control Panel.
2. Click on the Services tab.
3. Click on Add, and select Network Monitor Tools and Agent.
4. Click OK.
5. Reboot when the install is complete.

Monitor Network Performance

Before you begin with this scenario, it's important to understand that Network Monitor is an incredibly complex application. Although this book could spend the next 50 pages going through it in excruciating detail, fortunately, the exam does not ask you to know Network Monitor in quite that depth. In fact, just being able to analyze network traffic requires quite a bit more information than this book can cover. You should definitely explore this application in detail when you have Windows NT installed in a network environment. Now take a look at the next scenario.

Scenario 5.2

You have been told that there are problems with your server communicating to another server on the network. You need to get on the network and analyze the traffic, to ensure that traffic is moving correctly.

Required Results

- Prove that traffic is moving between the servers by capturing data.

Required Results

- Review the network traffic for errors or bad frames.

To get started with the objective, go to the Administrative Tools program group and open Network Monitor (see *Figure 5.14*).

FIGURE 5.14
The Network Monitor application.

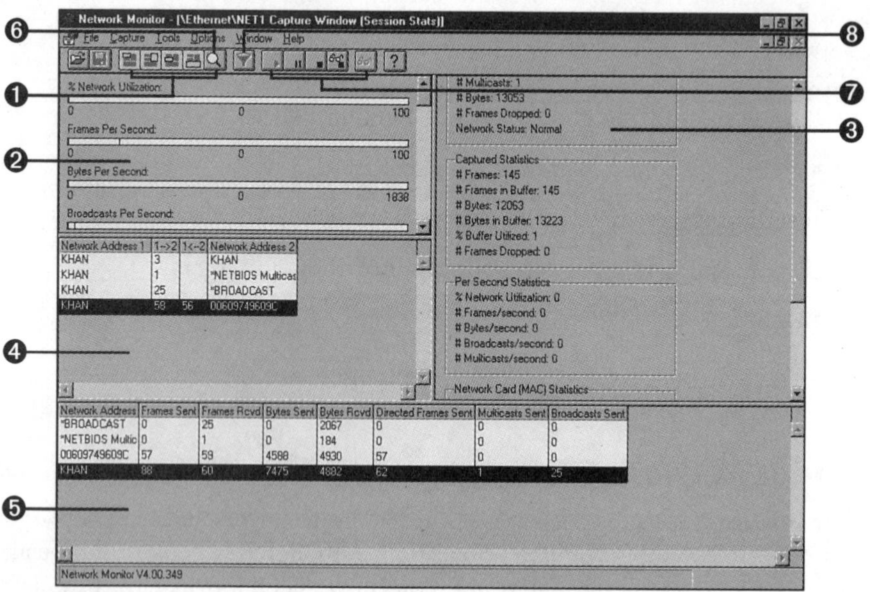

1. These buttons control the four panes in which Network Monitor presents information. The panes are Graph Pane, Total Statistics Pane, Session Statistics Pane, and Station Statistics Pane.
2. The Graph Pane displays a graphical view of the network activity that Network Monitor is monitoring.
3. The Total Statistics Pane shows the total statistics that Network Monitor has accumulated since it began monitoring during this session. It shows the time elapsed for this session, the network statistics, the capture statistics, the per-second statistics, the network interface card statistics, and the network error statistics. If you review this pane you have completed the secondary objective.
4. The Session Statistics Pane shows the sessions running between the monitoring server and other devices on the network.
5. The Station Statistics Pane shows all the stations that Network Monitor has found on the network, with their individual statistics.
6. The Zoom button allows you to zoom in on the pane you have selected.
7. The Start, Pause/Continue, Stop, and Stop and View buttons allow you to start, pause/continue, stop, and stop and view the traffic capture, respectively. These features are discussed in more detail later in the scenario.
8. The Edit Capture Filter button opens the Edit Capture Filter screen and allows you to configure the capture filter.

As soon as you start seeing statistics in Performance Monitor, you should see the other system appear in the Nodes portion of the screen. That's one way to determine whether there is traffic moving between the two systems.

Capture, Display, and Analyze Data

Now that you've looked at the high points of the application, it's time to finish configuring the capture portion of the scenario. When you click on the Capture Filter button on the toolbar, you will get the warning shown in *Figure 5.15*.

FIGURE 5.15

The warning message states that, for security reasons, this version of Network Monitor will only monitor traffic to and from the server.

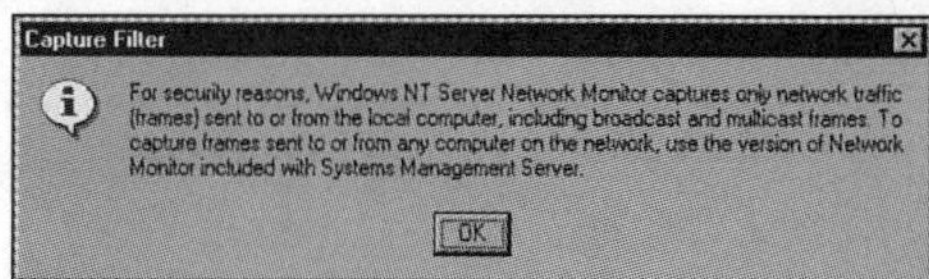

From *Figure 5.16* you can configure Network Monitor to capture traffic of a specific type, from a specific device or address, or for a specific protocol. In this scenario, the filter is in the Capture Everything mode.

FIGURE 5.16
Configuring a Capture Filter.

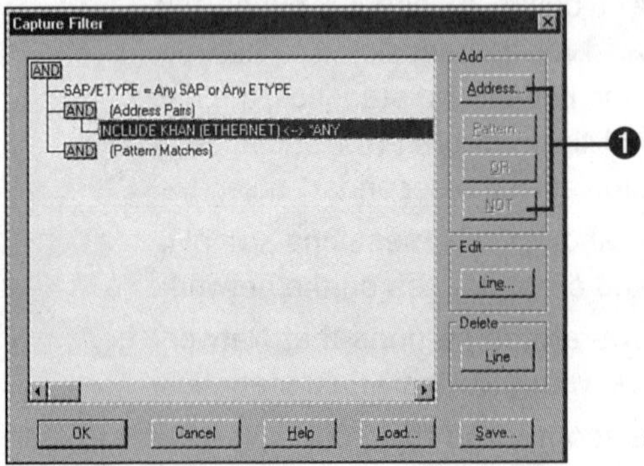

❶ Under the Add section, you can add addresses to the filter or configure the filter to capture certain patterns. These can replace the existing filter, or Boolean arithmetic can be used to add more conditions to the filter.

Click on Address in the Capture Filter dialog box to open the Address Expression dialog box, shown in *Figure 5.17*. This window brings up a list of the stations that the server has found on the network; you don't have to enter the devices manually.

FIGURE 5.17
Adding an address to the filter.

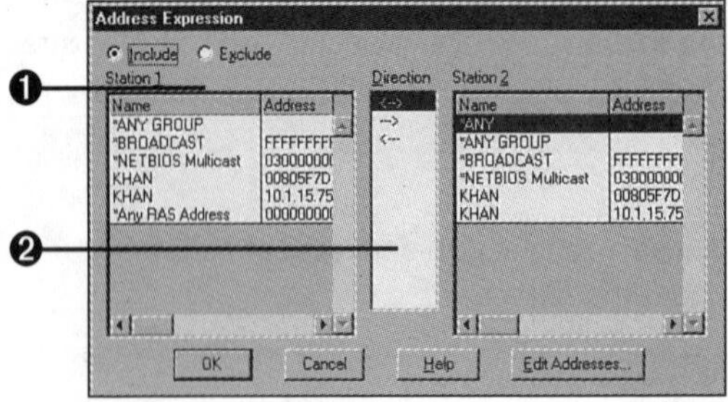

FIGURE 5.17 *cont.*

❶ You can either have machines included or excluded from the filter.

❷ You can also configure the direction of the traffic. You can capture traffic being sent to the server, being sent from the server, or both.

Once you have configured the Capture Filter, click on OK to return to the Network Monitor (see *Figure 5.18*).

FIGURE 5.18

The Network Monitor capture filter is capturing data.

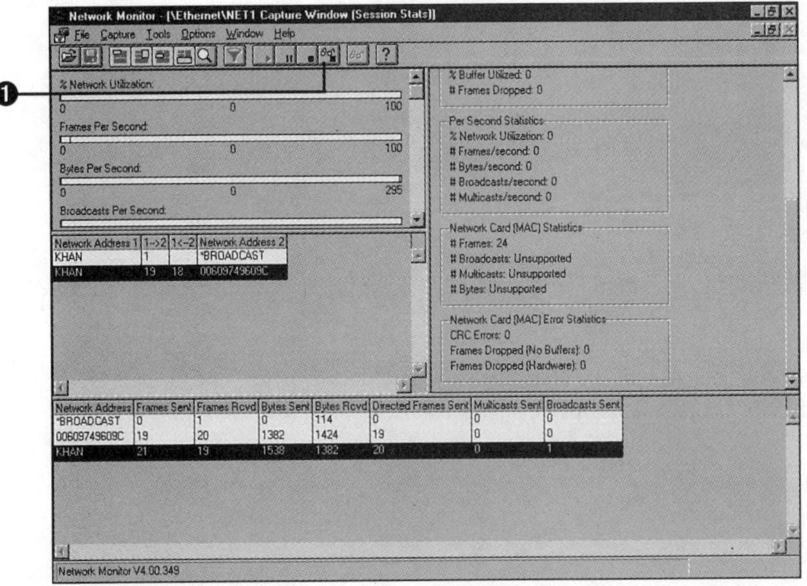

❶ Click on the Stop and View Icon to look at the data, shown in *Figure 5.19*.

FIGURE 5.19

The results of the traffic capture.

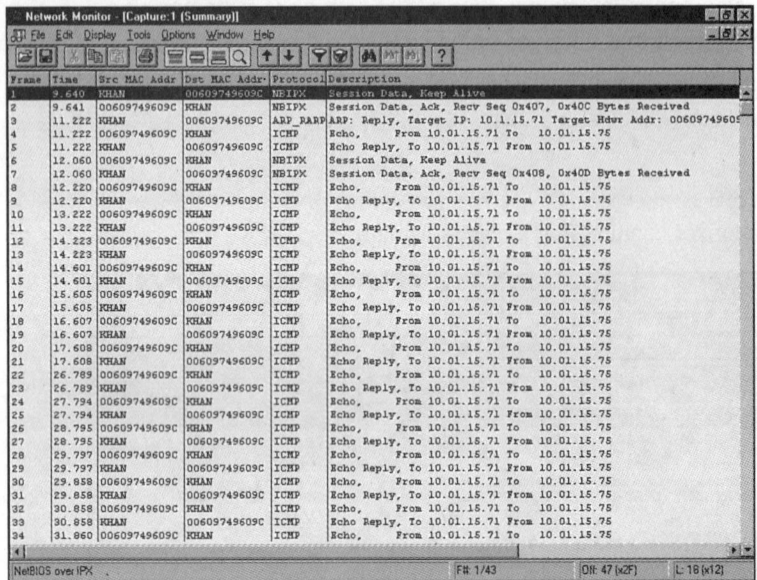

In *Figure 5.19*, you will see the results of the data capture configured during the scenario. Table 5.2 defines each of the fields.

TABLE 5.2

DESCRIPTION OF THE CAPTURE FIELDS

Field	*Purpose*
Frame	This is a counter of the number of frames captured.
Time	This is the elapsed time since the capture was started.
Src MAC Address	This is the MAC (Media Access Control) address of the source's network adapter.
Dst MAC Address	This is the same information for the destination's network adapter.
Protocol	This identifies the protocol family that the packet belongs to. It could be TCP/IP, IPX, and so on.
Description	This gives you a brief description of exactly what the packet you have captured is. In this example, a large number of the packets are ICMP. That's because there was a ping process running on the remote server to test connectivity. Ping uses the ICMP protocol of the TCP/IP protocol suite.

Double-click on one of the captured packets to view the detail shown in *Figure 5.20*.

FIGURE 5.20

The details of a captured data frame.

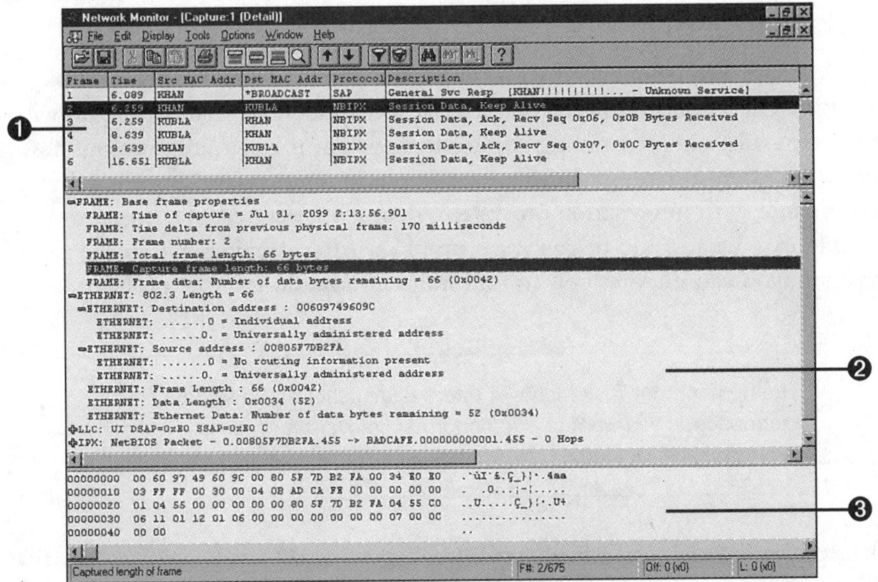

1. The top pane shows a smaller window of the same data in *Figure 5.19*.
2. The Detail Pane gives you all sorts of esoteric data (very useful if you know what you are looking for). From here you can get more protocol-specific information, as well as things like number of hops, frame sizes, or other session data.
3. The Hex Decode Pane shows every packet running across your network displayed as a hex decode. This is very hard for people new to network analysis to analyze, because it really doesn't mean anything unless you know what you are looking for. In some cases, you will see plain test ASCII characters as part of the hex decode. Before the use of encryption became more common, this was a favorite method for hackers to steal passwords from the network traffic.

That's it. You have successfully captured and examined traffic.

Other Tools for Performance Monitoring

Although the tools discussed up to this point can do very sophisticated server and network analysis, there are a number of other tools that can be used to obtain useful information without needing to get as involved as the previous tools.

Task Manager

Task Manager can be opened by pressing Ctrl + Alt + Del and selecting Task Manager. This application offers a very fast way to look at what's going on with the system. You can see running applications, what processes are running, how much CPU they are using, and finally a graphical representation of the CPU performance with information on system memory. It's a great way to get a quick look at what could be causing a problem. After it points you in the right direction, you can use the tools to find more information on the problem.

> **NOTE**
> Remember that Task Manager offers a snapshot of the system performance. If you want to see performance over time, you still need Performance Monitor.

The Applications tab of Task Manager (see *Figure 5.21*) can be used to identify what applications are running or not responding, and you can start and stop the same.

FIGURE 5.21
The Applications tab of Task Manager.

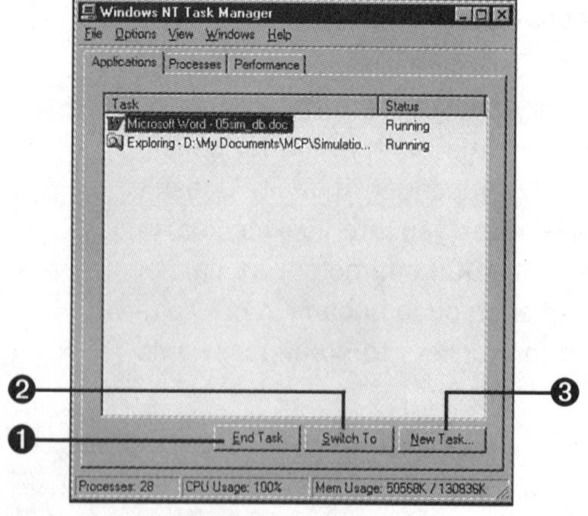

FIGURE 5.21 *cont.*

❶ The End Task button attempts to end the selected task. Depending on the status of the application, this may or may not be successful.

❷ The Switch To button causes the operating system to bring the selected application to the foreground as the active application.

❸ The New Task button functions like the File, Run command, allowing you to start a new application.

Click the Processes tab in the Task Manager (see *Figure 5.22*). From here, you can see what processes are running and how much CPU and memory each process is using, and you can end processes if necessary. Be careful with that last feature. Stopping processes can induce some unusual behavior in the system. The processes can be sorted by any parameter by clicking on the column title.

FIGURE 5.22

The Processes tab of Task Manager.

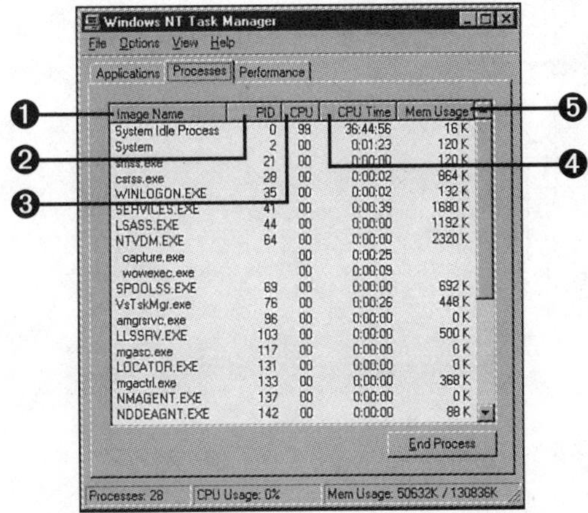

❶ The Image Name field shows you the name of the running process.

❷ The PID column shows the Process ID of the processes. The system uses this to keep track of the processes.

❸ The CPU column shows you how much CPU is being used by each process. This is a great place to identify which processes are using your CPU cycles, especially in a system that is running slowly.

cont.

FIGURE 5.22 *cont.*

❹ The CPU Time field shows you how long the process has been running.

❺ The Mem Usage field shows how much memory is being used by each process.

The Performance tab of Task Manager gives you a graphical record of the CPU and memory usage for the system (see *Figure 5.23*). You can get information on memory, processes, and threads. You can sort this view by any column, simply by clicking on the column title box.

FIGURE 5.23

The Performance tab of Task Manager.

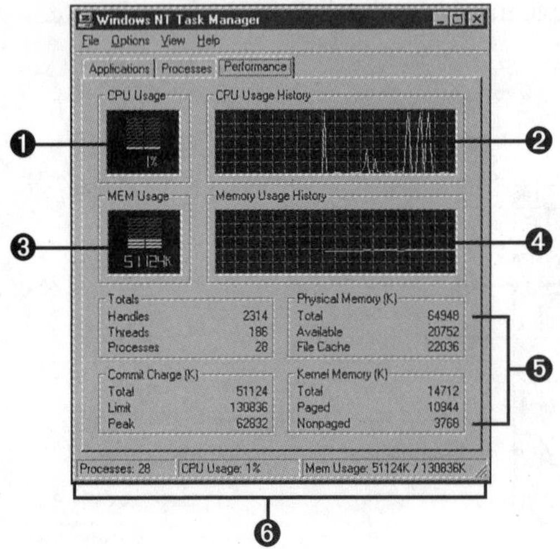

❶ The CPU Usage box shows you a snapshot of your CPU utilization. This is an "at this moment" number.

❷ CPU Usage History box charts the information available in the CPU Usage box, but over a period of time.

❸ The MEM Usage box is like the CPU Usage box, but for memory. It displays a snapshot of the memory usage.

❹ The Memory Usage History charts the MEM Usage box information over time.

❺ The bottom boxes show the specific statistics on the memory in use. You see a similar view in Chapter 6, "Troubleshooting," but in that chapter it's displayed by the WinMSD. This is discussed in the WinMSD section of Chapter 6.

❻ The number of processes, CPU Usage, and Mem Usage are all kept numerically in the status area, at the bottom of the screen.

Server Manager

Server Manager can be used to monitor some very basic server metrics. Server Manager can be used to monitor connected users, idle time, file shares in use, and active share names. You can also use it to monitor other servers on the network.

Now what do you do with this information? By monitoring these types of statistics, you are able to determine when server utilization peaks and where most of the access requests are. For example, suppose someone was nice enough to install a network game on your server in his personal directory and then he shared it. If you start to notice the same 10 users are accessing the Games share at 12:00 every day, and you also notice network utilization suddenly shoots through the roof, you'll be able to go right to the source of the problem. {*Server Manager is discussed in detail in Chapter 3, "Managing Resources."*}

System Optimization

There are a few places in the Windows NT system where you can configure how the system will perform. The two most important ones finish off the chapter.

Configuring Network Performance

In order to configure the network performance for the server, open the Networking applet in the Control Panel. Select the Services tab and open the Server service properties, as seen in *Figure 5.24*.

Figure 5.24
Configuring Network Performance in the Server service.

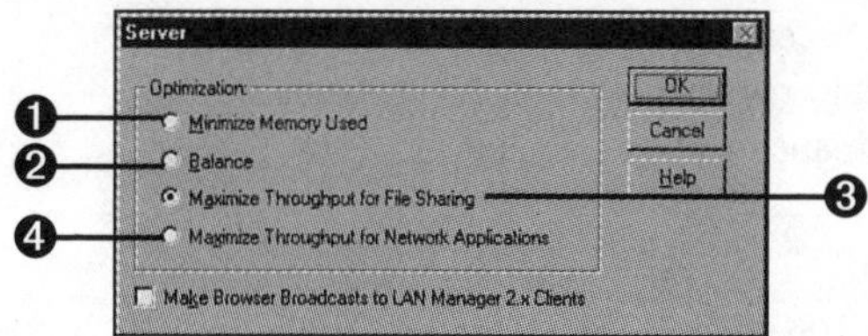

❶ The Minimize Memory Used selection makes network performance as slow as possible, but conserves memory for the rest of the server's processing. If you have people running local applications, and network processing is very low, this might be a good selection. This setting allows no more than 10 connections and essentially renders the server a workstation.

cont.

FIGURE 5.24 *cont.*

❷ Balance is a good selection for a general-purpose server that has some network traffic and some system processing. This setting allows 64 concurrent connections, and might be a member server in a workgroup or a domain.

❸ Maximize for File Sharing is the default and is recommended for file and print servers. This setting takes heavier network use into account.

❹ Maximize Throughput for Network Applications allocates the largest amount of memory possible for network usage, while limiting the amount of memory available for system use. This would be the setting for heavy client/server applications, in which a large number of users are accessing data on the server constantly. An SQL server, Web server, or Exchange server would be good examples of this.

Removing Bottlenecks

In this final section you learn how to remove bottlenecks when you find them:

> **NOTE**
>
> You can never remove all the bottlenecks from your server. By definition, *something* must be the slowest component of the system, and is therefore the bottleneck. The trick is to make sure that your bottleneck doesn't prevent the server from performing its function. For example, if you are running a high-end Web server and the hard drives are the bottleneck, you are probably okay if they are Ultra2 Wide SCSI. They may be the slowest component in the system, but at 80 MB of data transfer per second, you are probably going to be all right. The only time you really need to worry about bottlenecks is when you are having performance issues.

- *Disk Bottleneck.* This can be removed in several ways. You may want to implement a hardware RAID configuration to take advantage of the performance advantages of striping. You also want to make sure the controller card is running at an optimal configuration. Depending on the card, you might find a cache parameter that speeds things up. Refer to the vendor's documentation for specifics. Or, you can always replace the existing drives (and possibly controller) with faster ones (upgrade IDE disks for Ultra2 Wide SCSI, for example). If you are running multiple drives, you might also be able to add controllers to improve performance.

- *Memory Bottleneck.* This is usually an easy fix—just add more RAM. You can also increase the Level 2 cache on the processor if necessary. Finally, you can try to offload some of the functions of the server to another server. If your PDC is also your SQL server, you might want to think about moving SQL to another server.
- *Processor Bottleneck.* If the processor turns out to be the bottleneck, you can do one of two things. First, you can upgrade the CPU. If your application is multi-threaded and will support multiple processors, you can also add processors to resolve the issue.
- *Network Bottleneck.* Network bottlenecks frequently appear beyond the server (and are therefore beyond the scope of this book) but there are a few quick things you can do to speed up the server's performance. First, you can upgrade the network adapter. Many vendors are now putting processors on their adapters to relieve the CPU from processing network packets. You can also upgrade your LAN infrastructure. A 100 MB ethernet network has much higher performance than a 10 MB network. You can also add network adapters, which can help Windows NT process the incoming traffic more effectively.

CHAPTER 6

Troubleshooting

This chapter helps you prepare for the "Troubleshooting" sections of the Windows NT Server (Exam 70-067) and Windows NT Server Enterprise (Exam 70-068) exams. You'll see troubleshooting questions on both exams because Windows NT can have failures in any environment. The Enterprise exam adds some advanced troubleshooting objectives, beyond the failure resolution objectives common to both exams. It introduces Registry troubleshooting as well.

For Exam 70-067, the Windows NT Server Exam, Microsoft defines "Troubleshooting" objectives as follows:

- Choose the appropriate course of action to take to resolve installation failures.

  In a perfect world, Windows NT would install flawlessly every time. In reality, installations can be the first place you experience trouble with Windows NT. Microsoft wants you to understand the courses of action to take in case of this problem. Hardware issues play a large part in this objective.

- Choose the appropriate course of action to take to resolve boot failures.

  There are few things more frightening than turning on your server after a scheduled outage and instead of the Windows NT logon screen, you get an error message. This objective requires your understanding of the boot process, and what can go wrong with it.

- Choose the appropriate course of action to take to resolve configuration errors.

  In a sophisticated operating system like Windows NT, there are hundreds of configuration settings in even the simplest of installations. For the exam, Microsoft expects you to be able to take the appropriate actions when you have an error in one of these configurations. This can include hardware issues, driver issues, or configuration issues.

- Choose the appropriate course of action to take to resolve printer problems.

  Printing is one of the most important features of a Windows NT server utilized as a file and print server. This objective tests your familiarity with correcting printer issues, including hardware, software, and configuration issues.

- Choose the appropriate course of action to take to resolve RAS problems.

  Remote Access Server is one of Windows NT's most popular applications, and is a very sophisticated application. This objective tests your ability to resolve remote access and configuration issues with the server, including modems and configurations.

- Choose the appropriate course of action to take to resolve connectivity problems.

  The network brings its own complexity to a network operating system. Problems can occur with network interface cards, network drivers, network infrastructure, and application configuration.

- Choose the appropriate course of action to take to resolve resource access problems and permission problems.

  One of the largest problems in resource access issues is a conflict between share permissions and file permissions. In this objective, Microsoft expects you to be familiar with this issue, as well as other problems with resource access issues.

- Choose the appropriate course of action to take to resolve fault-tolerance failures, including tape backup, mirroring, stripe set with parity, and disk duplexing.

  Fault-tolerance is the cornerstone of a reliable Windows NT server because it enables the server to continue running after a drive failure. This objective requires you to know what to do if you have a failure and need to recover from it.

For Exam 70-068, the Windows NT Server in the Enterprise Exam, Microsoft defines "Troubleshooting" objectives as follows:

- Choose the appropriate course of action to take to resolve installation failures.

  This is the same objective as in the 70-67 exam.

- Choose the appropriate course of action to take to resolve boot failures.

  This is the same objective as in the 70-67 exam.

- Choose the appropriate course of action to take to resolve configuration errors by backing up, restoring, and editing the Registry.

  The Enterprise exam introduces you to the Registry, and how to save, restore, and edit it. You must be familiar with the Registry editor, as well as the major portions of the Registry.

- Choose the appropriate course of action to take to resolve printer problems.

  This is the same objective as in the 70-67 exam.

- Choose the appropriate course of action to take to resolve RAS problems.

  This is the same objective as in the 70-67 exam.

- Choose the appropriate course of action to take to resolve connectivity problems.

  This is the same objective as in the 70-67 exam.

- Choose the appropriate course of action to take to resolve resource access and permission problems.

  This is the same objective as in the 70-67 exam.

- Choose the appropriate course of action to take to resolve fault-tolerance including tape backup, mirroring, and stripe set with parity.

  This is the same objective as in the 70-67 exam.

- Perform advanced problem resolution. Tasks include diagnosing and interpreting a blue screen, configuring a memory dump, and using the Event Log service.

  Microsoft has taken a lot of abuse in the industry over its blue screen errors (nicknamed the "Blue Screen of Death"). What you need to know for the exam is that the blue screen errors actually provide a lot of information, which you should be able to interpret. You can also perform a memory dump, which can be valuable if you have to escalate to consulting a vendor (Microsoft or a third party) for technical support.

This chapter covers troubleshooting of the Windows NT network operating system. You'll learn some generic troubleshooting steps, walk through the different areas of Windows NT that you might have trouble with, starting with installation, and finish with some advanced troubleshooting information.

TROUBLESHOOTING TECHNIQUES—FIRST STEPS

Before you begin to look at the specifics of troubleshooting portions of Windows NT, it's worth taking a quick look at some general techniques for troubleshooting Windows NT (or any system):

- *Documentation:* Whenever you do anything on the server, document it thoroughly. When you perform the installation, you should document the amount of memory, number, and the size of hard drives, network adapters, and anything else you can think of. The more information you record before you experience a problem, the easier it will be to recover when there is an error. This is a good time to start a server logbook. Start with a configuration section. Then create an issues section. *Keep track of every error you receive on the system, and its resolution.* If you have a similar problem later on, you won't have to rediscover the resolution—just look it up. This practice saves time and reduces server down time. It also has the added benefit of information sharing in a large environment. If you have 10 administrators, you can all take advantage of one another's resolutions.
- *Back up configurations:* If you can back it up, do it. Store your backups somewhere away from the server, but keep them accessible. Use an Emergency Repair Disk with the boot parameters; back up the Registry every time you make a change to it, and use a tape or optical backup solution for storing the entire system configurations.
- *Test configurations:* Before you decide to make a change to a system, test it. This really isn't a troubleshooting technique, but it's a good way to avoid having to perform additional troubleshooting.
- *Be methodical:* As you approach a problem, take it one step at a time. If you have three possible solutions, try applying one solution at a time. For example, suppose you have a system that is unstable and keeps crashing. After troubleshooting, you determine that the next step is to apply the latest Service Pack, or replace memory. Don't do both at once. Even if the problem is corrected, you won't know which solution actually fixed the problem. If it was the Service Pack, you've just replaced good memory. If it was the memory, there's a chance the new Service Pack has introduced new problems. If you attempt one solution at a time and document each step, you'll usually reach a resolution faster than if you were to throw multiple fixes at the problem until it goes away.

- *Make a permanent fix:* In the highly demanding environment we work in today, it is very tempting to find a quick, easy workaround instead of fixing the problem itself. Occasionally, there is no way to fix a problem, and you're forced to come up with a workaround. In most cases, however, workarounds are put in place because they are easier or quicker to come up with. Suppose you have a multi-processor system that comes up with processor errors upon boot. Pressing F1 gets you around the problem, and lets the system boot. Problem solved? Clearly not. At this point, you should replace the processor or processor card, or consult the vendor. It may be a BIOS issue, or something else hardware related. Whatever you do, avoid the temptation to attach a note reading "Press F1 on boot to bypass error message." That's not a viable solution.

Troubleshooting Tools

You've now been introduced to some of the basics of troubleshooting. Windows NT gives you a number of specific tools to help you troubleshoot Windows NT services and components. You looked at a number service-specific tools such as RAS Manager for the Windows NT, and Network Monitor for connectivity, to name a few. Before you get into specifics, you should learn about a few tools that can be used in a number of troubleshooting situations.

Windows Diagnostics (WinMSD)

One of the biggest issues when troubleshooting a Windows NT server is determining just what is going on with the system. This is particularly true if you are walking up to a server you have never seen before, but it also holds true for servers you have installed yourself. Right off the top of your head, do you know the IRQ of the hard drive controller in the last server you worked with? Probably not—a lot of that information is assigned dynamically. What you need is a tool that allows you to locate this information quickly and accurately. WinMSD is a great tool for just that type of troubleshooting situation. Take a look at the following scenario, which illustrates one of the ways you can use WinMSD.

Scenario 6.1

You have been working on a problem with your Windows NT server. Ever since you installed a Compaq NetFlex Ethernet adapter, you have been experiencing intermittent drive failures, and you are unable to determine what the problem is. A quick search of the Microsoft KnowledgeBase suggests that it may be a resources issue. You must figure out if that is the case.

Required Results

- Figure out what resources your ethernet adapter is using, and determine if there is a possible conflict.

The best place to obtain this information (and a lot more) is to use the Windows NT Diagnostics utility.

To open the Windows NT Diagnostics utility, select Start, Run, and type in **winmsd**. *Figure 6.1* shows the Windows NT Diagnostics utility.

FIGURE 6.1
The Windows NT Diagnostics utility.

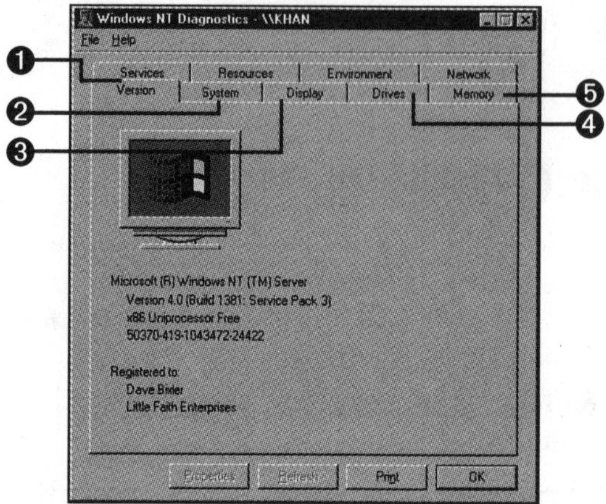

❶ The Version tab of the Windows NT Diagnostics utility provides the version of the operating system, installed Service Pack level, and registration information.

❷ The System tab shows system information like the system type, HAL (Hardware Abstraction Layer) version installed, BIOS information, and information on the installed processor, including type and speed.

FIGURE 6.1

❸ The Display tab provides information about the display adapter, including BIOS versions, configuration information, and amount of VRAM installed. It also shows information on the display driver, including the vendor, file(s) used, and version(s).

❹ The Drives tab shows all the drives available to the system, including network-attached drives. If you select a drive and click on Properties, you can find format information, including the amount of clusters and bytes that are used or available. You can also find information about the file system, including the partition type and the file system flags supported. File System Flags include Case Is Preserved in Filenames, Supports Case Sensitive Filenames, Unicode Characters Allowed in Filenames, File Based Compression Is Supported, and Security Is Preserved and Enforced.

❺ The Memory tab provides a snapshot of the memory information of Task Manager, discussed in Chapter 5, "Monitoring and Optimization." This includes information about Physical Memory, Kernel Memory, and running processes. The Windows NT Diagnostics utility also adds pagefile information, including total available and used memory.

To find the information you need to complete the scenario, look at the Resources tab shown in *Figure 6.2*. The Compaq ethernet adapter is device CpqNF3 and is using IRQ (Interrupt Request) 11. The disk controller in this system is device aic78xx and is also using IRQ 11. Although changing the IRQ used by one of the devices may not fix your problem, an IRQ conflict would be a good place to start the rest of your troubleshooting.

FIGURE 6.2
The Resources Tab of Windows NT Diagnostics Utility.

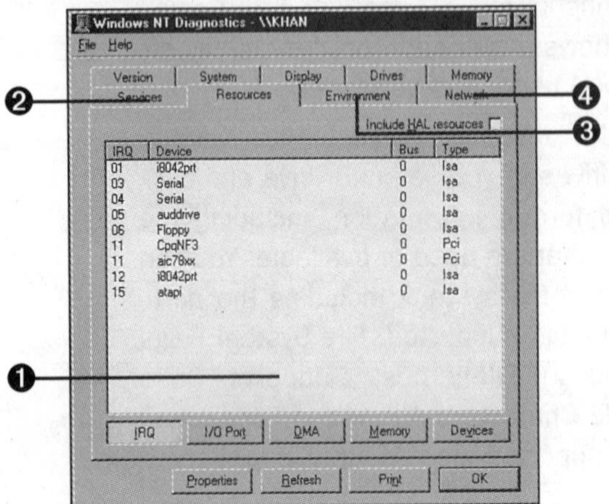

❶ The Resources tab can be used to show the IRQ, I/O port, DMA, memory, and a list of devices for the system. Select one of the devices and click on Properties for information on all the resources that particular device is using.

❷ The Services tab provides a list of all the system services or devices and their statuses. Select a service and click on Properties for information on the service and its dependencies. You can also display a list of devices to see similar information.

❸ The Environment tab shows the system and the local user's environment variables.

❹ The Network tab shows the information about users on the system, the transport protocols (this is a good place to find the MAC address for your adapter), driver settings, and statistics.

You've successfully completed the scenario, and with luck learned a little something about WinMSD. Keep in mind that WinMSD is for information gathering only. You cannot modify any of the information you viewed during the scenario.

Event Viewer

Another tool you will use quite a bit as you troubleshoot the system is the Event Viewer. Event Viewer is discussed in Chapter 3, "Managing Resources," as the way to determine whether domain synchronization has been completed successfully. Now take a look at another scenario and use the Event Viewer to figure out what's going on.

Scenario 6.2

You have just booted your Windows NT server and you get the error message shown in *Figure 6.3*. You need to resolve the issue.

Required Results

- Use the Event Viewer (shown in *Figure 6.4*) to identify the problem.

FIGURE 6.3
Sample of a Windows NT System Error.

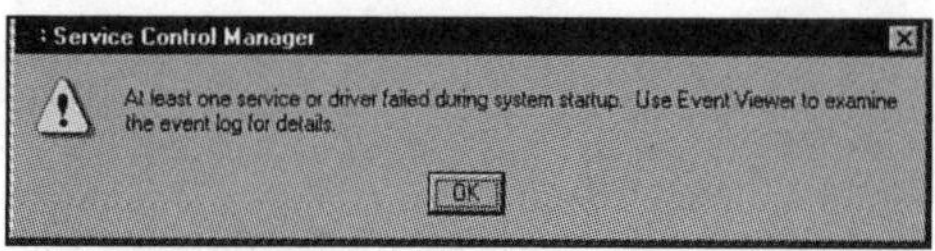

FIGURE 6.4
The Windows NT System Log shown in Event Viewer.

Event Viewer - System Log on \\KHAN

Log View Options Help

Date	Time	Source	Category	Event	User	Computer
8/3/98	10:19:01 PM	Service Control Mar	None	7026	N/A	KHAN
8/3/98	10:19:01 PM	BROWSER	None	8015	N/A	KHAN
8/3/98	10:19:01 PM	BROWSER	None	8015	N/A	KHAN
8/3/98	10:19:01 PM	BROWSER	None	8015	N/A	KHAN
8/3/98	10:19:01 PM	BROWSER	None	8015	N/A	KHAN
8/3/98	10:18:43 PM	NETLOGON	None	5712	N/A	KHAN
8/3/98	10:17:23 PM	EventLog	None	6005	N/A	KHAN
8/3/98	10:18:39 PM	Service Control Mar	None	7024	N/A	KHAN
8/3/98	10:15:52 PM	BROWSER	None	8033	N/A	KHAN
8/3/98	10:15:52 PM	BROWSER	None	8033	N/A	KHAN
8/3/98	10:15:52 PM	BROWSER	None	8033	N/A	KHAN
8/3/98	10:15:52 PM	BROWSER	None	8033	N/A	KHAN
8/3/98	10:15:20 PM	Service Control Mar	None	7024	N/A	KHAN
8/3/98	10:15:20 PM	Service Control Mar	None	7000	N/A	KHAN
7/28/98	7:31:07 PM	BROWSER	None	8015	N/A	KHAN
7/28/98	7:31:07 PM	BROWSER	None	8015	N/A	KHAN
7/28/98	7:31:06 PM	BROWSER	None	8015	N/A	KHAN
7/28/98	7:31:04 PM	BROWSER	None	8015	N/A	KHAN
7/28/98	7:30:46 PM	Service Control Mar	None	7024	N/A	KHAN
7/28/98	7:29:36 PM	EventLog	None	6005	N/A	KHAN
7/28/98	7:30:45 PM	NETLOGON	None	5712	N/A	KHAN
7/28/98	7:27:37 PM	BROWSER	None	8033	N/A	KHAN
7/28/98	7:27:36 PM	BROWSER	None	8033	N/A	KHAN

1 There are three types of errors that are logged in the Event Viewer. Events that are informational are represented by a blue *i* icon. Warning events are represented by a yellow *!* icon. Errors, which can generate error messages like the one is this scenario, are represented by a Stop sign icon.

The following are three logs that can be viewed in the Event Viewer:

- *System Event Log:* The System Log is used to record events that are generated by the Windows NT operating system. These messages are usually associated with services and drivers. This is the log to start in when you receive an error like the one found in *Figure 6.3*.

- *Application Event Log:* As you would imagine, this is the log in which you would find error messages generated by applications.
- *Security Event Log:* This is the log in which you would find auditable events recorded. Chapter 3 discusses configuring auditing; the results of those configurations are logged here.

Events can be sorted from newest to oldest, or vice-versa; in this example the newest event is on top. Double-clicking on the newest error message opens the Detail view, shown in *Figure 6.5*.

FIGURE 6.5
The Detail view of the newest error message.

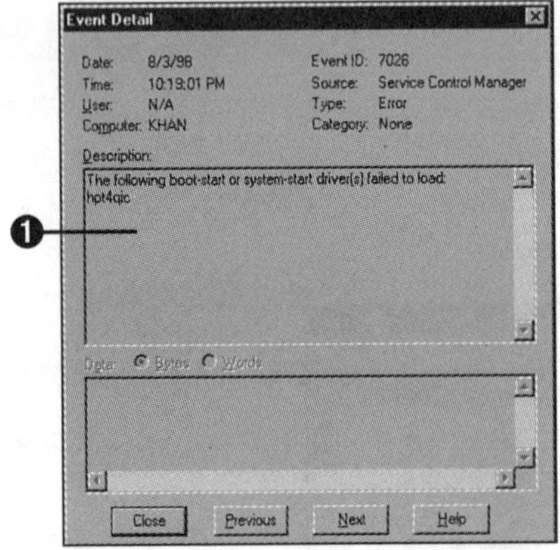

❶ The Description box is usually where you will find a message that you can identify. In this instance, notice that the *hpt4qic* driver didn't load. In this scenario, that's because there is not a Hewlett-Packard Colorado T4000 tape drive installed on this server. When Windows NT boots, it looks for the device; if the device can't be found, its driver can't be loaded.

Notice you have a lot of general information for the error in the detail screen:

- *Date:* The date on which the error occurred.
- *Time:* The time at which the error occurred.
- *User:* The user who caused the error to be generated, if applicable.
- *Computer:* The computer on which the error was generated.
- *Event ID:* A numeric value for the error message—useful for searching the Microsoft KnowledgeBase.
- *Source:* The service, device, or application that generated the error.

- *Type:* The informational, warning, or error classification as shown in *Figure 6.4*.
- *Category:* A further way in which the application can identify its error messages.
- *Description:* A description of the exact error message.
- *Data:* Some errors include the binary data associated with the error.

You have completed another scenario. There are a couple other features of the Event Viewer you should be aware of, however. *Figure 6.6* shows the configuration options for the log files. Go to Log, Log Settings to open this window.

FIGURE 6.6
Windows NT Event Viewer Log configuration options.

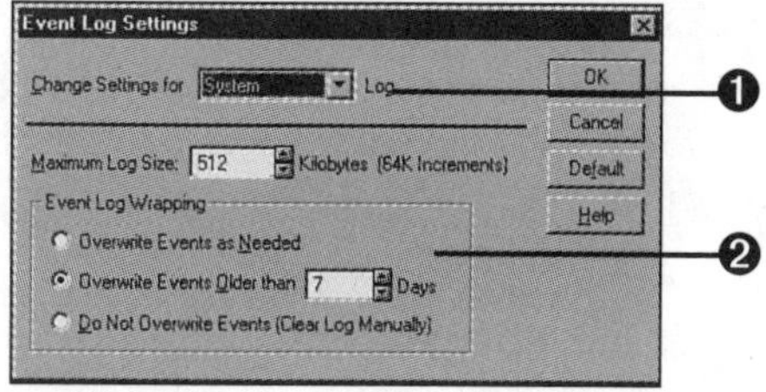

❶ From this pull-down menu, you can select the log for which to change the options. Each of the event logs can be configured differently.

❷ From here you can configure the size and actions of the log file. If you are having problems with a system, you should set the file size to 1024 or higher and set the log so that it must be cleared manually.

Figure 6.7 demonstrates Event Viewer's capability to view logs on other systems. You can open this by going to Log, Select Computer, and then use the standard browse interface to select the computer to view.

FIGURE 6.7
Selecting another computer's log file for viewing.

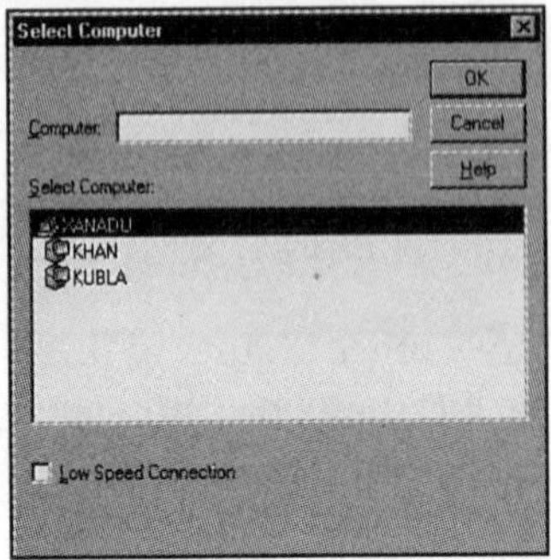

If you go to View, Filter Events, you see the Filter dialog box, shown in *Figure 6.8*.

FIGURE 6.8
Filtering the log events.

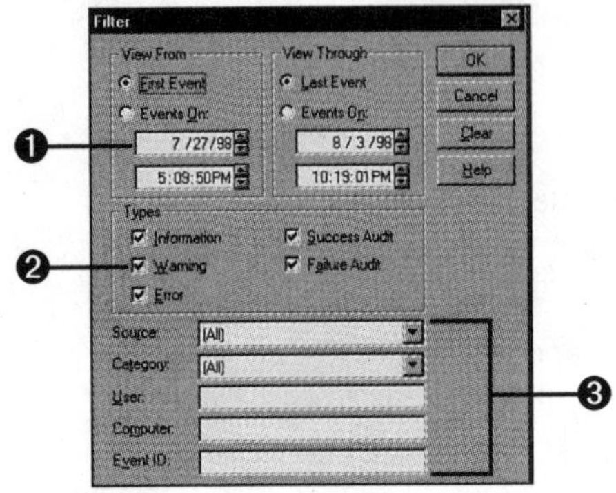

1. From here, you can set the length of time to view in the Event Log. You can set a start date and time, and an end date and time.
2. From here you can select the types of events to be viewed in the log. Notice that there are two event types that haven't been discussed yet. Success Audit and Fail Audit show up in the Security Log, and are related to events you have selected for auditing.
3. The bottom five fields allow you to search for strings in the various sections of the error message.

Now that you are familiar with the tools, you're ready to jump right into the actual troubleshooting, starting with troubleshooting installation problems.

TROUBLESHOOTING INSTALLATION ISSUES

There are a number of things that can cause the installation process to fail. One of the biggest is unsupported hardware. Microsoft publishes a document called the Hardware Compatibility List (HCL), which contains a list of all the hardware components that Microsoft has certified as being NT-compatible.

Scenario 6.3

You are installing Windows NT and walk away while the installation is running. When you return, the system is hung, and the installation has failed. You need to find the problem.

Required Results

- Troubleshoot and repair the installation issue.

If possible, always try to use components that have made the list. If you have just picked up a new Compaq server with the latest Intel processor, it may not be on the list yet. (It takes some time to certify a machine.) In this case, you must rely on the vendor to ensure that the hardware will work. A good rule of thumb is to check whether the vendor you are using has any other devices on the HCL. If it's a major vendor like Compaq, IBM, or Hewlett-Packard, you're probably OK. If you have purchased a custom-built PC from a local computer store, you might want to start checking components.

If your hardware is on the HCL, there are a few other areas to look at:

- Media errors
- Unsupported CD-ROM drive
- Hard disk errors
- Network adapter issues
- Miscellaneous hardware errors
- Server naming problems

These problems and errors are discussed in the following sections.

Media Errors

This is one of the easiest problems to troubleshoot. Sometimes the floppy disk or CD-ROM that comes out of the package has a problem. If it's a new copy of the software, you should be able to return it to your place of purchase for a new copy. There's one caveat, however: Make sure it's not a drive error. Try the media in another system before you take it back to the store.

Unsupported CD-ROM Drive

If you have a CD-ROM drive that is not supported by Windows NT, you will not be able to install directly from the installation CD. You do have another option—complete the following steps:

1. Access the CD-ROM drive from another operating system. DOS is usually a good candidate, unless you are interested in a dual-boot configuration.
2. Run WINNT.EXE with a `/b` option. This copies the system files that would ordinarily go on the system disks to the hard drive.
3. Copy the installation files from the CD-ROM to the hard drive. You obviously need a bit more than the required 110 MB of free space for this installation.
4. Run WINNT.EXE with the `/T:<installation path name>` option to install Windows NT from the hard drive.

Alternately, you can install from the network. {*For more information on the installation process, see Chapter 2, "Installation and Configuration."*}

Hard Disk Errors

There are a number of things that can cause drive problems during installation. Some of the more common issues you may run into include the following:

- *Drive cables:* Always check to make sure the CD-ROM, floppy drive, and hard drive cables are securely connected.
- *SCSI termination:* If you are using a SCSI hard drive (or drives) and you are seeing drive errors, make sure your SCSI bus has been properly terminated.
- *SCSI addressing:* Make sure each of your SCSI devices has a unique SCSI address.

- *Drive problems:* When Windows NT asks whether you want to do a thorough disk scan, say yes. If this is an upgrade, or the manufacturer was having a bad day, it's possible the hard drive is just bad. The scan should locate any actual disk problems.
- *Master/slave configuration:* If you are using IDE or EIDE drives, make sure the installation disk is the Master drive. That will always boot as the primary drive.
- *First EIDE controller:* If you are using a system with multiple EIDE controllers, be sure your drive is on the first controller in the system.
- *Viruses:* If this is an upgrade, or the drive came out of a different system, you should run a virus scan against the drive to ensure that there isn't a boot sector virus causing problems with your system. Some viruses will remain on the drive even after a format, hiding in the boot sector. A good virus scanner will find and clean those viruses.

Network Adapter Issues

Network adapters are another potential source for problems during the installation process. These errors can be broken into four basic categories:

- *Resource conflict:* Before you install Windows NT, make sure you know what resources the network adapter needs in order to operate properly. Ensure that they are available and don't conflict with any other devices.
- *Outdated drivers:* Make sure you have the latest drivers for Windows NT available when you install the adapter.
- *Network infrastructure:* There are a few things to look at under this category. First, check the cabling. 10BaseT, one of the more common media types, frequently suffers from poorly crimped cable connectors. Then check the network hardware. Make sure the port on the hub is active, if the token ring in not beaconing, and so on. Also, make sure the router(s) are routing.
- *Hardware failure:* Don't rule out a bad adapter. If you have checked the drivers, resources, and cabling, you might want to try a new adapter.

Miscellaneous Hardware Errors

A server is a complex hardware platform, and there are a number of other hardware devices that could cause problems during installation. Some generic tips for troubleshooting these devices include ensuring that their resource requirements do not conflict with any other devices, and that Windows NT will in fact support the device you are installing. For example, Windows NT does not support the Universal Serial Bus (USB) out of the box. If your system has a USB connector, you should disable it and free the resources it had reserved to operate.

Server Naming Problems

During the installation process, you are asked to name the server. The name of the computer must be unique to the domain. If you duplicate the name of a computer that already exists in the domain, you will start to experience authentication problems. If the server being installed is a Primary Domain Controller or a Backup Domain Controller, you must also provide a domain name. In the case of the PDC, you will need a unique name. In the case of the BDC, however, you must supply the name of an existing domain in order to complete the installation.

There are a few rules for these names:

- A number of invalid characters cannot be used in a Windows NT computer or domain name. This is due to the fact that these symbols are used in the computer system somewhere. The illegal characters are /\[]<>";:+=,*. and |.
- Names can be up to 15 characters in length.

> **NOTE**
> Windows NT does not allow you to create a computer with a name containing illegal characters or that exceeds 15 characters.

TROUBLESHOOTING SERVER BOOT FAILURES

After you've worked past any installation errors you may have encountered, the next big area of problems lies in server boot errors. There is nothing more frustrating than rebooting your server and receiving some obscure Windows NT error message instead of the familiar logon screen. Fortunately, there are some very easy, systematic ways to go about troubleshooting server boot problems. Take a look at the following scenario to understand these procedures.

Scenario 6.4

You've installed Windows NT and it has been running for several weeks. After installing some new applications and making some changes to the hardware, you reboot the server and you get an error message. The server will not boot.

Required Results

- Troubleshoot and repair the boot failure.

Before you can successfully troubleshoot and repair a boot failure, you should understand how the Windows NT boot process works.

Understanding the Boot Process

The boot process for Windows NT is relatively straightforward. Knowing this sequence and where key files and utilities are located should make a boot failure one of the easier Windows NT problems for you to troubleshoot. If you plan appropriately, recovering from a boot failure can be easy.

The Windows NT boot process is a sequential process, involving the boot phase and the loading phase.

Boot Phase

During the boot phase, the operating system is initialized, the hardware detection is performed, the Executive Services are loaded (Executive Services is the part of the kernel where processes and services execute), and the boot files are read. The Windows NT boot files are as follows:

- NTLDR
- BOOT.INI
- NTDETECT.COM
- NTOSKRNL.EXE
- NTBOOTDD.SYS (if necessary)
- HAL.DLL

The boot phase occurs like this:

1. NTLDR loads a mini-OS and changes memory to a flat, 32-bit memory model. FAT and NTFS drivers are loaded so the boot process can read the system partition.
2. NTLDR then reads the BOOT.INI file (discussed later in the chapter) and displays the Operating System Menu you see when NT boots.
3. After NT is selected, or the timer for the default operating system expires, the boot process continues with NTLDR loading NTDETECT.COM.
4. NTDETECT.COM analyzes the system hardware and creates the HKEY_LOCAL_MACHINE\HARDWARE Registry hive. (The Registry is discussed later in the chapter.)
5. If Windows NT is being loaded from a SCSI drive on a SCSI adapter with the BIOS disabled, NTDETECT.COM loads the NTBOOTDD.SYS driver to initialize the drive for access by the boot process.

> **NOTE** If you selected Windows 95 or MS-DOS from the menu, the boot process loads the BOOTSECT.DOS file. This file stores the location of the alternate operating system's boot files, and allows the selected OS to boot normally. This is the key to Windows NT multi-boot configurations.

6. NTLDR loads NTOSKRNL.EXE, which initializes the Executive Services loaded in the first part of the boot process. Some people liken this to the COMMAND.COM portion of the DOS boot process.
7. NTLDR loads the HAL.DLL and the SYSTEM hive, as well as any drivers needed to complete the boot sequence. After this is complete, NTLDR passes control of the process to NTOSKRNL.EXE.
8. You've reached the point where you should see a series of dots (.........) appearing across the top of the screen. It is at this point that you can select the Last Known Good configuration. This is also the end of the *boot phase* and the beginning of the *load phase.*

Load Phase

This is the phase during which the kernel is initialized, services are loaded, and the WIN32 subsystem is started. This portion of the process occurs as follows:

1. The kernel drivers are initialized and the CurrentControlSet is created and copied to the CLONE control set.
2. SMSS.EXE, the session manager, loads all the programs listed in HKEY_LOCAL_MACHINE\SYSTEM\CURRENTCONTROLSET\CONTROL\SESSIONMANAGE\BootExecute. If you have run CONVERT.EXE to convert a partition to NTFS, this is when the instruction to run the process is loaded.
3. The PAGEFILE is configured, and WIN32 is loaded. Once the WIN32 subsystem is loaded, WINLOGON.EXE is loaded. This service handles system logons.
4. WINLOGON starts the LSASS.EXE application (which displays the Ctrl+Alt+Del logon screen) and SCREG.EXE (The Service Controller), which starts all the automatic services.
5. Finally, the user is prompted to enter a user ID and password, and logon is complete. At this time, the CLONE control set is copied as the Last Known Good configuration.

> **NOTE** The Last Known Good configuration is not updated until after a successful logon.

Common Server Boot Sequence Problems

There are a large number of problems that can occur during the boot process, but they will generally break down into two categories: server problems (new or failed hardware, for example) or operating system problems.

Server Problems

Server problems are usually issues that involve a failed hardware device. Failed hard drives, hard disk controllers, mother boards, memory, or video adapters can all cause the boot process to fail. Usually these problems can be easily diagnosed with the server's hardware testing utilities. If you don't have diagnostics handy, contact the vendor or search the vendor's web page for that application. Replace the failed component, and you're up and running.

System Problems

System problems can range from corrupt system files to misbehaving drivers for newly installed hardware. There are a few things you can try to address this issue. First, select the Last Known Good configuration when prompted during the boot sequence. If there is a bad driver, this can often correct the problem and get you into the server, where you can work to address the issue. The last Known Good configuration is worth an in-depth look.

The *Last Known Good configuration* is a backup control set for the configuration of the last successful system boot. The Last Known Good configuration is updated after a successful boot without system critical errors involving the failure of a driver or system file and a successful logon.

The Last Known Good configuration can also be used when you install a new device driver that causes the system to hang upon restart. Because the Last Known Good configuration wouldn't have a reference to the new driver, it would allow the system to boot. You can also use this configuration if you have installed a new video driver, and upon reboot you have no video; powering the system off and using the Last Known Good configuration upon boot will restore your old settings.

Don't try to use this if you have had a successful logon since you made the change because the Last Known Good will have been overwritten. Only the configuration at the last logon is stored. You cannot go back beyond the last successful logon.

Another way to address system problems is to use Windows NT startup floppies (described in the "Performing an Emergency Repair" section) to boot the system from what should be a clean copy of the boot files. From here you should be able to access the system files to verify whether they are intact.

Finally, you can run an emergency repair.

Before you jump into running an emergency repair, take a look at a few of the more common boot errors:

- **BOOT: Couldn't find NTLDR**
  Please insert another disk.

  This error indicates that the NTLDR is missing or corrupt. It could also indicate that you left a floppy disk in the A: drive.

- **Windows NT could not start because the following file is missing or corrupt:**
  \winnt root\system32\ntoskrnl.exe
  Please reinstall a copy of the above file.

An error such as this frequently indicates there is a problem with the `BOOT.INI` file, and Windows NT is looking in the wrong directory for the boot files. Or the file could actually be missing.

- **I/O Error accessing boot sector file multi(0)disk(0)rdisk(0)partition(1):\bootsect.dos**

  This indicates the `BOOTSECT.DOS` file is missing or corrupt.

Because most of these errors can be fixed with an emergency repair, now is a great time to take a look at how you perform an emergency repair.

Performing an Emergency Repair

To perform a successful emergency repair, you need two things: a set of startup disks and a current Emergency Repair Disk (ERD). (RISC systems, however, start up from the system BIOS, and don't require startup disks.)

To generate a set of boot disks, place the Windows NT CD-ROM in the drive and run WINNT32 /b. This recreates the three boot disks.

To make sure your ERD is current, or to create an ERD, go to Start, Run and type in **`RDISK.EXE`**. The result is the utility shown in *Figure* 6.9. Here you can create or update an ERD, exit the utility, or read the Help file. When you create or update an ERD, the same information is stored on the hard drive in the `<%system_root%>/repair` subdirectory. This information can be copied to a floppy as a manual creation of an ERD.

> **NOTE**
>
> You must use the `/s` option when running RDISK.EXE if you want to copy the `SAM` and `SECURITY` portions of the Registry.

FIGURE 6.9

Creating or updating the Emergency Repair Disk.

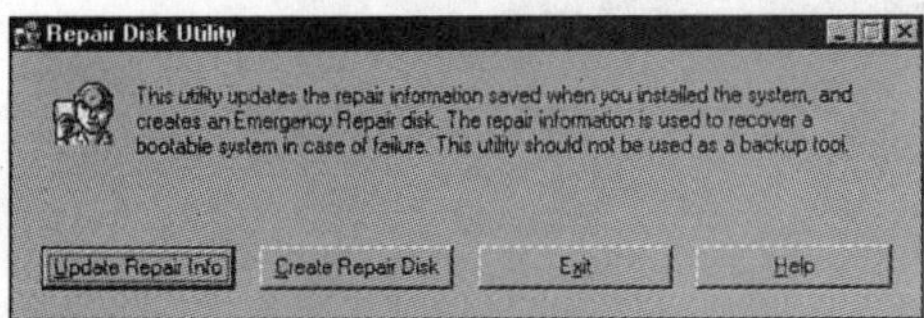

The ERD has the following files:

- SETUP.LOG: Contains a log of the files installed, with CRC checksums for each file to ensure integrity
- SYSTEM._: Contains the HKEY_LOCAL_MACHINE\SYSTEM Registry key in a compressed format
- SOFTWARE._: Contains the HKEY_LOCAL_MACHINE\SOFTWARE Registry key
- SECURITY._: Contains the HKEY_LOCAL_MACHINE\SECURITY Registry key
- SAM._: Contains the HKEY_LOCAL_MACHINE\SAM Registry key
- DEFAULT._[: Contains the HKEY_LOCAL_MACHINE\DEFAULT Registry key
- NTUSER.DA_: Contains the default user's profile information
- AUTOEXEC.NT and CONFIG.NT: MS-DOS configuration files

After you've got your updated ERD, you're ready to repair the system. To repair the system, boot from the first system floppy. Insert the second floppy when prompted, and you'll open the Setup window we saw in Chapter 2 (see *Figure 6.10*).

FIGURE 6.10
Running an emergency repair from the Setup screen.

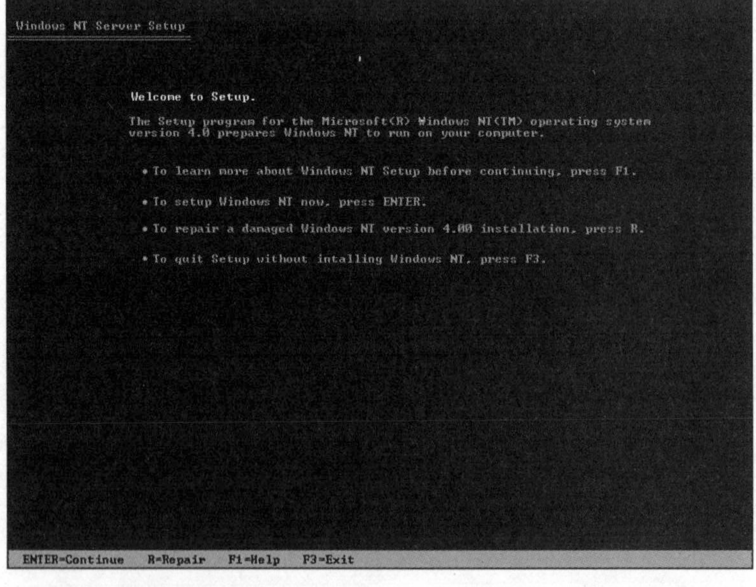

This time, select R for Repair. You are given four options:

- *Inspect Registry Files:* This option is used to repair a damaged Registry. You receive a list of Registry files that can be repaired, and are warned that information can be lost. You can repair the following Registry keys:
  - `SYSTEM`—System configuration information.
  - `SOFTWARE`—Software information.
  - `DEFAULT`—The Default User profile.
  - `NTUSER.DAT`—A New User profile.
  - `SECURITY`—The User Accounts database. Be careful with this one. You don't want to accidentally wipe out three or four hundred accounts because you repaired the User Accounts database with an old ERD.
- *Inspect Startup Environment:* This option ensures that the Windows NT boot files on the system partition are intact and in place. If you repair these files, you will need your original media. The repair process reinstalls these files from the installation media.
- *Verify Windows NT System Files:* This option ensures that the Windows NT system files are intact and in place. This is where the `SETUP.LOG` file is used. If a system file's checksum doesn't match the checksum in the `SETUP.LOG` file, you are asked whether you want to replace it. If you replace these files, you will need your original media. The repair process reinstalls these files from the installation media. You may also need to reapply any Service Packs you have installed.
- *Inspect Boot Sector:* This verifies that the `NTLDR` is configured correctly on the system partition to be loaded upon startup.

Creating an Emergency Boot Disk

If the system partition is protected by a mirror set and the primary drive fails, you can use an Emergency Boot Disk to start the server by using the mirror copy. First, you need to create a boot disk with the proper files. Then, you need to edit the `BOOT.INI` file so that it boots from another disk.

To create the boot disk for an x86 computer, perform the following steps:

1. Format a floppy using Windows NT Explorer.
2. Copy the following files to the floppy:

- NTLDR
- NTDETECT.COM
- NTBOOTDD.SYS (if present on your system)
- BOOT.INI

You now have a viable Emergency Boot Disk. If you are using this in conjunction with a failed mirror set, and the primary drive is the one that has failed, you must modify the BOOT.INI to point to the correct drive.

By this point, you should have found and repaired your boot problem, and successfully completed the primary objective. There are a few other things you should examine before moving on.

The BOOT.INI File

The BOOT.INI file contains information about the operating systems that can be booted, which OS is the default, and where the system files for each OS are located.

Your BOOT.INI file will look like this:

```
[boot loader]
timeout=30
default=multi(o)disk(o)rdisk(o)partition(3)\WINNT
[operating systems]
multi(o)disk(o)rdisk(o)partition(3)\WINNT="Windows NT Server Version 4.00"
multi(o)disk(o)rdisk(o)partition(3)\WINNT="Windows NT Server Version 4.00
[VGA mode]" /basevideo /sos
C:\="MS-DOS"
```

There are three important flags in the BOOT.INI that can help while troubleshooting boot issues:

- /SOS: This option displays kernel and driver names during startup. This can tell you what driver the system is crashing on.
- /MAXMEM: This option allows you to limit the amount of physical memory the system can use. This can be useful if you suspect bad memory, or to attempt to induce problems by setting available memory as low as possible.
- /BASEVIDEO: This sets the video to standard VGA, in case you start having problems with video.

Notice that the disk information is pretty obscure. That's because Windows NT uses ARC (Advanced RISC Computing) naming conventions.

The `BOOT.INI` file contains information that helps `NTLDR` find the system partition. The information is found in entries such as this:

```
multi(o)disk(o)rdisk(o)partition(1)
```

- `multi(n)/scsi(n)`: This field will be `multi(n)` for non-SCSI systems and for SCSI systems using a SCSI BIOS. This field will be `scsi(n)` for SCSI systems that do not use a SCSI BIOS. For the first hard drive controller `n` will be 0. Additional hard drive controllers will be numbered 1 through 3.

  If you are trying to recover from a failed mirror set as discussed in the "Breaking a Mirror Set" section, edit this field if the mirror partition is attached to a different disk controller.

- `disk(o)`: For systems using `scsi(n)`, `o` is the SCSI bus number for multiple-bus SCSI adapters. Edit `o` to reflect the SCSI address of the drive with the mirror partition. For systems using `multi(n)`, `o` is always 0.
- `rdisk(p)`: For `scsi(n)`, `p` is always 0. For `multi(n)`, `p` is the number of the disk on the adapter. With IDE or EIDE, the master drive will be 0 and the slave drive will be 1.
- `partition(q)`: `q` indicates the primary partition number on the drive that contains the mirror of the system partition (if the system drive is mirrored). Partitions are numbered 1 through 3. Extended partitions and unused partitions are not numbered.

TROUBLESHOOTING SYSTEM PROBLEMS

There are two pieces to troubleshooting system problems that you need to be familiar with. The first piece is the effective use of the Event Viewer, which is covered in the "Event Viewer" section. When you receive an error message, or have a service that is failing, a good place to start troubleshooting is the Event Logs.

The second place to go to troubleshoot and correct issues is the dreaded Registry.

The Registry is a database that stores most of Windows NT's configuration parameters as well as application settings. This takes the place of the legacy `.INI` files from the Windows 3.x days.

In order to view the Registry, open the Registry Editor, by going to Start, Run and type in **`REGEDT32.EXE`**. This opens the application shown in *Figure 6.11*.

FIGURE 6.11
The Registry Editor.

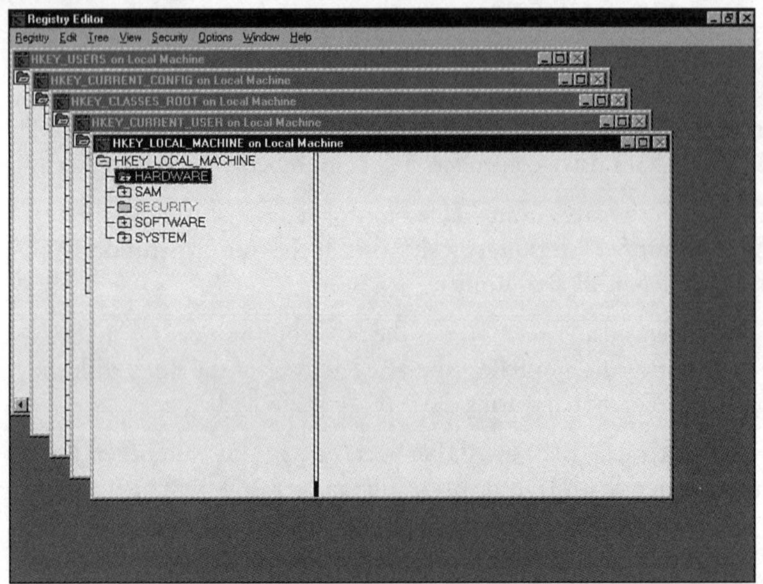

> **NOTE** Editing the Registry can be very dangerous if you don't know what you are doing. The Registry contains valuable data, and if you delete the wrong thing, you will be practicing your emergency repair knowledge before you know it. It's a good idea to place `Regedt32.exe` into read-only mode while you are learning your way around the Registry. This can be done by going to the Options menu, and selecting Read Only Mode.

The *Registry* is hierarchical database consisting of data stored in containers known as Registry keys. Each key contains data known as a value entry. Registry keys appear as folders and value entries show up in the right window of the Registry editor as you select keys.

There are five top-level keys in the Registry:

- `HKEY_LOCAL_MACHINE`: This key contains computer hardware information, as well as configuration information for software installed on the computer.
- `HKEY_CURRENT_CONFIG`: This key contains the current hardware configuration. This is built during the boot process.

- `HKEY_CLASSES_ROOT`: This key contains object linking and embedding (OLE) and file-class association data. Information in this subtree is duplicated in `HKEY_LOCAL_MACHINE\SOFTWARE\CLASSES`.
- `HKEY_CURRENT_USER`: This key contains user data for the current user.
- `HKEY_USERS`: This key contains all the actively loaded user profiles, including the default profile and a duplicate of information in `HKEY_CURRENT_USER`.

The key with which you will probably spend most of your time is `HKEY_LOCAL_MACHINE`. This is where most of the configuration information you will use during your troubleshooting is located. In *Figure 6.12*, you'll notice that a key can be expanded to reveal *subkeys*. Any subkey can contain other subkeys and can also contain values.

FIGURE 6.12
The Registry Editor—Expanded View.

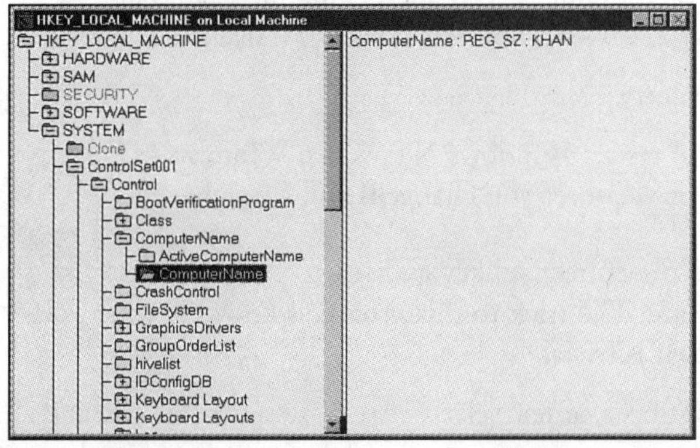

Each key and subkey can contain one or more *values*, and there are a number of different *data types*, which are used to store the data. The most common data types include the following:

- `REG_BINARY`: Used to store raw binary data and most hardware data.
- `REG_DWORD`: Used to store information that is represented by a number up to 4 bytes long. This data can be displayed in binary, hexadecimal, or decimal form.
- `REG_EXPAND_SZ`: Used to store a data string, which contains a system variable.

- `REG_MULTI_SZ`: Used to store a multiple value string consisting of lists or multiple values.
- `REG_SZ`: Used to store plain text.

Editing, Adding, and Deleting Registry Value Entries

To edit a registry setting, complete the following steps:

1. Start the Registry Editor by going to Start, Run and entering **`regedt32`** in the Open dialog box. Click on OK.
2. Locate the value you would like to edit, either by navigating through the appropriate key tree, or by performing a search.
3. Double-click the appropriate value. If you are looking for a safe value to change, try `HKEY_CURRENT_USER\ControlPanel\Desktop\Wallpaper`.
4. Choose OK to save the entry.
5. Quit Registry Editor and restart Windows NT. When Windows NT restarts, the wallpaper (or whatever you changed) will have changed.

To add an entry, navigate to the correct subkey and select either Add Key or Add Value from the Edit menu. The trick to this process is knowing what you need to enter. The action itself is trivial.

To delete a Registry value, it's even easier. Select what you want to delete, and press the Del key. Regedt32 gives you a warning to inform you that after the value is deleted, the information is gone.

Backing Up and Restoring the Registry

To back up the Registry be aware that you will need to back it up one key or subkey at a time. To back up the entire Registry, you'll need to use tape backup software, as described later in the chapter. Then, complete the following steps:

1. Start the Registry Editor by going to Start, Run and entering **`regedt32`** in the Open dialog box. Click on OK.
2. Select the key or subkey you would like to back up.
3. Go to File, Save Key, as shown in *Figure 6.13*.

4. Select a directory and file name, as shown in *Figure 6.14*.
5. Click on Save.

To restore the Registry key, complete the following steps:

1. Start the Registry Editor by going to Start, Run and entering **regedt32** in the Open dialog box. Click on OK.
2. Go to File, Restore.
3. Select the directory and file name for the key you would like to restore.
4. Click on Open.

FIGURE 6.13
Saving the Registry Subkey.

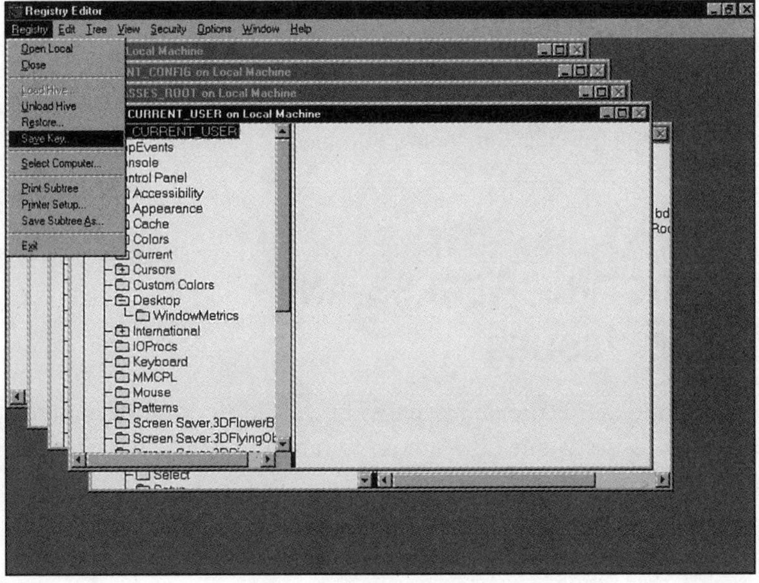

FIGURE 6.14
Select a directory and file name.

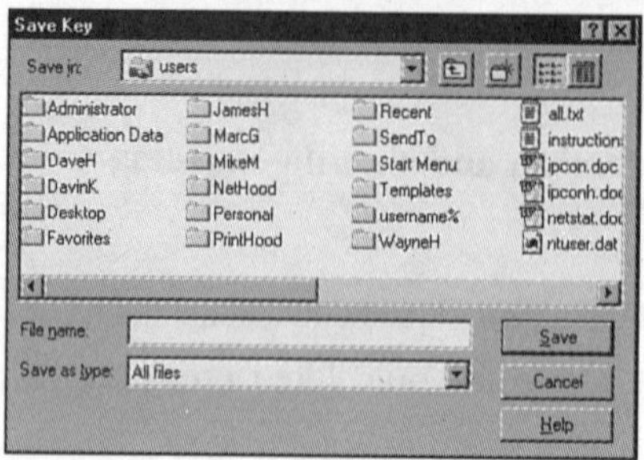

> **NOTE** While you study Regedt32 for editing the Registry, it's worth mentioning the 16-bit version of the Registry Editor: Regedit.exe. The nice thing about Regedit.exe is the fact that it aggregates all the hives, and allows you to search all the hives at once. The limitation of this editor is its inability to edit some of the Registry keys. It's not a bad idea to use this for searching, make a note of the path, and then perform the edits with the 32-bit version.

TROUBLESHOOTING ACCESS AND PERMISSIONS ISSUES

Some of the more troublesome problems you will be asked to troubleshoot are access and permission issues. Some of the more common problems to watch out for include the following:

- *User can't log on*: Make sure the user has the correct user ID and password, and is attempting to log on to the correct domain. Also, ensure that the Intruder Lockout hasn't been activated. If this still doesn't work, try logging on using a different account. If you still can't log on, you may want to verify the network connectivity for that machine.

> **NOTE** Make sure the CAPS Lock key isn't active when a user cannot log on. Windows NT passwords are case-sensitive.

- *No one can log on:* This could indicate a problem with your Security Accounts Manager database. You may have to perform an emergency repair and restore a backup copy of the database. Also be sure the Server service is running.
- *Too many people have access to a share:* Because every directory grants rights to the Everyone group, everyone has the right permissions to access the data. To solve this problem, remove the Everyone group from the Access Control List (ACL) for that directory.
- *One or more uUsers cannot access a shared resource:* Make sure the resource is shared, and that the permissions are set appropriately. You can also try accessing other resources on the same server. Be sure the user is spelling the resource name correctly. {*For more information on user creation and management, see Chapter 3, "Managing Resources."*}

There are a few other things to watch out for with user access issues in general:

- Make sure the Server, Workstation, and NetLogon services are running.
- Check User Manager for Domains and verify that the user has the rights he believes he does.
- Make sure you set the right permissions in the right place. Setting permissions on the file system doesn't do anything if the user is accessing the files across the network.
- Ensure that any necessary trust relationships have been established, and are still functioning.
- Check the System Policy Editor and the account policies in User Manager for Domains to verify that the user is allowed to log on at that time and from that particular machine.

TROUBLESHOOTING CONNECTIVITY ISSUES

Sometimes you'll get a call from a user who cannot connect to the server. Then another call, and another call, and so on. That's a pretty clear sign that you have a problem with connectivity to the server. The following are some key things to check to see where your connectivity issues are:

- *Check the media:* Before you do anything else, make sure the server is cabled properly—the connectors are securely seated and the ends are properly crimped on the cable. With most ethernet adapters, you should see a green light on the adapter indicating that you have a successful hardware link from the network adapter and the network.

- *Check the Network Adapter:* Run the diagnostics that came with the network adapter and make sure it is functioning correctly.
- *Check your protocol configurations:*
  - For TCP/IP, ensure that you have a valid IP address, subnet mask, and gateway.
  - For IPX/SPX, ensure that the proper frame type has been selected. Also make sure the Internal Network Number is unique.
  - Because NetBEUI doesn't have any configurable options, if you need to connect using NetBEUI, make sure it is loaded.
- *Check your services:* Make sure the Workstation and Server services are running. You should also check the binding in Network Properties to ensure that they are bound to at least one protocol.
- *Check your resources:* If a user is trying to map to a shared drive, make sure the drive is actually available. If that drive has failed or the share was inadvertently deleted, the network may be fine even though the user perceives a network-related problem.
- *Check the infrastructure:* Make sure you don't have any network problems beyond your server. If there is a router down, people will not be able to access your server.

Chapter 5 discusses a utility called Network Monitor. This is another excellent tool for advanced network troubleshooting.

TROUBLESHOOTING RAS ISSUES

A good place to start when you are experiencing RAS issues is the Dial-Up Monitor located in the Control Panel. This is shown in Figure 6.15. {*For more information on RAS configurations, see Chapter 4, "Connectivity."*}

FIGURE 6.15
The Dial-Up Monitor application.

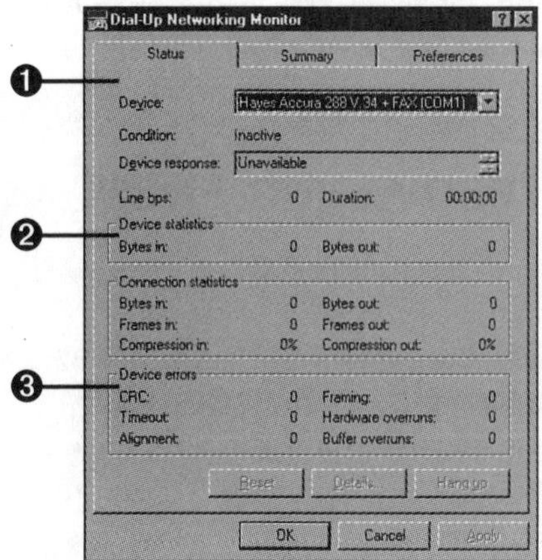

1. This section of the Status tab provides information about the devices connected to RAS.
2. These sections provide the total statistics for both the selected device as well as the connection statistics. This is a good place to look to quickly identify potential errors. Look for statistics that are out of line with what you would routinely expect.
3. This section can quickly identify problems with the hardware. If you see a lot of errors here, you almost assuredly have a hardware issue.

If you continue to have problems with your RAS connectivity, you can enable PPP logging by making the value of the Registry subkey `HKEY_LOCAL_MACHINE\System\CurtrentControlSet\Services\Rasman\PPP\Logging` to a value of 1.

A few other common RAS problems include the following:

- *Authentication issues:* Users frequently have authentication errors and find themselves unable to connect. First, try resetting their passwords. If that doesn't do it, set RAS to the lowest security possible (Allow Any Authentication Including Clear Text). If necessary you can then troubleshoot the problem with the more strict forms of authentication.
- *Hardware:* Check the hardware. Make sure everything is powered on and cabled appropriately. For a modem, turn up the volume and try to dial from it. You should get a dial tone, followed by the sound of dialing and a modem connection tone right before connecting. If you hear all this, your hardware should be functioning.

- *Callback:* Ordinarily, the Callback feature of RAS allows better security, and less expense to your remote users because the server is calling the user and absorbing the costs for the connection. However, this feature does not work if you are taking advantage of Windows NT's Multilink capabilities.

Troubleshooting and Recovering from Disk Problems

Troubleshooting a failed disk drive can be one of the easiest tasks in your day-to-day server maintenance. Failed disk drives tend to break in unmistakable ways. Some drives emit piercing whines before they fail. Others simply cease to respond to commands. No lights, no access sounds, or a failure to respond to system diagnostics are all terrific ways to determine whether a hard drive has failed. But after you've found your failed drive, what do you do? Well, if you're using some sort of fault-tolerance (I hope you are), you'll need to know how to recover from the failure.

Recovering from a Disk Failure

Depending on the level of fault-tolerance you have implemented, the method for recovering can vary widely. The least complicated is recovering from disk failure.

Breaking a Mirror Set

If you choose to use disk mirroring as your preferred method of fault-tolerance in a server, the day will come when one of those drives fails. In preparation, you should know how to break the mirror set so you can replace the failed drive. Take a look at how you would go about doing that. {*Creating a Mirror Set is discussed in Chapter 2.*}

Scenario 6.5

You have a mirrored drive set with a failed drive. You need to replace the drive, and re-establish the fault-tolerance.

Required Results

- Re-create the fault-tolerance by breaking the mirror set, replacing the failed drive, and then creating a new mirror set with the new drive. {*Creating a Mirror Set is discussed in Chapter 2.*}

To break a mirror set, perform the following steps:

1. Start Disk Administrator and select one of the mirror set partitions.
2. Select Fault-tolerance, Break Mirror.
3. A dialog box opens with the message "This will end mirroring and create two independent partitions. Are you sure you want to break the selected mirror?" Choose Yes.
4. The next message reads "Do you wish to continue with this operation?" Once again, choose Yes.
5. Select Partition, Commit Changes Now to complete breaking the mirror set.
6. If you are breaking a mirror for the system partition, you must restart the computer.

Re-create the mirror set following the procedure discussed in Chapter 2, and you will have successfully completed this scenario.

Fixing a Duplexing Issue

Duplexing consists of a mirror set with each drive on a separate controller. Replacing a failed disk is accomplished in the same manner as described in the "Breaking a Mirror Set" section because duplexed drives as a mirror set to the operating system.

If you have a controller failure, however, it's a little more complicated. Break the mirror set as discussed earlier, replace the failed controller, and then create a new mirror set between the two drives.

Repairing a Stripe Set with Parity

As good as hard drives are getting these days, you will eventually have one fail. When that occurs in a stripe set with parity, you need to know how to replace the drive and regenerate the stripe set. Take a look at the following scenario.

Scenario 6.6

You have a Windows NT server with a stripe set with parity. One of the drives has failed. You must re-establish the fault-tolerance of the stripe set.

Required Results

- Replace the failed drive in the stripe set and regenerate the data.

If a disk in a stripe set with parity fails, the set continues to function. Windows NT can read and write to the set by using the parity information that is contained on the remaining drives. However, there is a performance hit to the system due to the overhead associated with calculating information using the parity information. So you want to get that drive replaced as soon as possible.

After you replace the failed drive, you must regenerate the stripe set with parity. Regenerate the stripe set with parity as follows:

1. In Disk Administrator, select one of the segments of the stripe set with parity.
2. Hold down the Ctrl key and select an area of free space that is at least as large as the members of the stripe set with parity. This should be the drive that you just installed.
3. Go to the Fault Tolerance menu and choose Regenerate.
4. Restart the computer. Windows NT regenerates the stripe set with parity.

Backing Up and Restoring Data

OK, you've implemented full fault-tolerance on your system. You're running RAID-5 and you have extra controllers, so you're all set, right? *Wrong.* A common oversight by management is the belief that fault-tolerance is the same as a guarantee of data availability. The first time your building takes a lightning strike and burns up your server, you'll find the problem with that line of thinking. Always back up your data, no matter how fault-tolerant your system is.

There are a few things you should know about tape backup. *Figure 6.16* shows the backup application that is bundled with Windows NT. Because the exams ask only general questions about tape backup, and not this application in particular, this chapter omits the specifics of the application. Many people purchase third-party applications for tape backup. These applications offer sophisticated features such as scheduling, device management, support for a number of different drives and media, SNMP management, and a host of other features.

FIGURE 6.16
The Windows NT Backup utility.

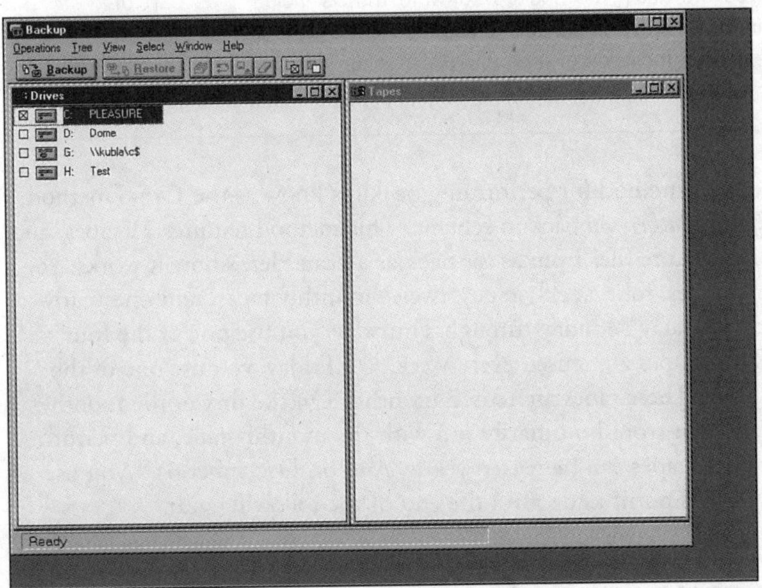

In general, you need to be aware of the three different types of tape backup used for performing backups:

- *Full:* This method backs up all the files you have selected, and marks the file as having been backed up. This is done by setting the archive bit. Because you are backing up all the files, this is the slowest of the backup methods. One advantage to this method is that you only need a single backup set to perform a restore. If you want to perform a restore on Wednesday, you just use the Tuesday tape set.
- *Differential:* This method backs up any files that have not been backed up up since the last full or incremental backup. A differential backup does not set an archive bit after the backup. This means that you would need two

backup sets to restore: the full backup and the latest differential backup. This is a faster method of backup than the full backup.

- *Incremental:* This method backs up all the files that have changed, and then resets the archive bit. This is the fastest backup method, but carries the drawback of requiring all the tapes since the last full backup in order to perform a restore. If one of those tapes goes bad, or gets lost, you will not be able to restore from that set of tapes.

> **NOTE** If you are using the backup software that is included as part of Windows NT, it's important to remember that you cannot back up Registries for remote servers. NT's Backup will only back up the Registry of the server that it is attached to.

There is a popular method for performing backups know as the *G-F-S* method, or the *grandfather-father-son* backup scheme. This method requires 21 tapes, and ensures you can restore files from as far back as a year. Here's how it works. You have four daily tapes, four weekly tapes, twelve monthly tapes, and one yearly tape. On each weekday Monday through Thursday, you use one of the four daily tapes. These tapes are reused every week. On Friday, you use one of the four weekly tapes. These tapes are reused monthly. On the first of the month, replace the tape that would ordinarily run with the monthly tape, and perform a full backup. These tapes can be reused yearly. And on December 31st you use the yearly tape, and put it aside until the end of the following year.

Troubleshooting Printer Issues

If you've ever used a Windows NT network printer, you may have noticed how easy it looks. You just run the wizard, make sure you have the right drivers loaded, and you're printing. Unfortunately for an administrator, the "under-the-hood" portion of printing is extremely complex, to give the appearance of simplicity from the front end. To effectively troubleshoot printing issues, you must be familiar with the entire printing process.

Scenario 6.7

You have a number of users who are unable to print to the network printer. You can't print from the server console, either.

Required Results

- Fix the printer and get the jobs in the queue printed.

Following the Printing Process

The printing process is one of the great "under-the-hood" features of Windows NT. From a user's perspective, a click on the printer icon magically produces a printout at a nearby printer. The underlying process that gets the document from the application to the printer is pretty complicated, and you need to understand how it works to effectively troubleshoot any problems with the process. {*To review Microsoft's terms for the printing mechanism, look in Chapter 2 for the specifics.*}

Take a moment to examine how your Word document gets from the application to the printer (or print device, in Microsoft terms):

1. First, your application (Word, in our example) makes a series of calls to the graphics device interface (GDI). The GDI communicates with the printer driver to take the document from Word and create the print job.
2. The print job is sent to the local print spooler.
3. The print job is then forwarded to the remote print device (your network printer).
4. The Windows NT print spooler receives the job from the workstation's print spooler.
5. Finally, the print job is sent to the print device (the actual printer) and the document is printed.

In addition to the process involved, you need to know what files and directories this process is using:

- The Print Spooler uses the `WINSPOOL.DRV`, `SPOOLSS.EXE`, and `SPOOLSS.DLL`.
- Local printers use the `LOCALMON.DLL` file to monitor the local print queue. Remote printers are monitored using printer-specific DLLs, such as `HPMON.DLL` for a Hewlett-Packard printer.

- The SPOOL Service uses the `<%systemroot%>\SYSTEM32\SPOOL\Printers` subdirectory to store jobs (by default—this can be redirected if necessary).
- Most of the rest of the files are located in the `SYSTEM` directory.

Locating a Printer Problem

Now that you know how a job gets printed, where do you look for printer problems?

Here's a list of common things to check while troubleshooting printer issues:

- Ensure that the printer is online, has toner or ink, is connected to the network, and has paper loaded. Also check for paper jams.
- Ensure that the users having the problem have the correct rights to access the printer. One easy way to test this is trying to print as an administrator.
- Make sure all the appropriate drivers are loaded. Remember that drivers for Windows 95 must be loaded locally.
- Make sure there is enough disk space available for the job to spool. If you are spooling jobs to the default directory, make sure your system partition isn't full.
- When a user is printing to a remote printer, make sure he or she can access the server. To spool a job to a remote printer, the user actually maps a drive to place the job on. Make sure he or she can make that connection.
- Ensure that the Spooler service is running. If a job gets hung up in the queue, try stopping and starting the Spooler service.

At this point you should have been able to track down your printer problem, completing the scenario.

Advanced Troubleshooting

There is one additional problem that Microsoft wants you to be familiar with for the exam. If you have worked with Windows NT for any period of time, you have probably been introduced to it already. Microsoft wants you to understand the blue screen errors.

Blue Screen Errors

If you have experienced a blue screen error during your experiences with Windows NT, you have probably handled it in one of two ways. If you are like many people, you powered the server off, powered it back on, and hoped the error went away. This is a mistake: The blue screen errors contain some good information for troubleshooting the problem. A blue screen error consists of five sections:

- *Debug Port Status Indicators:* This section describes the status of the serial port. Although this method is not covered in this book, advanced debugging can be done via the serial port.
- *BugCheck Information:* This contains the actual error message along with all associated parameters included with the error traps.
- *Driver Information:* This section shows the drivers loaded at the time of the error. You'll see the name, memory location, and date for each driver.
- *Kernel Build Number and Stack Dump:* This section gives you the OS build number and a dump of the last instructions executed.
- *Debug Port Information:* This contains all the information on the COM port being used by the DEBUG if used.

Almost all the blue screen errors you encounter are caused by poorly written or conflicting drivers, or a hardware error. Application errors will generally manifest in a different way. Now that you have an idea of what information the blue screen provides; you need to be familiar with doing a memory dump after the error.

Creating and Working with Memory Dump Files

If you follow the instructions in this chapter, you will have a good handle on troubleshooting errors with Windows NT. But what do you do when you are in over your head? Sometimes you create a *dump file*, which contains all the information the kernel debugger had at the time of the crash. To configure Windows NT to create a dump file, perform the following steps:

1. Right click on the My Computer icon and select Properties.
2. Choose the Startup/Shutdown tab (see *Figure 6.17*).
3. Under the Recovery section, select the Write Debugging Information To check box, and enter a directory path for the file.

FIGURE 6.17
Creating a dump file.

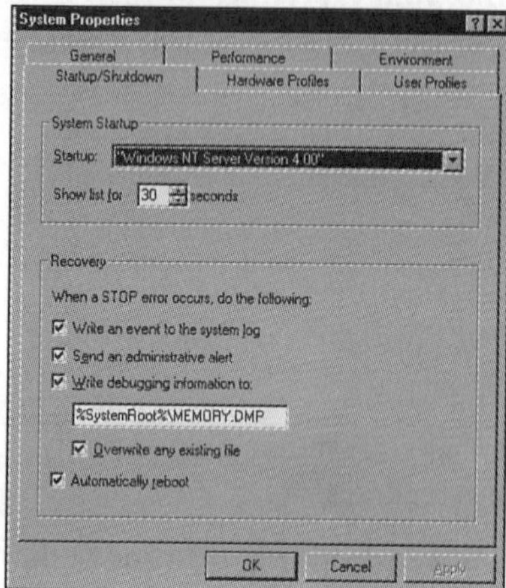

Now that the dump file is being written, there are three utilities you can use to work with the file:

- *DUMPCHK*: Ensures that the dump file is intact and readable.
- *DUMPEXAM*: Allows you to create a test file containing the same information as the dump file.
- *DUMPFLOP*: Backs up the dump file to a series of floppies in case you need to send it to Microsoft for further assistance.

APPENDIX A

Overview of the Certification Process

You must pass rigorous certification exams to become a Microsoft Certified Professional. These certification exams provide a valid and reliable measure of your technical proficiency and expertise. The closed-book exams are developed in consultation with computer industry professionals who have on-the-job experience with Microsoft products in the workplace. These exams are conducted by an independent organization—Sylvan Prometric—at more than 1,200 Authorized Prometric Testing Centers around the world.

Currently, Microsoft offers six types of certification, based on specific areas of expertise:

- *Microsoft Certified Professional (MCP).* Persons who attain this certification are qualified to provide installation, configuration, and support for users of at least one Microsoft desktop operating system, such as Windows NT Workstation. In addition, candidates can take elective exams to develop areas of specialization. MCP is the initial or first level of expertise.
- *Microsoft Certified Professional + Internet (MCP+Internet).* Persons who attain this certification are qualified to plan security, install and configure server products, manage server resources, extend service to run CGI scripts or ISAPI scripts, monitor and analyze performance, and troubleshoot problems. The expertise required is similar to that of an MCP, with a focus on the Internet.
- *Microsoft Certified Systems Engineer (MCSE).* Persons who attain this certification are qualified to effectively plan, implement, maintain, and support information systems with Microsoft Windows NT and other Microsoft advanced systems and workgroup products, such as Microsoft Office and Microsoft BackOffice. MCSE is a second level of expertise.

- *Microsoft Certified Systems Engineer + Internet (MCSE+Internet).* Persons who attain this certification are qualified in the core MCSE areas and are qualified to enhance, deploy, and manage sophisticated intranet and Internet solutions that include a browser, proxy server, host servers, database, and messaging and commerce components. In addition, MCSE+Internet-certified professionals will be able to manage and analyze web sites.
- *Microsoft Certified Solution Developer (MCSD).* Persons who attain this certification are qualified to design and develop custom business solutions by using Microsoft development tools, technologies, and platforms, including Microsoft Office and Microsoft BackOffice. MCSD is a second level of expertise with a focus on software development.
- *Microsoft Certified Trainer (MCT).* Persons who attain this certification are instructionally and technically qualified by Microsoft to deliver Microsoft Education Courses at Microsoft-authorized sites. An MCT must be employed by a Microsoft Solution Provider Authorized Technical Education Center or a Microsoft Authorized Academic Training site.

NOTE

Stay in Touch For up-to-date information about each type of certification, visit the Microsoft Training and Certification World Wide Web site at `http://www.microsoft.com/train_cert`. You must have an Internet account and a WWW browser to access this information. You also can call the following sources:

- Microsoft Certified Professional Program: 800-636-7544
- Sylvan Prometric Testing Centers: 800-755-EXAM
- Microsoft Online Institute (MOLI): 800-449-9333

How to Become a Microsoft Certified Professional (MCP)

To become an MCP, you must pass one operating system exam. The following list contains the names and exam numbers of each of the operating system exams that will qualify you for your MCP certification (an * denotes an exam that is scheduled to be retired):

- Implementing and Supporting Microsoft Windows 95, #70-064 (formerly #70-063)
- Implementing and Supporting Microsoft Windows NT Workstation 4.02, #70-073
- Implementing and Supporting Microsoft Windows NT Workstation 3.51, #70-042*
- Implementing and Supporting Microsoft Windows NT Server 4.0, #70-067
- Implementing and Supporting Microsoft Windows NT Server 3.51, #70-043*
- Microsoft Windows for Workgroups 3.11-Desktop, #70-048*
- Microsoft Windows 3.1, #70-030*
- Microsoft Windows Architecture I, #70-160
- Microsoft Windows Architecture II, #70-161

How to Become a Microsoft Certified Professional + Internet (MCP+Internet)

To become an MCP with a specialty in Internet technology, you must pass the following three exams:

- Internetworking Microsoft TCP/IP on Microsoft Windows NT 4.0, #70-059
- Implementing and Supporting Microsoft Windows NT Server 4.0, #70-067
- Implementing and Supporting Microsoft Internet Information Server 3.0 and Microsoft Index Server 1.1, #70-077

  OR Implementing and Supporting Microsoft Internet Information Server 4.0, #70-087

How to Become a Microsoft Certified Systems Engineer (MCSE)

MCSE candidates must pass four operating system exams and two elective exams. The MCSE certification path is divided into two tracks: the Windows NT 3.51 track and the Windows NT 4.0 track.

The following lists show the core requirements (four operating system exams) for the Windows NT 3.51, the core requirements for the Windows NT 4.0 track, and the elective courses (two exams) you can choose from for either track.

The four Windows NT 3.51 track core requirements for MCSE certification are as follows:

- Implementing and Supporting Microsoft Windows NT Server 3.51, #70-043*
- Implementing and Supporting Microsoft Windows NT Workstation 3.51, #70-042*
- Microsoft Windows 3.1, #70-030*

  OR Microsoft Windows for Workgroups 3.11, #70-048*

  OR Implementing and Supporting Microsoft Windows 95, #70-064

  OR Implementing and Supporting Microsoft Windows 98, #70-098
- Networking Essentials, #70-058

The four Windows NT 4.0 track core requirements for MCSE certification are as follows:

- Implementing and Supporting Microsoft Windows NT Server 4.0, #70-067
- Implementing and Supporting Microsoft Windows NT Server 4.0 in the Enterprise, #70-068
- Microsoft Windows 3.1, #70-030*

  OR Microsoft Windows for Workgroups 3.11, #70-048*

  OR Implementing and Supporting Microsoft Windows 95, #70-064

OR Implementing and Supporting Microsoft Windows NT Workstation 4.0, #70-073

OR Implementing and Supporting Microsoft Windows 98, #70-098

- Networking Essentials, #70-058

For both the Windows NT 3.51 and the Windows NT 4.0 track, you must pass two of the following elective exams for MCSE certification:

- Implementing and Supporting Microsoft SNA Server 3.0, #70-013

  OR Implementing and Supporting Microsoft SNA Server 4.0, #70-085

- Implementing and Supporting Microsoft Systems Management Server 1.0, #70-014*

  OR Implementing and Supporting Microsoft Systems Management Server 1.2, #70-018

  OR Implementing and Supporting Microsoft Systems Management Server 2.0, #70-086

- Microsoft SQL Server 4.2 Database Implementation, #70-021

  OR Implementing a Database Design on Microsoft SQL Server 6.5, #70-027

  OR Implementing a Database Design on Microsoft SQL Server 7.0, #70-029

- Microsoft SQL Server 4.2 Database Administration for Microsoft Windows NT, #70-022

  OR System Administration for Microsoft SQL Server 6.5 (or 6.0), #70-026

  OR System Administration for Microsoft SQL Server 7.0, #70-028

- Microsoft Mail for PC Networks 3.2-Enterprise, #70-037

- Internetworking with Microsoft TCP/IP on Microsoft Windows NT (3.5–3.51), #70-053

  OR Internetworking with Microsoft TCP/IP on Microsoft Windows NT 4.0, #70-059

- Implementing and Supporting Microsoft Exchange Server 4.0, #70-075*

  OR Implementing and Supporting Microsoft Exchange Server 5.0, #70-076

OR Implementing and Supporting Microsoft Exchange Server 5.5, #70-081

- Implementing and Supporting Microsoft Internet Information Server 3.0 and Microsoft Index Server 1.1, #70-077

  OR Implementing and Supporting Microsoft Internet Information Server 4.0, #70-087

- Implementing and Supporting Microsoft Proxy Server 1.0, #70-078

  OR Implementing and Supporting Microsoft Proxy Server 2.0, #70-088

- Implementing and Supporting Microsoft Internet Explorer 4.0 by Using the Internet Explorer Resource Kit, #70-079

How to Become a Microsoft Certified Systems Engineer + Internet (MCSE+Internet)

MCSE+Internet candidates must pass seven operating system exams and two elective exams. The following lists show the core requirements and the elective courses (of which you need to pass two exams).

The seven MCSE+Internet core exams required for certification are as follows:

- Networking Essentials, #70-058
- Internetworking with Microsoft TCP/IP on Microsoft Windows NT 4.0, #70-059
- Implementing and Supporting Microsoft Windows 95, #70-064

  OR Implementing and Supporting Microsoft Windows NT Workstation 4.0, #70-073

  OR Implementing and Supporting Microsoft Windows 98, #70-098

- Implementing and Supporting Microsoft Windows NT Server 4.0, #70-067
- Implementing and Supporting Microsoft Windows NT Server 4.0 in the Enterprise, #70-068
- Implementing and Supporting Microsoft Internet Information Server 3.0 and Microsoft Index Server 1.1, #70-077

  OR Implementing and Supporting Microsoft Internet Information Server 4.0, #70-087

- Implementing and Supporting Microsoft Internet Explorer 4.0 by Using the Internet Explorer Resource Kit, #70-079

You must also pass two of the following elective exams:

- System Administration for Microsoft SQL Server 6.5, #70-026
- Implementing a Database Design on Microsoft SQL Server 6.5, #70-027
- Implementing and Supporting Web Sites Using Microsoft Site Server 3.0, #70-056
- Implementing and Supporting Microsoft Exchange Server 5.0, #70-076

  OR Implementing and Supporting Microsoft Exchange Server 5.5, #70-081
- Implementing and Supporting Microsoft Proxy Server 1.0, #70-078

  OR Implementing and Supporting Microsoft Proxy Server 2.0, #70-088
- Implementing and Supporting Microsoft SNA Server 4.0, #70-085

How to Become a Microsoft Certified Solution Developer (MCSD)

MCSD candidates must pass two core technology exams and two elective exams. The following lists show the required technology exams, plus the elective exams that apply toward obtaining the MCSD.

You must pass the following two core technology exams to qualify for MCSD certification:

- Microsoft Windows Architecture I, #70-160
- Microsoft Windows Architecture II, #70-161

You must also pass two of the following elective exams to become an MSCD:

- Microsoft SQL Server 4.2 Database Implementation, #70-021

  OR Implementing a Database Design on Microsoft SQL Server 6.5, #70-027

  OR Implementing a Database Design on Microsoft SQL Server 7.0, #70-029

- Developing Applications with C++ Using the Microsoft Foundation Class Library, #70-024
- Implementing OLE in Microsoft Foundation Class Applications, #70-025
- Programming with Microsoft Visual Basic 4.0, #70-065

  OR Developing Applications with Microsoft Visual Basic 5.0, #70-165
- Microsoft Access 2.0 for Windows-Application Development, #70-051

  OR Microsoft Access for Windows 95 and the Microsoft Access Development Toolkit, #70-069
- Developing Applications with Microsoft Excel 5.0 Using Visual Basic for Applications, #70-052
- Programming in Microsoft Visual FoxPro 3.0 for Windows, #70-054

Becoming a Microsoft Certified Trainer (MCT)

To understand the requirements and process for becoming a Microsoft Certified Trainer (MCT), you must obtain the Microsoft Certified Trainer Guide document from the following WWW site:

```
http://www.microsoft.com/train_cert/mct/
```

From this page, you can read the document as web pages, or you can display or download it as a Word file. The MCT Guide explains the four-step process of becoming an MCT. The general steps for the MCT certification are described here:

1. Complete and mail a Microsoft Certified Trainer application to Microsoft. You must include proof of your skills for presenting instructional material. The options for doing so are described in the MCT Guide.
2. Obtain and study the Microsoft Trainer Kit for the Microsoft Official Curricula (MOC) course for which you want to be certified. You can order Microsoft Trainer Kits by calling 800-688-0496 in North America. Other regions should review the MCT Guide for information on how to order a Trainer Kit.
3. Pass the Microsoft certification exam for the product for which you want to be certified to teach.

4. Attend the Microsoft Official Curriculum (MOC) course for which you want to be certified. You do this so that you can understand how the course is structured, how labs are completed, and how the course flows.

WARNING

Be Sure to Get the MCT Guide! You should consider the preceding steps to be a general overview of the MCT certification process. The precise steps that you must take are described in detail on the WWW site mentioned earlier. Do not mistakenly believe the preceding steps make up the actual process you need to take.

If you are interested in becoming an MCT, you can receive more information by visiting the Microsoft Certified Training (MCT) WWW site at `http://www.microsoft.com/train_cert/mct/` or by calling 800-688-0496.

APPENDIX B

Fast Facts: Server

The fast facts listed in this section are designed as a refresher of key points and topics that are required to succeed on the Windows NT Server 4.0 exam. By using these summaries of key points, you can spend an hour prior to your exam to review key topics, and ensure that you have a solid understanding of the objectives and information required for you to succeed in each major area of the exam.

The following are the main categories Microsoft uses to arrange the objectives:

- Planning
- Installation and configuration
- Managing resources
- Connectivity
- Monitoring and optimization
- Troubleshooting

For each of these main sections, or categories, the assigned objectives are reviewed, and following each objective, review material is offered.

PLANNING

Remember: Here are the elements that Microsoft says they test on for the "Planning" section of the exam.

Planning Objective 1

Plan the disk drive configuration for various requirements. Requirements include choosing a file system and fault tolerance method.

Minimum requirement for installing NT Server on an Intel machine is 468DX/33, 16MB of RAM, and 130MB of free disk space.

The login process on an NT Domain is as follows:

1. WinLogon sends the user name and password to the Local Security Authority (LSA).
2. The LSA passes the request to the local NetLogon service.
3. The local NetLogon service sends the logon information to the NetLogon service on the domain controller.
4. The NetLogon service on the domain controller passes the information to the domain controller's Security Accounts Manager (SAM).
5. The SAM asks the domain directory database for approval of the user name and password.
6. The SAM passes the result of the approval request to the domain controller's NetLogon service.
7. The domain controller's NetLogon service passes the result of the approval request to the client's NetLogon service.
8. The client's NetLogon service passes the result of the approval request to the LSA.
9. If the logon is approved, the LSA creates an access token and passes it to the WinLogon process.
10. WinLogon completes the logon, thus creating a new process for the user and attaching the access token to the new process.

Your computer boots in the system partition, which must be on an active partition.

The WINNT folder is found in the boot partition, which contains the NT program files. It can be on any partition (other than on a volume set).

NT supports two forms of software-based fault tolerance: Disk Mirroring (RAID 1) and Stripe Sets with Paritiy (RAID 5).

Disk Mirroring uses two hard drives and provides 50% disk space utilization.

Stripe Sets with Parity uses between 3 and 32 hard drives and provides (n-1)/n*100% utilization (n = number of disks in the set).

Disk duplexing provides better tolerance than mirroring because it performs mirroring with separate controllers on each disk.

NT supports three file systems: NTFS, FAT, and CDFS. NT no longer supports HPFS, the OS/2 file system, or FAT32, a file system used by Windows 95.

Table B.1 shows a quick summary of the differencesbetween NTFS and FAT features.

TABLE B.1

FAT VERSUS NTFS COMPARISON

Feature	*FAT*	*NTFS*
File name length	255	255
8.3 file name compatibility	Yes	Yes
File size	4 GB	16 EB
Partition size	4 GB	16 EB
Directory structure	Linked list	B-tree
Local security	No	Yes
Transaction tracking	No	Yes
Hot fixing	No	Yes
Overhead	1 MB	>4 MB
Required on system partition for RISC-based computers	Yes	No
Accessible from MS-DOS/Windows 95	Yes	No
Accessible from OS/2	Yes	No
Case sensitive only	No	POSIX
Case preserving	Yes	Yes
Compression	No	Yes
Efficiency	200 MB	400 MB
Windows NT formatting	Yes	Yes
Fragmentation level	High	Low
Floppy disk formatting	Yes	No

Planning Objective 2

Choose a protocol for various situations. Protocols include TCP/IP, NWLink IPX/SPX Compatible Transport, and NetBEUI.

Table B.2 summarizes the protocols commonly used by NT for network communication.

TABLE B.2

PRIMARY PROTOCOL USES

Protocol	*Primary Use*
TCP/IP	Internet and WAN connectivity
NWLink	Interoperability with NetWare
NetBEUI	Interoperability with old LAN Manager networks

The main points regarding TCP/IP are as follows:

- Requires IP Address and Subnet Mask to function (default gateway if being routed)
- Can be configured manually or automatically by using DHCP server running on NT
- Common address resolution methods are WINS and DNS

INSTALLATION AND CONFIGURATION

Remember: Here are the elements that Microsoft says they test on for the "Installation and Configuration" section of the exam.

Installation and Configuration Objective 1

Install Windows NT Serveron Intel-based platforms.

The Hardware Compatibility list is used to ensure that NT supports all computer components.

Table B.3 is a summary of the WINNT and WINNT32 switches.

TABLE B.3

WINNT AND WINNT32 SWITCH FUNCTIONS

Switch	*Function*
/B	Prevents creation of the three setup disks during the installation process
/S	Indicates the location of the source files for NT installation (for example, /S:D:\NTFiles)
/U	Indicates the script file to use for an unattended installation (for example, /U:C:\Answer.txt)
/UDF	Indicates the location of the uniqueness database file, which defines unique configuration for each NT machine being installed (for example, /UDF:D:\Answer.UDF)
/T	Indicates where to place the temporary installation files
/OX	Initiates only the creation of the three setup disks
/F	Indicates to *not* verify the files copied to the setup disks
/C	Indicates to *not* check for free space on the setup disks before creating them

Three setup disks are required for installation when a CD-ROM is not supported by the operating system present on the computer at installation time. If no operating system exists but the computer will not boot from the CD-ROM, you'll also need to use the three setup disks.

To remove NT from a computer you must complete the following:

1. Remove all the NTFS partitions from within Windows NT and reformat them with FAT (this ensures that these disk areas will be accessible by non-NT operating systems).
2. Boot to another operating system, such as Windows 95 or MS-DOS.
3. Delete the Windows NT installation directory tree (usually `WINNT`).
4. Delete `pagefile.sys`.
5. Turn off the hidden, system, and read-only attributes for `NTBOOTDD.SYS`, `BOOT.INI`, `NTLDR`, and `NTDETECT.COM` and then delete them. (You might not have all of these on your computer, but if so, you can find them all in the root directory of your C drive.)

6. Make the hard drive bootable by placing another operating system on it (or SYS it with DOS or Windows 95 to allow the operating system that does exist to boot).

Installation and Configuration Objective 2

Install Windows NT Server to perform various server roles. Server roles include Primary domain controller, Backup domain controller, and Member server.

NT can be installed in three different configurations in a domain:

- **Primary Domain Controller.** The Primary Domain Controller (PDC) is the first domain controller installed into a domain. As the first computer in the domain, the PDC creates the domain. This fact is important to understand because it establishes the rationale for needing a PDC in the environment. Each domain can contain only one PDC. All other domain controllers in the domain are installed as Backup Domain Controllers. The PDC handles user requests and logon validation, and it offers all the standard Windows NT Server functionality. The PDC contains the original copy of the Security Accounts Manager (SAM), which contains all user accounts and security permissions for your domain.
- **Backup Domain Controller.** The Backup Domain Controller (BDC) is an additional domain controller used to handle logon requests by users in the network. To handle the logon requests, the BDC must have a complete copy of the domain database, or SAM. The BDC also runs the Netlogon service; however, the Netlogon service in a BDC functions a little differently than the same service within a PDC. In the PDC, the Netlogon service handles synchronization of the SAM database to all the BDCs.
- **Member server.** In both of the domain controllers (PDC or BDC) the computer has an additional function. The domain controllers handle logon requests and ensure that the SAM is synchronized throughout the domain. These functions add overhead to the system. A computer that handles the server functionality you require without the overhead of handling logon validation is called a *member server.* A member server is a part of the domain, but it does not need a copy of the SAM database and does not handle logon requests. The main function of a member server is to share resources.

A BDC can be promoted to a PDC, but a member server must have NT reinstalled in order to act as a Domain Controller.

Installation and Configuration Objective 3

Install Windows NT Server by using various methods. Installation methods include CD-ROM, Over-the-network, Network Client Administrator, and Express versus Custom.

Two sources can be used for installation files: CD-ROM or network share (which refers to the hardware specific files from the CD copied onto a server and shared).

WINNT and WINNT32 are used for network installation—WINNT32 for installations when NT is currently present on the machine you are installing to and WINNT when it is not.

Installation and Configuration Objective 4

Configure protocols and protocol bindings. Protocols include TCP/IP, NWLink IPX/SPX Compatible Transport, and NetBEUI.

You install a new protocol in Windows NT Server through the Network Properties dialog box. Select the Protocols Tab.

The protocols required for this exam are listed here, with their configuration options.

> **NOTE** Because there are no configuration options for NetBEUI, this protocol is not listed.

- **TCP/IP.** The following tabs are available for configuration in the Microsoft TCP/IP Properties dialog box:
  - **IP Address.** The IP Address tab enables you to configure the IP address, the subnet mask, and the default gateway. You also can enable the system to allocate IP address information automatically through the use of the DHCP server.

    An IP address is a 32-bit address that is broken into four octets and is used to identify your computer as a TCP/IP host. Each IP address must be unique. If you have any IP address conflicts on your computer (perhaps another device on the network is using the same address) you cannot use the TCP/IP protocol.

Your IP address is then grouped into a subnet. To subnet your network, you must assign a subnet mask. A *subnet mask* is used to identify the computers local to your network. Any address outside your subnet is accessed through the default gateway, also called the *router.* The default gateway is the address of the router that handles all routing of your TCP/IP information to computers, or *hosts,* outside your subnet.

- **DNS.** The DNS tab provides the options for configuring your TCP/IP protocol to use a DNS server. The Domain Name System (DNS) server translates TCP/IP host names of remote computers into IP addresses. Remember that an IP address is a unique address for each computer. The DNS server contains a database of all the computers you can access by host name. An example of this would be when you access a Web page on the Internet by name. The name is generally easier to remember and work with than using the IP address of the host.
- **WINS Address.** The WINS Address tab enables you to configure your primary and secondary Windows Internet Names Services (WINS) server addresses. WINS is used to reduce the number of NetBIOS broadcast messages sent across the network to locate a computer. By using a WINS server, you keep the names of computers on your network in a WINS database. The WINS database is dynamic.

  In configuring your WINS servers, you can enter your primary WINS server and a secondary WINS server. Your system searches the primary WINS server database first and if no match is found, searches the secondary database.
- **DHCP Relay.** The DHCP relay agent is used to locate your DHCP servers across routers. DHCP servers distribute the DHCP addresses. The client request, however, is made with a broadcast message. Broadcast messages do not cross routers; therefore, this protocol might place some restrictions on your systems. The solution is to use a DHCP relay agent to assist the clients in finding the DHCP server across a router.

  In configuring your DHCP relay agent, you can specify the seconds threshold and the maximum number of hops to use in searching for the DHCP servers. At the bottom of the tab, you can enter the IP addresses of the DHCP servers you want to use.
- **Routing.** In an environment in which multiple subnets are used, you can configure your Windows NT Server as a multihomed system. In other words, you can install multiple network adapters, each connecting

to a different subnet. If you enable the Enable IP Forwarding option, your computer acts as a router, forwarding the packets through the network cards in the multihomed system to the other subnet.

- **NWLINK IPX/SPX Compatible.** The configuration of the NWLink protocol is simple in comparison to the TCP/IP protocol. It is this simplicity that makes NWLink a popular protocol to use.

  The NWLink IPX/SPX Properties dialog box has two tabs:

  - **General.** On the General tab, you have the option to assign an internal network number. This eight-digit hexadecimal number format is used by some programs with services that can be accessed by NetWare clients.

    You also have the option to select a frame type for your NWLink protocol. The frame type you select must match the frame type of the remote computer with which you need to communicate. By default, Windows NT Server uses the Auto Frame Type Detection setting, which scans the network and loads the first frame type it encounters.

  - **Routing.** The Routing tab of the NWLink IPX/SPX Properties dialog box is used to enable or disable the Routing Information Protocol (RIP). If you enable RIP routing over IPX, your Windows NT Server can act as an IPX router.

The *binding order* is the sequence your computer uses to select which protocol to use for network communications. A protocol is listed for each network-based service, protocol, and adapter available.

The Bindings tab's Show Bindings For option can be used to select the service, adapter, or protocol you want to modify in the binding order. By clicking the appropriate button, you can enable or disable each binding, or move up or down in the binding order.

Installation and Configuration Objective 5

Configure network adapters. Considerations include changing IRQ, IObase, and memory addresses and configuring multiple adapters.

The Interrupt ReQuest (IRQ) is the address the adapter uses to request the attention of the CPU. Make sure the IRQ that is assigned to your adapter doesn't conflict with another device in the system.

When using multiple adapters, be sure they are not using the same address (IP or IPX). They must also use different IRQs, different IOBases, and different memory addresses.

If you are installing two network adapters so the server will act as a router, be sure to enable routing under the appropriate protocol through the Network Applet.

Network properties dialog box lets you install and configure the following:

- Computer and Domain names
- Services
- Protocols
- Adapters
- Bindings

When configuring NWLink, ensure that if more than one frame type exists on your network you don't use AutoDetect or only the first frame type encountered will be detected from then on.

Table B.4 shows you three TCP/IP command-line diagnostic tools and what they do.

TABLE B.4

TCP/IP COMMAND LINE DIAGNOSTIC TOOLS

Tool	*Function*
IPConfig	Displays the basic TCP/IP configuration of each adapter card on a computer (with **/all** displays detailed configuration information)
Ping	Determines connectivity with another TCP/IP host by sending a message that is echoed by the recipient if received
Tracert	Traces each hop on the way to a TCP/IP host and indicates points of failure if they exist

Network adapter card configuration of IRQ and I/O port addresses may or may not be configurable from the Network Properties dialog box; this capability depends on the card.

Installation and Configuration Objective 6

Configure Windows NT server core services. Services include Directory Replicator, License Manager, and other services.

In this objective, you look at configuring some of the core services in the Windows NT Server. These services are as follows:

- **License Manager.** The License Manager application is found in the Administrative Tools program group. It is used to display licensing information for the network, including client licenses—both Per Server and Per Seat licenses by BackOffice product. License Manager also allows you to browse for client license information across the network. You can monitor, add, or revoke licenses across the network.
- **Computer Browser service.** The Computer Browser service is responsible for maintaining a *browse list* of computers on the physical network. As a Windows NT Server, your system plays a large role in the browsing of a network. The Windows NT Server acts as a master browser or backup browser.

  The selection of browsers is made through an election. The election is called by any client computer or when a preferred master browser computer starts up. The election is based on broadcast messages. Every computer has the opportunity to nominate itself, and the computer with the highest settings wins the election.

  The election criteria are based on three things:

  - The operating system (Windows NT Server, Windows NT Workstation, Windows 95, or Windows for Workgroups)
  - The version of the operating system (NT 4.0, NT 3.51, or NT 3.5)
  - The current role of the computer (master browser, backup browser, or potential browser)
- **Directory Replicator service.** You can configure the Directory Replicator service to synchronize an entire directory structure across multiple servers.

  In configuring the directory service, you must select the export server and all the import servers. The export server is the computer that holds the original copy of the directory structure and files. Each import server receives a complete copy of the export server's directory structure. The Directory Replicator service monitors the directory structure on the export server. If the contents of the directory change, the changes are copied to all the import servers. The file copying and directory monitoring is completed by a special service account you create. You must configure the Directory Replicator service to use this service account. The following access is required for your Directory Replicator service account:

  - The account should be a member of the Backup Operators and Replicators groups.

- There should be no time or logon restrictions for the account.
- The Password Never Expires option should be selected.
- The User Must Change Password at Next Logon option should be turned off.

When configuring the export server, you have the option to specify the export directory. The default export directory is `C:\WINNT\system32\repl\export\`.

In the Import Directories section of the Directory Replication dialog box, you can select the import directory. The default import directory is `C:\WINNT\system32\repl\import`.

Remember that the default directory for executing logon scripts in a Windows NT system is `C:\WINNT\system32\repl\import\scripts`.

Installation and Configuration Objective 7

Configure peripherals and devices. Peripherals and devices include communication devices, SCSI devices, tape devices drivers, UPS devices and UPS service, mouse drivers, display drivers, and keyboard drivers.

These devices are all installed using various applets under the Control Panel.

You must reboot the server after installing a SCSI device.

A modem must be installed before you install Remote Access Server.

NT checking for serial mice at boot may disable a UPS. To disable that check, place `/noserialmice` in the boot line in the `BOOT.INI` file.

The SCSI adapters icon in the Control Panel lets you add and configure SCSI devices as well as CD-ROM drives.

Installation and Configuration Objective 8

Configure hard disks to meet various requirements. Requirements include allocating disk space capacity, providing redundancy, improving security, and formatting.

All hard disk configuration can be done using the Disk Administrator tool. The different disk configurations you need to understand for the Enterprise exam are as follows:

- **Stripe set.** A stripe set gives you improved disk read and write performance; however, it supplies no fault tolerance. A minimum of two disks is required, and the configuration can stripe up to 32 physical disks. A stripe set cannot include the system partition.
- **Disk mirroring.** A mirror set uses two physical disks and provides full data duplication. Often referred to as RAID level 1, disk mirroring is a useful solution to assigning duplication to the system partition, as well as any other disks that might be in the system.
- **Stripe set with parity.** A stripe set with parity enables fault tolerance in your system. A minimum of three physical disks is required, and a maximum of 32 physical disks can be included in a stripe set with parity. A stripe set with parity cannot include the system partition of your Windows NT system.

Of the preceding configurations, the solution that supplies the best duplication and optimization mix is the stripe set with parity (RAID 5).

Installation and Configuration Objective 9

Configure printers. Tasks include adding and configuring a printer, implementing a printer pool, and setting print priorities.

The installation of a printer is a fairly simple procedure involving the use of the Add Printer Wizard. Generally, wizard-driven tasks are not heavily tested because these tasks are usually fill-in-the-blank types of activities.

Use of a printer pool is a key point. The items to remember about printer pools are as follows:

- All printers in a printer pool must be able to function using the same printer driver.
- A printer pool can have a maximum of eight printers in the pool.

Printers can be assigned different priorities to print devices. In order to ensure someone has access to a print device when needed, he must be using a printer with a priority higher than that of any others in the pool. Priorities range from 1–99, with 99 being the highest priority.

To print to an NT-shared printer, Windows 95 and RISC clients need printer drivers installed on an NT Server acting as a print server.

By adjusting the printer schedule, you can ensure that jobs sent to particular printers are printed only at certain hours of the day.

A printer has permissions assigned to it. The following is a list of the permissions for printers:

- **No Access.** Completely restricts access to the printer.
- **Print.** Allows a user or group to submit a print job, and to control the settings and print status for that job.
- **Manage Documents.** Allows a user or group to submit a print job, and to control the settings and print status for all print jobs.
- **Full Control.** Allows a user to submit a print job, and to control the settings and print status for all documents as well as for the printer itself. In addition, the user or group may share, stop sharing, change permissions for, and even delete the printer.

MS-DOS users must have print drivers installed locally on their computers.

Installation and Configuration Objective 10

Configure a Windows NT Server computer for various types of client computers. Client computer types include Windows NT Workstation, Microsoft Windows 95, and Microsoft MS-DOS–based.

The Client Administrator allows you to do the following:

- **Make Network Installation Startup Disk.** Shares files and creates a bootable disk for initiating client installation.
- **Make Installation Disk Set.** Copies installation files to a disk for installing simple clients such as MS-DOS Network Client 3.0.
- **Copy Client-Based Network Administration Tools.** Creates a folder that can be attached to from Windows NT Workstation and Windows 95 clients to install tools for administering an NT Server from a workstation.

MANAGING RESOURCES

Remember: Here are the elements that Microsoft says they test on for the "Managing Resources" section of the exam.

Managing Resources Objective 1

Manage user and group accounts. Considerations include managing Windows NT groups, managing Windows NT user rights, administering account policies, and auditing changes to the user account database.

To allow NT computers to participate in a domain, a computer account must be created for each computer.

The assignment of permissions to resources should use the following procedure:

1. Create user accounts.
2. Create global groups for the domain and populate the groups with user accounts.
3. Create local groups and assign them rights and permissions to resources and programs in the domain.
4. Place global groups into the local groups you have created, thereby giving the users who are members of the global groups access to the system and its resources.

The built-in local groups in a Windows NT Domain are as follows:

- Administrators
- Users
- Guests
- Backup Operators
- Replicator
- Print Operators
- Server Operators
- Account Operators

The built-in global groups in an NT Domain are as follows:

- Domain Admins
- Domain Users
- Domain Guests

The system groups on an NT server are as follows:

- Everyone
- Creator Owner
- Network
- Interactive

The built-in users on an NT server are as follows:

- Administrator
- Guest

Table B.5 describes the buttons on the User Properties dialog box and their functions.

TABLE B.5

BUTTONS ON THE USER PROPERTIES DIALOG BOX

Button	*Function*
Groups	Enables you to add and remove group memberships for the account. The easiest way to grant rights to a user account is to add the account to a group that possesses those rights.
Profile	Enables you to add a user profile path, a logon script name, and a home directory path to the user's environment profile. You learn more about the Profile button in the following section.
Hours	Enables you to define specific times when the users can access the account. (The default is Always.)
Logon To	Enables you to specify up to eight workstations from which the user can log on. (The default is All Workstations.)
Account	Enables you to provide an expiration date for the account. (The default is Never.) You also can specify the account as Global (for regular users in this domain) or Domain Local.

Table B.6 is a summary of the account policy fields.

TABLE B.6

ACCOUNT POLICY FIELDS

Button	*Function*
Maximum Password Age	The maximum number of days a password can be in effect until it must be changed.
Minimum Password Age	The minimum number of days a password must stay in effect before it can be changed.

ACCOUNT POLICY FIELDS

Button	*Function*
Minimum Password Length	The minimum number of characters a password must include.
Password Uniqueness	The number of passwords that NT remembers for a user; these passwords cannot be reused until they are no longer remembered.
Account Lockout	The number of incorrect passwords that can be input by a user before the account becomes locked. Reset will automatically set the count back to 0 after a specified length of time. In addition the duration of lockout is either a number of minutes or Forever (until an administrator unlocks it).
Forcibly Disconnect Remote	In conjunction with logon hours, Users from Server when this checkbox enables forcible Logon Hours Expire disconnection of a user when authorized hours come to a close.
Users Must Log On in Order	Ensures that a user whose password to Change Password has expired cannot change his or her password; the user must have the password reset by an administrator.

Account SIDs are unique; therefore if an account is deleted, the permissions cannot be restored by recreating an account with the same name.

If a user is given permission to a resource and a group or groups of which the user is a member are also given access, then the user's effective permission is cumulative of all of the user permissions. This applies unless any of the permissions is No Access, in which case the user has no access at all to the resource, despite any other permissions.

If a user is given permission to a shared resource and is also given permission to that resource through NTFS permissions then the effective permission is the most restrictive permission.

The File Child Delete scenario manifests itself when someone has full control to a folder but is granted a permission that does not enable deletion (Read or No Access, for example). The effect is that the user will be able to delete files inside the folder even though sufficient access does not appear to be present.

To close the File Child Delete loophole, do not grant a user Full Control access to a folder; instead use special directory permissions to assign RXWDPO access, which eliminates the File Child Delete permission.

Access Tokens do not refresh and a user must log off and log back on if changed permissions are to take effect.

REGEDT32.EXE and REGEDIT are used to view and modify Registry settings in NT.

The five Registry subtrees are as follows:

- **HKEY_LOCAL_MACHINE.** Stores all the computer-specific configuration data.
- **HKEY_USERS.** Stores all the user-specific configuration data.
- **HKEY_CURRENT_USER.** Stores all configuration data for the currently logged-on user.
- **HKEY_CLASSES_ROOT.** Stores all OLE and file association information.
- **HKEY_CURRENT_CONFIG.** Stores information about the hardware profile specified at startup.

REGEDT32.EXE allows you to view and set security on the Registry. It also allows you to open the Registry in read-only mode, but does not allow you to search by key value.

Managing Resources Objective 2

Create and manage policies and profiles for various situations. Policies and profiles include local user profiles, roaming user profiles, and system policies.

Windows 95 clients need special profiles and policies created on a Windows 95 machine and then copied onto an NT Server to participate in domain profile and policy configuration.

Local profiles are only available from the machine on which they were created, whereas roaming profiles can be accessed from any machine on the network

A mandatory profile is a roaming profile that users cannot change. These profiles have the extension .MAN.

Hardware profiles can be used with machines that have more than one hardware configuration (such as laptops).

The System Policy Editor (POLEDIT) has two modes: Policy File mode and Registry mode.

The application of system policies is as follows:

1. When you log on, NTConfig.pol is checked. If there is an entry for the specific user, then any Registry settings indicated will be merged with, and overwrite if necessary, the user's Registry.
2. If there is no specific user entry, any settings for groups of which the user is a member will be applied to the user.
3. If the user is not present in any groups and is not listed explicitly, the default settings are applied.
4. If the computer that the user is logging on to has an entry then the computer settings are applied.
5. If there is not computer entry for the user then the default computer policy is applied.

Windows 95 policies are not compatible with NT. Therefore, to access a Windows 95 policy Windows 95 users must copy the Windows 95 policy to an NT machine and name it Config.Pol.

Managing Resources Objective 3

Administer remote servers from various types of client computers. Client computer types include Windows 95 and Windows NT Workstation.

This objective focuses on the remote administration tools available for your Windows NT Server. The following list summarizes the key tools:

- **Remote Administration Tools for Windows 95.** Allows User Manager, Server Manager, Event Viewer, and NTFS file permissions to be executed from the Windows 95 computer.
- **Remote Administration for Windows NT.** Allows User Manager, Server Manager, DHCP Manager, System Policy Editor, Remote Access Admin, Remote Boot Manager, WINS Manager, and NTFS file permissions to be executed from a Windows NT machine.

Managing Resources Objective 4

Manage disk resources. Tasks include copying and moving files between file systems, creating and sharing resources, implementing permissions and security, and establishing file auditing.

Many changes made in the Disk Administrator require that you choose Partition, Commit Changes for the changes to take effect.

Although you can set drive letters manually, the following list describes how NT assigns letters to partitions and volumes:

1. Beginning with the letter C, assign consecutive letters to the first primary partition on each physical disk.
2. Assign consecutive letters to each logical drive, completing assignments to all drives on one physical disk before moving on to the next.
3. Assign consecutive letters to the additional primary partitions, completing all assignments on one physical disk before moving on to the next.

Disk Administrator allows for the creation of two kinds of partitions: primary and extended. Table B.7 is a summary of their characteristics.

TABLE B.7

PARTITION CHARACTERISTICS

Object	*Characteristics*
Primary partition	Non-divisible disk unit that can be marked active and can be made bootable. Can have up to four on a physical drive. NT system partition must be on a primary partition.
Extended partition	Divisible disk unit that must be divided into logical disks (or have free space used in a volume) in order to function as space storage tool. Can have only one on a physical drive. Logical drive within can be the NT boot partition.

Disk Administrator can be used to format partitions and volumes as either FAT or NTFS.

The Net Use command line can be used to map a drive letter to a network share; using the `/persistent` switch ensures that it is reconnected at next logon.

FAT long file names under NT have 8.3 aliases created to ensure backward compatibility. The following is an example of how aliases are generated from five sample files that all have the same initial characters:

Team meeting Report #3.doc	TEAMME~1.DOC
Team meeting Report #4.doc	TEAMME~2.DOC
Team meeting Report #5.doc	TEAMME~3.DOC

Team meeting Report #6.doc	TEAMME~4.DOC
Team meeting Report #7.doc	TE12B4~1.DOC

A long file name on a FAT partition uses one file name for the 8.3 alias and then one more FAT entry for every 13 characters in the name.

A FAT partition can be converted to NTFS without loss of data through the following command line:

```
CONVERT <drive>: /FS:NTFS
```

NTFS supports compression as a file attribute that can be set in the file properties.

Compression can be applied to a folder or a drive and the effect is that the files within are compressed. Any file copied into that folder or drive will also become compressed.

Compression can be applied through the use of the COMPACT.EXE program through the following syntax:

```
COMPACT <file or directory path> [/switch]
```

The available switches for `COMPACT` are listed in Table B.8.

TABLE B.8

`COMPACT` SWITCHES

Switch	*Function*
`/C`	Compress
`/U`	Uncompress
`/S`	Compress an entire directory tree
`/A`	Compress hidden and system files
`/I`	Ignore errors and continue compressing
`/F`	Force compression even if the objects are already compressed
`/Q`	Display only summary information

Share-level permissions apply only when users access a resource over the network, not locally. The share-level permissions are as follows:

- **No Access.** Allows you to connect to the share, but nothing appears in File Manager except the message `You do not have permission to access this directory.`

- **Read.** Allows you to display folder and file names, display file content and attributes, run programs, and open folders inside the shared folder.
- **Change.** Allows you to create folders and files, change file content, change file attributes, delete files and folders, do everything the Read permission allows.
- **Full Control.** Allows you to change file permissions and do everything Change allows for.

Share-level permissions apply to the folder that is shared and apply equally to all the contents of that share.

Share-level permissions apply to any shared folder, whether on FAT or NTFS.

NTFS permissions can only be applied to any file or folder on an NTFS partition.

The actions that can be performed against an NTFS object are as follows:

- Read
- Write
- Execute
- Delete
- Change Permissions
- Take Ownership

The NTFS permissions available for folders are summarized in Table B.9.

TABLE B.9

NTFS FOLDER PERMISSIONS

Permission	*Action Permitted*
No Access	none
List	RX
Read	RX
Add	WX
Add & Read	RXWD
Change	RXWD
Full Control	RXWDPO

The NTFS permissions available for files are summarized in Table B.10.

TABLE B.10

NTFS FILE PERMISSIONS

Permission	*Action Permitted*
No Access	none
Read	RX
Add & Read	RX
Change	RXWD
Full Control	RXWDPO

CONNECTIVITY

Remember: Here are the elements that Microsoft says they test on for the "Connectivity" section of the exam.

Connectivity Objective 1

Configure Windows NT Server for interoperability with NetWare servers by using various tools. Tools include the following:

- Gateway Service for NetWare
- Migration Tool for NetWare

Gateway Service for NetWare (GSNW) performs the following functions:

- Enables Windows NT Servers to access NetWare file and print resources.
- Enables the Windows NT Servers to act as a gateway to the NetWare file and print resources. The Windows NT Server enables users to borrow the connection to the NetWare server by setting it up as a shared connection.

The Migration Tool for NetWare (NWCONV) transfers file and folder information, and user and group account information from a NetWare server to a Windows NT domain controller. The Migration Tool can preserve the folder and file permissions if it is being transferred to an NTFS partition.

Connectivity between Windows NT and a NetWare server requires the use of GSNW. If the user and file information from NetWare is to be transferred to a Windows NT Server, the NetWare Conversion utility, NWCONV, is used for this task. The following list summarizes the main points in this section on NetWare connectivity:

- GSNW can be used as a gateway between Windows NT clients and a NetWare server.
- GSNW acts as a NetWare client to the Windows NT Server, allowing the NT server to have a connection to the NetWare server.
- GSNW is a service in Windows NT, and is installed using the Control Panel.
- For GSNW to be used as a gateway into a NetWare server, a gateway user account must be created and placed in a NetWare group called NTGATEWAY.
- In configuring the GSNW as a gateway, you can assign permissions to the gateway share by accessing the GSNW icon in the Control Panel.
- For GSNW to be functional, the NWLINK IPX/SPX protocol must be installed and configured.
- To convert user and file information from a NetWare server to a Windows NT server, you can use the NWCONV.EXE utility.
- NWCONV requires that GSNW be installed prior to any conversion being carried out.
- To maintain the NetWare folder- and file-level permissions in the NWCONV utility, you must convert to an NTFS partition on the Windows NT system.

Connectivity Objective 2

Install and configure Remote Access Service (RAS). Configuration options include the following:

- Configuring RAS communications
- Configuring RAS protocols
- Configuring RAS security
- Configuring Dial-Up Networking clients

RAS supports the XE "Serial Line Interenet Protocol (SLIP)" Serial Line Internet Protocol (SLIP) and Point-to-Point Protocol (PPP) line protocols, and the NetBEUI, TCP/IP, and IPX network protocols.

RAS can connect to a remote computer using any of the following media:

- **Public Switched Telephone Network (PSTN).** (Also known simply as the phone company.) RAS can connect using a modem through an ordinary phone line.
- **X.25.** A packet-switched network. Computers access the network through a Packet Assembler Disassembler (PAD) device. X.25 supports dial-up or direct connections.
- **Null modem cable.** A cable that connects two computers directly. The computers then communicate using their modems (rather than network adapter cards).
- **ISDN.** A digital line that provides faster communication and more bandwidth than a normal phone line. (It also costs more, which is why not everybody has it.) A computer must have a special ISDN card to access an ISDN line.

RAS is designed for security. The following are some of RAS's security features:

- **Auditing.** RAS can leave an audit trail, enabling you to see who logged on when and what authentication they provided.
- **Callback security.** You can enable the RAS server to use callback (hang up all incoming calls and call the caller back), and you can limit callback numbers to prearranged sites that you know are safe.
- **Encryption.** RAS can encrypt logon information, or it can encrypt all data crossing the connection.
- **Security hosts.** If Windows NT's security is not secure enough, you can add an extra layer of security by using a third-party intermediary security host—a computer that stands between the RAS client and the RAS server and requires an extra round of authentication.
- **PPTP filtering.** You can tell Windows NT to filter out all packets except the encrypted Point-to-Point Tunneling Protocol (PPTP) packets.

RAS can be a very powerful and useful tool; it enables you to extend the reaches of your network to remote and traveling users. The following list summarizes main points for RAS in preparation for the exam:

- RAS supports SLIP and PPP line protocols.
- With PPP, RAS can support NetBEUI, NWLINK, and TCP/IP across the communication line.

- RAS uses the following media to communicate with remote systems: PSTN, X.25, null modem cable, and ISDN.
- The RAS security features available are auditing, callback security, encryption, and PPTP filtering.
- To install RAS, click the Network icon in the Control Panel.

MONITORING AND OPTIMIZATION

Remember: Here are the elements that Microsoft says they test on for the "Monitoring and Optimization" section of the exam.

Monitoring and Optimization Objective 1

Monitor performance of various functions by using Performance Monitor. Functions include processor, memory, disk, and network.

Performance Monitor has four views:

- **Chart view.** This view is very useful for viewing the objects and counters in a real-time mode. This mode enables you to view the data in a graphical format. You can also use the Chart view to view the contents of a log file.
- **Log view.** This view enables you to set all the options required for creating a log of your system resources or objects. After this log is created, you can view it by using the Chart view.
- **Alert view.** Use the Alert view to configure warnings or alerts of your system resources or objects. In this view, you can configure threshold levels for counters and can then launch an action should the threshold values be exceeded.
- **Report view.** The Report view enables you to view the object and counters as an averaged value. This view is useful for comparing the values of multiple systems that are configured similarly.

The subsystems that are routinely monitored are Memory, Disk, Network, and Processor.

Disk counters can be enabled through either of the following command lines:

```
Diskperf -y
Diskperf -ye (for RAID disks and volumes)
```

The following list summarizes the tools used to monitor your NT server that are available and are built in to Windows NT Server 4.0:

- Server Manager
- Windows NT Diagnostics
- Response Probe
- Performance Monitor
- Network Monitor

Monitoring and Optimization Objective 2

Identify performance bottlenecks.

Optimize performance for various results. Results include the following:

- Controlling network traffic
- Controlling the server load

To optimize the logon traffic in your Windows NT network, you should consider four main points:

- Determine the hardware required to increase performance.
- Configure the domain controllers to increase the number of logon validations.
- Determine the number of domain controllers needed.
- Determine the best location for each of the domain controllers.

The following are a few good points to follow in optimizing file-session traffic:

- Remove any excess protocols that are loaded.
- Reduce the number of wide area network (WAN) links required for file transfer.

The following are three points to consider when attempting to optimize server browser traffic:

- Reduce the number of protocols.
- Reduce the number of entries in the browse list.
- Increase the amount of time between browser updates.

Trust relationships generate a large amount of network traffic. When optimizing your system, attempt to keep the number of trusts very low.

TROUBLESHOOTING

Remember: Here are the elements that Microsoft says they test on for the "Troubleshooting" section of the exam.

Troubleshooting Objective 1

Choose the appropriate course of action to take to resolve installation failures.

The acronym DETECT can be used to define the troubleshooting process and stands for the following:

- Discover the problem.
- Explore the boundaries.
- Track the possible approaches.
- Execute an approach.
- Check for success.
- Tie up loose ends.

An NTHQ disk can test a computer to ensure that NT will successfully install on it.

The following list identifies possible sources of installation problems:

- Media errors
- Insufficient disk space
- Non-supported SCSI adapter
- Failure of dependency service to start
- Inability to connect to the domain controller
- Error in assigning domain name

Troubleshooting Objective 2

Choose the appropriate course of action to take to resolve boot failures.

The files involved in the boot process are identified in Table B.11 for both Intel and RISC machines.

TABLE B.11

FILES INVOLVED IN THE BOOT PROCESS

Intel	*RISC*
NTLDR	OSLOADER.EXE
BOOT.INI	NTOSKRNL.EXE
NTDETECT.COM	
NTOSKRNL.EXE	

In the NT boot process (in BOOT.INI), ARC paths define the physical position of the NT operating system files and come in two forms:

Scsidiskrdiskpartition\WINNT

Multidiskrdiskpartition\WINNT

SCSI ARC paths define hard drives that are SCSI and which have their bioses disabled. The relevant parameters are as follows:

- SCSI. The SCSI controller starting from 0
- DISK. The physical disk starting from 0
- PARTITION. The partition on the disk stating from 1
- \folder. The folder in which the NT files are located

MULTI ARC paths define hard drives which are non-SCSI or SCSI with their bioses enabled The relevant parameters are as follows:

- MULTI.The controller starting from 0
- RDISK. The physical disk starting from 0
- PARTITION. The partition on the disk stating from 1
- \folder. The folder in which the NT files are located

Partitions are numbered as follows:

- The first primary partition on each disk gets the number 0.

- Each additional primary partition then is given a number, incrementing up from 0.
- Each logical drive is then given a number according to the order in which they appear in the Disk Administrator.

Switches on boot lines in the `BOOT.INI` file define additional boot parameters. Table B.12 lists the switches you need to know about and their function.

TABLE B.12

BOOT.INI FILE SWITCHES

Switch	*Function*
`/basevideo`	Loads standard VGA video driver (640×480, 16 color)
`/sos`	Displays each driver as it is loaded
`/noserialmice`	Prevents autodetection of serial mice on COM ports that may disable a UPS connected to the port

A recovery disk can be used to bypass problems with system partition. Such a disk contains the files listed in Table B.13 (broken down by hardware platform).

TABLE B.13

FILES ON A FAULT-TOLERANT BOOT DISK

Intel	*RISC*
`NTLDR`	`OSLOADER.EXE`
`NTDETECT.COM`	`HAL.DLL`
`BOOT.INI`	`*.PAL` (for Alpha machines)
`BOOTSECT.DOS` (allows you to boot to DOS)	
`NTBOOTDD.SYS` (the SCSI driver for a hard drive with SCSI bios not enabled)	

Troubleshooting Objective 3

Choose the appropriate course of action to take to resolve configuration errors.

An emergency repair disk (ERD) can be used to recover an NT system if the Registry becomes corrupted and must be used in conjunction with the three setup disks used to install NT.

The RDISK program allows you to update the \REPAIR folder, which in turn is used to update your repair disk.

The Event Viewer allows you to see three log files: System Log, Security Log, and Application Log.

The Windows NT Diagnostics program allows you to see (but not modify) configuration settings for much of your hardware and environment.

The course of action to take when a stop error occurs (blue screen) can be configured from the System Properties dialog box (in the Control Panel) on the Startup/Shutdown tab.

Troubleshooting Objective 4

Choose the appropriate course of action to take to resolve printer problems.

To move the spool file from one partition to another, use the Advanced tab on the Server Properties dialog box; this can be reached from the File, Server Properties menu in the Printers dialog box.

If you have a hung job, stop and restart the Spooler service to clear it.

Troubleshooting Objective 5

Choose the appropriate course of action to take to resolve RAS problems.

Common RAS problems include the following:

- **User Permission.** User not enabled to use RAS in User Manager for Domains.
- **Authentication.** Often caused by incompatible encryption methods (client using different encryption than server is configured to receive).
- **Callback with Multilink.** Client is configured for callback but is using multilink; server will only call back to a single number, thereby removing multilink functionality.
- **Autodial at Logon.** Shortcuts on desktop referencing server-based applications or files causes autodial to kick in when logon is complete.

Troubleshooting Objective 6

Choose the appropriate course of action to take to resolve connectivity problems.

Users' failure to log on may be caused by a number of factors:

- Incorrect user name or password
- Incorrect domain name
- Incorrect user rights (inability to log on locally to an NT machine, for example)
- Netlogon service on server is stopped or paused
- Domain controllers are down
- User restricted in system policies from logging on at a specific computer

Troubleshooting Objective 7

Choose the appropriate course of action to take to resolve fault tolerance problems. Fault-tolerance methods include tape backup, mirroring, stripe set with parity, and disk duplexing.

The right to create backups and restore from backups using NT Backup is granted to the groups Administrators, Backup Operators, and Server Operators by default.

NT Backup will only back up files to tape; no other media is supported.

Table B.14 summarizes the backup types available in NT backup.

TABLE B.14

BACKUP TYPES AVAILABLE IN NT BACKUP

Type	*Backs Up*	*Marks?*
Normal	All selected files and folders	Yes
Copy	All selected files and folders	No
Incremental	Selected files and folders not marked as backed up	Yes
Differential	Selected files and folders not marked as backed up	No
Daily Copy	Selected files and folders changed that day	No

You can back up the local Registry of a computer by selecting the Backup Local Registry checkbox in the Backup Information dialog box.

Data from tape can be restored to the original location or to an alternate location, and NTFS permissions can be restored or not; however, you cannot change the names of the objects being restored until the restore is complete.

You can run Backup from a command line by using the NTBACKUP command in the following syntax:

```
Ntbackup backup path [switches]
```

Some command-line backup switches are shown in Table B.15.

TABLE B.15

NTBACKUP COMMAND-LINE SWITCHES

Switch	*Function*
`/a`	Append the current backup to the backup already on the tape.
`/v`	Verify the backed up files when complete.
`/d "text"`	Add an identifying description to the backup tape.
`/t option`	Specify the backup type. Valid options are Normal, Copy, Incremental, Differential, and Daily.

To recover from a failed mirror set you must take the following steps:

1. Shut down your NT server and physically replace the failed drive.
2. If required, boot NT using a recovery disk.
3. Start the Disk Administrator by selecting Start, Programs, Administrative Tools (Common), Disk Administrator.
4. Select the mirror set by clicking on it.
5. From the Fault Tolerance menu choose Break Mirror. This action exposes the remaining partition as a volume separate from the failed one.
6. Reestablish the mirror set if desired by selecting the partition you want to mirror and a portion of free space equal in size, and then choose Fault Tolerance, Establish Mirror.

To regenerate a stripe set with parity, follow these steps:

1. Shut down your NT server and physically replace the failed drive.
2. Start the Disk Administrator by selecting Start, Programs, Administrative Tools (Common), Disk Administrator.

3. Select the stripe set with parity by clicking on it.
4. Select an area of free space as large or larger than the portion of the stripe set that was lost when the disk failed.
5. Choose Fault Tolerance, Regenerate.

Hopefully, this has been a helpful tool in your final review before the exam. You might find after reading this that there are some portions of the book that you need to revisit. Just remember to stay focused and answer all the questions. You can always go back and check the answers for the questions you are unsure of. Good luck!

APPENDIX C

Fast Facts: Server Enterprise

The fast facts listed in this section are designed as a refresher of key points and topics required to succeed on the Windows NT Server 4.0 in the Enterprise exam. By using these summaries of key points, you can spend an hour before your exam to review key topics, and ensure that you have a solid understanding of the objectives and information required for you to succeed in each major area of the exam.

Following are the main categories Microsoft uses to arrange the objectives:

- Planning
- Installation and configuration
- Managing resources
- Connectivity
- Monitoring and optimization
- Troubleshooting

For each of these main sections, or categories, the assigned objectives are reviewed. Following each objective, review material is offered.

PLANNING

Planning Objective 1

Plan the implementation of a directory services architecture. Considerations include the following:

- Selecting the appropriate domain model
- Supporting a single logon account
- Enabling users to access resources in different domains

The main goals of directory services are the following:

- One user, one account
- Universal resource access
- Centralized administration
- Directory synchronization

To ensure that you are selecting the best plan for your network, always address each of the goals of directory services.

The requirements for setting up a trust are as follows:

- The trust relationship can be established only between Windows NT Server domains.
- The domains must be able to make an RPC connection. To establish an RPC connection, you must ensure that a network connection exists between the domain controllers of all participating domains.
- The trust relationship must be set up by a user with administrator access.
- You should determine the number and type of trusts prior to the implementation.
- You must decide where to place the user accounts because that location is the trusted domain.

Trust relationships enable communication between domains. The trusts must be organized, however, to achieve the original goal of directory services. Windows NT domains can be organized into one of four different domain models:

- The single-domain model
- The single-master domain model
- The multiple-master domain model
- The complete-trust model

Table C.1 summarizes the advantages and disadvantages of the domain models.

TABLE C.1

PROFILING THE DOMAIN MODELS

Domain Model	*Advantages*	*Disadvantages*
Single-domain model	Centralized administration.	Limited to 40,000 user accounts. No trust relationships. No distribution of resources.
Single-master domain model	Centralized administration.	Limited to 40,000 user accounts. Distributed resources.
Multiple-master domain model	Unlimited number of user accounts. each master domain can host 40,000 user accounts. Distributed resources. Complex trust relationships.	No centralized administration of user accounts.
Complete-trust model	Unlimited number of user accounts. Each domain can host 40,000 user accounts. Complex trust relationships.	No centralized administration of user accounts.

Planning Objective 2

Plan the disk drive configuration for various requirements. Requirements include choosing a fault-tolerance method.

Windows NT Server 4 supports the following solutions for fault-tolerance and/or performance:

- RAID Level 0 (disk striping)
- RAID Level 1 (disk mirroring)
- RAID Level 5 (disk striping with parity)

A comparison of the three configurations might help to summarize the information and to ensure that you have a strong understanding of the options available in Windows NT Server 4 (see Table C.2).

TABLE C.2

SUMMARY OF FAULT-TOLERANCE OPTIONS IN WINDOWS NT SERVER 4

Disk Striping	*Disk Mirroring/Disk Duplexing*	*Disk Striping with Parity*
No fault tolerance.	Complete disk duplication.	Data regeneration from stored parity information.
Minimum of two physical disks, maximum of 32 disks.	Two physical disks.	Minimum of three physical disks, maximum of 32 disks.
100 percent available disk utilization.	50 percent available disk utilization.	Dedicates the equivalent of one disk's space in the set for parity information. The more disks, the higher the utilization.
Cannot include a system/boot partition.	Includes all partition types.	Cannot include a system/boot partition.
Excellent read/write performance.	Moderate read/write performance.	Excellent read and moderate write performance.
No fault tolerance.	Complete disk duplication.	Data regeneration from stored parity information.
Minimum of two physical disks, maximum of 32 disks.	Two physical disks.	Minimum of three physical disks, maximum of 32 disks.
100 percent available disk utilization.	50 percent available disk utilization.	Dedicates the equivalent of one disk's space in the set for parity information. The more disks, the higher the utilization.
Cannot include a system/boot partition.	Includes all partition types.	Cannot include a system/boot partition.
Excellent read/write performance.	Moderate read/write performance.	Excellent read and moderate write performance.

Objective Planning 3

Choose a protocol for various situations. The protocols include the following:

- TCP/IP
- TCP/IP with DHCP and WINS
- NWLink IPX/SPX Compatible Transport Protocol

- Data Link Control (DLC)
- AppleTalk

Windows NT Server 4 comes bundled with several protocols that can be used for interconnectivity with other systems and for use within a Windows NT environment. You examine the various protocols, then try to define when each protocol best fits your network needs. The protocols discussed to prepare you for the enterprise exam are the following:

- **NetBEUI.** The NetBEUI protocol is the easiest to implement and has wide support across platforms. The protocol uses NetBIOS broadcasts to locate other computers on the network. This process of locating other computers requires additional network traffic and can slow down your entire network. Because NetBEUI uses broadcasts to locate computers, it is not routable; in other words, you cannot access computers that are not on your physical network. Most Microsoft and IBM OS/2 clients support this protocol. NetBEUI is best suited to small networks with no requirements for routing information to remote networks or to the Internet.
- **TCP/IP.** Transmission Control Protocol/Internet Protocol, or TCP/IP, is the most common protocol—more specifically, it is the most common suite of protocols. TCP/IP is an industry-standard protocol that is supported by most network operating systems. Because of this acceptance throughout the industry, TCP/IP enables your Windows NT system to connect to other systems with a common communication protocol.

  The following are advantages of using TCP/IP in a Windows NT environment:

  - The capability to connect dissimilar systems
  - The capability to use numerous standard connectivity utilities, including File Transfer Protocol (FTP), Telnet, and PING
  - Access to the Internet

  If your Windows NT system is using TCP/IP as a connection protocol, it can communicate with many non-Microsoft systems. Some of the systems it can communicate with are the following:

  - Any Internet-connected system
  - UNIX systems
  - IBM mainframe systems
  - DEC Pathworks
  - TCP/IP-supported printers directly connected to the network

- **NWLink IPX/SPX Compatible.** The IPX protocol has been used within the NetWare environment for years. By developing an IPX-compatible protocol, Microsoft enables Windows NT systems to communicate with NetWare systems.

  NWLink is best suited to networks requiring communication with existing NetWare servers and for existing NetWare clients.

  Other services must be installed, however, to enable the Windows NT Server system to gain access into the NetWare security. Gateway Services for NetWare/Client Services for NetWare (GSNW/CSNW) must be installed on the Windows NT server to enable the computer to be logged on to a NetWare system. GSNW functions as a NetWare client, but it also can share the connection to the Novell box with users from the Windows NT system. This capability enables a controlled NetWare connection for file and print sharing on the NetWare box, without requiring the configuration of each NT client with a duplicate network redirector or client.

- **DataLink Control.** The DLC protocol was originally used for connectivity in an IBM mainframe environment, and maintains support for existing legacy systems and mainframes. The DLC protocol is also used for connections to some network printers.

- **AppleTalk.** Windows NT Server can configure the AppleTalk protocol to enable connectivity with Apple Macintosh systems. This protocol is installed with the Services for the Macintosh included with your Windows NT Server CD-ROM. The AppleTalk protocol enables Macintosh computers on your network to access files and printers set up on the Windows NT server. It also enables your Windows NT clients to print to Apple Macintosh printers.

  The AppleTalk protocol is best suited to connectivity with the Apple Macintosh.

INSTALLATION AND CONFIGURATION

Installation and Configuration Objective 1

Install Windows NT Server to perform various server roles. Server roles include the following:

- Primary domain controller
- Backup domain controller
- Member server

The following are different server roles into which Windows NT Server can be installed:

- **Primary Domain Controller.** The Primary Domain Controller (PDC) is the first domain controller installed into a domain. As the first computer in the domain, the PDC creates the domain. This fact is important to understand because it establishes the rationale for needing a PDC in the environment. Each domain can contain only one PDC. All other domain controllers in the domain are installed as Backup Domain Controllers (BDCs). The PDC handles user requests and logon validation, and it offers all the standard Windows NT Server functionality. The PDC contains the original copy of the Security Accounts Manager (SAM), which contains all user accounts and security permissions for your domain.
- **Backup Domain Controller.** The Backup Domain Controller (BDC) is an additional domain controller used to handle logon requests by users in the network. To handle the logon requests, the BDC must have a complete copy of the domain database, or SAM. The BDC also runs the Netlogon service; however, the Netlogon service in a BDC functions a little differently than that in a PDC. In the PDC, the Netlogon service handles synchronization of the SAM database to all the BDCs.
- **Member server.** In both of the domain controllers (PDC or BDC), the computer has an additional function. The domain controllers handle logon requests and ensure that the SAM is synchronized throughout the domain. These functions add overhead to the system. A computer that handles the server functionality you require without the overhead of handling logon validation is called a *member server.* A member server is a part of the domain, but it does not need a copy of the SAM database and does not handle logon requests. The main function of a member server is to share resources.

After you have installed your computer into a specific server role, you might decide to change the role of the server. This can be a relatively easy task if you are changing a PDC to a BDC or vice versa. If you want to change a domain controller to a member server or member server to a domain controller, however, you must reinstall into the required server role. A member server has a local database that does not participate in domain synchronization. In changing roles, a member server must be reinstalled to ensure that the account database and the appropriate services are installed.

Installation and Configuration Objective 2

Configure protocols and protocol bindings. Protocols include the following:

- TCP/IP
- TCP/IP with DHCP and WINS
- NWLink IPX/SPX Compatible Transport Protocol
- DLC
- AppleTalk

You install a new protocol in Windows NT Server through the Network Properties dialog box.

The following list contains the protocols, and the configuration options available with each:

> NOTE
>
> Note: NetBEUI Not Discussed—This list does not include the NetBEUI protocol because there are no configuration options available for this protocol.

- **TCP/IP.** The following tabs are available for configuration in the Microsoft TCP/IP Properties dialog box:
  - **IP Address.** The IP Address tab enables you to configure the IP address, the subnet mask, and the default gateway. You also can enable the system to allocate IP address information automatically through the use of the DHCP server.

    An IP address is a 32-bit address that is broken into four octets and used to identify your network adapter card as a TCP/IP host. Each IP address must be a unique address. If you have any IP address conflicts on your computer, you cannot use the TCP/IP protocol.

    Your IP address is then grouped into a subnet. You must assign a subnet mask to subnet your network. A *subnet mask* is used to identify the computers local to your network. Any address outside your subnet is accessed through the default gateway, also called the *router.* The default gateway is the address of the router that handles all routing of your TCP/IP information to computers, or *hosts,* outside your subnet.
  - **DNS.** The DNS tab shows you the options available for configuring your TCP/IP protocol to use a DNS server. The Domain Name System (DNS) server translates TCP/IP host names of remote computers into

IP addresses. Remember that an IP address is a unique address for each computer. The DNS server contains a database of all the computers you can access by host name. This database is used when you access a Web page on the Internet. Working with the naming scheme is easier than using the IP address of the computer.

- **WINS Address.** The WINS Address tab enables you to configure your primary and secondary Windows Internet Names Services (WINS) server addresses. WINS is used to reduce the number of NetBIOS broadcast messages sent across the network to locate a computer. By using a WINS server, you keep the names of computers on your network in a WINS database. The WINS database is dynamic.

  In configuring your WINS servers, you can enter your primary WINS server and a secondary WINS server. Your system first searches the primary WINS server database , then the secondary database if no match was found in the primary one.

- **DHCP Relay.** The DHCP relay agent is used to find your DHCP servers across routers. The DHCP servers distribute DHCP addresses. The client request, however, is made with a broadcast message. Broadcast messages do not cross routers; therefore, this protocol might place some restrictions on your systems. The solution is to use a DHCP relay agent to assist the clients in finding the DHCP server across a router.

  When configuring your DHCP relay agent, you can specify the seconds threshold and the maximum number of hops to use in searching for the DHCP servers. At the bottom of the tab, you can enter the IP addresses of the DHCP servers you want to use.

- **Routing.** In an environment in which multiple subnets are used, you can configure your Windows NT Server as a multihomed system. In other words, you can install multiple network adapters, each connecting to a different subnet. If you enable the Enable IP Forwarding option, your computer acts as a router, forwarding the packets through the network cards in the multihomed system to the other subnet.

- **NWLINK IPX/SPX Compatible.** The configuration of the NWLink protocol is simple in comparison to the TCP/IP protocol. It is this simplicity that makes it a popular protocol to use.

The NWLink IPX/SPX Properties dialog box has two tabs:

- **General.** On the General tab, you have the option to assign an internal network number. This eight-digit hexadecimal number format is used by some programs with services that can be accessed by NetWare clients.

You also have the option to select a frame type for your NWLink protocol. The frame type you select must match the frame type of the remote computer with which you need to communicate. By default, Windows NT Server uses the Auto Frame Type Detection setting, which scans the network and loads the first frame type it encounters.

- **Routing.** The Routing tab of the NWLink IPX/SPX Properties dialog box is used to enable or disable the Routing Information Protocol (RIP). If you enable RIP routing over IPX, your Windows NT Server can act as an IPX router.

- **DLC.** The configuration of DLC is done through Registry parameters. The DLC protocol is configured based on three timers:
  - **T1.** The response timer.
  - **T2.** The acknowledgment delay timer.
  - **Ti.** The inactivity timer.

  The Registry contains the entries that can be modified to configure DLC. You can find the entries at `HKEY_LOCAL_MACHINE\SYSTEM\CurrentControlSet\Services\DLC\Parameters\ELNKIII` *`adapter name`*.

- **AppleTalk.** To install the AppleTalk protocol, you install Services for Macintosh.

Table C.3 reviews the protocols that you can configure for your NT enterprise (including the subcomponents—tabs—of each protocol).

TABLE C.3

PROTOCOLS TO CONFIGURE

Protocol	*Subcomponent (Tab)*
TCP/IP	IP Address DNS WINS Address DHCP Relay Routing
NWLink IPX/SPX Compatible	General Routing
AppleTalk	General Routing

The binding order is the sequence your computer uses to select which protocol to use for network communications. Each protocol is listed for each network-based service, protocol, and adapter available.

The Bindings tab contains an option, Show Bindings For, that can be used to select the service, adapter, or protocol you want to modify in the binding order. By clicking the appropriate button, you can enable or disable each binding, or move up or down in the binding order.

Installation and Configuration Objective 3

Configure Windows NT Server core services. Services include the following:

- Directory Replicator
- Computer Browser

In this objective, you look at configuring some of the core services in the Windows NT Server. These services are the following:

- **Server service.** The Server service answers network requests. By configuring Server service, you can change the way your server responds and, in a sense, the role it plays in your network environment. To configure Server service, you must open the Network dialog box. To do this, double-click the Network icon in the Control Panel. Select the Services tab. In the Server dialog box, you have four optimization settings. Each of these settings modifies memory management based on the role the server is playing. These options are as follows:
- **Minimize Memory Used.** The Minimize Memory Used setting is used when your Windows NT Server system is accessed by fewer than 10 users.

  This setting allocates memory so that a maximum of 10 network connections can be properly maintained. By restricting the memory for network connections, you make more memory available at the local or desktop level.
- **Balance.** The Balance setting can be used for a maximum of 64 network connections. This setting is the default when using NetBEUI software. Like the Minimize setting, Balance is best used for a relatively limited number of users connecting to a server that also can be used as a desktop computer.
- **Maximize Throughput for File Sharing.** The Maximize Throughput for File Sharing setting allocates the maximum amount of memory available for network connections. This setting is excellent for large networks in which the server is being accessed for file and print sharing.
- **Maximize Throughput for Network Applications.** If you are running distributed applications, such as SQL Server or Exchange Server, the network applications do their own memory caching. Therefore, you want

your system to enable the applications to manage the memory. You accomplish this by using the Maximize Throughput for Network Applications setting. This setting also is used for very large networks.

- **Computer Browser service.** The Computer Browser service is responsible for maintaining the list of computers on the network. The browse list contains all the computers located on the physical network. As a Windows NT Server, your system plays a big role in the browsing of a network. The Windows NT Server acts as a master browser or backup browser.

  The selection of browsers is through an election. The election is called by any client computer or when a preferred master browser computer starts up. The election is based on broadcast messages. Every computer has the opportunity to nominate itself, and the computer with the highest settings wins the election.

  The election criteria are based on three things:

  - The operating system (Windows NT Server, Windows NT Workstation, Windows 95, or Windows for Workgroups)
  - The version of the operating system (NT 4.0, NT 3.51, or NT 3.5)
  - The current role of the computer (master browser, backup browser, or potential browser)

- **Directory Replicator service.** You can configure the Directory Replicator service to synchronize an entire directory structure across multiple servers.

  In configuring the directory service, you must select the export server and all the import servers. The export server is the computer that holds the original copy of the directory structure and files. Each import server receives a complete copy of the export server's directory structure. The Directory Replicator service monitors the directory structure on the export server. If the contents of the directory change, the changes are copied to all the import servers. The file copying and directory monitoring is completed by a special service account you create. You must configure the Directory Replicator service to use this service account. The following access is required for your Directory Replicator service account:

  - The account should be a member of the Backup Operators and Replicators groups.
  - There should be no time or logon restrictions for the account.
  - The Password Never Expires option should be selected.

- The User Must Change Password At Next Logon option should be turned off.

When configuring the export server, you have the option to specify the export directory. The default export directory is `C:\WINNT\system32\repl\export\`.

In the Import Directories section of the Directory Replication dialog box, you can select the import directory. The default import directory is `C:\WINNT\system32\repl\import`.

Remember that the default directory for executing logon scripts in a Windows NT system is `C:\WINNT\system32\repl\import\scripts`.

Installation and Configuration Objective 4

Configure hard disks to meet various requirements. Requirements include the following:

- Providing fault-tolerance
- Improving performance

All hard disk configuration can be done with the Disk Administrator tool. The different disk configurations you need to understand for the enterprise exam are the following:

- **Stripe set.** A stripe set gives you improved disk read and write performance; however, it supplies no fault tolerance. A minimum of two disks is required, and the configuration can stripe up to 32 physical disks. A stripe set cannot include the system partition.
- **Volume set.** A volume set enables you to extend partitions beyond one physical disk; however, it supplies no fault tolerance. To extend a volume set, you must use the NTFS file system.
- **Disk mirroring.** A mirror set uses two physical disks and provides full data duplication. Often referred to as RAID level 1, disk mirroring is a useful solution to assigning duplication to the system partition, as well as any other disks that might be in the system.
- **Stripe set with parity.** A stripe set with parity enables fault tolerance in your system. A minimum of three physical disks is required, and a maximum of 32 physical disks can be included in a stripe set with parity. A stripe set with parity cannot include the system partition of your Windows NT system.

The solution that supplies the best duplication and optimization mix is the stripe set with parity.

Installation and Configuration Objective 5

Configure printers. Tasks include the following:

- Adding and configuring a printer
- Implementing a printer pool
- Setting print priorities

The installation of a printer is a fairly simplistic procedure and is not tested heavily on the exam; however, the printer pool is a key point. The items to remember about printer pools are as follows:

- All printers in a printer pool must be able to function using the same printer driver.
- A printer pool can have a maximum of eight printers in the pool.

Installation and Configuration Objective 6

Configure a Windows NT Server computer for various types of client computers. Client computer types include the following:

- Windows NT Workstation
- Windows 95
- Macintosh

The Network Client Administrator is found in the Administrative Tools group. You can use the Network Client Administrator program to do the following:

- **Make a Network Installation Startup Disk.** This option creates an MS-DOS boot disk that contains commands required to connect to a network server and that automatically installs Windows NT Workstation, Windows 95, or the DOS network clients.
- **Make an Installation Disk Set.** This option enables the creation of installation disks for the DOS network client, LAN Manager 2.2c for DOS, or LAN Manager 2.2c for OS/2.

- **Copy Client-Based Network Administration Tools.** This option enables you to share the network administration tools with client computers. The client computers that can use the network administration tools are Windows NT Workstation and Windows 95 computers.
- **View Remoteboot Client Information.** This option enables you to view the remoteboot client information. To install remoteboot, go to the Services tab of the Network dialog box.

When installing a client computer, you must ensure that your Windows NT system is prepared for and configured for the client. The Windows clients can connect to the Windows NT server without any configuration required on the server; however, some configuration is required on the client computers. For the Apple Macintosh client, the NT server must install the services for the Macintosh, which includes the AppleTalk protocol. This protocol enables the seamless connection between the Windows NT system and the Apple clients.

MANAGING RESOURCES

Managing Resources Objective 1

Manage user and group accounts. Considerations include the following:

- Managing Windows NT user accounts
- Managing Windows NT user rights
- Managing Windows NT groups
- Administering account policies
- Auditing changes to the user account database

AGLP stands for Accounts/Global Groups/Local Groups/Permissions. When you want to assign permissions to any resource, you should follow a few simple rules. All user accounts are placed into global groups, and global groups get assigned into local groups. The local groups have the resources and permissions assigned to them.

When you are working with groups across trust relationships, the following guidelines are useful:

- Always gather users into global groups. Remember that global groups can contain only user accounts from the same domain. You might have to create the same named global group in multiple domains.

- If you have multiple account domains, use the same name for a global group that has the same types of members. Remember that when multiple domains are involved, the group name is referred to as `DOMAIN\GROUP`.
- Before the global groups are created, determine whether an existing local group meets your needs. There is no sense in creating duplicate local groups.
- Remember that the local group must be created where the resource is located. If the resource is on a Domain Controller, create the local group in the Domain Account Database. If the resource is on a Windows NT Workstation or Windows NT Member Server, you must create the group in that system's local account database.
- Be sure to set the permissions for a resource before you make the global groups a member of the local group assigned to the resource. That way, you set the security for the resource.

Managing Resources Objective 2

Create and manage policies and profiles for various situations. Policies and profiles include the following:

- Local user profiles
- Roaming user profiles
- System policies

You can configure system policies to do the following:

- Implement defaults for hardware configuration—for all computers using the profile or for a specific machine.
- Restrict the changing of specific parameters that affect the hardware configuration of the participating system.
- Set defaults for all users in the areas of their personal settings that the users can configure.
- Restrict users from changing specific areas of their configuration to prevent tampering with the system. An example is disabling all Registry editing tools for a specific user.
- Apply all defaults and restrictions on a group level rather than just a user level.

Some common implementations of user profiles are the following:

- You can lock down display properties to prevent users from changing the resolution of their monitor. Display properties can be locked down as a whole or on each individual property page of display properties. You adjust this setting by clicking the Control Panel, Display, Restrict Display option of the Default User Properties dialog box.
- You can set a default color scheme or wallpaper by clicking the Desktop option of the Default User Properties dialog box.
- You can restrict access to portions of the Start menu or desktopby clicking the Shell, Restrictions option of the Default User Properties dialog box.
- You can limit the applications that the user can run at a workstation by clicking the System, Restrictions option of the Default User Properties dialog box. You can also use this option to prevent the user from modifying the Registry.
- You can prevent users from mapping or disconnecting network drives by clicking the Windows NT Shell, Restrictions option of the Default User Properties dialog box.

Profiles and policies can be very powerful tools to assist in the administrative tasks in your environment. The following list reviews each of the main topics covered in this objective:

- **Roaming profiles.** The user portion of the Registry is downloaded from a central location, allowing the user settings to follow the user anywhere within the network environment.
- **Local profiles.** The user settings are stored at each workstation and are not copied to other computers. Each workstation that you use will have different desktop and user settings.
- **System policies.** System policies enable the administrator to restrict user configuration changes on systems. This enables the administrator to maintain the settings of the desktop of systems without the fear that a user can modify them.
- **Computer policies.** Computer policies allow the lockdown of common machine settings that affect all users of that computer.

Managing Resources Objective 3

Administer remote servers from various types of client computers. Client computer types include the following:

- Windows 95
- Windows NT Workstation

This objective focuses on the remote administration tools available for your Windows NT Server. The following list summarizes the key tools:

- **Remote Administration Tools for Windows 95.** Allows User Manager, Server Manager, Event Viewer, and NTFS file permissions to be executed from the Windows 95 computer.
- **Remote Administration for Windows NT.** Allows User Manager, Server Manager, DHCP Manager, System Policy Editor, Remote Access Admin, Remote Boot Manager, WINS Manager, and NTFS file permissions to be executed from a Windows NT machine.
- **Web Based Administration.** Allows common tasks to be completed through a Web-based interface into the Windows NT Server.

Managing Resources Objective 4

Manage disk resources. Tasks include the following:

- Creating and sharing resources
- Implementing permissions and security
- Establishing file auditing

Windows NT has two levels of security for protecting your disk resources:

- Share permissions
- NTFS permissions

NTFS permissions enable you to assign more comprehensive security to your computer system. NTFS permissions can protect you at the file level. Share permissions, on the other hand, can be applied only to the folder level. NTFS permissions can affect users logged on locally or across the network from the system where the NTFS permissions are applied. Share permissions are in effect only when the user connects to the resource through the network.

The combination of Windows NT share permissions and NTFS permissions determines the ultimate access a user has to a resource on the server's disk. When share permissions and NTFS permissions are combined, no preference is given to one or the other. The key factor is which of the two effective permissions is the most restrictive.

For the exam, remember the following tips relating to managing resources:

- Users can be assigned only to global groups in the same domain.
- Only global groups from trusted domains can become members of local groups in trusting domains.
- NTFS permissions are assigned only to local groups in all correct test answers.
- Only NTFS permissions give you file-level security.

CONNECTIVITY

Connectivity Objective 1

Configure Windows NT Server for interoperability with NetWare servers by using various tools. The tools include the following:

- Gateway Service for NetWare
- Migration Tool for NetWare

Gateway Service for NetWare (GSNW) performs the following functions:

- Enables Windows NT Servers to access NetWare file and print resources.
- Enables the Windows NT Servers to act as a gateway to the NetWare file and print resources. The Windows NT Server enables users to borrow the connection to the NetWare server by setting it up as a shared connection.

The Migration Tool for NetWare (NWCONV) transfers file and folder information, and user and group account information from a NetWare server to a Windows NT domain controller. The Migration Tool can preserve the folder and file permissions if it is being transferred to an NTFS partition.

Connectivity between Windows NT and a NetWare server requires the use of GSNW. If the user and file information from NetWare is to be transferred to a

Windows NT Server, the NetWare Conversion utility, NWCONV, is used for this task. The following list summarizes the main points in this section on NetWare connectivity:

- GSNW can be used as a gateway between Windows NT clients and a NetWare server.
- GSNW acts as a NetWare client to the Windows NT Server, allowing the NT server to have a connection to the NetWare server.
- GSNW is a service in Windows NT, and is installed using the Control Panel.
- For GSNW to be used as a gateway into a NetWare server, a gateway user account must be created and placed in a NetWare group called NTGATEWAY.
- In configuring the GSNW as a gateway, you can assign permissions to the gateway share by accessing the GSNW icon in the Control Panel.
- For GSNW to be functional, the NWLINK IPX/SPX protocol must be installed and configured.
- To convert user and file information from a NetWare server to a Windows NT server, you can use the NWCONV.EXE utility.
- NWCONV requires that GSNW be installed prior to any conversion being carried out.
- To maintain the NetWare folder- and file-level permissions in the NWCONV utility, you must convert to an NTFS partition on the Windows NT system.

Connectivity Objective 2

Install and configure multiprotocol routing to serve various functions. Functions include the following:

- Internet router
- BOOTP/DHCP Relay Agent
- IPX router

Multiprotocol routing gives you flexibility in the connection method used by your clients, and in maintaining security. Check out the following:

- **Internet router.** Setting up Windows NT as an Internet router is as simple as installing two network adapters in the system, then enabling IP routing in the TCP/IP protocol configuration. This option enables Windows NT to act as a static router. Note that Windows NT cannot exchange Routing Information Protocol (RIP) routing packets with other IP RIP routers unless the RIP routing software is installed.
- **IPX router.** You enable the IPX router by installing the IPX RIP router software by choosing Control Panel, Networks, Services.

  After installing the IPX RIP router, Windows NT can route IPX packets over the network adapters installed. Windows NT uses the RIP to exchange its routing table information with other RIP routers.

The inclusion of the industry-standard protocols, and tools to simplify the configuration and extension of your NT network into other environments, makes this operating system a very powerful piece of your heterogeneous environment. The following are the main factors to focus on for this objective:

- A strong understanding of the functionality of each of the Windows NT protocols—with a strong slant toward TCP/IP and the configuration options available. Understanding and configuration of the DHCP server are also tested on this exam.
- The services used to resolve the IP addresses and names of hosts in a TCP/IP environment. DNS service, WINS Service, the Hosts file, and the LMHosts files are among the services tested.
- The routing mechanisms available in Windows NT. These mechanisms are powerful, and largely unknown to the vast majority of NT administrators. Ensure that you review the configuration and functionality of Internet or IP routing, as well as the IPX routing tools available.

Connectivity Objectives 3 and 4

Install and configure Internet Information Server.

Install and configure Internet services. Services include the following:

- The World Wide Web
- DNS
- Intranets

Internet Information Server (IIS) uses Hypertext Transfer Protocol (HTTP), File Transfer Protocol (FTP), and the Gopher service to provide Internet publishing services to your Windows NT Server computer.

IIS provides a graphical administration tool called the Internet Service Manager. With this tool, you can centrally manage, control, and monitor the Internet services in your Windows NT network. The Internet Service Manager uses the built-in Windows NT security model, so it offers a secure method of remotely administering your Web sites and other Internet services.

IIS is an integrated component in Windows NT Server 4.0. The IIS services are installed using the Control Panel or Networks icon or during the installation phase. The following list summarizes the key points in installing and configuring IIS:

- The three Internet services included in IIS are HTTP, FTP, and Gopher.
- HTTP is used to host Web pages from your Windows NT server system.
- FTP is a protocol used for transferring files across the Internet using the TCP/IP protocol.
- Gopher is used to create a set of hierarchical links to other computers or to annotate files or folders.
- The Internet Service Manager is the utility used to manage and configure your Internet services in IIS.
- The Internet Service Manager has three views that you can use to view your services: Report view, Servers view, and Services view.

Connectivity Objective 5

Install and configure Remote Access Service (RAS). Configuration options include the following:

- Configuring RAS communications
- Configuring RAS protocols
- Configuring RAS security

RAS supports the Serial Line Internet Protocol (SLIP) and Point-to-Point Protocol (PPP) line protocols, and the NetBEUI, TCP/IP, and IPX network protocols.

RAS can connect to a remote computer by using any of the following media:

- **Public Switched Telephone Network (PSTN).** Also known simply as the phone company. RAS can connect by using a modem through an ordinary phone line.
- **X.25.** A packet-switched network. Computers access the network through a Packet Assembler Disassembler (PAD) device. X.25 supports dial-up or direct connections.
- **Null modem cable.** A cable that connects two computers directly. The computers then communicate by using their modems (rather than network adapter cards).
- **ISDN.** A digital line that provides faster communication and more bandwidth than a normal phone line. (It also costs more, which is why not everybody has it.) A computer must have a special ISDN card to access an ISDN line.

RAS is designed for security. The following are some of RAS's security features:

- **Auditing.** RAS can leave an audit trail, enabling you to see who logged on when and what authentication they provided.
- **Callback security.** You can enable the RAS server to use callback (hang up all incoming calls and call the caller back), and you can limit callback numbers to prearranged sites that you know are safe.
- **Encryption.** RAS can encrypt logon information, or it can encrypt all data crossing the connection.
- **Security hosts.** If Windows NT's security is not secure enough, you can add an extra layer of security by using a third-party intermediary security host—a computer that stands between the RAS client and the RAS server and requires an extra round of authentication.
- **PPTP filtering.** You can tell Windows NT to filter out all packets except the encrypted Point-to-Point Tunneling Protocol (PPTP) packets.

RAS can be a very powerful and useful tool in enabling you to extend the reaches of your network to remote and traveling users. The following list summarizes main points for RAS in preparation for the exam:

- RAS supports SLIP and PPP line protocols.
- With PPP, RAS can support NetBEUI, NWLINK, and TCP/IP across the communication line.

- RAS uses the following media to communicate with remote systems: PSTN, X.25, null modem cable, and ISDN.
- The RAS security features available are auditing, callback security, encryption, and PPTP filtering.
- To install RAS, click the Network icon in the Control Panel.

MONITORING AND OPTIMIZATION

Monitoring and Optimization Objective 1

Establish a baseline for measuring system performance. Tasks include creating a database of measurement data.

You can use numerous database utilities to analyze the data collected. The following are some of the databases that Microsoft provides:

- Performance Monitor
- Microsoft Excel
- Microsoft Access
- Microsoft FoxPro
- Microsoft SQL Server

The following list summarizes the key items to focus on when you are analyzing your computer and network:

- Establish a baseline measurement of your system when functioning at its normal level. Later, you can use the baseline in comparative analysis.
- Establish a database to maintain the baseline results and any subsequent analysis results on the system. With this data, you can compare trends and identify potential pitfalls in your system.
- The main resources to monitor are memory, the processor, the disks, and the network.

The following list summarizes the tools used to monitor your NT server that are available and are built-in to Windows NT Server 4.0:

- Server Manager
- Windows NT Diagnostics

- Response Probe
- Performance Monitor
- Network Monitor

Monitoring and Optimization Objective 2

Monitor performance of various functions by using Performance Monitor. Functions include the following:

- Processor
- Memory
- Disk
- Network

To summarize the main views used within Performance Monitor, review the following list:

- **Chart view.** This view is very useful for viewing the objects and counters in a real-time mode. This mode enables you to view the data in a graphical format. You can also use the Chart view to view the contents of a log file.
- **Log view.** This view enables you to set all the options required for creating a log of your system resources or objects. After this log is created, you can view it by using the Chart view.
- **Alert view.** Use the Alert view to configure warnings or alerts of your system resources or objects. In this view, you can configure threshold levels for counters and can then launch an action based on the threshold values being exceeded.
- **Report view.** The Report view enables you to view the object and counters as an averaged value. This view is useful for comparing the values of multiple systems that are configured similarly.

When monitoring the disk, remember to activate the disk counters using the command `diskperf -y`. If you do not enter this command, you can select counter but will not see any activity displayed. In the case of a software RAID system, start `diskperf` with the `-ye` option.

When you want to monitor TCP/IP counters, make sure that SNMP is installed. Without the SNMP service installed, the TCP/IP counters are not available.

Performance Monitor is a graphical utility that you can use for monitoring and analyzing your system resources within Windows NT. You can enable objects and counters within Performance Monitor; these elements enable the logging and viewing of system data.

In preparing you for this objective, this section introduces numerous objects and counters that you use with Performance Monitor. To prepare for the exam, you need to understand the following key topics:

- The four views available in Performance Monitor are the Report view, Log view, Chart view, and Alert view.
- The main resources to monitor in any system are the disk, the memory, the network, and the processor.
- Each of the main resources are grouped as separate objects, and within each object are counters. A counter is the type of data available from a type of resource or object. Each counter might also have multiple instances. An instance is available if multiple components in a counter are listed.
- To enable the disk counters to be active, you must run the diskperf utility.

Monitoring and Optimization Objective 3

Monitor network traffic by using Network Monitor. Tasks include the following:

- Collecting data
- Presenting data
- Filtering data

Network Monitor is a network packet analyzer that comes with Windows NT Server 4. Actually two versions of Network Monitor are available from Microsoft. The first version comes with Windows NT Server 4 (simple version). This version can monitor the packets (frames) sent or received by a Windows NT Server 4 computer. The second version comes with Microsoft Systems Management Server (full version). This version can monitor all traffic on the network.

By fully understanding the various components found while analyzing traffic, you will be more successful in locating potential network bottlenecks and offering relevant optimization recommendations. The main components that need to be monitored with your network traffic analysis are the following:

- Locate and classify each service. Analyze the amount of traffic generated from each individual service, the frequency of the traffic, and the overall effect of the traffic on the network segment.
- Understand the three different types of frames: broadcast, multicast, and directed.
- Review the contents of a frame and ensure that you can find the destination address, source address, and data located in each frame.

The following points summarize the key items to understand in building a strong level of knowledge in using Network Monitor as a monitoring tool.

- Two versions of Network Monitor are available: the scaled-down version that is built in to the Windows NT Server operating system, and the full version that is a component of Microsoft Systems Management Server.
- The Network Monitor windows consist of four sections: Graph, Session Statistics, Station Statistics, and Total Statistics.
- After Network Monitor captures some data, you use the display window of Network Monitor to view the frames. The three sections of the display window are the Summary pane, the Detail pane, and the Hexadecimal pane.

Monitoring and Optimization Objectives 4 and 5

Identify performance bottlenecks.

Optimize performance for various results. Results include the following:

- Controlling network traffic
- Controlling the server load

To optimize the logon traffic in your Windows NT network, you should consider four main points:

- Determine the hardware required to increase performance.
- Configure the domain controllers to increase the number of logon validations.
- Determine the number of domain controllers needed.
- Determine the best location for each of the domain controllers.

Follow these good points to optimize file-session traffic:

- Remove any excess protocols that are loaded.
- Reduce the number of wide area network (WAN) links required for file transfer.

The following are three points to consider when attempting to optimize server browser traffic:

- Reduce the number of protocols.
- Reduce the number of entries in the browse list.
- Increase the amount of time between browser updates.

Trust relationships generate a large amount of network traffic. In optimizing your system, attempt to keep the number of trusts very low.

TROUBLESHOOTING

Troubleshooting Objective 1

Choose the appropriate course of action to take to resolve installation failures.

Troubleshooting a Windows NT system requires that you have a strong understanding of the processes and tools available to you. To be an effective troubleshooter, first you must have experience. The following is a list of some common installation problems:

- Hard disk problems
- Unsupported CD-ROMs
- Network adapter problems and conflicts
- Naming problems (each computer must be uniquely named, following the NetBIOS naming conventions)

Always use the hardware compatibility list to ensure that your components are supported by Windows NT.

Troubleshooting Objective 2

Choose the appropriate course of action to take to resolve boot failures.

For startup errors, try the following:

- Check for missing files that are involved in the boot process, including NTLDR, NTDETECT.COM, BOOT.INI, NTOSKRNL.EXE, and OSLOADER (RISC).
- Modify BOOT.INI for options.
- Create an NT boot disk for bypassing the boot process from the hard disk.
- Use the Last Known Good option to roll back to the last working set of your Registry settings.

Troubleshooting Objective 3

Choose the appropriate course of action to take to resolve configuration errors. Tasks include the following:

- Backing up and restoring the Registry
- Editing the Registry

You can resolve many problems that you encounter within Windows NT by configuring the Registry. However, before you make any Registry configurations, you must have a strong understanding of the keys within the Registry. Furthermore, you should always back up the Registry prior to making any modifications to ensure a smooth rollback if additional problems occur. The following are the main tools used to modify the Registry:

- REGEDT32
- REGEDIT

For configuration problems, remember the following:

- Using the Registry for configuration and troubleshooting can cause additional problems if you do not maintain a full understanding of the Registry.
- Always back up the Registry prior to editing the contents.
- You can back up and restore the local Registry by using REGEDT32.

Troubleshooting Objective 4

Choose the appropriate course of action to take to resolve printer problems.

To troubleshoot printers, you should do the following:

- Understand and review the overview of the printing process.
- Understand the files involved in the printing process.
- As a first step in troubleshooting a printer, always verify that the printer is turned on and online.
- Note that the most common errors associated with a printer are an invalid printer driver or incorrect resource permissions set for a user.

Troubleshooting Objective 5

Choose the appropriate course of action to take to resolve RAS problems.

The following is a list of some of the problems that you might encounter with RAS:

- You must ensure that the protocol you are requesting from the RAS client is available on the RAS server. There must be at least one common protocol or the connection will fail.
- If you are using NetBEUI, ensure that the name you are using on the RAS client is not in use on the network to which you are attempting to connect.
- If you are attempting to connect using TCP/IP, you must configure the RAS server to provide you with an address.

You can use the Remote Access Admin tool to monitor the ports as well as the active connections of your RAS server.

Numerous RAS settings can cause some problems with your RAS connections. Ensure that you understand the installation process, as well as any configuration settings required to enable your RAS server. You can avoid some of the common problems that can occur by taking the following steps:

- Ensure that the modem and communication medium are configured and functional prior to installing RAS. It can be very difficult to modify settings after the installation, so it is recommended to have all hardware tested and working first.

- Verify that dial-in permissions have been enabled for the required users. This small task is commonly forgotten in your RAS configuration.

Troubleshooting Objective 6

Choose the appropriate course of action to take to resolve connectivity problems.

To test and verify your TCP/IP settings, you can use the following utilities:

- IPCONFIG
- PING

The most effective method for troubleshooting connectivity is to understand thoroughly the installation and configuration options of each of the network protocols. If you understand the options available, you can narrow down the possible problem areas very quickly. Also ensure that you use utilities such as IPCONFIG and PING to test your connections.

Troubleshooting Objective 7

Choose the appropriate course of action to take to resolve resource access and permission problems.

You should keep in mind two main issues about permissions:

- The default permissions for both share and NTFS give the Windows NT group Everyone full control over the files and folders. Whenever you format a drive as NTFS or first share a folder, you should remove these permissions. The Everyone group contains everyone, including guests and any other user who, for one reason or another, can connect to your system.
- The NTFS folder permission delete takes precedence over any file permissions. In all other cases, the file permissions take precedence over the folder permissions.

Troubleshooting Objective 8

Choose the appropriate course of action to take to resolve fault-tolerance failures. Fault-tolerance methods include the following:

- Tape backup
- Mirroring
- Stripe set with parity

When using the NTBACKUP tool, the primary thing that you need to do is to determine the frequency and type of backup that you will do. There are three main types of backups that you might want to perform:

- **Full.** This backs up all the files that you mark, and marks the files as having been backed up. This is the longest of the backups because it transfers the most data.
- **Differential.** This backs up all the files that have changed since the last backup. A differential backup does not mark the files as being backed up. As time passes since the last full backup, the differentials become increasingly larger. However, you need only reload the full backup and the differential to return to the position of the last backup.
- **Incremental.** This backs up any files that have changed since the last backup, and then marks them as having been backed up. If your system crashes, you need to start by loading a full backup and then each incremental backup since that full backup.

If you are mirroring the system partition, the disks and partitions should be absolutely identical. Otherwise, the `MBR/DBR` (master boot record/disk boot record) that contains the driver information will not be correct.

Although ARC naming looks complicated, it is really rather simple. The name is in four parts, of which you use three. The syntax is as follows:

```
multi/scsidiskrdiskpartition
```

The following list outlines the parts of the name:

- **`multi/SCSI`.** You use either `multi` or `scsi`—not both. Use `multi` in all cases except when using a scsi controller that cannot handle int13 (hard disk access) BIOS routines. Such cases are uncommon. The number is the logical number of the controller with the first controller being 0, the second being 1, and so forth.
- **`disk`.** When you use a scsi disk, you use the `disk` parameter to indicate which of the drives on the controller is the drive you are talking about. Again, the numbers start at 0 for the first drive and then increase for each subsequent drive.
- **`rdisk`.** Use this parameter for the other controllers in the same way as you use the `disk` parameter for scsi.
- **`partition`.** This is the partition on the disk that you are pointing at. The first partition is 1, the second is 2, and so forth. Remember that you can have up to four primary partitions, or three primary and one extended

partition. The extended partition is always the last one, and the first logical drive in the partition will have the partition's number. Other drives in the extended partition each continue to add one.

The boot floppy will get the operating system up and running. You should immediately back up the mirrored copy of the mirror set. To back up the drive, you must break your mirror set. To do this, perform the following tasks:

1. Run the Disk Administrator.
2. From the Disk Administrator, click the remaining fragment of the mirrored set.
3. Choose Fault Tolerance, Break Mirror Set from the menu.

At the end of these three steps, you should notice that the mirror set has been broken, and you can now back up the drive.

Fixing a stripe set with parity is relatively simple. Perform the following tasks to regenerate your stripe set with parity:

1. Physically replace the faulty disk drive.
2. Start the Disk Administrator.
3. Select the stripe set with parity that you need to repair and then Ctrl+click the free space of the drive you added to fix the stripe set.
4. Choose Fault Tolerant, Regenerate. Note that this process can take some time, although the process takes less time than restoring from tape.

The drives regenerate all the required data from the parity bits and the data bits, and upon completion your stripe set with parity is completely functional.

- **Share permissions.** A common problem when troubleshooting share resources is found in the share permissions. Ensure that the minimum functional permissions have been assigned. Always remove the Everyone group to prevent full control of a share.
- **Combining NTFS and share permissions.** When combining these permissions, remember that NT uses the most restrictive of the permissions when combining. As a rule, use the NTFS permissions as the highest level of permissions, and use the share permissions mainly for access to the folder or share.
- **Tape backups.** In any system that you are using, ensure that you have a good backup strategy. Any component in your system can be faulty, and it is your responsibility to have a recovery plan in case of emergencies.

- **Disk mirroring.** If you are implementing disk mirroring in your system, ensure that you have created a fault-tolerant boot disk that you can use in case of drive failure. By having this disk preconfigured and handy, you can break the mirror set and replace the drive with very little downtime for your server.
- **Stripe set with parity.** This system automatically regenerates data if a drive is faulty. Although your system performance will dramatically decline, it is still a functional box and you risk no possibility of losing any data. If you find that a drive in your stripe set is faulty, replace the drive and use the `regenerate` command from the Disk Administrator.

Troubleshooting Objective 9

Perform advanced problem resolution. Tasks include the following:

- Diagnosing and interpreting a blue screen
- Configuring a memory dump
- Using the event log service

Three utilities are available on the Windows NT CD-ROM that enable you to work with the memory dump files that are created. The following list briefly describes these helpful tools:

- **DUMPCHK.** This utility checks that the dump file is in order by verifying all the addresses and listing the errors and system information.
- **DUMPEXAM.** This creates a text file that can provide the same information that was on the blue screen at the time the stop error occurred. You need the symbol files and the kernel debugger extensions as well as `IMAGEHLP.DLL` to run DUMPEXAM.
- **DUMPFLOP.** This utility backs up the dump file to a series of floppies so that you can send them to Microsoft.

The following list summarizes the key points required for this objective:

- The Event Viewer is a very powerful troubleshooting tool. The three logs that can be viewed through the Event Viewer are the system log, the application log, and the security log.
- Cross-reference the events in the Event Viewer with knowledge base articles found on Microsoft TechNet for troubleshooting help.

- Interpreting blue screens can be very difficult. Use memory dump files and the DUMPCHK, DUMPEXAM, and DUMPFLOP utilities to view your memory dumps to help you isolate the problems.

- If the problem persists, you might have to use the kernel debugger included on the NT server CD-ROM in the `\Support\debug` folder.

- You can use the kernel debugger to monitor a remote machine through a null modem, or by using the RAS service into a machine that is connected to the problematic computer through a null modem.

Index

A

B

C

D

E

F

G

H

I-J

K-L

M

N

O

P

Q-R

S

T

U

V

W-Z